Undergraduate Topics in Computer Science

'Undergraduate Topics in Computer Science' (UTiCS) delivers high-quality instructional content for undergraduates studying in all areas of computing and information science. From core foundational and theoretical material to final-year topics and applications, UTiCS books take a fresh, concise, and modern approach and are ideal for self-study or for a one- or two-semester course. The texts are all authored by established experts in their fields, reviewed by an international advisory board, and contain numerous examples and problems, many of which include fully worked solutions.

The UTiCS concept relies on high-quality, concise books in softback format, and generally a maximum of 275–300 pages. For undergraduate textbooks that are likely to be longer, more expository, Springer continues to offer the highly regarded Texts in Computer Science series, to which we refer potential authors.

More information about this series at http://www.springer.com/series/7592

Duncan Buell

Fundamentals of Cryptography

Introducing Mathematical and Algorithmic Foundations

 Springer

Duncan Buell
Department of Computer Science
and Engineering
University of South Carolina
Columbia, SC, USA

ISSN 1863-7310   ISSN 2197-1781   (electronic)
Undergraduate Topics in Computer Science
ISBN 978-3-030-73491-6   ISBN 978-3-030-73492-3   (eBook)
https://doi.org/10.1007/978-3-030-73492-3

This Springer imprint is published by the registered company Springer Nature Switzerland AG
The registered company address is: Gewerbestrasse 11, 6330 Cham, Switzerland

Preface

I taught in a computer science department. Our cryptography class, which I just finished teaching for the fourth time, is for upper-level undergraduates (juniors and seniors) and also for graduate credit. This is, I think, similar to what is available in a large number of universities in the United States. Our course is also cross-listed with the mathematics department, and we usually have a combination of math and computer science students taking the course.

The computer science students know how to program, but they are often not so good at the math. In contrast, the math students can usually do the math but don't have the same experience in programming. I have normally accepted programming assignments in any of Python, C++, or Java. I have pointed out that Python provides multiprecise integer arithmetic as a default, and have pointed the students using C++ to the gmp package and the students using Java to the BigNum package. I have also encouraged students to work in groups on the programming assignments, allowing groups to combine both the mathematical understanding and the ability to code up the algorithms and heuristics presented.

I have assumed some minimal background in asymptotic analysis of algorithms. I think I have kept the big-$\mathcal{O}(*)$ to a minimum, and I think virtually all the needed discrete math (modular arithmetic, groups, rings, and such) actually appears in this text.

I think most students in the United States see at least the rudiments of matrix reduction in high school; I have tried to make the linear algebra limited to what most students might actually see in high school; and I have not used any linear algebra beyond the mechanical process of matrix reduction.

Although there is a certain background in groups and rings, I have tried to make that as straightforward as possible. One advantage of this material is that it isn't pure theory; one can actually see concrete examples of the theorems and, I would hope, understand that the theory is mostly just a way of discussing the material and not the end in itself.

It is, in fact, precisely because this material does and should appear in both departments that I decided to write this book. There are several good crypto books that are suitable for a course that is just mathematics. There is at least one that is suitable for a lower-level course targeting a more general audience.

Cryptography, as done in this century, is heavily mathematical, but it also has roots in what is computationally feasible. What I would hope this text does, that I think other texts do not do, is balance the theorems of mathematics against the feasibility of computation. This is the essence of my including the material of Chap. 8 in the text. My background is mathematics. My experience (except for a first year in a math department after my doctorate) is in computer science departments, with 15 years at a research lab doing high performance computing research in support of the National Security Agency. My "take" on cryptography, including my time with NSA, is that it is something one actually "does", not a mathematical game one proves theorems about. There is deep math; there are some theorems that must be proved; and there is a need to recognize the brilliant work done by those who focus on theory. But at the level of an undergraduate course, I think the emphasis should be first on knowing and understanding the algorithms and how to implement them, and also to be aware that the algorithms must be implemented carefully to avoid the "easy" ways to break the cryptography.

Exercises

Most of the exercises in the later chapters are programming problems. This is largely due to the difficulty in posing realistic problems that can be done entirely by hand. As for computational resources: Many of the exercises, and many of the necessary exercises, require some computation. There are many tools that can be used. The (ancient, but certainly feasible) Unix tool bc will do the multiprecise arithmetic necessary for many of the computations and can be scripted using something like

```
bc < myscript.txt
```

to redirect from standard input. Some students will prefer Matlab® or Mathematica or Maple. Others may find SageMath a better tool. The key for some of the simpler problems is that students use the software as a sophisticated calculator but do the algorithms themselves rather than just calling functions built by someone else. The key for the genuine programming problems is that students learn the details of the algorithms, at least for small examples that would not require multiprecise arithmetic packages. Following the classic advice to "make it right before you make it better", if students can code single precision examples that work, then most of the work to code multiprecision examples will only be the transition from single to multiple precision, and the tracing of the single precision example can be used as ground truth for whether the multiple precision version has bugs.

Acknowledgements

It would be inappropriate for me not to thank my most recent cryptography class for which the first version of this was their textbook, and the previous classes for which earlier versions were written. I received great feedback from the most recent class, some corrections, and some suggestions for what should be changed and what had to be changed in order to become more readable. Everyone who teaches will complain about some of the students, but I have been fortunate to teach and work with a number of superstars; I am grateful to have had such students.

Columbia, SC, USA   Duncan Buell
February 2021

Contents

1 Introduction 1
  1.1   History 1
  1.2   Introduction 3
  1.3   Why Is Cryptography Used? 5
  1.4   Modes of Encryption 6
  1.5   Modes of Attack 7
  1.6   How Many Seconds in a Year? 7
  1.7   Kerckhoffs' Principle 9
  1.8   Exercises 9
  References 10

2 Simple Ciphers 11
  2.1   Substitution Ciphers 12
      2.1.1   Caesar Ciphers 12
      2.1.2   Random Substitutions 12
      2.1.3   Vigenère as an Example of Polyalphabetic
              Substitutions 13
  2.2   Language Characteristics and Patterns 14
      2.2.1   Letter Frequency 14
      2.2.2   Word Boundaries 15
      2.2.3   Cribbing 16
      2.2.4   Entropy 16
  2.3   Transposition Ciphers 19
      2.3.1   Columnar Transpositions 19
      2.3.2   Double Transposition 20
  2.4   Playfair 20
  2.5   ADFGX 21
  2.6   Cryptanalysis 22
      2.6.1   Breaking a Substitution Cipher 22
      2.6.2   Breaking a Transposition Cipher 23
  2.7   The Vernam One-Time Pad 23

	2.8	Exercises	24
		2.8.1 Cipher Text for Substitution Cipher Problems (3) and (4)	25
	References		26
3	**Divisibility, Congruences, and Modular Arithmetic**		**27**
	3.1	Divisibility	27
	3.2	The Euclidean Algorithm	29
		3.2.1 The Naive Euclidean Algorithm	30
		3.2.2 The Extended Euclidean Algorithm	31
		3.2.3 The Binary Euclidean Algorithm	32
		3.2.4 The Subtract-Three-Times Euclidean Algorithm	33
		3.2.5 GCDs of Large Integers	34
	3.3	Primes	35
	3.4	Congruences	36
	3.5	The Euler Totient	43
	3.6	Fermat's Little Theorem	43
	3.7	Exponentiation	44
	3.8	Matrix Reduction	45
	3.9	Exercises	46
	References		47
4	**Groups, Rings, Fields**		**49**
	4.1	Groups	49
	4.2	Rings	53
	4.3	Fields	54
	4.4	Examples and Expansions	54
		4.4.1 Arithmetic Modulo Prime Numbers	54
		4.4.2 Arithmetic Modulo Composite Numbers	57
		4.4.3 Finite Fields of Characteristic 2	60
	4.5	Exercises	60
	References		61
5	**Square Roots and Quadratic Symbols**		**63**
	5.1	Square Roots	63
		5.1.1 Examples	65
	5.2	Characters on Groups	67
	5.3	Legendre Symbols	67
	5.4	Quadratic Reciprocity	68
	5.5	Jacobi Symbols	68
	5.6	Extended Law of Quadratic Reciprocity	69
	5.7	Exercises	70
	Reference		71

6 Finite Fields of Characteristic 2 73
  6.1 Polynomials with Coefficients mod 2 73
    6.1.1 An Example 73
  6.2 Linear Feedback Shift Registers 75
  6.3 The General Theory 79
  6.4 Normal Bases 80
  6.5 Exercises 85
  References 85

7 Elliptic Curves 87
  7.1 Basics 87
    7.1.1 Straight Lines and Intersections 88
    7.1.2 Tangent Lines 90
    7.1.3 Formulas 90
    7.1.4 The Mordell-Weil Group. 91
  7.2 Observation 93
  7.3 Projective Coordinates and Jacobian Coordinates 94
  7.4 An Example of a Curve with Many Points 94
  7.5 Curves Modulo a Prime p 96
  7.6 Hasse's Theorem. 96
  7.7 Exercises 97
  Reference 98

8 Mathematics, Computing, and Arithmetic 99
  8.1 Mersenne Primes. 99
    8.1.1 Introduction 100
    8.1.2 Theory 100
    8.1.3 Implementation. 103
    8.1.4 Summary: Feasibility 104
    8.1.5 Fermat Numbers. 104
    8.1.6 The Arithmetic Trick Is Important 105
  8.2 Multiprecise Arithmetic and the Fast Fourier Transform 105
    8.2.1 Multiprecise Arithmetic. 105
    8.2.2 Background of the FFT. 106
    8.2.3 Polynomial Multiplication 106
    8.2.4 Complex Numbers as Needed for Fourier
        Transforms. 107
    8.2.5 The Fourier Transform 108
    8.2.6 The Cooley–Tukey Fast Fourier Transform 109
    8.2.7 An Example. 110
    8.2.8 The FFT Butterfly 116
  8.3 Montgomery Multiplication 117
    8.3.1 The Computational Advantage 120
  8.4 Arithmetic in General 120

8.5	Exercises	120
References		121

9   Modern Symmetric Ciphers—DES and AES 123
9.1	History	123
	9.1.1 Criticism and Controversy	124
9.2	The Advanced Encryption Standard	125
9.3	The AES Algorithm	127
	9.3.1 Polynomial Preliminaries: The Galois Field $GF(2^8)$	127
	9.3.2 Byte Organization	128
9.4	The Structure of AES	129
	9.4.1 The Outer Structure of the Rounds	129
	9.4.2 General Code Details	129
	9.4.3 KeyExpansion	130
	9.4.4 SubBytes	133
	9.4.5 ShiftRows	136
	9.4.6 MixColumns	137
	9.4.7 AddRoundKey	140
9.5	Implementation Issues	141
	9.5.1 Software Implementations	142
	9.5.2 Hardware Implementations	144
9.6	Security	145
9.7	Exercises	146
References		147

10   Asymmetric Ciphers—RSA and Others 149
10.1	History	149
10.2	RSA Public-Key Encryption	150
	10.2.1 The Basic RSA Algorithm	150
10.3	Implementation	151
	10.3.1 An Example	152
10.4	How Hard Is It to Break RSA?	153
10.5	Other Groups	153
10.6	Exercises	155
References		155

11   How to Factor a Number 157
11.1	Pollard rho	158
11.2	Pollard $p-1$	160
	11.2.1 The General Metaphysics of $p-1$	161
	11.2.2 Step Two of $p-1$	161

	11.3	CFRAC	162
		11.3.1 Continued Fractions	162
		11.3.2 The CFRAC Algorithm...........................	165
		11.3.3 Example.....................................	167
		11.3.4 Computation..................................	168
	11.4	Factoring with Elliptic Curves	169
	11.5	Exercises	170
		References	170

12 How to Factor More Effectively **173**
	12.1	Shortcomings of CFRAC..............................	173
	12.2	The Quadratic Sieve	173
		12.2.1 The Algorithm	174
		12.2.2 The Crucial Reasons for Success and Improvement over CFRAC	174
	12.3	Once More Unto the Breach	175
	12.4	The Multiple Polynomial Quadratic Sieve................	176
		12.4.1 Yet One More Advantage	177
	12.5	The Number Field Sieve	177
	12.6	Exercises	178
		References	178

13 Cycles, Randomness, Discrete Logarithms, and Key Exchange **179**
	13.1	Introduction	179
	13.2	The Discrete Logarithm Problem	180
	13.3	Difficult Discrete Log Problems	181
	13.4	Cycles	182
	13.5	Cocks-Ellis-Williamson/Diffie-Hellman Key Exchange	182
		13.5.1 The Key Exchange Algorithm...................	183
	13.6	The Index Calculus	183
		13.6.1 Our Example	184
		13.6.2 Smooth Relations	184
		13.6.3 Matrix Reduction	185
		13.6.4 Individual Logarithms.........................	187
		13.6.5 Asymptotics	187
	13.7	Key Exchange with Elliptic Curves	187
	13.8	Key Exchange in Other Groups	188
	13.9	How Hard Is the Discrete Logarithm Problem?...........	189
	13.10	Exercises	189
		References	190

14   Elliptic Curve Cryptography   191
   14.1   Introduction   191
            14.1.1   Jacobian Coordinates   192
   14.2   Elliptic Curve Discrete Logarithms.   193
   14.3   Elliptic Curve Cryptography   193
   14.4   The Cost of Elliptic Curve Operations   194
            14.4.1   Doubling a Point   194
            14.4.2   Left-to-Right "Exponentiation"   195
   14.5   The NIST Recommendations   196
   14.6   Attacks on Elliptic Curves   198
            14.6.1   Pohlig-Hellman Attacks   198
            14.6.2   Pollard Rho Attacks   198
            14.6.3   Pollard Rho for Curves   200
            14.6.4   Pollard Rho in Parallel   201
   14.7   A Comparison of Complexities   202
   14.8   Exercises   202
   References   202

15   Lattice-Based Cryptography and NTRU   205
   15.1   Quantum Computing   205
   15.2   Lattices: An Introduction   207
   15.3   Hard Lattice Problems.   208
   15.4   NTRU   209
   15.5   The NTRU Cryptosystem   210
            15.5.1   Parameters   210
            15.5.2   Creating Keys   211
            15.5.3   Encrypting a Message.   211
            15.5.4   Decrypting a Message.   211
            15.5.5   Why This Works   213
            15.5.6   Preventing Errors in Decryption   213
   15.6   Lattice Attacks on NTRU   214
   15.7   The Mathematics of the Lattice Reduction Attack   216
            15.7.1   Other Attacks on NTRU   217
            15.7.2   Lattice Reduction   217
   15.8   NTRU Parameter Choices   218
   15.9   Exercises   220
   References   220

16   Homomorphic Encryption   223
   16.1   Introduction   223
   16.2   Somewhat Homomorphic Encryption   224
   16.3   Fully Homomorphic Encryption.   224
   16.4   Ideal Lattices   224
   16.5   Learning with Errors   227

16.6   Security, and Homomorphic Evaluation of Functions   228
16.7   An Apologetic Summary   228
References   228

Appendix A: An Actual World War I Cipher   231

Appendix B: AES Code   253

Index   275

Introduction

1

Abstract

The desire of governments, generals, and even private individuals to communicate in a fashion that prevents private communications from being read by others goes back millennia. The ability of third parties to read messages not intended for them, or for messages to be unreadable by third parties, has frequently changed the path of history. The use of technology in the last 200 years has changed the process of communicating messages, first with the telegraph, then with wireless, and now with the internet. With telegraph systems based on wires, a third party needed physical access to the communication medium. With wireless radio, the transmission became public, and the need for secure communications increased. With messages sent in packets over the internet, literally anyone can be eavesdropping from anywhere in the world. In this chapter we will briefly cover some of the history, and we will define basic terms and uses that will continue through the book.

1.1 History

The problem of secure communication is probably almost as old as civilization itself. In sending a message to a distant correspondent, with adversaries somewhere along the way, it has always been necessary to ensure that the messages cannot be understood by the adversaries in the middle. In other instances, it is only for the purpose of privacy (or, as one might say today, protection of intellectual property), information is written in a code that cannot be read except by those in the know. Leonardo da Vinci, for example, wrote his notes in mirror image, from right to left. Some have suggested this was to protect the content from prying eyes, although another suggestion is just that he was left-handed and by writing right to left he would not smudge the page as he wrote.

D. Buell, *Fundamentals of Cryptography*, Undergraduate Topics in Computer Science,
https://doi.org/10.1007/978-3-030-73492-3_1

Secure communications have been crucial for those who plot and scheme. Mary, Queen of Scots, for example, was found in 1586 to be plotting against Elizabeth of England. As it turned out, Elizabeth's cryptanalyst, Thomas Phelippes, was better at his job than was Mary's cryptographer, and coded messages connecting Mary to the plot against Elizabeth were read, leading to Mary's execution.

Thomas Jefferson devised a ciphering machine that was apparently never built in his lifetime, but was largely reinvented in the early 20th century and used, as the M-94, by the United States Army.

One of the classics of literature on cryptography, and as controversial at the time as it is now a classic, is *The American Black Chamber*, by Herbert O. Yardley [1]. Yardley was a cryptographer during and after the First World War, working for Army intelligence during the war and then for a joint black chamber[1] office of the Army and the U. S. Department of State, until Secretary of State Henry Stimson, famously saying, "Gentlemen do not read each other's mail", ended the funding and effectively terminated the office. One of the primary accomplishments of Yardley's office came during the negotiations of the Washington Naval Conference of 1921–1922. Under discussion at the conference were the ratios of ship tonnage that the major powers were to adhere to, and decrypted Japanese communications revealed the lower limit that Japan was willing to accept at the time.

While Yardley worked for the Army and the State Department, the other preeminent American cryptographers of the era were William and Elizabeth Friedman, husband and wife. They worked together at the Riverbank Laboratories, a privately funded operation near Chicago of wealthy businessman George Fabyan, and wrote many of the early papers on cryptography that are still viewed as classics of the modern literature. William Friedman led the Army's Signals Intelligence Service and played a key role in cracking Purple, the Japanese diplomatic code. Among the famous messages decrypted from Purple was the seventeen-part communication to the Japanese Embassy on the day before the Pearl Harbor attack. The message on its last pages clearly indicated that war was about to begin, but the last part of the message never reached Washington officials in time. Conspiracy theories persist that in fact officials knew, but wanted to allow Japan to attack so as to force public opinion in favor of going to war.

Codebreaking played crucial roles in the Second World War. The British work at Bletchley Park (following early breakthroughs by three Polish mathematicians) on the German naval cipher, code-named Enigma, has been the subject of many books and movies [2]. Although the most recent film, *The Imitation Game*, has received the most attention, there is more Hollywood than fact in the script; the earlier film *Enigma* is much closer to the truth. It was for decrypting Enigma and subsequent German ciphers that the first electronic computers, named Colossus, were built by the British, but since their existence was classified until the mid-1970s, the American-built ENIAC has been usually taken to be the first real computer.

---

[1]The term *black chamber* is a translation of the French term *cabinet noire* that was established in France in the late 16th century.

Perhaps the greatest triumph of cryptanalysis in the war in the Pacific was the ability of the American naval group, led by Joseph Rochefort in Hawaii, to decrypt the Japanese communications leading to the battle at Midway. Famously, Rochefort and his team had cracked one of the Japanese naval codes and had decrypted the time and the order of battle of the Japanese fleet, but knew the location only by the code letters "AF". Suspecting it was Midway, and in the midst of a heated discussion with other naval intelligence officers, a message was sent to the base at Midway by secure undersea cable. The Midway base was told to send back to Hawaii, in the clear so it would be picked up by the Japanese, the (false) message that a desalination plant had broken down and there was a shortage of fresh water. Within 24 h, Rochefort's group decrypted a Japanese message that "AF is short on water" and thus knew the attack would be on Midway. Barely six months after Pearl Harbor, the Japanese lost four aircraft carriers and their naval expansion was halted.

Cryptanalysis also played a key role in the D-Day landings in Normandy. Gathering intelligence was much more difficult on the European continent, since land lines were used and not the wireless communications of Enigma to ships at sea. But there were German wireless communications using a cipher that was code-named TUNNY, that had been cracked and whose messages could be decrypted. And in addition to the direct information on German plans and positions from reading German ciphers, the Allies had the advantage of collateral information. The Japanese ambassador and the military attache had been given tours of the coastal defenses along the English Channel. They had written extensive reports that were sent back to Japan, by radio, using a cipher that had been broken, so the Allies had first-hand information as to the German defenses.

Cryptography has also always been political. Governments often do not want just the ability to read the messages of other countries or groups; they want to read the messages of their own citizens, and occasionally they have law-enforcement reasons for doing so. Courts have not completely settled on whether one can be required to divulge a password, or whether that would constitute a required self-incrimination forbidden in the United States by the Fifth Amendment. Encryption is useful for business transactions, but some of those transactions are illegal. The United States effort to create the CLIPPER chip failed miserably in the early 1990s, and there have been several studies of the benefits and pitfalls of private encryption [3–5]. Major technology companies have refused to implement back doors in the security of their consumer products, despite repeated efforts to pass laws mandating such back doors [6].

1.2 Introduction

We shall begin with some terms. The *crypt* part of our terms means *secret*. An *ology* is a study, so *cryptology* is etymologically the study of secrets. We will restrict to the study of *cryptography*, where the *graphy* means *writing*, so *cryptography* thus means *secret writing*. The other term that is often seen is *cryptanalysis*, which we shall take to mean the analysis of a cryptographic endeavor. We may well conflate the terms cryptography and cryptology, but will try to reserve cryptanalysis for the process of attacking a cryptographic system so as to read the hidden messages.[2]

In using a cryptographic system, one starts with the original message to be sent, called the *plaintext*. By using the cryptographic system one converts plaintext into *ciphertext* that the sender intends not to be understandable by anyone but the intended recipient. We shall interchangeably use the words *encrypting* and *enciphering* for the process of changing plaintext into ciphertext, and interchangeably use the words *decrypting* and *deciphering* for the process of converting ciphertext back into plaintext. Encryption and decryption always use some sort of *key*. Until very recently, cryptosystems were symmetric, with the same key being used for encryption and for decryption. This made it necessary that the key be information known only to sender and receiver, and it made preservation of that secrecy of paramount importance. Modern cryptography now relies on asymmetric systems for which the key to encrypt is not the same as the key to decrypt; a public key is used by the sender, and a private key known only to the receiver (and thus logistically much less likely to be compromised) is used for decryption.

A small bit of simplifying jargon is also useful. We assume that the sender creates the ciphertext, and that the ciphertext could be intercepted by an adversary. Clearly, then, the adversary can observe the pattern of bits that is the ciphertext. However, we will say that the adversary (or even the intended recipient) can *read* the ciphertext only if the reader can turn the ciphertext back into the original plaintext.

Part of cryptography, although not something we will spend time on here, is the idea of a *codebook*, which historically has often been a book that provides code sequences (often five-digit numbers) for each word to be used in the plaintext. The plaintext is transformed from text into a sequence of code words transmitted in the clear. The secrecy of the coded text relies on an adversary's being unable to obtain a copy of the code book and being unable to use frequency analysis or cribbing to guess the code words being used, *cribbing* being the term for guessing a match between known or expected words in the plaintext (like days of the week or times of day) and parts of the ciphertext or coded text and using that guess to try to see if more of the message can thus be decrypted/decoded.

Finally, we mention *coding theory*, yet another discipline not really related to what we present here. The primary purpose of coding theory is to permit unambiguous reception of transmitted messages even in the presence of garbling. Perhaps the simplest technique in coding theory is that of a parity bit appended to the end of a bit string. With "even parity", an extra 0 or 1 bit, as appropriate, would be added to a bit string so that all strings would have an even number of 1 bits. A string that arrived at its destination with an odd number of 1 bits would be known to have been garbled in transmission. The research and substance of coding theory is to find and analyze codes that provide the maximum ability to transmit unambiguously and to

---

[2]And we will never use the incorrect word "crypto-analysis", because that would seem instead to mean analysis done in secret, which is something quite different.

detect and possibly be able to correct garbles while using the fewest number of bits beyond the minimum necessary to provide unique codes for each of the symbols being transmitted. We can do most of what we need in English using 8-bit ASCII codes, for example, and a single extra parity bit would permit us to determine to flag as garbled characters any character for which an odd number of bits were flipped in transmission. We would not, however, know which bit or bits were incorrect.

1.3   Why Is Cryptography Used?

It is reasonable to ask about the various purposes for cryptography. We can identify four basic ways in which cryptographic functions are used in the modern world. Many of these exist outside the world of internet communication and transaction, but we will focus on those uses.

- The obvious reason for using cryptography is to preserve *confidentiality*, that is, to make communications between two parties understandable only by the two parties involved.
- In the world of the internet, important documents like contracts and real-estate transactions are sent over the internet, which is not secure. Variants of the same functions used to maintain confidentiality can be used to ensure the *integrity* of the documents transmitted, so, for example, the dollar value of a contract could not be changed by a malicious interceptor as the document was being sent from one party to another. Cryptography is also used to encrypt databases and disk files, so that if a malicious actor stole a laptop or was able to obtain unauthorized access to a desktop, the files would not be understandable to anyone except the owner of the files.
- In addition to the issue of the integrity of a document is the issue of *authentication* of the identity of someone on the other end of an internet transaction. Cryptographic functions can be used to ensure that one can authenticate with whom one is communicating.
- The traditional method for ensuring that a person's commitment cannot be repudiated has been a wet signature on a document. Knowing, as we do, that malicious actors populate the internet in great numbers, it is necessary that *non-repudiation* of transmitted documents not be possible. We need an analog of a wet signature.

As part of a discussion about the uses for cryptography, we can distinguish two basic, and often complementary, ways in which cryptographic algorithms are used. If the goal is to ensure that the contents of a message cannot be read by anyone other than the intended recipient, then the process will be to take an unknown (to the interceptor) plaintext and to convert it into ciphertext that only the intended recipient can read.

The goals of authentication or non-repudiation work in the opposite direction. When a sender authenticates her identity, any receiver or interceptor can be assumed to know the plaintext (or at least to crib part of the plaintext). The ciphertext thus needs to be something that only the assumed sender could have sent. This is often combined with a *hash function* that produces an apparently random short signature for a document that could only have been produced by the original document. Although there are variations in algorithms for these two different purposes, there is substantial commonality.

1.4 Modes of Encryption

Algorithms for cryptography operate in different ways, and sometimes the differences are very important.

A *block cipher* is an algorithm that operates on a block of bits at a time, producing a block of ciphertext from a block of plaintext. For example, AES operates on 128-bit blocks of plaintext to produce 128-bit blocks of ciphertext. An RSA cryptosystem, with a 2048-bit key, would likely operate on blocks of size 2048.

In an *electronic codebook* implementation, the blocks would be treated independently, with each pair of plaintext/ciphertext blocks independent of one another. This can be insecure in many instances. AES, for example, has only a 16-byte block, and if the "text" to be encrypted is an image, there might well be large parts of the image that have the same background plaintext and thus would be encrypted as the same ciphertext. This can make the outlines of the underlying image identifiable.

To prevent the encryption of identical plaintext blocks into identical ciphertext blocks, one can implement *cipher block chaining*. In this, an initialization vector of random bits is XOR-ed with the first block of plaintext, which is encrypted. The ciphertext of block n is then used as if it were an initialization vector for block $n + 1$ before that block is encrypted. By doing this, even identical blocks of original text are modified by a bit pattern that is more random before the blocks are encrypted, and thus it is not the case that one creates the same ciphertext from the same blocks of identical plaintext.

In contrast to block ciphers, with a *stream cipher* a sequence of "random" bits is XOR-ed to a stream of plaintext bits to create the ciphertext. This requires, of course, that one has a deterministic algorithm, known to both sender and receiver, that generates a stream of bits that appear for all intents and purposes to be random. Stream ciphers have often been constructed using linear feedback shift registers, for example, as will be discussed in Chap. 6.

We remark that with the digital age has come a standardization. Unlike a message sent entirely on paper, all messages that are sent electronically will be sent as coded zeros and ones, and thus all messages can be treated as numbers. Text stored in a computer is usually stored as Unicode numbers that represent the characters to be stored. Unicode is the multi-byte extension to the ASCII (American Standard Code for Information Interchange) that assigned one-byte (originally not using all the bits) codes to letters, numbers, punctuation, and control characters. Such coding began with Samuel F. B. Morse and Emile Baudot in the nineteenth century for use with telegraphs. Morse code is variable length, with the more frequent letters getting shorter code words. Baudot and subsequent codes before Unicode were fixed-length codes. Unicode, still in progress, has been developed to provide codes for all the alphabets and diacriticals for all the world's languages as well as such new things as emojis. Unicode is variable length: the original codes deriving from ASCII are single-byte. If more bytes are needed (since a single byte can only encode 256 different values), the first byte has a signal encoded in it that indicates that the next byte is a continuation of the first. Three-byte codes simply do this continuation twice.

Modern cryptography, then, takes one of two different forms. In most public-key cryptography, the bit patterns of the underlying text are taken to be the binary number represented by the pattern, and computation is done on that number. In systems such as AES, the Advanced Encryption Standard, the bit patterns are made to appear random by reordering and application of binary functions like an XOR.

1.5   Modes of Attack

In doing cryptanalysis, there are four basic kinds of attack that can be mounted.

- In a *ciphertext only attack* we are presented only with ciphertext.
- In a *known plaintext attack* we know the decrypted plaintext and we have the corresponding ciphertext. Our goal here is to discover the encryption algorithm, if we don't know it yet, and the key if we have found the encryption algorithm by some other methods.
- In a *chosen ciphertext attack* it is possible to gain information about how to decrypt by having the decryptions of chosen instances of ciphertext.
- In a *chosen plaintext attack* the cryptanalyst can choose the plaintext and from that obtain the ciphertext for that plaintext. With public key encryption schemes, for example, the ability to encrypt a message is possible for anyone who has plaintext, because the encryption key itself is public knowledge.

1.6   How Many Seconds in a Year?

In measuring the brute-force complexity of a cryptosystem, one often has to compute a ballpark estimate for the time needed to crack the system with a totally naive attack. The United States Data Encryption Standard (DES) cryptosystem, for example, had a 56-bit key. There were thus $2^{56} \approx 7.2 \times 10^{16}$ possible keys. If one were to attack DES by brute force, one would simply test each key in sequence. In a large scale operation with many possible messages to decipher, we would expect on average only to go halfway up the key space before we hit the correct key, so on average we would expect to have to test $2^{55} \approx 3.6 \times 10^{16}$ possible keys before we were able to decrypt a message.

Table 1.1 Brute force time to crack, for varying bit lengths

Key size	Years	Key size	Years
56	1.14	320	3.39×10^{79}
64	292.47	352	1.45×10^{89}
96	1.26×10^{10}	384	6.25×10^{98}
128	5.40×10^{21}	416	2.68×10^{108}
160	2.32×10^{31}	448	1.15×10^{118}
224	4.27×10^{50}	480	4.95×10^{127}
256	1.84×10^{60}	512	2.13×10^{137}
288	7.89×10^{69}		

How long would this take us? As was once said, one test of whether a speaker has really been doing supercomputing is whether she knows how many seconds there are in a year. There are $86,400$ s in a day and $31,536,000 \approx 3 \times 10^7$ s, or 3×10^{16} ns, in a non-leap year. When doing rough calculations such as this in binary, we also notice that $2^{25} = 33,554,432$, so for rough back-of-the-envelope calculations that are easier to do in binary, one can use that as the number of seconds in a year.

Modern computers run with about a 3 GHz clock, which means that each clock period is about 0.33 ns. But modern computers are highly pipelined, so it's not the case that instructions only take 0.33 ns to complete. For convenience, let's say we can test a single DES key in 1 ns, which means we can test 10^9 keys every second. At that rate we could exhaust the DES key space in 3.6×10^7 s, which is a little over a year.

It is only now we need to worry about being less sloppy in our estimates. A little over a year is within range of a concerted attack. Since testing keys is embarrassingly parallel, we could hand off different parts of the key space to different computers and run the entire computation in parallel. With 1000 computers, at 10^9 keys tested per second on each computer, our brute force time is down to about $36,000$ s, which is about ten hours. And now we start working to be less sloppy. One key per nanosecond? That's probably optimistic, but if we are only off by a factor of 5, then we are still finding keys about once every two days. Can we get 1000 computers? If we are a major player in the computing world, that's not unreasonable, assuming that decrypting messages is important to The Powers That Be. Adjusting the estimates up and down still results in the basic conclusion that DES can be cracked by brute force in some reasonably small number of days.

We can contrast DES with AES. Since AES has a 128-bit key, and $2^{128} \approx 3.4 \times 10^{38}$, we know that a brute force attack isn't going to work no matter what we do. With 1000 computers testing 10^9 keys per second, and 30 million seconds in a year, going halfway up the key space would take

$$\frac{1.7 \times 10^{38}}{10^3 \times 10^9 \times 3.0 \times 10^7} \approx 5 \times 10^{18}$$

years to find one key. And now it doesn't help to fix the sloppiness in our estimates. Getting 100 times as many computers each of which goes 100 times faster only gets the exponent down to 14. Planet Earth has only been around for about 4.5×10^9 years; and our brute force attack will still take about 100 thousand times longer than that.

Just to put things in perspective, we provide in Table 1.1 the expected time needed for a brute force attack on a cryptosystem with varying key lengths. This assumes that we test one key in one nanosecond and that on average we only need to test half the keys to get success. The lesson is clear; brute force is not going to work.

1.7 Kerckhoffs' Principle

Finally, we cite the principle enunciated by the Dutch cryptographer Auguste Kerckhoff in the nineteenth century: A cryptosystem should be secure even if everything is known about the system except the key that is used to encrypt a particular message.

Claude Shannon reiterated that in a different way in 1949, stating that in communications one must assume that the enemy knows everything about the system.

These principles would seem self-evident. The contrasting view is what is referred to (in a deprecating way) as "security through obscurity". Companies often naturally have trade secrets. Patents are mechanisms whereby inventions beneficial to the inventor are made public but which cannot be used without licensing. It is a general rule in security, and no less for communications security, that one cannot assume that secrets in the design of a system will stay secret. If there is something of value to be found, the conservative approach to security is to assume that attempts will be made to uncover that which has value. And the conservative approach is to assume that even if outside spies cannot break in, insiders in the know could be corrupted or blackmailed. As Benjamin Franklin put it, "Three can keep a secret, if two of them are dead."

1.8 Exercises

Present an analysis, using reputable sources, on the importance of cryptography regarding the following:

1. Mary, Queen of Scots.
2. The Washington Naval Treaty.
3. The attack on Pearl Harbor.
4. The use of Enigma decrypts in the Battle of the Atlantic in World War 2.
5. The use of decrypts in the Battle of Midway.
6. The Venona decrypts and the trials and execution of Julius and Ethel Rosenberg.

7. The work of William and Elizabeth Friedman at Riverbank Laboratories.
8. The work of Elizabeth Friedman during the era of Prohibition in the United States.
9. The controversy over the publication in the late 1970s by Rivest, Shamir, and Adleman of the RSA encryption method.
10. The CLIPPER chip proposed in the 1990s by the United States government.
11. The current controversy over whether individuals can be forced to decrypt information on laptop hard drives when crossing the border into another country.
12. The current controversy over whether technology companies should be required to implement a back door in the security and cryptography so that law enforcement can obtain access to information connected to a cell phone.

References

1. H.O. Yardley, *The American Black Chamber* (Bobbs-Merrill, Indianapolis, 1931), pp. 140–171
2. G. Welchman, *The Hut Six Story* (McGraw-Hill, New York, 1982).
3. W. Hollingsworth, H. Sachs, A.J. Smith, The CLIPPER processor: instruction set architecture and implementation. Commun. ACM **32**, 200–219 (1989)
4. S. Landau, S. Kent, C. Brooks, S. Charney, D. Denning, W. Diffie, A. Lauck, D. Miller, P. Neumann, D. Sobel, Crypto policy perspectives. Commun. ACM **37**, 115–121 (1994)
5. S. Landau, S. Kent, C. Brooks, S. Charney, D. Denning, W. Diffie, A. Lauck, D. Miller, P. Neumann, D. Sobel, *Codes, Keys, and Conflicts: Issues in U.S. Crypto Policy*. Association for Computing Machinery Report (1994)
6. H. Abelson, R. Anderson, S.M. Bellovin, J. Benaloh, M. Blaze, W. Diffie, J. Gilmore, M. Green, P.G. Neumann, S. Landau, R.L. Rivest, J.I. Schiller, B. Schneier, M. Specter, D.J. Witzner, Keys under doormats: mandating insecurity by requiring government access to all data and communications. Commun. ACM **58**, 24–26 (2015)

Simple Ciphers

2

Abstract

Until the computer age, making and breaking ciphers was a task that required extreme concentration and care. Search trees based on guesses can be programmed on computers and run at high speed, where we can use the computer's speed and the ease of keeping track of the data in data structures to allow us not to care too much about following low probability paths. The cost in time and effort to search using pencil and paper would have demanded much better guesses as to the correct path down the tree. Cryptanalysis in the first half of the twentieth century required knowledge of language patterns and frequency statistics, and both encryption and decryption had to be processes that could easily be remembered and followed. In this chapter we will describe some classical ciphers (that would be easily attacked with a program running on a desktop computer) as well as some statistical characteristics of language that could be used to attack these now-outdated ciphers. There are two basic forms of simple cipher. In a *substitution cipher*, one substitutes for each letter in the underlying alphabet another symbol (perhaps a different letter in the same alphabet, or sometimes another symbol entirely). In a *transposition cipher*, the letters of the underlying alphabet remain the same, but their order is transposed into a different order. In this, one can take the term "letter" to mean a single letter or perhaps a pair of letters. We distinguish at the outset a *codebook* from a *cipher*, although the two can be closely related. Traditional codebooks were a form of making communications secret by substituting a fixed length (often five) sequence of numbers for each of the individual words in the message. One can think of such a codebook as a substitution cipher in which the symbols are words (of variable length, of course) for which one substitutes numerical symbols. We will also mention only briefly (right here) the notion of *steganography*, where a message is hidden in some seemingly innocuous communication. One version of this would be a letter in which the hidden message was the sequence of first letters of words of the text. A more modern reverse version of steganography is *digital watermarking*, in which a digital pattern is inserted into a document, usually an image document, so that the provenance of the image

D. Buell, *Fundamentals of Cryptography*, Undergraduate Topics in Computer Science,
https://doi.org/10.1007/978-3-030-73492-3_2

can be authenticated if it is illegally taken without attribution or royalty. This is not unlike the apparent inclusion of intentional errors in maps, say, so that the owner of the map's copyright could argue that the map had been illegally copied. The author wishes very much that he had kept the road map of Louisiana (where he grew up) that showed a road south from Venice, Louisiana, and a bridge across the Mississippi to reach Pilottown. No such road or bridge has ever existed; Pilottown is where the Mississippi River pilots meet the incoming vessels and take the conn on the way up the river to the Port of New Orleans, and where on the outward voyage they turn over the conn to the seagoing pilots. The "city" can only be reached by water; there is no road south from Venice and no bridge across the Mississippi.

2.1 Substitution Ciphers

2.1.1 Caesar Ciphers

Perhaps the simplest and most historic of the substitution ciphers is that attributed to Julius Caesar. The classic Caesar cipher is a shift, modulo 26, of the letters of the alphabet:

Plaintext	a b c d e f g h i j k l m
Ciphertext	d e f g h i j k l m n o p
Plaintext	n o p q r s t u v w x y z
Ciphertext	q r s t u v w x y z a b c

In other words, every letter of plaintext is simply shifted down three letters to produce the ciphertext.

We might see

Plaintext	i a m t h e m e s s a g e
Ciphertext	l d p w k h p h v v d o h

2.1.2 Random Substitutions

The Caesar cipher has the major advantage of being easy to be used for encrypting a message. One need only know that encrypting is shifting down by three letters. On the other hand, the pattern of "every letter shifts by 3" is a pattern that is a weakness in the cipher. Once a cryptanalyst found that several letters seemed to have been shifted down by three, she might surmise that this was true for all the letters, and the encryption would be broken.

Consider instead a substitution in which one permutation of the $26! \approx 15 \times 10^{24}$ possible permutations of the 26 letters of the English alphabet is chosen as the encryption mechanism. With a randomly chosen permutation, there would be no pattern of "shift by three" that would be apparent, and the cipher would be much harder to break.

2.1.3 Vigenère as an Example of Polyalphabetic Substitutions

Both the Caesar cipher and a random substitution cipher use a single alphabet with which to encrypt symbols. The Vigenère cipher, first described by Giovan Battista Bellaso but then later misattributed to Vigenère, is a *polyalphabetic cipher*, in which (not surprisingly given the name) multiple alphabets are used to substitute one set of symbols for another.

We start with a table of symbols shifted for each of the possible shifts of a Caesar-like cipher.

	a	b	c	d	e	f	g	h	i	j	k	l	m	n	o	p	q	r	s	t	u	v	w	x	y	z
a	a	b	c	d	e	f	g	h	i	j	k	l	m	n	o	p	q	r	s	t	u	v	w	x	y	z
b	b	c	d	e	f	g	h	i	j	k	l	m	n	o	p	q	r	s	t	u	v	w	x	y	z	a
c	c	d	e	f	g	h	i	j	k	l	m	n	o	p	q	r	s	t	u	v	w	x	y	z	a	b
d	d	e	f	g	h	i	j	k	l	m	n	o	p	q	r	s	t	u	v	w	x	y	z	a	b	c
e	e	f	g	h	i	j	k	l	m	n	o	p	q	r	s	t	u	v	w	x	y	z	a	b	c	d
f	f	g	h	i	j	k	l	m	n	o	p	q	r	s	t	u	v	w	x	y	z	a	b	c	d	e
g	g	h	i	j	k	l	m	n	o	p	q	r	s	t	u	v	w	x	y	z	a	b	c	d	e	f
h	h	i	j	k	l	m	n	o	p	q	r	s	t	u	v	w	x	y	z	a	b	c	d	e	f	g
i	i	j	k	l	m	n	o	p	q	r	s	t	u	v	w	x	y	z	a	b	c	d	e	f	g	h
j	j	k	l	m	n	o	p	q	r	s	t	u	v	w	x	y	z	a	b	c	d	e	f	g	h	i
j	k	l	m	n	o	p	q	r	s	t	u	v	w	x	y	z	a	b	c	d	e	f	g	h	i	j
k	l	m	n	o	p	q	r	s	t	u	v	w	x	y	z	a	b	c	d	e	f	g	h	i	j	k
l	m	n	o	p	q	r	s	t	u	v	w	x	y	z	a	b	c	d	e	f	g	h	i	j	k	l
m	n	o	p	q	r	s	t	u	v	w	x	y	z	a	b	c	d	e	f	g	h	i	j	k	l	m
n	o	p	q	r	s	t	u	v	w	x	y	z	a	b	c	d	e	f	g	h	i	j	k	l	m	n
o	p	q	r	s	t	u	v	w	x	y	z	a	b	c	d	e	f	g	h	i	j	k	l	m	n	o
p	q	r	s	t	u	v	w	x	y	z	a	b	c	d	e	f	g	h	i	j	k	l	m	n	o	p
q	r	s	t	u	v	w	x	y	z	a	b	c	d	e	f	g	h	i	j	k	l	m	n	o	p	q
r	s	t	u	v	w	x	y	z	a	b	c	d	e	f	g	h	i	j	k	l	m	n	o	p	q	r
s	t	u	v	w	x	y	z	a	b	c	d	e	f	g	h	i	j	k	l	m	n	o	p	q	r	s
t	u	v	w	x	y	z	a	b	c	d	e	f	g	h	i	j	k	l	m	n	o	p	q	r	s	t
u	v	w	x	y	z	a	b	c	d	e	f	g	h	i	j	k	l	m	n	o	p	q	r	s	t	u
v	w	x	y	z	a	b	c	d	e	f	g	h	i	j	k	l	m	n	o	p	q	r	s	t	u	v
w	x	y	z	a	b	c	d	e	f	g	h	i	j	k	l	m	n	o	p	q	r	s	t	u	v	w
x	y	z	a	b	c	d	e	f	g	h	i	j	k	l	m	n	o	p	q	r	s	t	u	v	w	x
y	z	a	b	c	d	e	f	g	h	i	j	k	l	m	n	o	p	q	r	s	t	u	v	w	x	y
z	a	b	c	d	e	f	g	h	i	j	k	l	m	n	o	p	q	r	s	t	u	v	w	x	y	z

We now use an easy-to-remember word as the key, say "buell", and repeat it over the extent of the message:

```
Key        b u e l l b u e l l b u e
Plaintext  i a m t h e m e s s a g e
Ciphertext j v q f t f g i e e b b i
```

To encrypt, we start with the first letter, "i", and the first letter of the key, "b". We can take column "i" and row "b" and find the cipher letter "j". We then take the second letter and key letter, and under the column "a" for row "u" we find the cipher letter "v". And so forth. Decryption is just the opposite.

2.2   Language Characteristics and Patterns

Before going on to transposition ciphers and then the cryptanalysis of these simple ciphers, it is worth making a slight digression into the observation (and mathematics) of patterns that appear in any human language.

2.2.1   Letter Frequency

The first thing to note is that the letters do not appear equally often in text, and then that letter frequency is a strong indicator of language. We present in Table 2.1 three frequency percentages for English. The first column comes from a Cornell University website [1] and the second and third come from a frequency count of the Gutenberg Project [2] versions of Charles Dickens's *David Copperfield* and Charles Darwin's *Voyage of the Beagle*. We have blocked off sections where the letters in a block are the same but the frequencies slightly different; only in the penultimate block, of letters u, c, m, f, y, w, g, and p, do we see a significant difference in the ordering.

For cryptanalytic purposes, such frequency counts can almost immediately distinguish a substitution cipher from a transposition cipher. Since a transposition cipher does not change the frequency of the letters in the text, the frequency count should be roughly the same as a benchmark frequency count. In the case of a substitution cipher, one could almost immediately guess that the most common letter was the substitute in English for the letter "e".

In the case of a transposition cipher, the frequencies of the letters can serve to identify the underlying language, at least for the major European languages.

A similar frequency count on words themselves can also be used for guessing, especially when a codebook is used. The eight most common words in *David Copperfield*, for example, are, in order, "the", "I", "and", "to", "of", "a", "in", and "my", together accounting for nearly 21% of the total words in the text. For this reason,

Table 2.1 Three frequency distributions for English text

Cornell		Dickens		Darwin	
e	12.02	e	12.08	e	13.06
t	9.10	t	8.84	t	9.23
a	8.12	a	8.17	a	8.36
o	7.68	o	7.74	o	7.23
i	7.31	i	7.24	n	6.87
n	6.95	n	6.84	i	6.80
s	6.28	h	6.06	s	6.63
r	6.02	s	6.05	r	6.27
h	5.92	r	5.75	h	5.87
d	4.32	d	4.70	l	4.08
l	3.98	l	3.79	d	3.95
u	2.88	m	3.15	c	2.95
c	2.71	u	2.83	u	2.62
m	2.61	w	2.60	f	2.57
f	2.30	y	2.26	m	2.28
y	2.11	c	2.25	w	2.05
w	2.09	f	2.17	g	1.93
g	2.03	g	2.10	p	1.77
p	1.82	p	1.70	y	1.57
b	1.49	b	1.52	b	1.65
v	1.11	v	0.93	v	1.13
k	0.69	k	0.90	k	0.55
x	0.17	x	0.14	x	0.18
q	0.11	j	0.10	q	0.13
j	0.10	q	0.09	z	0.10
z	0.07	z	0.02	j	0.08

most codebooks have been created with multiple code words to be used for the very common words in order to hide the frequencies with which they occur.

2.2.2   Word Boundaries

We remark that it has been customary with either substitution or transposition ciphers to leave out the spaces between words and run the text together. English, for example, only has two words of one letter, "a" and "I", and relatively few words of two or of three letters. This makes guessing very much easier.[1,2]

---

[1]In the 1992 movie "Sneakers" the cryptanalysis takes place on a computer screen, with blank spaces separating words. This was the cause of some serious derision among the various cryppies of my acquaintance.

[2]We certainly admit that there could appear in plaintext something like "the letter b" but these are infrequent.

2.2.3 Cribbing

Simple ciphers, if done badly, can be extremely insecure. The following is a version of a cipher the author was actually asked to decrypt. The letter was formatted as a letter, complete with punctuation and spaces between words. The "collateral information" was that this was known to be a letter from the sender to a receiver with a known romantic connection.

```
pase zhic,
xqasta fchy mism u qhva dhj scp mism u kutt dhj s qhm.
qhva,
ksemis
```

It is not hard to crib this. How does one end a letter with a romantic connection? With the word "love", of course, so we crib qhva to be love. That gives us guesses for two vowels, "o" and "e". We can guess "u" and "s" to be "a" and "i" or the other way around. After that, it is easy, even with a message this short.

The lesson is that one cannot expect communications security if one doesn't obscure information that isn't part of the actual cipher system but that can be inferred, guessed, or cribbed.

2.2.4 Entropy

The extent to which a natural language has underlying patterns can be made mathematical, using the concept of *entropy* in information theory developed by Claude Shannon and described brilliantly in Hamming's book [3]. Assuming that we have "text" as a sequence of "symbols" (which we will take in this instance to be letters), the idea is this. We want a mathematical function that will measure the extent to which a new symbol provides more "information". For example, in English, seeing a "u" follow a "q" provides relatively little information except for the fact that one seems to be reading an English word. Seeing something other than a "u" following a "q" does provide information, since it indicates that the word is probably not English.

2.2.4.1 Information
We will assume that we have an alphabet of symbols

$$\{a_1, \ldots, a_k\}$$

each of which appears in text with fixed probabilities

$$p_i = p(a_i),$$

and we assume that these cover the space:

$$\sum_{i=1}^{k} p_i = 1$$

We want to measure the amount of information $I(p)$, or surprise, in seeing a symbol a that occurs with probability p. We assume three properties of the function $I(p)$.

1. Information is always nonnegative, that is, $I(p) \geq 0$.
2. Information is additive for independent events, that is,

$$I(p_i p_j) = I(p_i) + I(p_j).$$

3. $I(p)$ is a continuous function of p.

We can now determine what kinds of function $I(p)$ have these properties. First, we notice that we must have

$$I(pp) = I(p^2) = I(p) + I(p) = 2I(p).$$

From this we can extend recursively to get

$$I(p^n) = I(pp^{n-1}) = I(p) + I(p^{n-1}) = I(p) + (n-1)I(p) = nI(p).$$

Since $I(p)$ is continuous, we can substitute $q = p^n$, so $p = q^{1/n}$ and thus

$$I(q) = nI(q^{1/n}).$$

and then apply the argument above using the second condition to get

$$I(p^{m/n}) = (m/n)I(p).$$

We conclude that $I(p)$ for rational numbers behaves exactly as does a logarithm. Since we have assumed that $I(p)$ is continuous, we can extend from all rational numbers to all real numbers, and thus that

$$I(p) = r \log p.$$

Now, since p is in the range 0 to 1, we know that $\log p$ is negative, and thus that r must be negative in order for the first property to hold. Considering the second property, that $I(p)$ is additive, we have that

$$I(p_1 \ldots p_m) = I(p_1) + \ldots + I(p_m) = r(\log p_1 + \ldots + \log p_m).$$

We can choose r to be anything we want without changing the behavior of the function $I(p)$; different values of r would only scale the absolute numbers without changing any relative difference, so there is no reason to consider a value of r other than -1. We this we have

$$I(p) = -\log p = \log(1/p),$$

and this is the standard function used to measure the quantity of information.

2.2.4.2 Entropy

We can use the information function to provide a measure of the average information one gets when reading symbols from a fixed alphabet. If the symbols

$$\{a_1, \ldots, a_k\}$$

from an alphabet S appear in text with fixed probabilities

$$p_i,$$

then one gets

$$p_i \log(1/p_i)$$

units of information, on average, from the symbol a_i. Summing over all symbols, we have

$$H(S) = \sum_{i=1}^{k} p_i \log(1/p_i)$$

as the average information conveyed by an average text over the alphabet S. We call this the *entropy* of the alphabet, or of text written using that alphabet.

2.2.4.3 Examples

Consider what happens when a fair coin is tossed, and let's imagine (since computing is done in a binary world) that an outcome of heads corresponds to a 1 bit and an outcome of tails corresponds to a 0. If the coin is fair, then 0 and 1 will appear with equal probability 1/2. We get exactly the same information from the appearance of either of the possible outcomes. The entropy of this system is

$$H(S) = \sum_{i=1}^{2} (1/2)\lg 2 = \lg 2 = 1$$

if we decide to use binary logarithms, as we quite often do in computing (a different choice of logarithms will only change the result by a fixed multiplicative factor).

Now consider instead a loaded coin in which heads will appear twice as often as tails. Thus 1 occurs with probabilities 2/3 and 0 appears with probabilities 1/3. The entropy of this system is

$$\begin{aligned}
H(S) &= (2/3)\lg(3/2) + (1/3)\lg(3/1) \\
&= (2/3)\lg(3/2) + (1/3)\lg 3 \\
&= (2/3)\lg 3 - (2/3)\lg 2 + (1/3)\lg 3 \\
&= \lg 3 - (2/3)\lg 2 \\
&\approx 1.585 - (2/3) \\
&\approx 0.918
\end{aligned}$$

We remind ourselves of the intuitive notion of entropy from physics: a measure of the randomness of the system. The entropy of the fair die is greater than that of the loaded die, because the outcomes of the fair die are more random and less biased than are the outcomes of the loaded die.

2.2.4.4 The Entropy of English

Using the frequencies from Table 2.1, we can compute the entropy of English. Using the Cornell frequencies, and a binary logarithm, we get about 2.898 bits of information per letter. If the letter frequency was uniform, the entropy of a 26-letter language would be about

$$H(S) = \lg 26 \approx 4.7$$

bits per letter. Thus, about

$$100 \left(1 - \frac{2.898}{4.7} \right),$$

or 38% of the letters used in English are redundant.[3]

2.2.4.5 Entropy for Equal Distributions

It is worth as a benchmark to think of what the entropy is for a distribution that is "fair" in the sense above of a fair coin. Consider a set of n symbols $S = \{a_1, \ldots, a_n\}$, each of which has equal probability $1/n$. For such a distribution, the entropy is

$$H(S) = \sum_{i=1}^{n}(1/n) \lg n = \lg n \sum_{i=1}^{n}(1/n) = \lg n.$$

Thinking of entropy as the measure of surprise, or the measure of the quantity of information received from seeing a_k as the next symbol in a sequence, this value is the maximum that can be achieved. Any uneven distribution of symbols, like the frequency counts of letters in any human language, will cause the entropy to be smaller than this maximum.

2.3 Transposition Ciphers

In a substitution cipher, the original letters are replaced by different letters. In a transposition cipher, the letters remain the same but their ordering is changed.

2.3.1 Columnar Transpositions

Probably the simplest form of transposition is just to write the plaintext in the normal order across a page, but then to transmit as ciphertext the message letters read down in columns. For example, "A simple message like this sentence" could be written as

---

[3] Years prior to Shannon's work on entropy, Mark Twain published his humorous piece "A Plan for the Improvement of Spelling in the English Language", part of which was to combine letters with similar purpose and pronunciation; this would have increased the entropy, although we are unaware that a formal computation has ever been done.

```
asimxpl
emessxa
gelxike
thissex
nxtence
```

and then could be transmitted by reading down the columns:

```
aegtn smehx ielit msxse xsise pxkec laexe
```

where we have padded the message with "x" characters and then shown spaces (that would not be part of the transmitted message) in order to make it more readable in this text.

Variations on this theme have been used for millennia. The Spartans of ancient Greece used a *scytale*; by winding a paper strip around a rod of a fixed diameter, one could write the message across the rod, separating the individual letters by the circumference of the rod. A recipient not in possession of a rod of the same diameter would not be able to line up the letters as they had originally been written.

2.3.2 Double Transposition

Ciphers such as Playfair and ADFGX described below can readily be broken by using statistics on letter digrams or letter frequencies. For this reason, many transposition ciphers were done as double transpositions, with the first obscuring the underlying plaintext and the second doing the randomization needed for security.

2.4 Playfair

Purportedly the first cipher system to encrypt two letters at a time was invented by Sir Charles Wheatstone (he of the eponymous bridge) and named for his friend Baron Playfair, who was a major proponent of the cipher. One lays out a table of letters, perhaps

```
d u  n c  a
b e  l f  g
h i  k m  o
p q  r s  t
v w  x y  z
```

starting with a keyword (in this case the author's name), dropping letters if repeated, finishing with letters not in the keyword, and then conflating "i" with "j" to produce a square tableau.

Encryption now takes place as follows. Start with a message

```
this is the message
```

and break that into pairs of letters

```
th is is th em es sa ge
```

Three rules govern the production of ciphertext.

1. If the two letters of the pair lie in different rows and columns, they will form opposite corners of a rectangle, and the ciphertext pair is the letters on the other two corners. We will choose the corner letter that is in the same row as the plaintext letter.
2. If the two letters of the pair lie in the same row, shift each right one letter.
3. If the two letters of the pair lie in the same column, shift each down one letter.

Thus th becomes po, is becomes mq, em becomes fi, es becomes fq, sa becomes tc, ge becomes bl, and the ciphertext is

```
po mq mq fi fq tc bl
```

.

2.5 ADFGX

A substitution-transposition cipher that was used extensively by the Germans in World War I was called "ADFGX". In its simplest version it is simply a digram-for-digram substitution. Given a tableau

	A	D	F	G	X
A	d	u	n	c	a
D	b	e	l	f	g
F	h	i	k	m	o
G	p	q	r	s	t
X	v	w	x	y	z

with a random choice for the 5×5 matrix of letters, one replaces each letter with the row-column pair where that letter is found. Our previous message,

```
this is the message
```

would be sent as the ciphertext

```
GX FA FD GG FD GG GX FA DD FG DD GG GG AX DX DD
```

More complicated versions of the cipher would then apply transpositions to the letters of the substitution ciphertext.

2.6 Cryptanalysis

2.6.1 Breaking a Substitution Cipher

Breaking a substitution cipher is largely a matter of statistics, and with computer assistance, the tedious parts need no longer be done by hand. A combination of brute force, a small amount of tree search and pruning of unlikely branches, and some guessing and cribbing using frequency counts of letters, bigrams, and such, and a simple substitution can be cracked almost immediately.

We remark that statistics work best when there is data on which to do statistics, and thus that longer messages are more susceptible to statistical attacks than are short messages. However, messages don't have to be that long to expose their frequency counts.

Let's take the Gettysburg Address as an example. The nine most common letters in Lincoln's address are listed, in Table 2.2, along with the nine most common letters, in order, from Table 2.1.

The four most common letters match up, and they account for 42% of the letters in the Address. The next five account for almost another 32% of the total letters. We would expect that even if all $10! = 3628800$ different permutations were tried, it would be relatively easy to score the resulting letter sequences against English and prune the tree to something quite feasible. With more than 70% of the letters accounted for in the most common nine letters, it seems hard to believe that any reasonable attack would fail.

And we do point out that in this argument, the ability to use a computer is an enormous advantage. Human cryptanalysts are not going to try three million possi-

Table 2.2 Frequencies in the Gettysburg address

Lincoln	e	t	a	o	h	r	n	i	d
Cornell	e	t	a	o	i	n	s	r	h
Dickens	e	t	a	o	i	n	h	s	r
Darwin	e	t	a	o	n	i	s	r	h

bilities, but computers can do this quite readily. Prior to the computer era, and today for those who might do the daily newspaper cryptogram by hand, a great deal of good guesswork is needed. With computers and frequency counts, the time honored tradition of BFI[4] makes simple substitution completely breakable.

We point out here once again that having the text separated into words makes a brute force attack even easier. In the entire Brown corpus from the Natural Language Tool Kit [4], there are only 212 two-letter and 879 three-letter combinations, and many of these show up as chemical element or other abbreviations.

2.6.2 Breaking a Transposition Cipher

Breaking a transposition cipher is also largely a matter of statistics and some language guesswork. One example of breaking such a cipher is the World War I cipher in Appendix A.

2.7 The Vernam One-Time Pad

All but one cryptosystem, even when considering the modern ones, relies not on the ability to be perfectly secure but on the belief that it is computationally infeasible to decrypt a message. The general goal in encrypting a message is to make the text appear to be random. It is hard to be totally random, however, so both classic and modern cryptosystems use a pattern, or a function, that makes the text appear random. That pattern makes encrypting easier for humans, but also indicates to those attacking the encryption that a pattern exists.

The only truly secure cryptosystem is a one-time pad. One version of a one-time pad would be essentially a Vigenère cipher that chooses the alphabet based on an infinite sequence of random numbers. The Vigenère cipher has 26 alphabets, but for convenience a keyword is used to determine which alphabet is used for any given letter. If the keyword is chosen from any of some hundreds of thousands of dictionary words, place names, names of people, etc., an apparent randomness results, but it is the finite length of the keyword that leads to repetition in the choice of alphabets and the likelihood that in a long message the same letter will be encrypted with the same alphabet. If that "keyword" were in fact randomly generated and of infinite length, the repetition, that leads to detecting the length, would not be present in the ciphertext.

The Vernam one-time pad [5] was invented at about the same time as the use of teletypes for transmission of messages. With the original teletype, letters were converted to 5-bit integers and transmitted as such, often using punched paper tape. One version of a Vernam one-time pad would have a companion tape with a random

---

[4]Brute force and ignorance.

sequence of 5-bit integers, and the bits of the random integers XOR-ed with the text bits to produce the ciphertext. The receiver, with an identical paper tape, would XOR again to produce the plaintext.

Security of the Vernam cipher is 100% guaranteed, as mentioned in [5], provided that

- there are only two copies of the key-tape;
- both sides of the communications link have the same key-tape;
- the key-tape is used only once;
- the key-tape is destroyed immediately after use;
- the key-tape contains truly random characters;
- the equipment is TEMPEST proof;
- the key tape was not compromised during transport.

All these criteria are necessary. In order for the tape to be genuinely random, there must be only the two copies of the tape, which must be identical and not intercepted in transmission. In order to prevent repetitions such as are used to break a Vigenère cipher, the tape must be used only once and then destroyed. In order for the ciphertext to be read, the two tapes must of course be identical and synchronized to start at the same place for the XOR process. TEMPEST-ing is the mechanism for preventing a third party from monitoring the electrical signals generated by a device such as a teletype or computer terminal, and both encryption and decryption processes must be proof against "listening in" by an adversary.

And finally, of course, in order to be a random XOR-ing that will not have the sort of repetition used in breaking a Vigenère cipher, the sequence really does need to be truly random. There are mechanisms for generating random numbers. It has been alleged that the British Lottery once had a Geiger counter on the roof of its building, recording the random pattern of cosmic rays hitting the counter. Many lottery systems really do generate random results with physical ping-pong balls that are carefully checked to be identical in size and weight. Random numbers have been generated from a noisy diode.

We will discuss later the generation of pseudo-random numbers using a periodic function whose period is so long as to appear random. Much of public key cryptography relies on the fact that functions exist to generate numbers that satisfy randomness tests but can be generated deterministically with a function.

2.8 Exercises

1. The following are believed to be ciphertext from Caesar ciphers. Decrypt them.

   a. `alirmrxligsyvwisjlyqerizirxw`
   b. `sdgkcdrolocdypdswocsdgkcdrogybcdypdswoc`
   c. `hzruvadohafvbyjvbuayfjhukvmvyfvbhzrdohafvbjhukvmvyfvbyjvbuayf`

2. (Programming exercise) From some legitimate source (perhaps Project Guten-berg), obtain text in a language other than English. (French and German are easy to get from Project Gutenberg.) Compute letter frequencies for these other lan-guages, and compare them with English to determine how you would recognize the underlying language of text encrypted with either a substitution or transposi-tion cipher.

3. (Programming exercise) Write a program to assist a human observer in decrypting ciphertext from an English document encrypted with a substitution cipher. You may assume that the word boundaries are present in the ciphertext, so you can use established lists of short words as cribs and score longer words based on English letter patterns.

4. (Programming exercise) Write a program to do a ciphertext decryption from an English document encrypted with a substitution cipher. Unlike the previous exer-cise, this will probably require a depth-first search through possible substitutions and a much more sophisticated scoring function to determine the likelihood that the particular assignment of letters at that point in the search tree is correct.

5. (Programming exercise) Write a program to compute, not the single letter fre-quencies, but the frequencies of two-letter and three-letter sequences in English. You might use as source text any of the corpora from the Brown corpus, or a text from the Gutenberg project. If you do the frequency counts with and without word boundaries, are they different? This would affect how you would attack an encrypted message with a search program.

2.8.1 Cipher Text for Substitution Cipher Problems (3) and (4)

- mia zhjecad hg s mihjtscp kuqat baouct yumi s behfac gsc baqm scp qasfd muea
- ph chm ba ueeaxqsnasbqa ug dhj nscchm ba eaxqsnap dhj nscchm ba xehkhmap
- ug dhj miucf chbhpd nseat ug dhj sea squva med kuttuco s nhjxqa hg nse xsdkacmt
- baghea dhj neumunuwa thkahca dhj tihjqp ysqf s kuqa uc miaue tihat mism ysd yiac dhj neumunuwa miak dhj sea s kuqa sysd scp dhj isva miaue tihat
- ug sm guetm dhj ph chm tjnnaap tfdpuvuco ut chm ghe dhj
- ug dhj maqq mia mejmi dhj ph chm isva mh eakakbae scdmiuco
- mia ljunfatm ysd mh phjbqa dhje khcad ut mh ghqp um uc isqg scp xjm um bsnf uc dhje xhnfam
- pjnm msxa ut qufa mia ghena um ist s quoim tupa scp s psef tupa scp um ihqpt mia jcuvaeta mhoamiae
- oacaesqqd txasfuco dhj sea chm qasecuco kjni yiac dhje quxt sea khvuco
- arxaeuacna ut thkamiuco dhj phc m oam jcmuq zjtm sgmae dhj caap um
- cavae kutt s ohhp niscna mh tijm jx
- ouva s ksc s guti scp ia yuqq asm ghe s psd masni iuk ihy mh guti scp ia yuqq tum uc s bhsm scp peucf baae sqq psd

References

1. Cornell University, English letter frequency, http://pi.math.cornell.edu/~mec/2003-2004/cryptography/subs/frequencies.html
2. Project Gutenberg, The Gutenberg Project, https://www.gutenberg.org
3. R. W. Hamming, *Coding and Information Theory*, 2nd edn. (Prentice-Hall, Hoboken, 1986), p. 103ff
4. Natural Language Tool Kit, Brown Corpus, http://www.nltk.org
5. The Crypto Museum, The Vernam cipher, https://www.cryptomuseum.com/crypto/vernam.htm. Accessed 24 Jan 2020

Divisibility, Congruences, and Modular Arithmetic

3

Abstract

Modern cryptography is largely based on the mathematicals of modular arithmetic, congruences, and the arithmetic in the integers modulo prime numbers or products of (usually) two large prime numbers. In this chapter we cover the basic number theory that appears in both symmetric and asymmetric cryptographic systems: divisibility and congruences, greatest common divisor, exponentiation, and the Euler totient. Our emphasis is on mathematical theorems that must be understood and used, rather than on their proofs, unless the method or constructions in the proofs are relevant to cryptography itself. Although we treat this as background mathematics, we point out that the reader can readily generate examples for all the principles that are covered as well as find examples that demonstrate why the assumptions made are necessary and the conclusions tightly drawn.

3.1 Divisibility

We operate in this chapter on the assumption, which may not always be explicitly stated, that everything is an integer.

Definition 3.1 We say that an integer a *divides* an integer b, and write $a|b$, if there is a third integer d such that $b = ad$. We call such an a a *divisor* or *factor* of b. If a is a divisor of integers b and c, then we say that a is a *common divisor* of b and c. If we have $a|c$ and $b|c$, then we call c a *common multiple* of a and b.

Theorem 3.1 *1. For all c, $a|b$ implies that $a|bc$.*
2. If $a|b$ and $b|c$, then $a|c$.
3. For all integers x and y, if $a|b$ and $a|c$, then $a|(bx + cy)$.
4. If $a|b$ and $b|a$, then $a = \pm b$.
5. If $a|b$ and both $a > 0$ and $b > 0$, then $a \leq b$.

© The Author(s), under exclusive license to Springer Nature Switzerland AG 2021
D. Buell, *Fundamentals of Cryptography*, Undergraduate Topics in Computer Science,
https://doi.org/10.1007/978-3-030-73492-3_3

Proof 1. If $a|b$, then there is a d such that $b = ad$. For all c, then, we have $bc = adc$, and dc is the multiplier that satisfies the condition in the definition of "divides".

2. If $b = ad_1$ and $c = bd_2$ for integers d_1, d_2, then $c = ad_1d_2 = a(d_1d_2)$ and we again have satisfied the condition for "divides".

3. If $b = ad_1$ and $c = ad_2$ for integers d_1, d_2, then for all $x, y \in \mathbb{Z}$ we have

$$bx + cy = ad_1x + ad_2y = a(d_1x + d_2y)$$

and again we have satisfied the condition.

4. If $b = ad_1$ and $a = bd_2$ for integers d_1, d_2, then we have $b = ad_1 = bd_1d_2$ and thus $d_1d_2 = 1$. This can only hold if $d_1 = d_2 = +1$ or $d_1 = d_2 = -1$.

5. If $b = ad$, and these are positive, then the only possible values for b are $a, 2a, 3a, \ldots$, all of which are larger than a except the first, which is equal.

Definition 3.2 (*The Division Algorithm*) Given two elements $a, b \in \mathbb{Z}$, the *division algorithm* is the process by which we find integers q and r, the *quotient* and *remainder*, with $0 \le r < a$, such that

$$b = qa + r$$

1. Among the finitely many values $r = b - qa$, for $|q| \le |b|$, we choose the nonnegative value of least magnitude.

2. Return r and $q = (b - r)/a$.

Theorem 3.2 *Given integers a and $b \neq 0$, the division algorithm returns values q and r such that $b = qa + r$ and $0 \le r < |a|$.*

Theorem 3.3 *There are only finitely many divisors of any integer a.*

Definition 3.3 For a and b integers not both zero, the largest common divisor of a and b is called the *greatest common divisor*, written $\gcd(a, b)$. The smallest common multiple of a and b is called the *least common multiple*, written $\mathrm{lcm}(a, b)$.

Remark 3.1 The gcd is frequently written just (a, b) and the lcm is frequently written just $[a, b]$. There are too many things without sufficient labelling, however, so we will not write them that way but will write them as in the definition.

Theorem 3.4 *Given a and b not both zero, the values of $\gcd(a, b)$ and $\mathrm{lcm}(a, b)$ are unique.*

Theorem 3.5 *The $\gcd(a, b)$ is the least positive value of $ax + by$ as x and y run through all integers.*

Proof This is a useful constructive proof, so we'll do it.

First off, let $g = \gcd(a, b)$. We then have $g|(ax + by)$ for all x and y by Theorem 3.1, part 3.

Let's let $\ell = ax_0 + by_0$ be the least positive value of $ax + by$ as x and y run through all the integers. Since g divides all such values, we have that $g|\ell$. Since both g and ℓ are positive, we know there is an integer $k \geq 1$ such that $\ell = gk$. But if $k > 1$, then g is strictly less than ℓ, which is contrary to our assumption. So it has to be that $k = 1$ and $g = \ell$. □

Remark 3.2 Note that the preceding theorem says that if $g = \gcd(a, b)$, then we can find x_0 and y_0 such that $g = ax_0 + by_0$. This is a very big deal.

Remark 3.3 Note that if a divides b, then $\gcd(a, b) = |a|$ and is not zero, because we have defined the gcd to be positive and not nonnegative.

Theorem 3.6 *Assume that a and b are both nonzero.*

1. *If $g = \gcd(a, b)$, then g divides every common divisor of a and b.*
2. *If $m > 0$, then $\gcd(ma, mb) = m \cdot \gcd(a, b)$.*
3. *If $m > 0$, then $\mathrm{lcm}(ma, mb) = m \cdot \mathrm{lcm}(a, b)$.*
4. *If $d > 0$, $d|a$, and $d|b$, then $\gcd(a, b) = d \gcd(a/d, b/d)$.*
5. *If $g = \gcd(a, b)$, then $\gcd(a/g, b/g) = 1$.*
6. $\gcd(a, b) = \gcd(b, a)$.
7. $\mathrm{lcm}(a, b) = \mathrm{lcm}(b, a)$.
8. $\gcd(a, -b) = \gcd(a, b)$.
9. $\mathrm{lcm}(a, -b) = \mathrm{lcm}(a, b)$.
10. $\gcd(a, b + xa) = \gcd(a, b)$ *for all integers x.*
11. $\gcd(a, 0) = \gcd(0, a) = \gcd(a, a) = \mathrm{lcm}(a, a) = |a|$.
12. $\gcd(a, b, c) = \gcd(a, \gcd(b, c))$.
13. *If $c|ab$, and if $\gcd(b, c) = 1$, then $c|a$.*

Definition 3.4 If $\gcd(a, b) = 1$, then we say that a and b are *relatively prime* or *prime to one another.*

3.2 The Euclidean Algorithm

The Euclidean algorithm is perhaps the oldest algorithm on the planet. Certainly it is likely the oldest algorithm still being used in its original form. The naive version here is presented almost exactly as in Euclid's *Elements*.

3.2.1 The Naive Euclidean Algorithm

Algorithm 3.1 Naive algorithm to calculate $g = \gcd(a, b)$

Require: $a, b \in \mathbb{Z}$, not both zero
1: $r_{-1} \leftarrow a$
2: $r_0 \leftarrow b$
3: $j \leftarrow 0$
4: **while** $r_j \neq 0$ **do**

5:    $j \leftarrow j + 1$
6:    Use the division algorithm to obtain q_j and r_j: $r_{j-2} \leftarrow q_j r_{j-1} + r_j$

7: **end while**
8: Output $g \leftarrow r_{j-1}$

Example 3.1 Let's compute the gcd of 366 and 252.

$$
\begin{aligned}
r_{-1} &= 366 \\
r_0 &= 252 \\
j &= \quad 0 \\
j &= \quad 1 \\
q_1 &= \quad 1 \; r_1 = 114 \quad 366 = 1 \cdot 252 + 114 \\
j &= \quad 2 \\
q_2 &= \quad 2 \; r_2 = 24 \quad 252 = 2 \cdot 114 + 24 \\
j &= \quad 3 \\
q_3 &= \quad 4 \; r_3 = 18 \quad 114 = 4 \cdot 24 + 18 \\
j &= \quad 4 \\
q_4 &= \quad 1 \; r_4 = 6 \quad\;\; 24 = 1 \cdot 18 + 6 \\
j &= \quad 5 \\
q_5 &= \quad 3 \; r_5 = 0 \quad\;\; 18 = 3 \cdot 6 + 0
\end{aligned}
$$

We output $r_4 = 6$ as the gcd.

Remark 3.4 We observe that the algorithm must terminate, because the division algorithm produces a smaller, nonnegative, value of r_j with each step, so the process cannot continue forever.

Remark 3.5 We observe that a worst case running time of this version of the Euclidean algorithm occurs when a and b are successive Fibonacci numbers, because in that case all the quotients are 1 and the number of steps is maximized. Since there is a closed form for the Fibonacci numbers,

$$F_n = \frac{\left(\frac{1+\sqrt{5}}{2}\right)^n - \left(\frac{1-\sqrt{5}}{2}\right)^n}{\sqrt{5}}$$

and the gcd operation will descend n steps until we get to the base value of 1, which is the gcd of any two adjacent Fibonacci numbers, we know that the number of steps to be taken in this worst case example, n, is logarithmic in the size of F_n. Indeed, knowing that we can write $\gcd(a, b) = \gcd(b, a - b)$, if we assume that $a > b$ to begin with and that all quotients are 1 in the descent to the gcd, we have

$$\gcd(a, b) = \gcd(b, a - b)$$
$$= \gcd(a - b, 2b - a)$$
$$= \gcd(2b - a, 2a - 3b)$$
$$= \gcd(2a - 3b, 5b - 3a)$$

and so forth. The coefficients are the Fibonacci numbers, with alternating signs, and the logarithmic number of steps is independent of the values of a and b.

3.2.2 The Extended Euclidean Algorithm

Our example above deserves a more explicit elucidation. The naive Euclidean algorithm will find the greatest common divisor g of integers a and b. The extended algorithm will find values x and y such that $ax + by = g$, and it requires only that we keep track of the necessary coefficients. If we compute in sequence, using the division algorithm,

$$a = r_{-1}$$
$$b = r_0$$
$$r_{-1} = r_0 q_1 + r_1$$
$$r_0 = r_1 q_2 + r_2$$
$$r_1 = r_2 q_3 + r_3$$
$$r_2 = r_3 q_4 + r_4$$

This allows us to keep track of how to compute r_i from the original values of a and b:

$$r_1 = a - q_1 b$$
$$r_2 = b - q_2 r_1 = b - q_2(a - q_1 b) = (q_1 q_2 + 1)b - q_2 a$$
$$r_3 = r_1 - q_3 r_2 = a - q_1 b - q_3((q_1 q_2 + 1)b - q_2 a)$$
$$= (q_2 q_3 + 1)a - (q_1 q_2 q_3 + q_3 + q_1 + 1)b$$

and so forth. The algebra gets ugly, but done recursively as a computer program, each step is straightforward. Each of the remainders in the Euclidean algorithm can be expressed as an integer linear combination of the original a and b. For our example above, we compute

$$114 = 366 - 252$$
$$24 = 3 \cdot 252 - 2 \cdot 366$$
$$18 = 9 \cdot 366 - 13 \cdot 252$$
$$6 = 16 \cdot 252 - 11 \cdot 366$$

This leads us to a hugely important fact.

Theorem 3.7 *Let x_0 and y_0 be any result obtained from the extended Euclidean algorithm to determine*

$$ax_0 + by_0 = \gcd(a, b)$$

Then the set of all solutions of $ax + by = \gcd(a, b)$ is exactly the set

$$(x, y) = (x_0 + \lambda b, y_0 - \lambda a)$$

for $\lambda \in \mathbb{Z}$.

3.2.3 The Binary Euclidean Algorithm

The naive version of Euclid requires division, which is on a computer very much the slowest of all arithmetic operations. Even in ancient days,[1] the relative cost of addition versus multiplication versus division was on the order of one to five or one to ten.[2] On modern computers, since the advent of RISC architectures in the 1980s, integer division can take as many as 100 individual machine instructions. This cost is somewhat mitigated by the long pipelines on modern CPUs, but the cost of integer division is still very high compared to addition or multiplication. This is to some extent made even worse by the fact that much attention is paid to floating point arithmetic, in hopes of improving the performance of scientific computing, but little attention is paid to integer arithmetic, for which cryptography is almost the only real computing-intensive application that uses integer arithmetic for something other than controlling loops or indexing into arrays in memory.

We observe three things:

1. If a and b are both odd, then $\gcd(2^i a, 2^j b) = 2^{\min(i,j)} \gcd(a, b)$;
2. If a and b are both odd, then $b - a$ is even;
3. $\gcd(a, b) = \gcd(a, b - a)$.

Our binary gcd algorithm is thus the following.

---

[1] The 1970s?

[2] On the IBM System 370 Model 158 of the early 1970s, for example, integer multiplication cost 6.5 times as much as integer addition, and integer division cost 47 times as much, with division thus about 7 times the cost of multiplication.

Algorithm 3.2 Binary algorithm to calculate $g = \gcd(a, b)$

Require: $a, b \in \mathbb{Z}$, not both zero

1: $a_s \leftarrow a$ right shifted i bits until the rightmost bit of a_s is a 1
2: $b_s \leftarrow b$ right shifted j bits until the rightmost bit of b_s is a 1
3: Comment: Note that $g = 2^{\min(i,j)} \gcd(a_s, b_s)$
4: **while** a_s and b_s are both nonzero **do**

5:   **if** $a_s > b_s$ **then**

6:     exchange a_s and b_s

7:   **end if**
8:   $b_s \leftarrow b_s - a_s$
9:   $b_s \leftarrow b$ right shifted k bits until the rightmost bit of b_s is a 1

10: **end while**
11: Output $g \leftarrow 2^{\min(i,j)} a_s$

The algorithm, briefly, is this. We know that the gcd of a and b is the smaller power of 2 dividing a and b times the gcd of the odd parts of a and b. We thus first clear off the powers of 2, which in binary are the rightmost zero bits. We then subtract the smaller from the larger. Since the difference of two odd numbers is even, we know we can shift off at least one zero bit from the difference, and then repeat on the now-smaller pair of integers. When we subtract to get zero, then the positive value of a_s is the odd part of the gcd.

What is significant is that this algorithm requires no multiplication and no division. It uses only the addition, bit test, and subtraction instructions, which are about the fastest of any instructions on any computer.

The disadvantage of this algorithm on 64-bit integers is that we would have to iterate the loop many times; the pathological worst cases would be those for which every time we subtract we get only one zero bit to shift off from the difference, and if one operand is much smaller than the other, the subtract-and-shift looks more like what the hardware would do much more efficiently. The potential for that many loop iterations would have to be balanced against the relative costs of the machine instructions used inside the loop.

3.2.4 The Subtract-Three-Times Euclidean Algorithm

Paul Lévy [1] showed that for random integers a and b of the same maximum bit length, the quotient a/b was 1 about 41.5% of the time, 2 about 17.0% of the time, and 3 about 9.3% of the time, and thus was 1, 2, or 3 just over two-thirds of the time. This leads to a hybrid algorithm in which one subtracts the smaller of a or b until the result is negative, or up to four times. In about 2/3 of the cases, then, the division can be avoided.

3.2.5 GCDs of Large Integers

Algorithm 3.3 Subtraction algorithm to calculate $g = \gcd(bigger, smaller)$

Require: $bigger, smaller \in \mathbb{Z}$, not both zero, with $bigger > smaller$
  while $smaller > 0$ **do**

    $bigger \leftarrow bigger - smaller$
    if $bigger < smaller$ **then**

      $q \leftarrow 1$
      Exchange $bigger$ and $smaller$

    else

      $bigger \leftarrow bigger - smaller$
      if $bigger < smaller$ **then**

        $q \leftarrow 2$
        Exchange $bigger$ and $smaller$

      else

        $bigger \leftarrow bigger - smaller$
        if $bigger < smaller$ **then**

          $q \leftarrow 3$
          Exchange $bigger$ and $smaller$

        else

          Compute q and r using the division algorithm

        end if

      end if

    end if
    Exchange $bigger$ and $smaller$ if necessary so $bigger > smaller$

  end while
  Output $g \leftarrow bigger$

Public-key cryptography, as we will discuss later in this book, relies on arithmetic modulo large integers, perhaps of 1024, 2048, or even 4096 bits in length. As one might imagine, good algorithms for computing the greatest common divisor for such large integers might be different from more naive algorithms. The basic version of Euclid's algorithm requires division, which for long integers can be very expensive.

The binary algorithm can only be guaranteed to reduce the size of the integers one bit at a time. Division itself is different from addition, subtraction, and multiplication in that schoolchild arithmetic for division works from the most down to the least significant digits, not the other way around, and unlike the other three operations, with division it can happen that trial quotient digit turns out to be too large. Dividing 30 into 60, for example, using schoolchild arithmetic, the trial quotient of $6/3 = 2$ is correct, but dividing 31 into 60 doesn't yield the correct quotient of 1 until one looks at the first two digits. One can easily show that for integers of many digits, no fixed-size set of trial digits will always produce the correct quotient. However, an improved version of Euclid's algorithm, suitable for gcds of very long integers but using only fixed single-precision arithmetic, was given by Lehmer [2] and is also presented and analyzed in Knuth [1, pp. 328ff]. Lehmer's improvement to Euclid's algorithm provides a predicted quotient that is almost always correct but can be computed using single-precision arithmetic of the leading digits of divisor and dividend.

Lehmer's version of Euclid's algorithm works from the most significant to the least significant digits. An alternative algorithm for computing the gcd comes from the work of Sorenson and then Jebelean, Weber, and Sedjelmaci [3–6]. This algorithm works from low digits to high, solving

$$au + bv \equiv 0 \pmod{k}$$

for values a, b, that are bounded by $\sqrt{k}$. Using values for k that are powers of 2 permits computing the reduction modulo k by extracting bits; we shall see this approach used more extensively in Chap. 8.

3.3 Primes

Definition 3.5 An integer p is said to be *prime* if the only divisors of p are 1 and p. An integer $p \neq 1$ that is not prime is said to be *composite*.

Remark 3.6 We will assume by convention that we only apply the term "prime" to positive integers.

Remark 3.7 We note that modern convention is that 1 is not a prime. This has not always been the convention. D. N. Lehmer counted 1 as a prime.

Theorem 3.8 (Fundamental Theorem of Arithmetic) *The factoring of an integer n into a product of primes is unique up to the order of the primes and multiplication by +1 or −1.*

Theorem 3.9 (Euclid) *The number of primes is infinite.*

Proof (This is exactly the proof given in Euclid, Book IX, proposition 20.) We do a proof by contradiction. Assume that the number of primes is finite, and let the finite set P be the set of all primes. Consider the integer $N = \left(\prod_{p \in P} p\right) + 1$. Now, this can be written, due to Theorem 3.8, as a product of primes, and thus there is some prime p that divides N. However, $p \notin P$, because then we would have $p|N$ and $p|\prod_{p \in P}$, and thus $p|1$, which is impossible. So this prime p is a prime not in P; our supposed set P of all primes is not a set of all the primes, and that is a contradiction. Our assumption that the number of primes is finite must be false.   □

We finally have a theorem that shows that the primes are in fact the building blocks of divisibility of the integers.

Theorem 3.10 *If p is a prime, and if $p|ab$, then either $p|a$ or $p|b$.*

3.4 Congruences

Definition 3.6 Two integers a and b are said to be *congruent* modulo a positive integer m if $m|(a - b)$. We write $a \equiv b \pmod{m}$ and say that a is *congruent to b modulo m*. The integer m is called the *modulus*.

Definition 3.7 If $a \equiv b \pmod{m}$ and if we have $0 \le a < b$, we say that a is the *least positive residue* modulo m.

Definition 3.8 A *complete set of residues* modulo m is a set S such every integer n is congruent to some element of S modulo m but no two elements of S are congruent to each other modulo m.

We normally take as our complete set of residues modulo m either the set of least positive residues

$$S = \{r : 0 \le r < m\}$$

or (occasionally, when it suits us) the set of least-magnitude residues

$$S' = \{r : -m/2 < r <= m/2\}.$$

The next set of propositions and theorems state in concrete terms results we would know to be true if we first covered the material of Chap. 4 and proved that the integers modulo m form a ring.

Theorem 3.11 *Congruence modulo m is an equivalence relation.*

1. *(Reflexivity) $a \equiv a \pmod{m}$;*
2. *(Symmetry) $a \equiv b \pmod{m}$ if and only if $b \equiv a \pmod{m}$;*
3. *(Transitivity) $a \equiv b \pmod{m}$ and $b \equiv c \pmod{m}$ implies that $a \equiv c \pmod{m}$.*

Theorem 3.12 *1.* $a \equiv b$ (mod m) *and* $c \equiv d$ (mod m); *implies that for all integers*
   x, y *we have* $ax + cy \equiv bx + dy$ (mod m);
2. $a \equiv b$ (mod m) *and* $c \equiv d$ (mod m) *implies that* $ac \equiv bd$ (mod m);
3. $a \equiv b$ (mod m) *implies that for any polynomial* $f(x)$ *with integer coefficients*
   we have $f(a) \equiv f(b)$ (mod m).

The statements in the previous theorem are about what happens when we multiply, and we know that multiplication makes sense.

In general, however, we are not in what we will learn in Chap. 4 to be a field, and division is not guaranteed to be possible with the original modulus; division in congruences involves the gcd of the modulus and the dividend.

Theorem 3.13 *The following are true.*

1. $ax \equiv ay$ (mod m) *if and only if* $x \equiv y$ (mod $m/(\gcd(a, m))$);
2. $ax \equiv ay$ (mod m) *and* $\gcd(a, m) = 1$ *implies that* $x \equiv y$ (mod m);
3. *Solving a linear congruence*

$$ax \equiv b \quad (\text{mod } m)$$

is equivalent to performing the extended Euclidean algorithm. If we have

$$\gcd(a, m) \nmid b$$

then no such solution exists.

Proof We will prove only the last of these. Assume we have a linear congruence

$$ax \equiv b \quad (\text{mod } m)$$

to be solved for the indeterminate x. This is equivalent to determining x such that

$$ax - b = my$$

for some indeterminate y, and this is the same as searching for x and y such that

$$ax - my = b.$$

Clearly, if $\gcd(a, m) \nmid b$ then the equation cannot be solved, because the gcd divides the left hand side but not the right hand side.

If $\gcd(a, m)|b$ then we can perform the extended Euclidean algorithm to compute x_0 and y_0 such that

$$ax_0 - my_0 = g,$$

where $g = \gcd(a, m)$. This is the same as solving the equation

$$(a/g)x_0 - (m/g)y_0 = 1.$$

We can now multiply back to obtain

$$a(b/g)x_0 - m(b/g)y_0 = b,$$

where $a, b/g, x_0, m, b/g, y_0$ are all integers, and we have an integral solution to the necessary equation.

The fact that the extended Euclidean algorithm produces all the solutions to the linear congruence comes from Theorem 3.7. $\qquad\square$

Remark 3.8 It should be noted that the term is *modular arithmetic* and not *modulo arithmetic*. The former has been in use in English since about the 1830s, and it is unfortunate that the incorrect term seems to have come into common use.

Remark 3.9 We will refer to the least-residue solution of

$$ax \equiv 1 \pmod{m}$$

as $a^{-1} \pmod{m}$ so that we can represent multiplication by an inverse modulo m, when that is well defined, as integer arithmetic modulo m, and we will continue to write something like $1/a$ when the "division" might not produce an integer.

Theorem 3.14 (Chinese Remainder Theorem (CRT)) *Let $m_1, m_2, \ldots, m_k$ be k positive integers that are pairwise relatively prime (that is, for which $\gcd(m_i, m_j) = 1$ for any $i \neq j$). Then for any set of integers $a_1, a_2, \ldots, a_k$, the simultaneous congruences*

$$x \equiv a_i \pmod{m_i}$$

have a unique solution X modulo $M = \prod_{i=1}^{k} m_i$.

Proof (*First version*) The first proof is a variation on Lagrange interpolation and is done by pulling the rabbit out of the hat in one step.

Let $M_j = M/m_j$. Since the m_i are pairwise relatively prime, we know that $\gcd(M_j, m_j) = 1$ and thus that we can find b_j such that $M_j b_j \equiv 1 \pmod{m_j}$. (We alleged that Theorem 3.5 was a big deal. We have just used it here.)

We then let

$$X = \sum_{i=1}^{k} a_i b_i M_i.$$

Now, for any m_j, we have that $m_j | M_i$ for $i \neq j$, and thus that

$$X \equiv a_j b_j M_j \equiv a_j \cdot 1 \pmod{m_j}.$$

Proof (*Second version*) The first congruence is simple: the solutions of

$$x \equiv a_1 \pmod{m_1}$$

comprise exactly the integers

$$x_1 = a_1 + m_1 x_2$$

for $x_2 \in \mathbb{Z}$.

The second of our congruences,

$$x \equiv a_2 \pmod{m_2},$$

can be rewritten as

$$a_1 + m_1 x_2 \equiv a_2 \pmod{m_2},$$

which can be rewritten as

$$m_1 x_2 \equiv a_2 - a_1 \pmod{m_2},$$

Since we know that $\gcd(m_1, m_2) = 1$, we know that this congruence has solutions

$$x_2 \equiv (a_2 - a_1) \cdot m_1^{-1} \pmod{m_2}$$

which are

$$x_2 = A_1 + m_2 x_3$$

for $x_3 \in \mathbb{Z}$, and where we write A_1 for the least positive reduced residue $(a_2 - a_1) \cdot m_1^{-1}$ taken modulo m_2.

We now repeat the process:

$$x \equiv a_3 \pmod{m_3}$$

becomes

$$a_1 + m_1(A_1 + m_2 x_3) \equiv a_3 \pmod{m_3}$$

which becomes

$$m_1 m_2 x_3 \equiv a_3 - a_1 - m_1 A_1 \pmod{m_3}$$

Remark 3.10 We remark that the first proof is a beautiful example of an existential mathematical proof, and that it is very much the wrong thing to do if one actually wants to use the CRT to solve some simultaneous equations. The problem with the first proof is that the modulus M grows exponentially with the number of individual moduli m_i, and the first proof requires the use of full-length arithmetic throughout the computation.

On the other hand, the second proof, which is relatively easy to do but ungainly to state, is constructive and algorithmic and never requires doing arithmetic of size larger than the square of the largest of the moduli.

Example 3.2 We use the CRT to solve the following system of congruences.

$$x \equiv 3 \pmod{5}$$
$$x \equiv 2 \pmod{7}$$
$$x \equiv 4 \pmod{11}$$

and we will do this first in the computationally efficient way.

We have $x \equiv 3 \pmod{5}$, which means that $x = 3 + 5a$ for some integer a. We thus have

$$3 + 5a \equiv 2 \pmod{7}$$
$$5a \equiv 6 \pmod{7}$$
$$a \equiv 4 \pmod{7}$$

and thus $x = 3 + 5a = 3 + 5(4 + 7b) = 23 + 35b$ for some integer b.

We continue

$$23 + 35b \equiv 4 \pmod{11}$$
$$2b \equiv 3 \pmod{11}$$
$$b \equiv 7 \pmod{11}$$

and thus $x = 23 + 35b = 23 + 35(7 + 11c) = 268 + 385c$ for some integer c.

We check that $268 \equiv 3 \pmod 5$, then that $268 \equiv 2 \pmod 7$, and finally that $268 \equiv 4 \pmod{11}$; our solution

$$x \equiv 268 \pmod{385}$$

is unique modulo $385 = 5 \times 7 \times 11$.

Example 3.3 Let's do the same computation using the method analogous to Lagrange interpolation. We want

$$x \equiv 3 \pmod 5$$
$$x \equiv 2 \pmod 7$$
$$x \equiv 4 \pmod{11}$$

We have $M_1 = 77$, $M_2 = 55$, $M_3 = 35$, say, and we determine that $b_1 \equiv 3 \pmod 5$, $b_2 \equiv 6 \pmod 7$, $b_3 \equiv 6 \pmod{11}$. We can write

$$X = 3 \times (3 \times 77) + 2 \times (6 \times 55) + 4 \times (6 \times 35)$$
$$= 693 + 660 + 840$$
$$= 2193$$

and we notice that $2193 = 268 + 5 \times 385$.

Remark 3.11 The CRT is an extremely powerful computational tool. Let's say that we have a polynomial equation $f(x) = 0$ that we wish to solve in integers. Finding a solution in integers could be a computationally painful thing, in part because one might very quickly need to use multiprecise arithmetic. However, finding a solution to the congruence $f(x) \equiv 0 \pmod p$ for a prime p is much simpler and would not require arithmetic of values larger than p^2. The power lies in the fact that the modulus is growing as the *product* of the individual prime moduli, so if the fraction of possible solutions is a relatively constant fraction of the primes, the possible solution set gets very thin very fast.

We illustrate this with an example. Let's say we want to solve

$$x^2 + x - 10100 = 0$$

Modulo 8, we have

$$0 : 0 + 0 - 4 \equiv -4 \equiv 4 \neq 0$$
$$1 : 1 + 1 - 4 \equiv -2 \equiv 6 \neq 0$$
$$2 : 4 + 2 - 4 \equiv 2 \neq 0$$
$$3 : 1 + 3 - 4 \equiv 0$$
$$4 : 0 + 4 - 4 \equiv 0$$
$$5 : 1 + 5 - 4 \equiv 2 \neq 0$$
$$6 : 4 + 6 - 4 \equiv 6 \neq 0$$
$$7 : 1 + 7 - 4 \equiv 4 \neq 0$$

and thus $x \equiv 3, 4 \pmod 8$ is necessary.

Modulo 3, we have

$$0 : 0 + 0 - 2 \equiv -2 \equiv 1 \neq 0$$
$$1 : 1 + 1 - 2 \equiv 0$$
$$2 : 1 + 2 - 2 \equiv 1 \neq 0$$

and thus $x \equiv 1 \pmod 3$ is necessary.

Modulo 5, we have

$$0 : 0 + 0 - 0 \equiv 0$$
$$1 : 1 + 1 - 0 \equiv 2 \neq 0$$
$$2 : 4 + 2 - 0 \equiv 1 \neq 0$$
$$3 : 4 + 3 - 0 \equiv 2 \neq 0$$
$$4 : 1 + 4 - 0 \equiv 0$$

and thus $x \equiv 0, 4 \pmod 5$ is necessary.

So let's build our solution. (And let's be careful to notice when we have equalities and when we have congruences.)

Start with $X = 3a + 1$ for a variable a.

We need $X \equiv 0, 4 \pmod 5$

The first option is

$$X = 3a + 1 \equiv 0 \pmod 5$$
$$3a \equiv -1 \equiv 4 \equiv 9 \pmod 5$$
$$a \equiv 3 \pmod 5$$
$$a = 5b + 3$$
$$X = 3a + 1 = 3(5b + 3) + 1 = 15b + 10$$

for any value of b.

The second option is

$$X = 3a + 1 \equiv 4 \pmod 5$$
$$3a \equiv 3 \pmod 5$$
$$a \equiv 1 \pmod 5$$
$$a = 5b + 1$$
$$X = 3a + 1 = 3(5b + 1) + 1 = 15b + 4$$

for any value of b.

We now use these two and solve modulo 8. The first option is

$$X = 15b + 10 \equiv 3 \pmod 8$$
$$15b \equiv -b \equiv -7 \pmod 8$$
$$b \equiv 7 \pmod 8$$
$$b = 8c + 7$$
$$X = 15b + 10 = 15(8c + 7) + 10 = 120c + 115$$

for any value of c.

The second option is

$$X = 15b + 10 \equiv 4 \quad (\text{mod } 8)$$
$$15b \equiv -b \equiv -6 \quad (\text{mod } 8)$$
$$b \equiv 6 \quad (\text{mod } 8)$$
$$b = 8c + 6$$
$$X = 15b + 10 = 15(8c + 6) + 10 = 120c + 100$$

for any value of c.

The third option is

$$X = 15b + 4 \equiv 3 \quad (\text{mod } 8)$$
$$15b \equiv -b \equiv -1 \quad (\text{mod } 8)$$
$$b \equiv 1 \quad (\text{mod } 8)$$
$$b = 8c + 1$$
$$X = 15b + 4 = 15(8c + 1) + 4 = 120c + 19$$

for any value of c.

Finally, the fourth option is

$$X = 15b + 4 \equiv 4 \quad (\text{mod } 8)$$
$$15b \equiv 0 \quad (\text{mod } 8)$$
$$b \equiv 0 \quad (\text{mod } 8)$$
$$b = 8c$$
$$X = 15b + 4 = 15(8c) + 4 = 120c + 4$$

for any value of c.

Modulo 120, we have possible solutions

$$4, 19, 100, 115$$

We note that

$$4 \equiv 1 \quad (\text{mod } 3)$$
$$\equiv 4 \quad (\text{mod } 5)$$
$$\equiv 4 \quad (\text{mod } 8)$$
$$19 \equiv 1 \quad (\text{mod } 3)$$
$$\equiv 4 \quad (\text{mod } 5)$$
$$\equiv 3 \quad (\text{mod } 8)$$
$$100 \equiv 1 \quad (\text{mod } 3)$$
$$\equiv 0 \quad (\text{mod } 5)$$
$$\equiv 4 \quad (\text{mod } 8)$$
$$115 \equiv 1 \quad (\text{mod } 3)$$
$$\equiv 0 \quad (\text{mod } 5)$$
$$\equiv 3 \quad (\text{mod } 8)$$

With a little bit of up front CRT calculation, we have reduced the brute force search for a solution by a factor of 30, since we need only test four possible solutions every 120 integers.

If we were to carry this one prime more, we would discover that we would need

$$X \equiv 2, 4 \pmod 7$$

If we extended the CRT to include the prime 7, we would get only 8 possible solutions every 840 integers. With only four applications of the CRT, the brute force search is improved by a factor of more than 100.

And this was all done with arithmetic only as bad as the square of the largest prime in the modulus. The key observation is that congruence-solving modulo primes p is roughly of cost $\mathcal{O}(\lg p)$ in number of arithmetic steps, but the solution is guaranteed modulo the product of the primes. With the solution for each prime p costing $\mathcal{O}(\lg p)$ operations, we *multiply* the modulus by which the solution is unique by all of p.

3.5 The Euler Totient

Definition 3.9 The *Euler phi function* also referred to as the *totient*, is defined for any positive integer n as

$$\phi(n) = |\{a : 0 \leq a < n, \gcd(a, n) = 1\}|$$

That is, $\phi(n)$ is the number of integers in a least positive residue set modulo n that are relatively prime to n.

We observe that $\phi(p) = p - 1$ for primes p.

Theorem 3.15 *The phi function is multiplicative. That is, if m and n are relatively prime, then*

$$\phi(mn) = \phi(m)\phi(n).$$

3.6 Fermat's Little Theorem

Theorem 3.16 (Fermat's Little Theorem (FLT)) *If p is a prime, then for any integer a, we have $a^{p-1} \equiv 1 \pmod p$.*

We mention that FLT is just a special case of Lagrange's theorem, to be presented in Chap. 4. Lagrange's theorem says that any element in a group, raised to the order of the group, is the identity. Since the order of the group of residues modulo a prime p is $p - 1$, then clearly FLT is a special case of Lagrange.

We note that FLT works only in one direction: if p is prime, then $a^{p-1} \equiv 1 \pmod p$ holds for all a. There are pathological numbers n, called *Carmichael numbers*, which are not prime but for which $a^{n-1} \equiv 1 \pmod n$ holds for all a. The smallest and most famous of these is 561. There is a large literature on Carmichael numbers. We shall see later that one special case in which one can make FLT work both as an "if" and as an "only if" we get a powerful test for primality that is the way in which one finds new examples of "the largest known prime numbers".

3.7 Exponentiation

We will frequently need to compute a^n for some element a in a multiplicative structure and some integer n. The naive way to exponentiate is to multiply a times itself n times.

The right way to exponentiate is to do it in binary.

Let's compute 3^{13} modulo 17.

We write $13 = 8 + 4 + 1$ in binary as 1101. We need a running product P, which we initialize to 1, and a running multiplier M, which we initialize to $a = 3$.

We now look at the rightmost bit. It's a 1, so we multiply $P \leftarrow M \cdot P$ to get $P = 3$.

We shift left one bit and square the multiplier $M \leftarrow M \cdot M$. So now $M = 9 = 3^2$.

The bit we are looking at is a 0, so we do not multiply in to the running product.

We shift left one bit and square the multiplier $M \leftarrow M \cdot M$. So now $M = 81 = 13 = 3^4$.

The bit we are looking at is a 1, so we multiply $P \leftarrow M \cdot P$ to get $P = 3 \cdot 13 = 39$, which we mod down by 17 to get 5.

Let's pause and think. The rightmost three bits of 13 are 101, which is 5 in binary. And we have as our running product the value $3^5 = 243$, mod down by 17 to 5. This is the steady state; our running product is the correct value for the exponentiation up through the bits that have been processed so far.

We shift left one bit and square the multiplier $M \leftarrow M \cdot M$. So now $M = 169 = 16 = -1$. The bit we are looking at is a 1, so we multiply $P \leftarrow M \cdot P$ to get $P = 5 \cdot 16 = 80$, which we mod down by 17 to get 12.

One version of Python code for this algorithm for exponentiation is Fig. 3.1.

There is a variation of this in which one processes the bits from left to right instead of right to left. In this version, one squares the running product as one moves across the bits of the exponent. This version has the disadvantage that you have to have a way to get at the bits in the middle of an exponent (in contrast to the right-to-left version above in which mod-by-2 and divide-by-2 do exactly what is needed for dealing with the bits). However, in the left to right version, the multiplier never changes. This is the version that is used in elliptic curve cryptography, because elliptic curve group operations are expensive. In elliptic curves the squaring is much cheaper than multiplication, and if one is clever one can choose the multiplier to make the group operation especially simple, so the left-to-right version is more common.

```
###################################################################
## MODULAR INTEGER EXPONENTIATION
## computes a^b mod n
def starstar(a_value, b_value, n_value):
    running_prod = 1
    multiplier = a_value
    local_exponent = b_value
    while local_exponent > 0:
        rightmost_bit = local_exponent % 2
        if rightmost_bit == 1:
            running_prod = (running_prod * multiplier) % n_value
        multiplier = (multiplier * multiplier) % n_value
        local_exponent = local_exponent // 2
    return running_prod
```

Fig. 3.1 Modular integer exponentiation

3.8 Matrix Reduction

Finally, we remark on a computation that shows up in several places in doing modern cryptography. Consider a matrix equation with integer coefficients, such as

$$
\begin{pmatrix} 2 & 1 & 6 & 5 & 8 \\ 5 & 7 & 3 & 9 & 1 \\ 1 & 2 & 1 & 0 & 3 \\ 1 & 4 & 7 & 2 & 5 \\ 3 & 2 & 1 & 4 & 2 \end{pmatrix} \begin{pmatrix} a \\ b \\ c \\ d \\ e \end{pmatrix} = \begin{pmatrix} 37 \\ 53 \\ 0 \\ 22 \\ 25 \end{pmatrix}
$$

If we were solving this over the real numbers we would (naively) use Gaussian elimination. Over the integers, we can swap rows, and we can add rows to other rows, but we are not permitted to divide unless the division results in a row that continues to have integer coefficients. We might begin the matrix reduction by swapping the first and third rows and then subtracting 5, 2, 1, and 3 times the new first row from the other rows, obtaining an augmented matrix

$$
\begin{pmatrix} 1 & 2 & 1 & 0 & 3 & | & 0 \\ 0 & -3 & -2 & 9 & -14 & | & 53 \\ 0 & -3 & 4 & 5 & 2 & | & 37 \\ 0 & 2 & 6 & 2 & 2 & | & 22 \\ 0 & -4 & -2 & 4 & -7 & | & 25 \end{pmatrix}
$$

We can continue, doing what amounts to a greatest-common-divisor process on column 2 and rows 2 through 5, then column 3 and rows 3 through 5, finally obtaining

$$
\begin{pmatrix} 1 & 2 & 1 & 0 & 3 & | & 108 \\ 0 & 1 & 10 & 13 & -10 & | & -479 \\ 0 & 0 & 2 & 24 & -54 & | & -1032 \\ 0 & 0 & 0 & 4 & 89 & | & -2341 \\ 0 & 0 & 0 & 0 & 89 & | & -1951 \end{pmatrix}
$$

The fact that we get no rows of zeros shows that the determinant of the matrix is nonzero and that there is a solution over the reals to the matrix equation. We could try now to back-solve for integer values for a, b, c, d, e, or we could continue to reduce until we reached the *Hermite Normal Form* that is an upper triangular matrix whose coefficients above the main diagonal are all smaller (at least in absolute value) than the entry for that column along the diagonal.

$$\begin{pmatrix} 1\ 0\ 1\ 2\ 17 \mid & -290 \\ 0\ 1\ 0\ 1\ 82 \mid & -1947 \\ 0\ 0\ 2\ 0\ 35 \mid & -643 \\ 0\ 0\ 0\ 4\ 0\ \mid & -390 \\ 0\ 0\ 0\ 0\ 89 \mid & -1951 \end{pmatrix}$$

It will almost always happen, as it does here, that we cannot back-solve and get integer solutions. All is not lost, however. In most uses in cryptography, we are not actually solving the system over the integers, but rather modulo a prime p. In that case, we can usually solve for solutions to the matrix equation; since all primes except 2 are odd, modulo any odd prime p we have $d = (-195 + p)/2$ as the solution.

We will see a version of this matrix reduction in Chap. 6, where we will in fact be reducing only modulo 2, in Chaps. 11 and 12, also working modulo 2, in Chap. 13, working modulo very large primes, and in Chap. 15, working modulo more moderately sized primes. In some uses, we will use the solutions modulo primes, and in some cases we will have more rows than columns and use the necessary rows of all zeros for further work.

3.9 Exercises

1. Find the greatest common divisor of the following pairs of integers, using some version of the Euclidean algorithm.

   a. 101 and 73
   b. 221 and 85
   c. 96 and 27
   d. 152 and 86
   e. 199 and 200

2. Find the x and y values of the extended Euclidean algorithm.

   a. 101 and 73
   b. 221 and 85
   c. 96 and 27
   d. 152 and 86
   e. 199 and 200

3. Solve for x:
$$23x \equiv 2 \pmod{37}$$

4. Solve for x:
$$23x \equiv 2 \pmod{111}$$

5. Solve for x:
$$23x \equiv 2 \pmod{343}$$

6. Find a primitive root of the primes 941, 1009, and 1013.

7. Show that if r is a primitive root modulo an odd prime p, then either r or $r + p$, whichever is odd, is a primitive root of $2p$.

8. Consider the integers modulo $N = pq$, for distinct odd primes p and q, with $p < q$. Show that there must exist an element modulo N of order at least $q - 1$. Show, by looking at examples for small values of p and q, that there could be elements modulo n of order larger than $q - 1$.

9. Consider the integers modulo $N = pq$, for distinct odd primes p and q, with $p < q$. Show that the largest possible order of any element modulo N is the least common multiple of $p - 1$ and $q - 1$.

10. (Programming exercise) Write a program that is an "endless sieve" to produce prime numbers. Determine a "block size" of size 10^5, say, with the subscript of the first occurrence of a prime less than the block size dividing a value in the block. This allows your program to determine that an integer in the k-th block of integers k will have the first occurrence of divisibility by a small prime at subscript j in the block. This allows you to sieve endlessly, using memory only equal to the block size, for all primes less than the square of the block size.

11. (Programming exercise) Write code to compute the smallest primitive root modulo a prime, using a naive method, or perhaps a naive method with some enhancements.

12. (Programming exercise) Write code to do the Euclidean algorithm and the extended Euclidean algorithm.

13. (Programming exercise) Write code to solve congruences. Be sure to include the error traps for when a congruence cannot in fact be solved.

References

1. D.E. Knuth, *The Art of Computer Programming, Volume 2, Seminumerical Algorithms*, 2nd edn. (Addison-Wesley, Boston, 1981)
2. D.H. Lehmer, Euclid's algorithm for large numbers. Am. Math. Mon. 227–233 (1938)
3. T. Jebelean, A generalization of the binary GCD algorithm, in *Proceedings of the International Symposium on Symbolic and Algebraic Computation, ISSAC*, vol. 93 (1993), pp. 111–116
4. J. Sorenson, Two fast GCD algorithms. J. Algorithms **16**, 110–144 (1994)

5. S.M. Sedjelmaci, Jebelean-Weber's algorithm without spurious factors. Inf. Process. Lett. **102**, 247–252 (2007)
6. K. Weber, Parallel implementation of the accelerated GCD algorithm. J. Symb. Comput. **21**, 457–466 (1996)

Groups, Rings, Fields

4

Abstract

Modern cryptography relies, for its ability to convert plaintext into ciphertext
that appears to be random sequences of symbols, on the basic notions of abstract
algebra. We introduce in this chapter the basics of groups, rings, and fields, including subgroups, cyclic groups, the order of elements, and Lagrange's Theorem. A
group is a set that is closed under an operation that is usually referred to (and often
is) either as addition or as multiplication, with additional properties. A *ring* has
both an addition and a multiplication, but which may not have an operation that
resembles division. A *field* has all the characteristics we normally associate with
doing arithmetic. All three are in some sense merely descriptions in the abstract
of ordinary arithmetic. Proofs will to a large extent be left to later, or not done
at all. And since we are interested more in using groups, rings, and fields than
in proving theorems about them as algebraic objects, this chapter can be viewed
largely as simply providing definitions for and formal statements of the truth of
what we observe when doing the operations for encrypting and decrypting.

4.1 Groups

Definition 4.1 A *group* $G = (S, *)$ is a set S of elements together with a binary
operation

$$* : S \times S \to S$$

such that

- the operation $*$ is *associative*, that is,

$$(a * b) * c = a * (b * c)$$

  for all $a, b, c \in S$;

- there is an *identity* element e such that for all $a \in S$, we have $a * e = e * a = a$;
- every element $a \in S$ has an *inverse* a^{-1} for which $a * a^{-1} = a^{-1} * a = e$.

Definition 4.2 We say a group G is *abelian* (or *commutative*) if for all pairs $a, b \in S$ we have $a * b = b * a$.

When we insist on being formal, we will write the group as

$$G = (S, *)$$

but much of the time we will just write S and assume that the group operation is known.

Sometimes we speak of the group operation as "multiplication" and sometimes we speak of the group operation as "addition". If we are thinking of the operation as multiplication, we will write $a * b$ for the operation, a^{-1} for the inverse, and 1 for the identity. If we are thinking of the operation as addition, we will write $a + b$ for the operation, $-a$ for the inverse, and 0 for the identity.

Example 4.1 The classic example of a group would be the integers $\mathbb{Z}$ under addition. This is clearly an abelian group, with zero as the identity, and $-n$ the inverse for any integer n.

Example 4.2 Another useful example of a group would be the positive integers modulo 16, say, under addition. For the moment, we simply point out that, for integers a and b, both less than n, taken modulo n, we have that the "sum" of a and b is $a + b$ if this sum is less than n, and is $a + b - n$ if this sum is greater than or equal to n. Thus, for example, 11 plus 9 taken modulo 16 is

$$11 + 9 = 20 \equiv 20 - 16 = 4.$$

Taking things using addition modulo 16, the integers

$$\{0, 1, 2, 3, 4, 5, 6, 7, 8, 9, 10, 11, 12, 13, 14, 15\}$$

clearly form an abelian group, with zero as the identity, and $16 - n$ the inverse for any integer n in the range 0 through 15.

We remark that any complete set of residues works, although the specification of the result of the group operation would be somewhat more complicated. One could, for example, choose the least-magnitude residues, as

$$\{-8, -7, -6, -5, -4, -3, -2, -1, 0, 1, 2, 3, 4, 5, 6, 7\}$$

Definition 4.3 A *subgroup* of a group G is a group $G' = (S', *)$ such that $S' \subseteq S$ as a set of elements, the identity $1_{S'}$ of the subgroup is the same as the identity 1_S of the group $G = (S, *)$, and the inverse of any element in the subgroup is the same as the inverse of that element in $G = (S, *)$.

Example 4.3 A classic example of a subgroup would be the even integers under addition, or more generally the integers divisible by any fixed integer n. The sum of two even integers is an even integer, so that closure is satisfied, and the other requirements are inherited from ordinary addition of integers.

Example 4.4 Another example would be the subgroup of multiples of 4 in the group of integers modulo 16. These integers would be

$$\{0, 4, 8, 12\}$$

Definition 4.4 A group $G = (S, *)$ is said to be *cyclic* if there is a *generator* g such that for every element $a \in S$ there is an integer power k such that $a = g^k$.

This is the definition in multiplicative notation. In additive notation we would say that there is a generator g such that for every element a there is an integer multiple n such that $a = ng$. Continuing with our classic example, we observe that the integers under addition $\mathbb{Z}$ are cyclic with the generator 1, the even integers similarly cyclic with the generator 2, and so forth.

Theorem 4.1 *Every subgroup of a cyclic group is cyclic.*

Proof Let S' be the set of elements of G that form the subgroup. We will be a little sloppy here and refer to "the group S'" just by its elements and not as a pair with the operation listed explicitly. We are going to prove this using material that won't appear in these notes until Chap. 3 on congruences. If G is cyclic, and we write G as a multiplicative group, then we have a generator g and we can refer to every element of the group using the exponent of g for that element. That is, we can write every element of the group as

$$\{g^0, g^1, g^2, \dots, \}$$

So let h be the element in S' that is $h = g^k$ for the least nonnegative k. We claim that $S' = \{h^n | n \in \mathbb{Z}\}$. Consider any element $t \in S'$. We must have an s such that $t = g^s$. By the division algorithm for integers (which we will get to later), we can write

$$s = q \cdot k + r$$

with r nonnegative and less than k.

Now, since we have $g^s \in S$, and we have $g^k \in S$, we must have $g^s * g^{-qk} = g^r \in S$. Thus $r = 0$; the existence of a nonnegative r would contradict our choice of k as the least nonnegative exponent of an element in the subgroup. This means that $t = g^{qk} = (g^k)^q = h^q$, which is what we have claimed; every element in S can be written as a power of h, and the subgroup S' is in fact cyclic. □

Example 4.5 In our example of the subgroup

$$\{0, 4, 8, 12\}$$

we note that every element in the group is generated by multiples of 4, which is 4 times the generator of the entire group.

Definition 4.5 The *order* of an element a in a group G is the least integer k such that (written multiplicatively) we have $a^k = 1$. If no such integer exists, then the element is said to have *infinite order*.

We note that if the group is finite, then the order of an element is well-defined. Since the group is finite, the sequence of elements (written multiplicatively)

$$a, a^2, a^3, \ldots, a^k, \ldots$$

must repeat (note that we are not claiming the group is cyclic, only that the powers of any particular element must form a cycle). That is, there are exponents i and j such that $a^i = a^j$. But then we have

$$1 = a^{i-i} = a^{j-i}.$$

If we have chosen i and j to be the least integers such that $a^i = a^j$, then $j - i$ is the order of the element a.

Definition 4.6 The *order* of a group G is $|S|$, the cardinality of the set S.

We note that there are groups of finite order, such as the integers modulo 16, of order 16, and groups of infinite order, such as the set of all integers under addition.

Theorem 4.2 (Lagrange) *The order of any element of a finite group G divides the order of the group.*

Proof Writing the group multiplicatively, choose an element a of G and compute its powers. We have that

$$A = \{1, a, a^2, \ldots a^{k-1}\}$$

is, for some k, a subgroup of k elements, with $a^k = 1$. If this exhausts the set of elements in the group, then we are done.

If not, choose any element b in G that is not in A, and consider

$$B = \{b, ba, ba^2, \ldots ba^{k-1}\}.$$

None of these are elements in A, because if it were the case that $ba^i = a^j$, then we would have $b = a^{j-i} \in A$, contrary to our choice of b.

Thus $A \cup B$ is a set of $2k$ elements in G. If this is all of G, we are done.

If not, choose any element c in G that is not in A or in B, and consider

$$C = \{c, ca, ca^2, \ldots ca^{k-1}\}.$$

None of these are elements in A or in B. If it were the case that $ca^i = a^j$, then we would have $c = a^{j-i} \in A$. If it were the case that $ca^i = ba^j$, then we would have $c = ba^{j-i} \in B$. Either of these would be contrary to our choice of c.

And so forth. Each time we go out to find another element not yet found, we actually add k elements into our set of elements in G. Since we are adding k elements at a time, it must be the case that when we have accounted for all the elements in the group, we have for some m a total of km elements. Thus the order the group is km and is clearly divisible by k.

Corollary 4.1 (Lagrange) *If G is a group with n elements, and we write G as a multiplicative group, then for any element $a \in G$ we have a^n equal to the identity of the group.*

Proof For any element $a \in G$, we know that a^k, for some k that is the order of a, is the identity. We can thus write

$$a^n = (a^k)^{n/k} = 1^{n/k} = 1,$$

which proves the corollary.

Definition 4.7 The *exponent* of a group G is the least integer k such that $a^k = 1$ for all elements $a \in G$.

4.2 Rings

Definition 4.8 A *ring* $R = (S, +, \times)$ is a set S with two binary operations, that we shall call addition $(+)$ and multiplication $(\times)$, such that

- $(S, +)$ is an abelian group with identity 0;
- multiplication is associative, that is,

$$(a \times b) \times c = a \times (b \times c)$$

for all $a, b, c \in S$;
- multiplication distributes over addition, that is,

$$a \times (b + c) = (a \times b) + (a \times c)$$

and

$$(a + b) \times c = (a \times c) + (b \times c)$$

for all $a, b, c \in S$;

Definition 4.9 A *multiplicative identity* in a ring $R = (S, +, \times)$ is a nonzero element 1 such that $1 \times a = a \times 1 = a$ for all $a \in S$.

Definition 4.10 A ring is said to be *commutative* if the multiplication operation is commutative, that is, if

$$r \times s = s \times r$$

for all $r, s \in S$.

Example 4.6 Continuing with our classic example, we notice that the integers form a ring under the usual addition and multiplication. This is a commutative ring with the additive identity 0 and the multiplicative identity 1.

4.3   Fields

We have now done all the preliminaries, and it remains to finish off the algebraic background. We have described ordinary arithmetic in an abstract way, with addition, multiplication, subtraction (the addition of an inverse), commutivity, and distribution.

The one thing we cannot do in the integers and still stay within the set of integers is to divide one integer by another. There is an additive inverse for every integer, but the only integers with a multiplicative inverse are 1 and -1, each of which is its own inverse.

To finish our description of the general properties of arithmetic, we need to extend our set to include all the rational numbers.

Definition 4.11 A *field* is a ring $R = (S, +, \times)$ for which multiplication is commutative and every nonzero element in S has an inverse under multiplication. That is, a field is a ring that is a group under addition and for which the elements other than the additive identity form an abelian group under multiplication.

With this, we have just described the rational numbers $\mathbb{Q}$. Under addition, the integers form an abelian group. Under addition and multiplication, the integers form a ring. Extending the set to include all rational numbers, we can divide by all integers except 0 and stay within the set of rational numbers, and thus get a field.

We will mostly be dealing with finite fields   that come from the integers modulo prime numbers p or from polynomials, with coefficients taken modulo 2, with the polynomials taken modulo some polynomial $f(x)$. (These constructions are the subjects of Chaps. 3 and 6.) Finite fields are often written as fields $GF(p)$ in the former case, or $GF(2^n)$ in the latter case, where n is the degree of $f(x)$. The notation GF is short for "Galois Field" in tribute to the celebrated French mathematician Évariste Galois.

4.4   Examples and Expansions

One of the great advantages of working with the mathematics that is the underpinning of cryptography is that it is very concrete. There are examples.

4.4.1   Arithmetic Modulo Prime Numbers

The classic example of a field is the set of rational numbers. We will also have great use to be made of the fields of integers modulo prime numbers. We will prove these things later, but will use these examples as concrete things to fix the notions we will be using.

Theorem 4.3 *Let p be a prime number. The integers modulo p, written $\mathbb{Z}_p$, form a finite field under the usual modular addition and multiplication. Further, the group of integers modulo p is a cyclic group under multiplication.*

Definition 4.12 Any generator of the multiplicative group of integers modulo a prime number p is referred to as a *primitive root* modulo p.

Theorem 4.4 *An integer n has a primitive root if and only if $n = 2, 4, p^k, 2p^k$, for odd primes p.*

Finding a primitive root is a big deal, and this is one instance in which theory diverges from practice. The current best theorem without qualifications says that the smallest primitive root modulo a prime p is only guaranteed to be smaller than about $p^{1/4}$. With qualifications, Victor Shoup has shown [1] that, under the assumption of the Generalized Riemann Hypothesis (which of course pretty much everyone believes to be true), the smallest primitive root modulo a prime p is less than $\log^6 p$.

In practice, we might do nothing much more sophisticated than a naive search. The integers modulo p are a single cycle of $p - 1$ elements under multiplication, so they form a set

$$\{1, 2 = g^{a_1}, 3 = g^{a_2}, \ldots\}$$

It turns out there is a fast and simple way to determine if the exponent a_i is even, and if the exponent is even, then the integer cannot be a primitive root because its powers would only be the residues of even exponent. So the usual practical approach to finding a primitive root is just to start with 2, 3, 5, etc., check that the exponent is not even, and if not, to check by powering up whether one gets the identity any earlier than the power $p - 1$.

It is often the case in number theory that asymptotic results that one can prove are achieved very slowly, so the results of computations on relatively small numbers can be misleading. Nonetheless, we can remark that for the 78497 odd primes less than one million, we have 2, 3, 5, 6, and 7 occurring as least primitive roots for a total of 86.51% of the time, and only 19 primes have a least primitive root larger than 50. Among the 487 primes between 10^9 and $10^9 + 10000$, 85.6% have 2, 3, 5, 6, or 7 as the least primitive root.

For example, for $p = 11$, we observe that 7 is a primitive root, with

$$7^1 = 7,$$
$$7^2 \equiv 49 \equiv 5,$$
$$7^3 \equiv 35 \equiv 2,$$
$$7^4 \equiv 14 \equiv 3,$$
$$7^5 \equiv 21 \equiv 10,$$

$$7^6 \equiv 70 \equiv 4,$$
$$7^7 \equiv 28 \equiv 6,$$
$$7^8 \equiv 42 \equiv 9,$$
$$7^9 \equiv 63 \equiv 8,$$
$$7^{10} \equiv 56 \equiv 1$$

We observe that the order of the multiplicative group modulo a prime p is $p - 1$ and that if we have a primitive root we can do the multiplication by adding exponents modulo $p - 1$, that is,

$$24 = 8 \times 3 \equiv 7^9 \times 7^4 \equiv 7^{13} \equiv 7^3 \equiv 2 \pmod{11}$$

This will be very important in cryptography. The use of the exponents in this way is called the *index calculus*. The unraveling of the index calculus is called the *discrete logarithm problem*. That is, if we are given a cyclic group G, a group generator g, and a random element $a \in G$, the discrete logarithm problem in G is to determine the exponent k such $g^k = a$.

We note that the sequence of powers of 7 modulo 11 appears reasonably random:

$$5, 2, 3, 10, 4, 6, 9, 8, 1$$

The discrete logarithm problem is important in cryptography because there are groups, such as the integers modulo large primes, for which this apparent randomness can be exploited: given a prime p, an exponent e, and a primitive root r, it is computationally easy to compute the power $s \equiv r^e \pmod{p}$, but computationally difficult to do the discrete log problem that reverses that exponentiation and computes e given s, r, and p.

We also note that any of the elements $7^1, 7^3, 7^7, 7^9$, are primitive roots. As can be seen, multiplication of integers modulo p can be written as multiplication of powers of a primitive root. And since

$$a^m \cdot a^n = a^{m+n}$$

by the rules of exponents, the use of primitive roots transforms a multiplication problem modulo p into a problem of addition of exponents modulo $p - 1$. In our example, we notice that generating a subcycle with 7^2 means that we get a cycle of elements

$$7^2, 7^4, 7^6, 7^8,$$

and then we short-cycle because $7^{10} \equiv 1$. Similarly, generating a subcycle with 7^4 means that get a cycle of elements

$$7^4, 7^8, 7^{12} \equiv 7^2, 7^6,$$

and then we short-cycle because $7^{10} \equiv 1$. The fact that $7^1, 7^3, 7^7, 7^9$, are primitive roots is because their exponents are relatively prime to 10.

Hold this thought; we will do a lot more of this later. In fact, most of the mathematics behind modern cryptography is essentially this kind of a multiplication table.

4.4.2 Arithmetic Modulo Composite Numbers

Arithmetic modulo a prime results in a field. Arithmetic modulo a composite number results in a ring, not a field, because not every element has a multiplicative inverse. Elements that do not have inverses are called *zero divisors*. For example, let's look at Table 4.1, of multiplication modulo 15.

We observe that the zero divisors are those integers with factors of 3 or 5 in them, and that if we look only at the eight integers 1, 2, 4, 7, 8, 11, 13, and 14, that have no factors of 3 or 5, then we get a multiplication table without zero divisors, as in Tables 4.2 and 4.3.

More to the point, we observe that the multiplication modulo $15 = 3 \times 5$ can be done as the product of a 2-cycle and a 4-cycle. That is, it's the product of a $3 - 1 = 2$-cycle and a $5 - 1 = 4$-cycle, where the 3 and the 5 are exactly the primes 3 and 5 that show up in the factoring of 15. The arithmetic modulo 15 can be written as $11^i \times 2^j$, with $i = 0, 1$ and $j = 0, 1, 2, 3$. In general, if $n = p \cdot q$ with p and q prime numbers (to be defined in a moment), then the multiplication modulo n can be written as the product of an element of order $p - 1$ and an element of order $q - 1$. We will use this later on, and we rearrange the multiplication table modulo 15 accordingly as Table 4.3.

We can also view this structure in an abstract way. Consider the group generated by concatenating symbols a and b under the constraint that $ab = ba$, and $1a = a1 = a$,

Table 4.1 Multiplication table modulo 15

	1	2	3	4	5	6	7	8	9	10	11	12	13	14
1	1	2	3	4	5	6	7	8	9	10	11	12	13	14
2	2	4	6	8	10	12	14	1	3	5	7	9	11	13
3	3	6	9	12	0	3	6	9	12	0	3	6	9	12
4	4	8	12	1	5	9	13	2	6	10	14	3	7	11
5	5	10	0	5	10	0	5	10	0	5	10	0	5	10
6	6	12	3	9	0	6	12	3	9	0	6	12	3	9
7	7	14	6	13	5	12	4	11	3	10	2	9	1	8
8	8	1	9	2	10	3	11	4	12	5	13	6	14	7
9	9	3	12	6	0	9	3	12	6	0	9	3	12	6
10	10	5	0	10	5	0	10	5	0	10	5	0	10	5
11	11	7	3	14	10	6	2	13	9	5	1	12	8	4
12	12	9	6	3	0	12	9	6	3	0	12	9	6	3
13	13	11	9	7	5	3	1	14	12	10	8	6	4	2
14	14	13	12	11	10	9	8	7	6	5	4	3	2	1

Table 4.2 Multiplication mod 15, without zero divisors

	1	2	4	7	8	11	13	14
1	1	2	4	7	8	11	13	14
2	2	4	8	14	1	7	11	13
4	4	8	1	13	2	14	7	11
7	7	14	13	4	11	2	1	8
8	8	1	2	11	4	13	14	7
11	11	7	14	2	13	1	8	4
13	13	11	7	1	12	6	4	2
14	14	13	11	8	7	4	2	1

Table 4.3 Multiplication mod 15, reordered

	1	2	4	8	11	7	14	13
1	1	2	4	8	11	7	14	13
2	2	4	8	1	7	14	13	11
4	4	8	1	2	14	13	11	7
8	8	1	2	4	13	11	7	14
11	11	7	14	13	1	2	4	8
7	7	14	13	11	2	4	8	1
14	14	13	11	7	4	8	1	2
13	13	11	7	14	8	1	2	4

and $1b = b1 = b$, and $aa = 1$ and $bbbb = 1$. That is, we have elements

$$1$$
$$a$$
$$b$$
$$bb$$
$$bbb$$
$$ab$$
$$abb$$
$$abbb$$

That is, we have the *direct product*

$$\{1, a\} \times \{1, b, bb, bbb\}$$

If we now substitute $a = 11$ (or 7 or 13 or 14) and $b = 2$ (or 8), this abstract group is the same group as the group of integers modulo 15 under multiplication.

We can rewrite Table 4.3 more abstractly as Table 4.4.

Table 4.4 Multiplication mod 15, abstracted

	1	b	b^2	b^3	a	ab	ab^2	ab^3
1	1	b	b^2	b^3	a	ab	ab^2	ab^3
b	b	b^2	b^3	1	ab	ab^2	ab^3	a
b^2	b^2	b^3	1	b	ab^2	ab^3	a	ab
b^3	b^3	1	b	b^2	ab^3	a	ab	ab^2
a	a	ab	ab^2	ab^3	1	b	b^2	b^3
ab	ab	ab^2	ab^3	a	b	b^2	b^3	1
ab^2	ab^2	ab^3	a	ab	b^2	b^3	1	b
ab^3	ab^3	a	ab	ab^2	b^3	1	b	b^2

Definition 4.13 A *homomorphism* of a group $(G, \circ_G)$ into a group $(H, \circ_H)$ is a mapping $f : G \to H$ such that if $g_1 \circ_G g_2 = g_3$ for any two elements g_1, g_2 in the group G, then $f(g_1) \circ_H f(g_2) = f(g_3)$ in the group H. The homomorphism is an *isomorphism* of if the mapping f is one-to-one and onto.

A homomorphism of groups is thus a mapping that preserves the group operation, and the mapping is an isomorphism if it is 1-1 and onto. We note several examples from what we have covered already.

1. Let G be the group of integers under addition, and let $H = \{1, -1\}$ under multiplication, with even integers mapping to 1 and odd integers mapping to -1. This is a homomorphism.
2. Let G be the integers under addition modulo a composite integer n, p a prime divisor of n, and H be the integers under addition modulo p. Then G mapping to H by $f(m) = m \pmod{p}$ is a homomorphism.
3. One of the most important isomorphisms we will use is the following. Let G be a cyclic group of n elements, written multiplicatively, with a generator g, so the set

$$\{g^0, g^1, \ldots, g^{n-1}\}$$

   lists all the group elements. Let H be the group $\{0, 1, \ldots, n-1\}$ under addition modulo n. Then $f : G \to H$ defined by $f(g^k) = k$ is an isomorphism of groups.
4. Let $n = pq$ for primes p and q, and let G be the integers modulo n that are relatively prime to both p and q, under multiplication. Let

$$H = \{(r, s) : r = 1, \ldots, p-1, s = 1, \ldots, q-1\},$$

   and define the group operation on H to be

$$(r, s) \circ_H (t, u) = (rt \pmod{p}, su \pmod{q})$$

   This is an isomorphism of G and H.

4.4.3   Finite Fields of Characteristic 2

A field is said to have *characteristic n*, for n an integer, if it is the case that $na = 0$ for all a in the field. The field of integers modulo a prime p, described in Sect. 4.4.1, has exactly p elements and is of characteristic p. We will see later in Chap. 6 that for for any prime p and integer k, one can construct finite fields, of characteristic p, of p^k elements. We will make use of this for characteristic 2, since that involves binary arithmetic that can be done in computer hardware in especially efficient ways. The curious reader should consult the classic book on this subject by Lidl and Niederreiter [2].

4.5   Exercises

1. Consider the group of non-zero integers modulo 11 under multiplication. What is the order of the group?
2. Consider the non-zero integers modulo 11 under multiplication. What is the largest order of any element in the group?
3. Show that for any prime number p, all multiplicative groups G of order p are isomorphic to one another.
4. Show that there are exactly two non-isomorphic groups of order 4, and they are both abelian. One of these is the cyclic group

$$G = \{1, a, a^2, a^3\}$$

   for some generator a such that a^4 is the identity, and the other is the abelian *Klein-4 group*

$$H = \{1, a, b, ab\}$$

   for which $a^2 = b^2 = (ab)^2$ is the identity.
5. Show that any cyclic group is abelian.
6. Prove from the definition and first principles that the integers, modulo a prime number p, form a field under ordinary addition and multiplication, with the additive identity being 0 and the multiplicative identity being 1.
7. Prove from the definition and first principles that the integers, modulo a product pq of prime numbers p and q, form a ring but not a field under ordinary addition and multiplication, with the additive identity being 0 and the multiplicative identity being 1.
8. Build the table of least nonnegative residues modulo 17 and their exponents using 3 as the primitive root. Build the table using 5 as the primitive root. Then find the function mapping exponents based on 3 to the exponents based on 5.
9. Extend the example above into a proof for all prime numbers p: If r_1 and r_2 are two primitive roots for p, and if we have

$$r_2 \equiv r_1^i \pmod{p},$$

then we have

$$r_2^\ell \equiv (r_1)^{i\ell \pmod{p-1}} \pmod{p}.$$

References

1. V. Shoup, Searching for primitive roots in Finite Fields. Math. Comput. **58**, 369–380 (1992)
2. R. Lidl, H. Niederreiter, *Introduction to Finite Fields and Their Applications*, 2nd edn. (Cambridge University Press, Cambridge, 1997)

Square Roots and Quadratic Symbols

5

Abstract

We will do square roots modulo primes using primitive roots and exponents. This is a little different from the way that is done in many references, but we want to emphasize that it is the world of additive exponent arithmetic that is important. Modulo a prime p, the exponents work additively modulo $p - 1$. When we get to RSA encryption, in which we have a modulus $N = pq$ for two large and unknown primes p and q, we cannot play the same exponent games as with primes because $\phi(N) = (p - 1)(q - 1)$ is not $N - 1$, and it is the $\phi(N)$ that determines the arithmetic on the exponents. In the later chapters on factoring and elliptic curves, it will be computationally beneficial to be able to determine whether an integer is or is not congruent to a square modulo a modulus N. Fortunately, determining whether an integer is a square modulo a prime, or determining that an integer is not a square modulo a composite number, can be done by a process that resembles the gcd and has the same logarithmic complexity.

5.1 Square Roots

Theorem 5.1 *Let p be an odd prime. Let a be an integer, with a not congruent to 0 modulo p. Then*

$$x^2 \equiv a \pmod{p}$$

has either no solutions or two solutions modulo p.

Proof Consider a primitive root g. Then all the linear residues are in the list

$$g, g^2, g^3, \ldots, g^{p-1} \equiv 1$$

There is one integer k, $1 \le k \le p - 1$, such that $a = g^k$.

We have two cases.

Case 1: If k is odd, then we have no solutions.

There are no solutions because we would have to have, for some t,

$$(g^t)^2 \equiv g^{2t} \equiv g^k$$

which would imply that we had

$$2t \equiv k \pmod{(p-1)}$$

This means that

$$2t = k + m \cdot (p-1)$$

for some integer m. But since $p-1$ is even, and k is odd, this can't possibly happen.

Case 2: If $k = 2\ell$ is even, then

$$(g^\ell)^2 \equiv a$$

and

$$(-g^\ell)^2 \equiv a$$

So we clearly have at least two solutions.

Can there be any others?

Well, if there's an m that is any solution, we have

$$(g^m)^2 \equiv g^{2\ell} \pmod{p}$$

which implies that

$$2m \equiv 2l \pmod{p-1}$$

and thus that

$$m \equiv l \pmod{(p-1)/2}$$

But if we have chosen ℓ, m such that $0 \leq \ell, m, < p-1$, then as integers (and not just congruences)

$$m = \ell$$

$$m = \ell + (p-1)/2$$

$$\ell = m + (p-1)/2$$

are the only options, depending on the relative sizes of ℓ and m. The first of these and exactly one of the second two are possible, so we know there are only the two solutions.   □

Theorem 5.2 *Let p be an odd prime and g a primitive root. Then*

$$g^{(p-1)/2} \equiv -1 \pmod{p}$$

Proof Clearly
$$(g^{(p-1)/2})^2 \equiv g^{p-1} \equiv 1 \pmod{p}$$

We know there are two roots of 1, namely ± 1, and we know from the previous theorem that there are only these two roots. And we know that
$$g^{(p-1)/2}$$

is not $+1$, because modulo an odd prime we don't get a primitive root powering up to 1 until we get to the $(p-1)$-st power. So it has to be the case that
$$g^{(p-1)/2}$$

is the other square root of 1, and is -1.   □

5.1.1   Examples

Let's look at things modulo 11 and modulo 13.

Modulo 11, with exponents in the first row and powers of 2 in the second:

$$1\ 2\ 3\ 4\ 5\ \ 6\ \ \ 7\ 8\ 9\ 10$$
$$2\ 4\ 8\ 5\ 10\ 9\ \ \ 7\ 3\ 6\ \ 1$$
$$-1\ -2\ -4$$

Modulo 13, with exponents in the first row and powers of 2 in the second:

$$1\ 2\ 3\ 4\ 5\ \ \ 6\ \ 7\ \ \ 8\ 9\ 10\ 11\ 12$$
$$2\ 4\ 8\ 3\ 6\ \ 12\ 11\ \ 9\ 5\ 10\ \ 7\ \ 1$$
$$-1\ -2\ -4$$

Notice the exponents. They suggest the following theorem, whose proof is easy using the exponents.

Theorem 5.3 *Let p be an odd prime. Then -1 is a square modulo p if and only if $p \equiv 1 \pmod 4$*

Proof Since we know that
$$g^{(p-1)/2} \equiv -1 \pmod{p}$$

we know that
$$x^2 \equiv -1 \pmod{p}$$

has no solutions or it has solutions
$$\pm 1 g^{(p-1)/4}$$

But now
$$(p-1)/4$$

is an integer if and only if $p \equiv 1 \pmod 4$.   □

This is what we see modulo 11, which is 3 modulo 4, and modulo 13, which is 1 modulo 4.

Obviously, the residues that are even powers of a primitive root are squares and the residues that are odd powers are not. Since we know that the $(p-1)/2$-st power is -1, we know that -1 is a square exactly when $(p-1)/2$ is even, which is exactly when p is 1 modulo 4.

Theorem 5.4 *Let p be a prime, $p \equiv 3 \pmod 4$, let y be an integer, and let*

$$x = y^{(p+1)/4}.$$

Then

$$z^2 \equiv y \pmod p$$

has no solutions or two solutions. If it has two solutions they are $\pm x$. If it has no solutions, then

$$z^2 \equiv -y \pmod p$$

has the two solutions $\pm x$.

Proof We know that

$$(\pm x)^2 = y^{(p+1)/2} = y \cdot y^{(p-1)/2}$$

If y is a square, then $y = g^{2k}$ for some k. Thus

$$(\pm x)^2 = y^{(p+1)/2} = y \cdot (g^{2k})^{(p-1)/2} = y \cdot g^{k(p-1)} = y \cdot (g^{p-1})^k = y \cdot (1)^k = y$$

If y is not a square, then $y = g^{2k+1}$.

Then

$$-y = (g^{2k+1})(g^{(p-1)/2}) = g^{2k+1+(p-1)/2}$$

Now, since p is 3 modulo 4, $(p-1)/2$ is odd, so $1 + (p-1)/2$ is even, so the entire exponent above is even. That means that $-y$ is the square as claimed.   □

Theorem 5.5 *Let p be an odd prime, and a any integer not 0 modulo p. Then*

$$a^{(p-1)/2} \equiv \pm 1 \pmod p$$

Proof We know that

$$x^2 \equiv a \pmod p$$

has solutions if and only if

$$a^{(p-1)/2} \equiv +1 \pmod p$$

Let $a = g^k$ for whatever k works. So if a is a square, then $a = g^{2m}$, and then

$$a^{(p-1)/2} \equiv g^{m(p-1)} \equiv 1 \pmod p$$

On the other hand, if a is not a square, then it is $a = g^{2m+1}$, and then

$$a^{(p-1)/2} \equiv g^{(2m+1)(p-1)/2} \equiv g^{m(p-1)+(p-1)/2} \equiv g^{(p-1)/2} \equiv -1 \pmod p$$

□

5.2 Characters on Groups

Given any group $G = (S, *)$ which we shall write multiplicatively, a *character* on the group is a mapping

$$\chi : S \to \mathbb{C}$$

that preserves the group operation, that is, for which

$$\chi(ab) = \chi(a)\chi(b)$$

where the "multiplication" inside the parentheses on the left hand side is in the group, and the multiplication outside the parentheses on the right hand side is in the complex numbers.

We will use the Legendre symbols and the Jacobi symbols as characters on the group of integers modulo an integer.

5.3 Legendre Symbols

Let p be an odd prime. The *Legendre symbol*

$$\left(\frac{a}{p}\right)$$

is defined to be

$$\left(\frac{a}{p}\right) = +1 \quad \text{if} \quad x^2 \equiv a \pmod{p} \quad \text{is solvable}$$

$$= -1 \quad \text{otherwise}$$

The following theorem shows, among other things, that the Legendre symbol is a character on the group of integers modulo p.

Theorem 5.6 *Let p be an odd prime and a and b integers prime to p.*

1. If $a \equiv b \pmod{p}$, then

$$\left(\frac{a}{p}\right) = \left(\frac{b}{p}\right)$$

2. If a is not zero modulo p, then

$$\left(\frac{a}{p}\right) = a^{(p-1)/2} \pmod{p}$$

3. If $ab \neq 0$ modulo p, then

$$\left(\frac{a}{p}\right)\left(\frac{b}{p}\right) = \left(\frac{ab}{p}\right)$$

4.
$$\left(\frac{-1}{p}\right) = (-1)^{(p-1)/2}$$

which is 1 for primes p that are 1 modulo 4, and −1 for primes that are 3 modulo 4.

5.
$$\left(\frac{2}{p}\right) = (-1)^{(p^2-1)/8}$$

which is 1 for primes p that are 1 or 7 modulo 8, and −1 otherwise.

Proof We have basically done all of these except the last, and we will leave that to the reader. ◻

5.4 Quadratic Reciprocity

Gauss's *law of quadratic reciprocity* [1] makes all this simple and computationally efficient.

Theorem 5.7 *Let p and q be distinct odd primes. Then*

$$\left(\frac{p}{q}\right) = -\left(\frac{q}{p}\right) \quad if \ \ p \equiv q \equiv 3 \pmod 4$$
$$= \left(\frac{q}{p}\right) \quad otherwise$$

5.5 Jacobi Symbols

The Legendre symbol is defined for primes in the "denominator". The *Jacobi symbol* is the extension by multiplicativity to composites in the "denominator". Thus if we have n that factors as n = rs, then

$$\left(\frac{a}{n}\right) = \left(\frac{a}{rs}\right) = \left(\frac{a}{r}\right) \cdot \left(\frac{a}{s}\right)$$

Caveat

Note that having the Jacobi symbol come up +1 does *not* mean that the quadratic congruence is solvable, because it could be that there are an even number of nonsolutions making up the product. One such example is this.

$$\left(\frac{2}{15}\right) = \left(\frac{2}{3}\right) \cdot \left(\frac{2}{5}\right) = (-1)(-1) = 1$$

The symbol is $+1$, but the quadratic congruence

$$x^2 \equiv 2 \pmod{15}$$

has no solutions.

5.6   Extended Law of Quadratic Reciprocity

Gauss's *law of quadratic reciprocity* [1] extends to composite integers.

Theorem 5.8 *Let M and N be odd, positive, and relatively prime. Then*

$$\left(\frac{M}{N}\right) = -\left(\frac{N}{M}\right) \quad if \ M \equiv N \equiv 3 \pmod{4}$$

$$= \left(\frac{N}{M}\right) \quad otherwise$$

We also note, without proof, that the last of the points in Theorem 5.6 carries over to composites. If Q is odd, then

$$\left(\frac{2}{Q}\right) = (-1)^{(Q^2-1)/8}$$

which is 1 for Q that are 1 or 7 modulo 8, and -1 otherwise.

We note that the reciprocity law allows quadratic symbols to be computed essentially as quickly as the greatest common divisor, because the division algorithm can be applied to reduce the size of the integers involved. For example,

$$\left(\tfrac{10102}{7815}\right) = \left(\tfrac{2287}{7815}\right) \qquad\qquad = (-1)\left(\tfrac{7815}{2287}\right) \quad = (-1)\left(\tfrac{954}{2287}\right)$$

$$= (-1)\left(\tfrac{2}{2287}\right)\left(\tfrac{477}{7815}\right) = (-1)(+1)\left(\tfrac{185}{477}\right) = (-1)\left(\tfrac{477}{185}\right)$$

$$= (-1)\left(\tfrac{107}{185}\right) \qquad\qquad = (-1)\left(\tfrac{185}{107}\right) \qquad = (-1)\left(\tfrac{78}{107}\right)$$

$$= (-1)\left(\tfrac{2}{107}\right)\left(\tfrac{39}{107}\right) \quad = (-1)(-1)\left(\tfrac{39}{107}\right) = (-1)\left(\tfrac{107}{39}\right)$$

$$= (-1)\left(\tfrac{29}{39}\right) \qquad\qquad = (-1)\left(\tfrac{39}{29}\right) \qquad = (-1)\left(\tfrac{10}{29}\right)$$

$$= (-1)\left(\tfrac{2}{29}\right)\left(\tfrac{5}{29}\right) \quad = (-1)(-1)\left(\tfrac{5}{29}\right) \ = \left(\tfrac{29}{5}\right)$$

$$= \left(\tfrac{4}{5}\right) \qquad\qquad\qquad = +1$$

However, we notice again that the Jacobi symbol is $+1$ but it is not the case that we have a solution to

$$x^2 \equiv 10102 \pmod{7815}.$$

This is most easily seen by factoring the "denominator":

$$\left(\frac{10102}{7815}\right) = \left(\frac{10102}{3}\right)\left(\frac{10102}{5}\right)\left(\frac{10102}{521}\right)$$

and we can see that

$$\left(\frac{10102}{5}\right) = -1$$

so the congruence cannot be solved.

We can contrast the above with

$$\left(\tfrac{17194}{7815}\right) = \left(\tfrac{1564}{7815}\right) \qquad\qquad = \left(\tfrac{4}{7815}\right)\left(\tfrac{391}{7815}\right)$$

$$= (+1)(-1)\left(\tfrac{386}{391}\right) = (-1)\left(\tfrac{2}{391}\right)\left(\tfrac{193}{391}\right)$$

$$= (-1)\left(\tfrac{5}{193}\right) \qquad\quad = (-1)\left(\tfrac{193}{5}\right)$$

$$= (-1)\left(\tfrac{3}{5}\right) \qquad\qquad = (-1)(-1) = +1$$

In this case, when we factor $7815 = 3 \cdot 5 \cdot 521$, we see that

$$17194 \equiv 1 \quad (\text{mod } 3)$$
$$17194 \equiv 1 \quad (\text{mod } 5)$$
$$17194 \equiv 4 \quad (\text{mod } 521).$$

These have easy solutions, so we can build the solutions using the Chinese Remainder Theorem

$$x \equiv \pm1 \quad (\text{mod } 3)$$
$$x \equiv \pm1 \quad (\text{mod } 5)$$
$$x \equiv \pm2 \quad (\text{mod } 521).$$

to get eight solutions modulo 7815:

$$x \equiv 1043, 1562, 2083, 3127, 4688, 5732, 6253, 6772 \quad (\text{mod } 7815)$$

We get eight solutions because the two solutions for each of the factors 3, 5, 521 are independent.

5.7 Exercises

1. Show that any quadratic polynomial $x^2 + ax + b$ has exactly two roots or no roots modulo an odd prime p.
2. Modulo a prime p, and given a primitive root r modulo p, we know that $r^{(p-1)/2}$ is -1 and thus is "the other" square root of 1 besides 1 itself. Show that -1 modulo p is itself a square if and only if $p \equiv 1 \pmod{4}$.
3. By looking at the factoring of $(p - 1)/2$, explain exactly when -1 is a cube, a fourth power, a fifth power, etc., modulo p.

4. Compute the Jacobi and/or Legendre symbols $\left(\frac{a}{b}\right)$ for the following and then state whether or not the congruences $x^2 \equiv a \pmod{b}$ are solvable.

    a. $\left(\frac{23}{59}\right)$

    b. $\left(\frac{59}{23}\right)$

    c. $\left(\frac{19}{39}\right)$

    d. $\left(\frac{141}{221}\right)$

    e. $\left(\frac{31}{55}\right)$

    f. $\left(\frac{79}{97}\right)$

Answer:

5. (Programming exercise) Write code to compute quadratic symbols. Start with the Legendre symbol and then expand it to the Jacobi symbol.

Reference

1. I. Niven, H.S. Zuckerman, H.L. Montgomery, *An Introduction to the Theory of Numbers*, 5th edn. (Wiley, 1991)

Finite Fields of Characteristic 2

6

Abstract

In this chapter we extend beyond integers modulo primes to consider finite fields of characteristic 2. For a more extensive presentation of finite fields, the reader should consult Lidl and Niederreiter [1]. For a different presentation of finite fields of characteristic 2, the reader could consult Golomb [2]. Finite field arithmetic in characteristic 2 is used in the Advanced Encryption Standard (AES). It can be preferable in other cryptosystems, because computer hardware works in binary, and thus the underlying arithmetic operations needed to encrypt and decrypt can be very fast.

6.1 Polynomials with Coefficients mod 2

6.1.1 An Example

We consider polynomials with coefficients taken modulo a prime number p, taken modulo "the right kind" of polynomial of degree n. This will generate a finite field of p^n elements whose multiplicative group of $p^n - 1$ elements is cyclic and generated by a primitive element entirely analogous to a primitive root modulo a prime integer.

We are going to do a congruence computation using polynomials with coefficients taken modulo 2.

We start with

$$n_{00} = 1$$

We multiply by x:

$$n_{01} = x$$

© The Author(s), under exclusive license to Springer Nature Switzerland AG 2021
D. Buell, *Fundamentals of Cryptography*, Undergraduate Topics in Computer Science,
https://doi.org/10.1007/978-3-030-73492-3_6

and then again

$$n_{02} = x^2$$

and again

$$n_{03} = x^3$$

But we're going to take the polynomials modulo

$$m = 1 + x + x^3$$

which is the same thing (with coefficients mod 2) as saying that

$$1 + x \equiv x^3$$

so we have

$$n_{03} = x^3 \equiv 1 + x \quad (\text{mod } m)$$

We continue multiplying by x modulo m.

$$n_{04} = x + x^2$$
$$n_{05} = x^2 + x^3 \equiv 1 + x + x^2 \quad (\text{mod } m)$$

Multiplying one more time by x modulo m we get

$$n_{06} = x + x^2 + x^3 \equiv x + x^2 + 1 + x \equiv 1 + x^2 \quad (\text{mod } m)$$

and then multiplying by x one more time we get

$$n_{07} = x + x^3 \equiv x + 1 + x \equiv 1 \quad (\text{mod } m)$$

and we are back where we started.

The Special Theory: We take $p = 2$ because binary arithmetic is especially easy to do in computer hardware, and we hope for every degree n to find an example of "the right kind" of polynomial so that the hardware to be implemented is even more especially easy.

In this example, the powers of x taken modulo the *primitive trinomial*

$$m = 1 + x + x^3$$

of degree 3 generate all seven not-all-zero bit patterns of 3 bits in length (which is the same as all seven nonzero integers modulo 8). These bit patterns, reading from lowest degree to highest, are

$$n_0 = 100$$
$$n_1 = 010$$
$$n_2 = 001$$
$$n_3 = 110$$
$$n_4 = 011$$
$$n_5 = 111$$
$$n_6 = 101$$
$$n_7 = 100$$

The polynomial is a trinomial because it has only three nonzero coefficients. Since the degree 0 term (the 1) and the degree n term are nonzero, a polynomial is a trinomial if there is only one nonzero coefficient between the terms of lowest and of highest degree. We say that such a polynomial $f(x)$ of degree n is *primitive* if the powers of x generate, modulo $f(x)$, all the $2^n - 1$ distinct polynomials of degree less than or equal to n.

What this gives us is a field structure entirely analogous to the structure of the integers modulo a prime p, complete with generators of the multiplicative cycle and the same "reasonably random" sequence of bit patterns that makes the discrete log problem hard.

We note further that we can run the bits going either direction. That is, we could write $1 + x + x^3$ or $x^3 + x + 1$, depending on personal tastes in such things, and as long as we do things "the same way" in both representations, we get the same bit patterns.

6.2 Linear Feedback Shift Registers

We will in this section describe what is true, but not necessarily prove the theorems. The proofs and a much more extended discussion of this material can be found in Golomb [2] and in Lidl and Niederreiter [1].

The *linear feedback shift register (LFSR)* representation of the first example generates the same set of bit patterns, but in a different order.

Let's imagine an initial sequence of bits of length 3, viewed in a window of width 3:

$$n_0 = |100|$$

We add bits to the right by adding in the sum mod 2 of the two leftmost bits in the window.

$$n_0 = |100|$$
$$n_1 = 1|001|$$
$$n_2 = 10|010|$$
$$n_3 = 100|101|$$
$$n_4 = 1001|011|$$
$$n_5 = 10010|111|$$
$$n_6 = 100101|110|$$
$$n_7 = 1001011|100|$$

At this point the sequence begins again; we have an LFSR of *period* 7.

This is an example of a LFSR with two *taps* at x^0 and x^1. The polynomial we are using is still $m = 1 + x + x^3$ and we are applying that polynomial to the window for n_i in order to generate as the next bit the coefficient of x^3 necessary to make $m \equiv 0$.

That is, the LFSR is a degree three recurrence relation

$$x_{n+3} = x_{n+1} + x_n$$

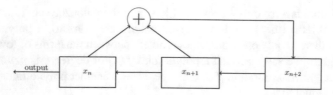

Fig. 6.1 LFSR of $x_{n+3} = x_{n+1} + x_n$

An LFSR can be viewed, not surprisingly given its name, as a shift register with an XOR, as in Fig. 6.1. We have a register of bits with an initial fill (100, say). The register is shifted left, with the leftmost bit becoming the output, and the rightmost bit is filled in as the XOR (the modulo 2 sum) of the two leftmost bits. The output bits thus become eventually the sequence of bits that precede the window in n_7 above.

It is the shift register version that is a favorite of hardware designers. Registers are easy to build, shifts are easy, and the XOR of two bits to fill in the empty slot on the right end is easy. One can show that the same characteristics of randomness that are displayed by taking powers of a generator modulo an irreducible polynomial (we will define "irreducible" later in this chapter) are inherent in the sequence of output bits of an LFSR (although the bit sequence is, of course, deterministic, and it does repeat eventually). For this reason, they have been used as a means of generating "random" bits of cipher key to be XORed with plaintext bits to produce ciphertext bits.

The crucial fact here is that if the integer $P = 2^r - 1$ is a prime, that is, is a Mersenne prime, then an degree r LFSR will generate a sequence of P bits before repeating.[1]

Let us look more closely at the mathematics of an LFSR, which can be done using matrix algebra modulo 2.

If we have a degree three recurrence relation, say, then we have an equation

$$x_{n+3} = a_2 x_{n+2} + a_1 x_{n+1} + a_0 x_n$$

and we can write the recurrence as a matrix

$$M = \begin{pmatrix} 0 & 0 & a_0 \\ 1 & 0 & a_1 \\ 0 & 1 & a_2 \end{pmatrix}$$

with a 2×2 identity matrix below the main diagonal, zeros above the identity matrix, and the coefficients of the recurrence down the last column. For any 3-bit window, $(x \ y \ z)$, we have

$$(x \ y \ z) \begin{pmatrix} 0 & 0 & a_0 \\ 1 & 0 & a_1 \\ 0 & 1 & a_2 \end{pmatrix} = (y \ z \ a_0 x + a_1 y + a_2 z)$$

---

[1] The first several Mersenne primes are for $r = 2, 3, 5, 7, 13, 17, 19, 31, 61, 89, 107$ and 127; certainly from the last four of these we would get extremely long sequences of deterministically-produced bits that do happen to satisfy standard tests for being a random sequence of bits.

More to the point, if we have the sequence of output bits, we can take those bits 3 at a time, form a matrix from them, and use that to produce the coefficients of the recurrence. Continuing with our example, and choosing the first three windows, we have

$$
\begin{pmatrix} 1 & 0 & 0 \\ 0 & 0 & 1 \\ 0 & 1 & 0 \end{pmatrix} \begin{pmatrix} a_0 \\ a_1 \\ a_2 \end{pmatrix} = \begin{pmatrix} 1 \\ 0 \\ 1 \end{pmatrix}
$$

From this set of three windows it is trivial to compute the coefficients. But we could use any set of three windows, as a matrix, with the column vector on the right hand side being the modulo-2 sum.

Thus, perhaps $x_n + x_{n+1}$ for each row for our running example.

$$
\begin{pmatrix} 0 & 1 & 0 \\ 0 & 1 & 1 \\ 1 & 1 & 0 \end{pmatrix} \begin{pmatrix} a_0 \\ a_1 \\ a_2 \end{pmatrix} = \begin{pmatrix} 1 \\ 1 \\ 0 \end{pmatrix}
$$

from which we would get simultaneous equations

$$
a_1 = 1
$$
$$
a_1 + a_2 = 1
$$
$$
a_0 + a_1 = 0
$$

and a unique solution for the coefficients a_i.

This approach works in general. If we have a sequence of bits generated by an LFSR of degree r, we can set up the matrix equation

$$
\begin{pmatrix} x_0 & \cdots & x_{r-1} \\ & \cdots & \\ x_{r-1} & \cdots & x_{2r-1} \end{pmatrix} \begin{pmatrix} a_0 \\ \cdots \\ a_{r-1} \end{pmatrix} = \begin{pmatrix} x_r \\ \cdots \\ x_{2r} \end{pmatrix}
$$

and solve uniquely for the coefficients.

The question then arises as to how we can determine the appropriate degree r of the recurrence. This is also a problem in matrix algebra. If we overconstrain the matrix, assuming perhaps that we should have

$$
\begin{pmatrix} x_0 & \cdots & x_r \\ & \cdots & \\ x_r & \cdots & x_{2r} \end{pmatrix} \begin{pmatrix} a_0 \\ \cdots \\ a_r \end{pmatrix} = \begin{pmatrix} x_r \\ \cdots \\ x_{2r} \\ x_{2r+1} \end{pmatrix} \tag{6.1}
$$

We will find that the matrix has determinant 0 and the system cannot be solved. We can find zero determinants for r that are too small, just by chance, but if we really do have only r linearly independent coefficients, then matrices that are too large must reduce to matrices with rows of zeros. If the determinants of the matrices (6.1) and larger are all zero for a sequence of larger matrices, then the size of the matrix with the last nonzero is probably the appropriate degree. We can check that this is the appropriate degree by solving for the coefficients and running the putative recurrence to check against our known sequence of output bits.

Indeed, we can make this precise. Consider the leftmost column of a matrix like (6.1) or a matrix that is not just $r \times r$ but even larger. Assume the recurrence is

$$x_{n+r} = a_{r-1}x_{n+r-1} + \ldots + a_0 x_n.$$

What we have in the leftmost column is $(x_0 \ldots x_{n+r})^T$, so if we sum the entries for which the a_i are nonzero, the sum must be 0. Shifting right one column, we have $(x_1 \ldots x_{n+r+1})^T$, and the same property must hold. That is, adding the rows for which the a_i are nonzero produces exactly the r-th row, so adding the rows for which the a_i are nonzero to the r-th row produces a row of all zeros, and thus a zero determinant.

We note, but will not prove, that we can find a correspondence between an LFSR of degree r and period $2^r - 1$ by computing the characteristic polynomial

$$det(M + xI).$$

In the case of our example, this would be the determinant of

$$\begin{pmatrix} x & 0 & 1 \\ 1 & x & 1 \\ 0 & 1 & x \end{pmatrix}$$

which is, taking coefficients modulo 2, exactly what we expect:

$$x^3 + x + 1.$$

The actual theorem is this [2, p. 37].

Theorem 6.1 *If an LFSR has an irreducible characteristic polynomial of degree r, then the period of the sequence is a factor of $2^r - 1$. If $P = 2^r - 1$ is prime, then every irreducible polynomial of degree r corresponds to an LFSR of period P.*

Theorem 6.1 builds on a theorem usually proved earlier, that we also will not prove.

Theorem 6.2 *Every irreducible polynomial modulo 2 of degree r divides the polynomial*

$$x^{2^r-1} + 1.$$

We note that

$$x^{2^3-1} + 1 = (x + 1)(x^3 + x + 1)(x^3 + x^2 + 1).$$

For completeness, as an example of the two theorems above, we note that the "other" recurrence of degree 3,

$$x_{n+3} = x_{n+2} + x_n,$$

has a matrix representation of

$$M = \begin{pmatrix} 0 & 0 & 1 \\ 1 & 0 & 0 \\ 0 & 1 & 1 \end{pmatrix}$$

and that the characteristic polynomial is

$$det(M + xI) = det \begin{pmatrix} x & 0 & 1 \\ 1 & x & 0 \\ 0 & 1 & 1+x \end{pmatrix} = x^3 + x^2 + 1,$$

which is the other irreducible of degree 3 in the polynomial factoring above.

6.3 The General Theory

We are not going to prove everything here, in part because the proofs are fairly simple. What we will do is point out that polynomial arithmetic is entirely analogous to arithmetic modulo ordinary integers and modulo primes. We will restrict our study to polynomials with coefficients modulo 2, but versions of these results work for coefficients modulo any prime.

We work modulo 2 because the arithmetic can be done very efficiently in hardware, and therefore *if* we can get the mathematical structures we want working modulo 2, we will do that. Working modulo odd primes produces similar mathematical structures, but this would require adders and multipliers for each of the coefficients, where working modulo 2 requires only OR and AND capability. If working in a finite field based on polynomial arithmetic is part of the plan for a cryptographic system, then there will be a strong preference for working modulo 2 because that is the way that hardware works.

We do note that there are some concerns that there might be structure in these fields that has not yet been seen to be exploitable when used in a cryptographic setting, but with that caveat, it is clear that a great computational advantage comes from working with bits on a computer.

We observe that the "less than" condition has been useful, for example, in guaranteeing that the division algorithm (and thus the Euclidean algorithm) terminates after a finite number of steps. The analogous purpose is served for polynomials $f(x)$ by the degree of the polynomial, $deg(f)$.

Theorem 6.3 *The division algorithm works for polynomials. That is, for any two polynomials $f(x)$ and $g(x)$, there exist polynomials $q(x)$ and $r(x)$ such that*

$$f(x) = q(x) \cdot g(x) + r(x),$$

with $deg(r) < deg(g)$.

Theorem 6.4 *The Euclidean algorithm works for polynomials.*

Definition 6.1 A polynomial $p(x)$ is called *irreducible* or *prime* if it has positive degree and if $p(x) = a(x)b(x)$ implies that one of $a(x)$ and $b(x)$ is a constant. (And given that we are working with polynomials with coefficients mod 2, that constant would have to be 1.)

Theorem 6.5 *If we have, for an irreducible polynomial $p(x)$, that $p(x)|a(x)b(x)$, then either $p(x)|a(x)$ or $p(x)|b(x)$.*

Theorem 6.6 *The ring of polynomials with coefficients mod 2, taken modulo a polynomial $m(x)$, is a field if and only if $m(x)$ is irreducible.*

As a convenience to the reader, we cross reference terminology of the field of residues modulo primes and of finite fields of characteristic 2.
For primes:

- We say an integer p is prime if there are no divisors of p other than 1 and p.
- If an integer p is prime, then the least positive linear residues $0, 1, \ldots, p-1$ form a field of p elements under modular addition and multiplication. The multiplicative group of the non-zero linear residues is of order $p - 1$ and can be generated as the powers modulo p of a primitive root, and multiplication modulo p is the same as addition of the exponents of any fixed primitive root. The primitive roots modulo p are the least linear residues whose exponents, as powers of any primitive root, are relatively prime to $p - 1$.

For polynomials:

- We say that a polynomial $f(x)$, with coefficients 0, 1 taken modulo 2, is primitive if all polynomials taken modulo $f(x)$, and with coefficients taken modulo 2, can be generated as powers of x.
- We say that a polynomial $p(x)$, with coefficients taken modulo 2, is prime, or (equivalently) irreducible if no writing $p(x) = a(x)b(x)$ as polynomials can be done without either $a(x) = 1$ or $b(x) = 1$.
- The ring of polynomials with coefficients taken modulo 2 and taken modulo a polynomial $f(x)$ is a field if and only if $f(x)$ is irreducible.

Displayed in Tables 6.1, 6.2, 6.3, 6.4 and 6.5 are the irreducible polynomials $f(x)$ of small degree, together with the least generator. Since the powers of x generate the entire set of residues of $f(x)$, a primitive polynomial is necessarily irreducible. We note that if a polynomial is irreducible, then its reverse is also irreducible, so of the pairs of polynomials we could list, we present the one with the least nonzero coefficients. Further tables can be found in Zierler and Brillhart [3,4].

6.4   Normal Bases

It should come as no surprise to anyone who does computation that "ordinary" computers are not designed for the purpose of expediting computations in number theory. Computers intended for serious computation invariably are targeted at floating point computations, usually for solving differential equations, solving problems in linear

Table 6.1 Degree 2, 3, 4 irreducibles and least generators

0	1	2	3	4		0	1
1	1	1				0	1
1	1	0	1			0	1
1	0	1	1			0	1
1	1	1	1	1		1	1
1	1	0	0	1		0	1
1	0	0	1	1		0	1

Table 6.2 Degree 5 irreducibles and least generators

0	1	2	3	4	5	0	1
1	1	1	1	0	1	0	1
1	1	1	0	1	1	0	1
1	1	0	1	1	1	0	1
1	0	1	1	1	1	0	1
1	0	1	0	0	1	0	1
1	0	0	1	0	1	0	1

Table 6.3 Degree 6 irreducibles and least generators

0	1	2	3	4	5	6	0	1
1	1	1	0	1	0	1	1	1
1	1	1	0	0	1	1	0	1
1	1	0	1	1	0	1	0	1
1	1	0	0	1	1	1	0	1
1	1	0	0	0	0	1	0	1
1	0	1	1	0	1	1	0	1
1	0	1	0	1	1	1	1	1
1	0	0	1	0	0	1	1	1
1	0	0	0	0	1	1	0	1

algebra, or Monte Carlo simulations requiring random numbers. Integer arithmetic is usually very much a secondary priority, and arithmetic in finite fields modulo polynomials is thought of not much at all. Because of this, it has been normal in discrete mathematics and in number theory, including the mathematics that supports cryptography, to devise algorithms and representations that facilitate computation.

We have in this chapter represented the elements of a finite field $GF(2^n)$ as polynomials in the ordinary way, with coefficients of 0 or 1 that multiply times the powers of x. For computational purposes there is an alternative presentation that

Table 6.4 Degree 7 irreducibles and least generators

0	1	2	3	4	5	6	7	0	1
1	1	1	1	1	1	0	1	0	1
1	1	1	1	0	1	1	1	0	1
1	1	1	1	0	0	0	1	0	1
1	1	1	0	1	1	1	1	0	1
1	1	1	0	0	1	0	1	0	1
1	1	0	1	0	1	0	1	0	1
1	1	0	1	0	0	1	1	0	1
1	1	0	0	1	0	1	1	0	1
1	1	0	0	0	0	0	1	0	1
1	0	1	1	1	1	1	1	0	1
1	0	1	1	1	0	0	1	0	1
1	0	1	0	1	0	1	1	0	1
1	0	1	0	0	1	1	1	0	1
1	0	0	1	1	1	0	1	0	1
1	0	0	1	0	0	0	1	0	1
1	0	0	0	1	1	1	1	0	1
1	0	0	0	1	0	0	1	0	1
1	0	0	0	0	0	1	1	0	1

permits more efficient computation. Following Mullin, et al. [5] we rewrite the field in terms of a normal basis and then in terms of an optimal normal basis.

Definition 6.2 A *normal basis* for a finite field $GF(2^n)$ is a basis

$$N = \{\beta, \beta^2, \beta^4, \ldots, \beta^{2^{n-1}}\}$$

so that every element α of $GF(2^n)$ can be written as a linear combination

$$A = \sum_{i=0}^{n-1} a_i \beta^{2^i}$$

with a_i either 0 or 1 for all i.

Every finite field $GF(2^n)$ has a normal basis [1], and using a normal basis is an exercise in linear algebra. We note that this is really only a special variation on the choice of a primitive generator for the multiplicative group of a field. If one were interested only the speed of computation in the field of residues modulo a very large prime number, of 1024 bits, for example, then using 2 as a primitive root would have the advantage that multiplication would be a bit shift usually followed by a subtraction.

Table 6.5 Degree 8 irreducibles and least generators

0	1	2	3	4	5	6	7	8	0	1	2	3
1	1	1	1	1	1	0	0	1	1	1		
1	1	1	1	1	0	1	0	1	0	1		
1	1	1	1	1	0	0	1	1	1	1		
1	1	1	1	0	0	1	1	1	0	1		
1	1	1	0	1	1	1	0	1	1	1		
1	1	1	0	1	0	1	1	1	1	1	1	
1	1	1	0	0	1	1	1	1	0	1		
1	1	1	0	0	0	0	1	1	0	1		
1	1	0	1	1	1	1	0	1	1	0	0	1
1	1	0	1	1	0	0	0	1	1	1		
1	1	0	1	0	1	0	0	1	0	1		
1	1	0	1	0	0	0	1	1	0	1	1	
1	1	0	0	1	1	1	1	1	0	1	1	
1	1	0	0	0	1	1	0	1	0	1		
1	1	0	0	0	1	0	1	1	1	1		
1	1	0	0	0	0	1	1	1	0	1		
1	0	1	1	1	1	0	1	1	1	1	1	
1	0	1	1	1	0	1	1	1	0	1	1	
1	0	1	1	1	0	0	0	1	0	1		
1	0	1	1	0	1	0	0	1	0	1		
1	0	1	1	0	0	1	0	1	0	1		
1	0	1	1	0	0	0	1	1	0	1		
1	0	1	0	1	1	1	1	1	0	1		
1	0	1	0	0	1	1	0	1	0	1		
1	0	0	1	1	1	1	1	1	1	1		
1	0	0	1	1	1	0	0	1	1	1		
1	0	0	1	0	1	1	0	1	0	1		
1	0	0	1	0	1	0	1	1	0	1		
1	0	0	0	1	1	1	0	1	0	1		
1	0	0	0	1	1	0	1	1	0	1	1	

Without going into the details of the linear algebra, we notice that a normal basis permits us to play games with the coefficients, and thus to make computation simpler and faster, especially when done, as in this case, with binary coefficients for which computer hardware is naturally suited.

We recall the classic algorithm for exponentiation, attributed by Knuth [6, pp. 441ff.] to the Arabs, for which we had Python code in Chap. 3. To compute a^e, we write e in binary. We keep a running multiplier m and a running product p, with m initialized to a and p initialized to 1. Reading the bits of e from right to left, we replace p with $p * a$ if the bit is a 1, do nothing if the bit is a 0, and then move left in the bits of e while squaring the running multiplier $m = m * m$.

Exponentiation is a crucial part of modern cryptography, and the first thing we can say about exponentiation is that the squaring in the middle of the iteration is especially easy when the finite field is written in a normal basis: If

$$A = \sum_{i=0}^{n-1} a_i \beta^{2^i}$$

which we can write more simply as

$$A = (a_0, a_1, \ldots, a_{n-1}),$$

then

$$A^2 = \sum_{i=0}^{n-1} a_i^2 \beta^{2^{i+1}},$$

and, since we are working modulo 2, this is

$$A^2 = \sum_{i=0}^{n-1} a_i \beta^{2^{i+1}},$$

which we write more simply as

$$A = (a_{n-1}, a_0, a_1, \ldots, a_{n-2}).$$

That is, squaring an element in the finite field can be done with a circular shift of the bits representing the element in a normal basis. Coefficients for general terms A^{2^k} are similarly just circular bit shifts, and we observe that the arithmetic is indeed simple, since modulo 2 we have $x = x^2$ for $x = 0, 1$, and the cross products disappear.

One can further simplify the arithmetic to allow for all products of elements in the finite field to be done by coefficient shifting by adopting an *optimal normal basis* [5], which exists for all the finite fields $GF(2^k)$ relevant to cryptography.

6.5 Exercises

In all these exercises, we assume the coefficients are simply 0 and 1.

1. List the irreducible polynomials of degree 4.
2. List the primitive polynomials of degree 4.
3. Give one representation for the finite field $GF(2^5)$.
4. Give a normal basis for the finite field $GF(2^5)$.
5. There are three polynomials that can be used to generate the finite field $GF(2^4)$. Two of these are primitive: $x^4 + x + 1$ and $y^4 + y^3 + 1$. According to the theorem, these fields are isomorphic. Give the explicit isomorphism mapping one field to the other.
6. You are given the sequence of bits

$$1\,0\,0\,0\,0 \quad 1\,0\,0\,1\,0 \quad 1\,1\,0\,0\,1 \quad 1\,1\,1\,1\,0$$

which you suspect are generated by an LFSR. Find the recurrence. (The blank spaces are present only to help readability.)
7. (Programming exercise) Write programs to assist with the solution to problem 6. These would largely be matrix reductions over the integers modulo 2.

References

1. R. Lidl, H. Niederreiter, *Introduction to Finite Fields and Their Applications*, 2nd edn. (Cambridge University Press, Cambridge, 1997)
2. S. Golomb, *Shift Register Sequences* (Aegean Park Press, 1982)
3. N. Zierler, J. Brillhart, On primitive trinomials (mod 2). Inform. Control **13**, 541–554 (1968)
4. N. Zierler, J. Brillhart, On primitive trinomials (mod 2) (part 2). Inform. Control **14**, 566–569 (1969)
5. R.C. Mullin, I.M. Onyszchuk, S.A. Vanstone, R.M. Wilson, Optimal normal bases in GF(pn). Discrete Appl. Math. **22**, 149–161 (1989)
6. D.E. Knuth, *The Art of Computer Programming, Volume 2, Seminumerical Algorithms*, 2nd edn. (Addison-Wesley, 1981)

Elliptic Curves

7

Abstract

Elliptic curves are one of the more elegant objects in algebra. A background of the underlying arithmetic of curves is necessary for cryptography, because they are used for (at least) three purposes: for factoring integers, for cryptography itself, and for key exchange. The arithmetic of elliptic curves parallels in many ways the arithmetic of integers modulo primes or composites, at least. In this chapter we present an introduction to elliptic curves as background for later chapters that use them for cryptographic purposes.

7.1 Basics

Definition 7.1 An *elliptic curve* $\mathcal{E}$ over a field K is the set of points satisfying an equation with integer coefficients that is quadratic in one variable and cubic in another.

$$\mathcal{E} : y^2 = x^3 + ax + b$$

An excellent more extended reference for the material in this chapter is [1].

We will see that the points on a curve form a group. We will be concerned at the beginning of this chapter only with points on $\mathcal{E}$ in the field of rational numbers $\mathbb{Q}$, but will then shift to consider points that lie in fields of integers modulo a large prime P and finite fields $GF(2^k)$ of characteristic 2. We will also consider points on a curve that come from the ring of integers modulo a composite integer N. In that case, the mechanics of computing the group operation are the same, but taking the points modulo a composite number has much the same effect as does working with zero divisors in the ring of integers modulo N.

© The Author(s), under exclusive license to Springer Nature Switzerland AG 2021   87
D. Buell, *Fundamentals of Cryptography*, Undergraduate Topics in Computer Science,
https://doi.org/10.1007/978-3-030-73492-3_7

Remark 7.1 In general we might think we would have to consider the more general form

$$\mathcal{E}' : y^2 + ay = x^3 + bx^2 + cx + d$$

However, we can get rid of the linear term in y and the quadratic term in x provided we can divide by 2 and 3. Since we are going to start by being interested in *rational* number solutions, with $K = \mathbb{Q}$, we can substitute

$$y = y' - a/2$$

and

$$x = x' - b/3$$

and get a rationally equivalent polynomial without the linear y term or the quadratic x term. We are about to define the process by which we treat the points on a curve as a group, and one can readily show that the group of points on $\mathcal{E}'$ with rational coordinates is isomorphic to the group of points on $\mathcal{E}$ with rational coordinates.

Later on we will be dealing with curves whose points are taken not from the rational numbers but from elements in a finite field whose coefficients are taken mod 2. In those cases we won't be able to divide by 2; we thus may have a linear term in y.

Remark 7.2 This is only one of several "standard" representations for the curve. We also sometimes see the Weierstrass form

$$\mathcal{E}'' : y^2 = 4x^3 - g_2 x - g_3$$

The mathematical structures are the same regardless of the formulation. It's only the high-school-level algebraic formulas that have to be redone.

An elliptic curve often has a graph like the one shown in Fig. 7.1. This is really the plane cutting through a three-dimensional surface at a particular value of the z coordinate, and the general surface is similar to that of a saddle. As one pushes down in z, the isolated oval elongates and eventually connects with the curved section on the right.

7.1.1   Straight Lines and Intersections

Since this is a cubic in x, a straight line should cut the graph of the curve in three points (counting multiplicities). That is, if we intersect the line

$$y = Mx + B$$

with the curve, we get

$$M^2 x^2 + 2MBx + B^2 = x^3 + ax + b$$

which is

$$x^3 - M^2 x^2 + (a - 2MB)x + b - B^2 = 0$$

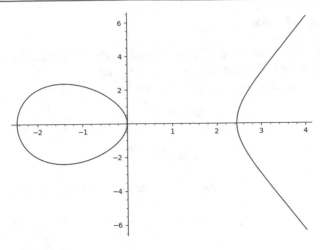

Fig. 7.1 Graph of $y^2 = x^3 - 6x + 9$

and if we factor the cubic, we get

$$0 = (x - x_1)(x - x_2)(x - x_3)$$
$$= x^3 - (x_1 + x_2 + x_3)x^2 + x(*) - x_1 x_2 x_3$$

where we don't really care about the linear terms. What we do care about are the Newton equations

$$x_1 + x_2 + x_3 = M^2$$
$$x_1 x_2 x_3 = B^2 - b.$$

Therefore, given two points (x_1, y_1) and (x_2, y_2) with *rational* coordinates, then

$$M = \frac{y_2 - y_1}{x_2 - x_1}$$

is rational, and so is

$$B = y_1 - x_1 \cdot \left(\frac{y_2 - y_1}{x_2 - x_1} \right)$$

Since x_1 is rational, x_2 is rational, and M is rational, x_3 must also be rational. And since x_3 is rational, and B is rational, we have that y_3 is rational.

That is, two points with rational coordinates determine a straight line, with rational slope and intercept, that intersects the curve in a third point that also has rational coordinates. We note that this is not a property only of rational numbers; if we consider solutions whose coordinates lie in any field, the same result obtains: since arithmetic in a field has well-defined division, the third point intersecting a straight line that joins two points with coordinates in the field will also have coordinates in the field.

7.1.2 Tangent Lines

The formulas above work for looking at the straight line determined by two different points. What about two points that are the same point?

For this we need the tangent, so we differentiate.

$$2yy' = 3x^2 + a$$

and thus

$$y' = \frac{3x^2 + a}{2y}$$

which says that the slope M of the tangent line at a point (x_1, y_1) is

$$M = \frac{3x_1^2 + a}{2y_1}$$

and thus that

$$x_3 = \left(\frac{3x_1^2 + a}{2y_1} \right)^2 - 2x_1$$

Again, if we start with rational coordinates, then the third point has rational coordinates.

7.1.3 Formulas

We use the curve

$$\mathcal{E} : y^2 = x^3 + ax + b$$

If we have two points with rational coordinates

$$P_1 = (x_1, y_1)$$
$$P_2 = (x_2, y_2)$$

then they determine a line

$$y = Mx + B$$

with

$$M = \frac{3x_1^2 + a}{2y_1}$$

or

$$M = \frac{y_2 - y_1}{x_2 - x_1}$$

depending on whether $P_1 = P_2$ or not, and

$$B = y_1 - Mx_1$$

By the Newton equations for the roots, we have that the straight line intersects the curve in a third point

$$P_3 = (x_3, y_3)$$

with
$$x_3 = M^2 - x_1 - x_2.$$

This is enough to determine y_3 up to sign, and we can determine the sign by

$$M = \frac{y_3 - y_1}{x_3 - x_1}.$$

We remark that this formula determines a value for y_3 that is the y-coordinate of the third point on the straight line. In the next subsection, we will negate that y-coordinate, reflecting the point across the x-axis, in order to put the structure of an additive group on the rational points of an elliptic curve.

7.1.4   The Mordell-Weil Group

The method described above, referred to as the chord-and-tangent method, has been known for a long time to be a method by which to find more points on a curve with rational coordinates, given at least one point on the curve with rational coordinates. It was a major result of Louis Mordell, published in 1922, that the points on an elliptic curve, under the chord-and-tangent process, form an abelian group generated by a finite number of base points.

The group law, which is normally written additively, is that

1. the identity of the group is the "point at infinity".
2. the negative (group inverse) of a point $P = (x, y)$ is the point $-P = (x, -y)$ that is the reflection about the x-axis.
3. the three points collinear on a straight line sum to the identity.

The last item is the same as saying that if we have three collinear points

$$P_1 = (x_1, y_1), \quad P_2 = (x_2, y_2), \quad P_3 = (x_3, y_3)$$

then we have in the group that

$$P_1 + P_2 = -P_3 = (x_3, -y_3)$$

The reader should be very careful to notice whether we want y_3 or $-y_3$ in the various formulas. This is important, and easy to get wrong if one is not careful.

Example 7.1 Let
$$y^2 = x^3 - 36x$$

and consider the points
$$P = (-3, 9)$$
$$Q = (-2, 8)$$

Summing $P + Q$:

For $P + Q$ we get

$$M = \frac{9 - 8}{-3 + 2} = \frac{1}{-1} = -1$$

so

$$x_3 = 1 + 3 + 2 = 6$$

In this case we don't have to worry about the sign of y_3 because

$$y_3^2 = 216 - 216 = 0$$

so we have

$$y_3 = 0$$

and

$$P + Q = (6, 0)$$

Doubling P:

To compute $2P$, we need

$$y' = \frac{3x^2 - 36}{2y}$$

and thus

$$M = \frac{27 - 36}{18} = \frac{-1}{2}$$

from which we get

$$x_3 = \frac{1}{4} + 3 + 3 = \frac{25}{4}$$

and then

$$\frac{-y_3 - 9}{25/4 + 3} = \frac{-1}{2}$$

$$-y_3 = 9 + \frac{-1}{2}\frac{37}{4} = \frac{72}{8} - \frac{37}{8} = \frac{35}{8}$$

so

$$2P = (25/4, -35/8)$$

Example 7.2 Now let

$$y^2 = x^3 + 1$$

and consider the point

$$P = (2, 3)$$

Then for $2P$ we have

$$M = 3x^2/2y = 12/6 = 2$$

and thus

$$x_3 = 4 - 2 - 2 = 0$$

This means $y_3 = \pm 1$ and we determine from the slope that $y_3 = 1$.
   We then find

$$3P = (2, 3) + (0, 1)$$

getting

$$M = 1$$
$$x_3 = -1$$
$$y_3 = 0$$

so

$$3P = (2, 3) + (0, 1) = (-1, 0)$$

We then find

$$4P = (2, 3) + (-1, 0)$$

getting

$$M = 1$$
$$x_3 = 0$$
$$y_3 = -1$$

so

$$4P = (2, 3) + (-1, 0) = (0, -1)$$

We then find

$$5P = (2, 3) + (0, -1)$$

getting

$$M = 2$$
$$x_3 = 2$$
$$y_3 = -3$$

so

$$5P = (2, 3) + (-1, 0) = (2, -3)$$

Now, when we try to add to get

$$6P = (2, 3) + (2, -3)$$

we get a zero in the denominator for M. The two points lie on a vertical line, so they are inverse to each other in the group, and the third point on the line is the point at infinity. What is somewhat cute about this is that we will find the answer we want exactly at the point that the arithmetic fails.

7.2 Observation

One should note that since we have

$$x_3 = \left(\frac{y_2 - y_1}{x_2 - x_1} \right)^2 - x_1 - x_2$$

the denominators in the fractions are essentially being squared with each addition of points. So the arithmetic, as rational number arithmetic, is pretty horrible; with every addition or doubling, the number of bits needed to represent the coordinates of a point essentially doubles.

7.3   Projective Coordinates and Jacobian Coordinates

In many cases, it is simpler to shift to *projective coordinates* or *Jacobian coordinates* X, Y, Z instead of standard coordinates x, y. This is actually quite simple: We choose not to work with

$$\mathcal{E} : y^2 = x^3 + ax + b$$

because it would require us to do rational arithmetic. Instead, we notice that if a and b are integers, then the rational numbers that are the coordinates

$$(x, y)$$

will be

$$(X/Z^2, Y/Z^3)$$

for integers X, Y, and Z If we clear denominators, we get the equation for the curve as

$$\mathcal{E} : Y^2 = X^3 + aXZ^4 + bZ^6$$

We consider a point on the curve to be the triple

$$(X : Y : Z)$$

all of which are integers.

    What this really does, after one rewrites all the formulas for doubling or adding points, is provide a gentler way (gentler, that is, than division by zero) to determine that one is about to add two points that lie on a vertical line. We will present an algorithmic process for point addition and duplication in Chap. 14.

7.4   An Example of a Curve with Many Points

A nontrivial curve with a surprisingly large number of integer points is

$$\mathcal{E} : y^2 = x^3 - 3024x - 1353456$$

which has the large number of integer-coordinate points of Table 7.1.

    And we find a very large number of collineations of points all with integer coordinates. This is not common. We notice the patterns in the collineations of Table 7.2: if all subscripts are odd, the collineation that comes from negating all the y-coordinates is the same as adding one to each of the subscripts. Similarly, negating the y-coordinates of the collineation

$$P_1 + P_4 + P_{20} = \mathcal{O}$$

corresponds to the collineation

$$P_2 + P_3 + P_{19} = \mathcal{O}$$

where the y-coordinates have similarly been negated.

Table 7.1 Integer-coordinate points on $\mathcal{E} : y^2 = x^3 - 3024x - 1353456$

P_1	$= (120, 108)$	P_2	$= (120, -108)$
P_3	$= (156, 1404)$	P_4	$= (156, -1404)$
P_5	$= (192, 2268)$	P_6	$= (192, -2268)$
P_7	$= (228, 3132)$	P_8	$= (228, -3132)$
P_9	$= (436, 8956)$	P_{10}	$= (436, -8956)$
P_{11}	$= (552, 12852)$	P_{12}	$= (552, -12852)$
P_{13}	$= (588, 14148)$	P_{14}	$= (588, -14148)$
P_{15}	$= (777, 21573)$	P_{16}	$= (777, -21573)$
P_{17}	$= (1020, 32508)$	P_{18}	$= (1020, -32508)$
P_{19}	$= (1488, 57348)$	P_{20}	$= (1488, -57348)$
P_{21}	$= (3585, 214623)$	P_{22}	$= (3585, -214623)$
P_{23}	$= (10056, 1008396)$	P_{24}	$= (10056, -1008396)$
P_{25}	$= (22080, 3280932)$	P_{26}	$= (22080, -3280932)$
P_{27}	$= (34356, 6368004)$	P_{28}	$= (34356, -6368004)$
P_{29}	$= (561360, 420593148)$	P_{30}	$= (561360, -420593148)$

Table 7.2 Point subscripts for collineations

(1 3 17)	(1 4 20)	(1 5 13)	(1 6 16)
(1 7 9)	(1 8 12)	(2 3 19)	(2 4 18)
(2 5 15)	(2 6 14)	(2 7 11)	(2 8 10)
(3 5 7)	(3 6 24)	(3 8 22)	(3 10 16)
(3 12 14)	(4 5 23)	(4 6 8)	(4 7 21)
(4 9 15)	(4 11 13)	(5 8 26)	(5 10 20)
(5 12 18)	(6 7 25)	(6 9 19)	(6 11 17)
(7 14 20)	(7 16 18)	(8 13 19)	(8 15 17)
(9 12 28)	(9 14 26)	(9 18 22)	(10 11 27)
(10 13 25)	(10 17 21)	(11 14 30)	(11 16 26)
(11 20 22)	(12 13 29)	(12 15 25)	(12 19 21)
(13 16 28)	(13 18 24)	(14 15 27)	(14 17 23)
(15 20 24)	(16 19 23)	(17 20 28)	(18 19 27)
(21 24 26)	(22 23 25)	(25 28 30)	(26 27 29)

7.5 Curves Modulo a Prime p

What we have been discussing above are curves whose points are taken from the field of rational numbers.

We can equally well look at curves whose points are taken from a field of integers modulo a prime p, or from a field generated by an irreducible polynomial with coefficients taken modulo 2.

For example, if we consider points modulo 11 on the curve

$$\mathcal{E} : y^2 = x^3 + x + 6$$

then the points are

$$(2, 4), \quad (2, 7)$$
$$(3, 5), \quad (3, 6)$$
$$(5, 2), \quad (5, 9)$$
$$(7, 2), \quad (7, 9)$$
$$(8, 3), \quad (8, 8)$$
$$(10, 2), \quad (10, 9)$$

and doing the curve arithmetic, but this time doing all arithmetic modulo 11, we get

$$P = (2, 4) \qquad 7P = (7, 9)$$
$$2P = (5, 9) \qquad 8P = (3, 6)$$
$$3P = (8, 8) \qquad 9P = (10, 2)$$
$$4P = (10, 9) \qquad 10P = (8, 3)$$
$$5P = (3, 5) \qquad 11P = (5, 2)$$
$$6P = (7, 2) \qquad 12P = (2, 7)$$
$$13P = \mathcal{O}$$

We observe what must be true: since this is a cyclic group with 13 elements, then if $kP = (x, y)$, we have $(13 - k)P = (x, -y)$, because the additive inverse of a point is the point with the same x coordinate but the negative of the y coordinate.

7.6 Hasse's Theorem

We shall see later in Sect. 11.2.1 and beyond that cryptography can be done in finite groups modulo a large prime p, provided that the order of the group is about the same size as p and that the identity of the group can be connected to some algebraic expression that can easily be recognized modulo p. We have seen with the projective representation of the curve that the second condition is met: the identity of the curve group can be recognized when the z-coordinate becomes zero modulo p.

That the first condition, on the size of the group, is met is Hasse's Theorem [1, p. 82] .

Theorem 7.1 (Hasse's Theorem) *Let $\#\mathcal{E}(F_p)$ be the number of points on an elliptic curve $\mathcal{E}$ taken modulo a prime p. Then*

$$\#\mathcal{E}(F_p) = p + 1 - t$$

where we have

$$|t| < 2\sqrt{p}$$

That is to say, the number of points on a curve modulo p is within $2\sqrt{p}$ of $p + 1$.

This becomes important for cryptographic purposes because it says that the size of the group, $\mathcal{O}(p)$, is large enough to ensure a group on the curve that is computationally infeasible to exhaustively examine. It will not be the case that all groups are suitable for use in cryptographic applications, but there will be sufficiently many that are that we can use curve groups for cryptographic purposes.

7.7 Exercises

1. For the curve of Sect. 7.4, compute the sums

$$2P_1$$
$$2P_3$$
$$P_1 + P_3$$
$$P_2 + P_5$$

   and note that the last two are listed in the collineations of Table 7.2.
2. Given an elliptic curve

$$\mathcal{E} : y^2 = x^3 + Ax + B,$$

   show that the rational points (x, y) on $\mathcal{E}$ are of the form $(a/e^2, b/e^3)$, where a, b, and e are integers and the fractions are expressed in lowest terms.
3. Compute the points modulo 11 and 13 on the curve

$$y^2 = x^3 - 6x + 9$$

   Compute the group modulo 11.
4. (Programming exercise.) Write a program to count the number of points on a curve modulo a prime p. For small primes, this isn't difficult: run the loop on possible values x, computing the right hand side $RHS = x^2 + Ax + B$ modulo p, and then determining using the quadratic residue symbol whether RHS is a square modulo p. If it is, then that x contributes one or two points to the count depending on whether RHS is 0 or not.
5. (Programming exercise.) Write the code to do arithmetic on an elliptic curve modulo a prime p. Test your code on curves modulo the prime 257 by finding points on the curve and then finding the orders of those points by the additive analog of "exponentiation". You should be able to tell that your code is working by verifying that for any point P, there is an n such that nP is the identity.

You might well want to do the initial computation using Jacobian coordinates, but then reduce the points to points with $z = 1$, because that will more easily allow you to recognize points and their inverses in the cycle.

6. (Probable programming exercise.) Many of the curve groups we have used as examples are single cycles. Compute the group for $\mathcal{E} : y^2 = x^3 + x + 18$ modulo 31 to show that the group is not a single cycle. (Hint: Look at points $(1, 12)$ and $(2, 11)$).

Reference

1. D. Hankerson, A. Menezes, S. Vanstone, *Guide to Elliptic Curve Cryptography* (Springer, Berlin, 2004)

Mathematics, Computing, and Arithmetic

8

Abstract

We have remarked earlier that actually doing cryptography requires combining mathematics and computing. In this chapter we describe several algorithms and computational tricks that make it possible to do the discrete mathematics that is cryptography on computers that have not necessarily been designed to provide robust support for discrete mathematics. This chapter covers a few of these tricks and algorithms necessary for understanding how one might actually do cryptography in the real world. The first set of tricks has been used extensively in testing integers for primality, using the bit patterns of the integers to eliminate the need for modular reduction. Multiprecise arithmetic is needed for much of modern cryptography, with modular reduction and multiplication dominating the cost of arithmetic. Multiplication itself is done with fast methods like the FFT, which we cover here, and reduction can be dealt with by Montgomery multiplication, which essentially extends the Mersenne prime trick to all integer moduli.

8.1 Mersenne Primes

Every so often (for example, on 7 December 2018) it is announced that a new Mersenne prime is discovered. This is a brief introduction of how and why that happens, why it is that the largest known prime numbers are almost invariably Mersenne numbers, and why this apparently esoteric activity in some sense a model for how computing is done in the real world. The lesson to be learned is the interplay between the mathematics and the computing. One can prove that testing certain numbers for primality can be done more quickly (in theory, with a big-$\mathcal{O}$ estimate) than testing a random number, and fortunately, for these certain numbers, there is a computational trick that can be used to make primality testing not just theoretically feasible but actually feasible in practice.

© The Author(s), under exclusive license to Springer Nature Switzerland AG 2021 99
D. Buell, *Fundamentals of Cryptography*, Undergraduate Topics in Computer Science,
https://doi.org/10.1007/978-3-030-73492-3_8

8.1.1　Introduction

The largest known prime number as of this writing is
$$2^{82589933} - 1,$$
a number of 24, 862, 048 decimal digits, found on 7 December 2018.

This is the seventh number of more than ten million decimals that has been proved prime. (A number of the form $2^N - 1$ is called a *Mersenne number*.)

Although this may seem like a rather abstract enterprise, proving such numbers prime is a combination of theory, algorithm, and implementation that serves as a good model for how to think about solving problems, especially problems in discrete mathematics, on a computer.

It also happens to be the case that if one analyzes the computational cost of finding the largest known prime number, that cost tracks fairly well the raw computing power of the best available computing platforms. In essence, since this computation is so huge, and yet so completely predictable, one can argue that the narrow group of extreme Mersenne fans do us a favor by running a computation that tracks an otherwise difficult measurement of the raw capability of computing power.

8.1.2　Theory

8.1.2.1　General Purpose Theory

First off, how is it that we prove a number to be prime? There is a general purpose algorithm call the AKS algorithm (after the initials of the inventors) that runs reasonably quickly [1]. This caused quite a stir back in 2002 by being the first algorithm for testing primality of integers that could be proved to run in polynomial time. In the case of primality testing, this means polynomial in the number of bits in the number to be tested. If the number is P, and has N bits (and thus we have $2^{N-1} \leq P < 2^N$), then AKS runs in time polynomial in N, which is polynomial in $\lg P$. Actually, the current best version runs in time $\mathcal{O}((\lg P)^6)$.

As good as this algorithm is, however, the algorithm is too complicated to be used to test a number of nearly 25 million decimals. Instead, we have to rely on simpler methods if we are going to test these huge numbers.

The basis for this kind of heroic computation is Fermat's Little Theorem.

8.1.2.2　More General Purpose Theory

We repeat Fermat's Little Theorem from Chap. 3.

Theorem 8.1 (Fermat's (Little) Theorem) *For any prime integer P, and any integer a, then P divides $a^{P-1} - 1$.*

Actually, as mentioned early, this is really just Lagrange's theorem that any element in a group, raised to the order of the group, is the identity. The order of the multiplicative group modulo a prime P is just $P - 1$, so this is just Lagrange.

This is a very useful theorem, but it is not a theorem that can be used to prove a number is prime. What this says is that if for any a we have that a^{P-1} is *not* 1 modulo P, then P is *not* a prime. But for general numbers it only works in that direction and is not an "if and only if" theorem. In fact, there is an infinite set of what are called *Carmichael numbers* which are integers C that are *not* prime but for which N divides $a^{C-1} - 1$ for all a. The smallest Carmichael number is 561.

8.1.2.3 Special Purpose Theory

One of the reasons that the largest known primes have (almost) always been Mersenne primes is that for this special kind of number it is in fact possible to get an if-and-only-if variation on Fermat's Little Theorem to work.

Theorem 8.2 ((Lucas–Lehmer Test) [2, pp. 223–225]) *Let N be an odd prime congruent to 3 modulo 4. Let $P = 2^N - 1$ be a Mersenne number, define $s_1 = 3$, and recursively compute*

$$s_i = s_{i-1}^2 - 2 \quad (\text{mod } P)$$

for $i > 1$. If P divides s_{N-1}, that is, if the residue s_{N-1} is zero modulo P, then P is prime. Otherwise, P is not prime.

This isn't really just Lagrange (or Fermat Little), but it is quite similar, and we get to determine primality both yes or no based on the outcome of this test.

This is a test, requiring a number of arithmetic steps that is logarithmic in the size of $2^N - 1$ (that is, linear in N–we need $\mathcal{O}(N)$ squarings). This is asymptotically not much different from the general AKS algorithm, but of course this only works for Mersenne numbers.

The condition that N is an odd prime is not an important condition, because high school algebra shows that

$$2^{ab} - 1 = (2^a - 1) \cdot (2^{ab-a} + 2^{ab-2a} - 2^{ab-3a} \ldots + 1)$$

so there is an algebraic factoring of $2^{ab} - 1$ if both a and b are larger than 1 and we wouldn't even need to do a real test for primality.

8.1.2.4 Preprocessing

In any real search for primes, we want to filter out as soon as possible the integers that can't possibly be primes. For example, if $N \equiv 4 \pmod 5$, then $2^N - 1$ will be zero modulo 5. There is a similar set of conditions that can be applied for all primes, so a search for Mersenne primes starts by filtering out all the exponents that can't possibly work. In general, the mantra is that one filters until one just can't stand it any more, or until the cost benefit of running the filter drops below the cost of testing an exponent that remains after the filter.

8.1.2.5 Algorithms

Now, given that we have a theorem that allegedly runs in polynomial time in the number of bits, how can we make this computationally effective?

Fact We do not need to compute s_{N-2} to full precision; we only need to compute s_{N-2} modulo P, so we can reduce modulo P with every squaring. Our arithmetic only gets twice as large as P itself. That is, we only need to deal with integers of size $2N$ bits.   □

This is an obvious fact to a number theorist, but it's also very powerful in computation because it keeps the size of the numbers down. If a is a number of n bits, then a^2 is a number of $2n$ bits (give or take one or two based on carries or no carries), and a^4 is a number of $4n$ bits. The actual number that would be s_{N-2} without reduction would be a number of $2^{N-2} \approx P$ *bits*, exponentially larger than P itself.

But because we are allowed to reduce modulo P, we could keep the arithmetic necessary down to about 25 million decimals at every stage, if we were to be testing what is now the largest known prime.

The headliner algorithm we use is *fast multiplication with the Fast Fourier Transform (FFT)* [3,4]. If we were not to think too hard, we would do the squarings using naive schoolchild arithmetic, which is basically multiplying one array of numbers times another array of numbers, accumulating the products into a third array, and settling the carries (Fig. 8.1).

On modern computers, we would do this not base 10, but base 2^{32}, since on a serious computer we can accumulate a $32 \times 32 = 64$-bit product without overflow. For this largest Mersenne prime, a single calculation of an intermediate value of s_i would take $82589933/32 = 2580936$ "digits" (rounding up for the last digit). Naively, multiplication of an n-digit number times an m-digit number takes $n \times m$ multiplications. Squaring is twice as fast as multiplication, because we don't have distinct cross-products, but a naive squaring is still $\mathcal{O}(n^2)$ multiplications.

Fig. 8.1 Naive multiplication of integers

However, the *Fast Fourier Transform*, or FFT, can be adapted from its usual signal processing use to produce a multiplication algorithm that runs not in $\mathcal{O}(n^2)$ time but in the much faster $\mathcal{O}(n \log n)$ time.

Algorithmically, then, proving any particular Mersenne number $2^N - 1$ to be prime requires about N squarings (and then a one-digit subtraction) of a number that is N bits long, and each of these squarings can be done in something like $(N/32) \cdot \log(N/32)$ integer multiplications of single-precision 32-bit numbers. After each squaring, we must reduce a double-length product of $2N$ bits down to a single-length result of N bits.

8.1.3   Implementation

We are still not able to test for primality in feasible time using only these simplifications. If the complexity of FFT multiplication were exactly $n \log n$, then a single squaring of a number of 82589933 bits would take about 55 million integer multiplication machine instructions, and the total number of multiplications would be more than 10^{15}. At 10 ns per multiplication, this puts the cost of multiplication in the ballpark of 10^7 s, which is about four months. This would be acceptable, if this were all that we have to do, and if we only needed to test a single exponent, but in fact we have this nasty business of reducing a double length product down to single length. Unfortunately, a genuine multiprecise division is usually maybe 50–100 times more expensive than a multiplication. If we had to do a genuine division by $2^N - 1$ in order to reduce the double-length squared value down to a single length number for the next squaring, we would not be able to finish the test of a Mersenne number for primality.

At this point we rely on an implementation trick based on the nature of computers built with binary arithmetic. Any of the values s_i computed in the intermediate steps of the Lucas–Lehmer test can be written as a single "digit" D base 2^N. When we square D, we get a "two-digit" number $A \cdot 2^N + B$, where each of A and B are single digits base 2^N, that is, they are integers of N bits in length. We now do a minor bit of algebraic sleight of hand:

$$A \cdot 2^N + B =$$
$$A \cdot 2^N - A + A + B =$$
$$A \cdot (2^N - 1) + A + B \equiv$$
$$\equiv A + B \pmod{2^N - 1}.$$

If we are interested in reducing the product modulo $2^N - 1$, then the task is easy. The remainder of this expression upon dividing by $2^N - 1$ is clearly $A + B$, with possibly one subtraction by $2^N - 1$ if the addition generated a carry.

Think for a moment what this means. In steady state we have an intermediate value s_i that is a remainder modulo $2^N - 1$, that is, an integer of N bits. When we square this number as part of the process of computing $s_{i+1} = s_i^2 - 2$ modulo $2^N - 1$, we get an integer of $2N$ bits, or of two digits base 2^N. In order to compute the remainder modulo $2^N - 1$, however, we do not need to do any divisions at all. Instead, we take the left "digit" A, that is to say, the left half of the product, shift it over, and add it to the right half of the product, the right "digit" B. Addition is a linear-time operation, not a quadratic time operation (like multiplication), and certainly not as expensive as is division itself.

We note that in adding A and B together, we will on average half the time have a carry and get a number of $N + 1$ bits, larger than $2^N - 1$. To complete the reduction we would then have to subtract $2^N - 1$, but we would have to subtract only once. The cost of the "division", which is really a modular reduction, is thus for Mersenne numbers only $3/2$ times the linear cost of a single addition. (One addition all the time is one linear cost, plus one more linear cost half the time on average for the cases in which the addition generates a carry, comes out to $3/2$ linear operations on average.)

8.1.4 Summary: Feasibility

The ability to prove huge Mersenne numbers to be prime thus comes from the convergence of several factors.

1. First, for these numbers there is a theoretical result (the Lucas–Lehmer test) that allows for one test to determine for a number of this special form either if the number is prime or is not prime.
2. Second, there is a basic algorithm (the FFT) that cuts a naively n^2 number of "steps" down to a more tractable $n \log n$ number of "steps".
3. Finally, there is an implementation trick that turns an otherwise intractable modular division in the innermost loop into a very tractable linear time addition.

Without all of these working together, it would not be possible to prove that numbers of this magnitude were prime.

8.1.5 Fermat Numbers

The discussion above has been about Mersenne numbers, of the form

$$M_n = 2^n - 1.$$

A similar discussion can be had about the Fermat numbers

$$F_n = 2^{2^n} + 1.$$

Fermat conjectured that these were prime for all n. In fact, they have been seen to be prime only for $n = 0, 1, 2, 3, 4$.

There is an analogous test, due to Pépin, for testing these to be prime: F_n is prime if and only if

$$3^{(F_n - 1)/2} \equiv -1 \pmod{F_n}.$$

The same arguments apply here as for Mersenne numbers. We have an if-and-only-if test for primality that is a refinement of Lagrange's theorem in groups, and we can apply the arithmetic trick

$$A \cdot 2^N + B =$$
$$A \cdot 2^N + A - A + B =$$
$$A \cdot (2^N + 1) - A + B \equiv$$
$$\equiv B - A \quad (\mathrm{mod} \; 2^N + 1).$$

to do a modular reduction not by division but by a subtraction of the two N-bit halves of a $2N$-long product.

8.1.6 The Arithmetic Trick Is Important

We will talk later about elliptic curve cryptography. The elliptic curves recommended by NIST for use in cryptography all have primes that have Mersenne/Fermat like shape as

$$2^n + f(.) + 1$$

where $f(.)$ is a polynomial that is at most a few powers of 2, so that analogous fast reduction games can be played with the arithmetic by using additions or subtractions instead of division.

8.2 Multiprecise Arithmetic and the Fast Fourier Transform

8.2.1 Multiprecise Arithmetic

Much of modern cryptography relies on arithmetic modulo large integers, usually either prime integers or the product of two prime integers. Computer hardware at present normally does 32-bit or 64-bit arithmetic. Although Python does arithmetic on integers of any length, most programming languages have integer data types of limited precision. For example, an unsigned int_64 variable in C++ handles positive integers of size no larger than $2^{64} = 18,446,744,073,709,551,616$. General purpose arithmetic will not produce the correct product of two integers unless they are less than $2^{32} = 4,294,967,296$, although a small number times a larger number produces the correct product if the product is less than 2^{64}.

At present, the arithmetic needed for number-theory-based modern cryptography uses integers of several hundred to perhaps 4096 bits in length. The underlying software to do multiplication, division, addition, and subtraction would treat such numbers as arrays of digits in as large a base as would be feasible given the computer hardware and the programming language; base 2^{32} as unsigned integers in C++ would be reasonable. Addition and subtraction are relatively fast, because they are linear operations; adding two integers of d digits each takes d additions when done digit-by-digit. Multiplication of two integers of d digits each, however, requires d^2 digit-by-digit multiplications if done using naive schoolchild multiplication.

Division is much worse, and fortunately most cryptography is done as modular arithmetic and does not need actual integer division. What would be the division step is modular reduction, which is why arithmetic tricks are used as for Mersenne primes, or as will be discussed as Montgomery multiplication in Sect. 8.3. For the most part, we can avoid actual division, and we can reduce the naive d^2 individual multiplication steps for a multiprecise multiplication by using the Fast Fourier Transform (or other methods that are algorithmically faster than schoolchild algorithms).

8.2.2   Background of the FFT

One of the major theorems in signal processing, that we won't prove, or even state in an overly formal way, is the Fourier Theorem.

Theorem 8.3 *Any oscillatory squiggle can be written as a sum of sine waves.*

That is, any function with $f(t)$ a function of time t "in the time domain" (like the output on an oscilloscope) can also be written "in the frequency domain" as

$$f(\theta) = \sum_{n \in \mathbb{N}} a_n exp(2\pi i \theta / n)$$

Going from $f(t)$ to get the coefficients a_n for $f(\theta)$ and back again is done by the *Fourier transform* and its inverse.

8.2.3   Polynomial Multiplication

Polynomial multiplication is actually the same problem.
   Let $f(x) = \sum a_i x^i$ and $g(x) = \sum b_i x^i$
   Then $h(x) = f(x) \cdot g(x) = \sum c_i x^i$ where

$$c_0 = a_0 b_0$$
$$c_1 = a_0 b_1 + a_1 b_0$$
$$c_2 = a_0 b_2 + a_1 b_1 + a_2 b_0$$
$$c_3 = a_0 b_3 + a_1 b_2 + a_2 b_1 + a_3 b_0$$
$$c_4 = a_0 b_4 + a_1 b_3 + a_2 b_2 + a_3 b_1 + a_4 b_0$$

The coefficients c_i are *convolution products*.

In general, then, to multiply two polynomials of degrees n and m would take nm multiplies of all coeffs against all other coeffs (and then some adds that we don't count because addition is so much cheaper than multiplication).

But maybe we can do it faster?

1. Evaluate the polynomials f and g at $2n + 1$ points (assuming $n > m$) This costs time linear in n.
2. Multiply the $2n + 1$ values together coordinatewise. This costs time linear in n.
3. We know from Lagrange interpolation (and other results) that there is a unique polynomial of degree $2n$ passing through $2n+1$ points, and this unique polynomial must therefore be the product h of f and g
4. Interpolate to determine this unique h.

Doing Lagrange interpolation in the naive way, we have $2n$ summands, each of which takes $2n$ multiplies. so this is naively order n^2 multiplications. This sounds like *more* work—how can this be faster?

The trick that is the "fast" part of "Fast Fourier Transform" is that if we interpolate at the right sort of points (in this case, roots of unity, to be explained in a moment), then the sums of the cross product terms collapse to zero and don't need to be computed.

And, of course, it's a trivial jump from polynomial multiplication to multiprecise multiplication of integers. The decimal integer 2345, for example, is simply the polynomial

$$2x^3 + 3x^2 + 4x + 5$$

evaluated at the radix 10. Multiplication of two k-digit numbers (in whatever radix is used) is done by multiplying the two polynomials of degrees $k - 1$ together and then evaluating the product polynomial for x equal to the radix.

8.2.4   Complex Numbers as Needed for Fourier Transforms

We define $i = \sqrt{-1}$ and do simple algebra with this, so we have

$$i^2 = (\sqrt{-1})^2 = -1,$$
$$i^3 = (\sqrt{-1})^3 = (\sqrt{-1})^2 \cdot (\sqrt{-1}) = -\sqrt{-1} = -i,$$
$$i^4 = (i^2)^2 = (-1)^2 = 1.$$

Consider points in the *Argand plane* with axes x and $iy = \sqrt{-1}y$. We then *define* $e^{i\theta}$ to be $\cos\theta + i\sin\theta$. With this definition, $e^{i\theta}$ is a vector of length 1 in the Argand plane, thus a unit vector with an angle of θ above the x-axis.

Then $(e^{i\theta})^2 = e^{2i\theta} = \cos 2\theta + i\sin 2\theta$ (do the trigonometry...).

All we need of complex arithmetic is that the *n-th roots of unity*, which are the solutions to the equation $x^n = 1$, are the complex numbers $e^{2\pi i/n}$. These are the points on the unit circle with angles $2\pi k/n$, for $k = 0, 1, \ldots, n - 1$. Multiplying these roots of unity can be done just by adding the exponents, which is the same as adding the angles. And of course values of k larger than n can be reduced modulo n, since we're just going around in a circle ...

8.2.5 The Fourier Transform

We'll use an 8-point Fast Fourier Transform (FFT) as an example.

Let ω be a primitive 8-th root of unity, that is, $\omega = \exp(2\pi i/8)$, so we have $\omega^8 = 1$. Part of the mathematical trick we will use, to get the convolution products to collapse to zero, is the observation that

$$0 = (\omega^8 - 1) = (\omega - 1)(\omega^7 + \omega^6 + \omega^5 + \omega^4 + \omega^3 + \omega^2 + \omega^1 + \omega^0).$$

Since we have 0 on the left hand side, one of the two factors on the right hand side must be 0. It can't be $\omega - 1$, because we specifically chose ω to be $e^{2\pi i/8}$, which is most definitely not 1. Therefore, the sum of the roots of unity in the second term of the right hand side must be zero. This is why the cross product terms in the Fourier transform will disappear.

Consider the matrix

$$
F = \left(\omega^{ij}\right) =
\begin{pmatrix}
\omega^0 & \omega^0 & \omega^0 & \omega^0 & \omega^0 & \omega^0 & \omega^0 & \omega^0 \\
\omega^0 & \omega^1 & \omega^2 & \omega^3 & \omega^4 & \omega^5 & \omega^6 & \omega^7 \\
\omega^0 & \omega^2 & \omega^4 & \omega^6 & \omega^0 & \omega^2 & \omega^4 & \omega^6 \\
\omega^0 & \omega^3 & \omega^6 & \omega^1 & \omega^4 & \omega^7 & \omega^2 & \omega^5 \\
\omega^0 & \omega^4 & \omega^0 & \omega^4 & \omega^0 & \omega^4 & \omega^0 & \omega^4 \\
\omega^0 & \omega^5 & \omega^2 & \omega^7 & \omega^4 & \omega^1 & \omega^6 & \omega^3 \\
\omega^0 & \omega^6 & \omega^4 & \omega^2 & \omega^0 & \omega^6 & \omega^4 & \omega^2 \\
\omega^0 & \omega^7 & \omega^6 & \omega^5 & \omega^4 & \omega^3 & \omega^2 & \omega^1
\end{pmatrix}
$$

$$
=
\begin{pmatrix}
1 & 1 & 1 & 1 & 1 & 1 & 1 & 1 \\
1 & \omega^1 & \omega^2 & \omega^3 & -1 & -\omega^1 & -\omega^2 & -\omega^3 \\
1 & \omega^2 & -1 & -\omega^2 & 1 & \omega^2 & -1 & -\omega^2 \\
1 & \omega^3 & -\omega^2 & \omega^1 & -1 & -\omega^3 & \omega^2 & -\omega^1 \\
1 & -1 & 1 & -1 & 1 & -1 & 1 & -1 \\
1 & -\omega^1 & \omega^2 & -\omega^3 & -1 & \omega^1 & -\omega^2 & \omega^3 \\
1 & -\omega^2 & -1 & \omega^2 & 1 & -\omega^2 & -1 & \omega^2 \\
1 & -\omega^3 & -\omega^2 & -\omega^1 & -1 & \omega^3 & \omega^2 & \omega^1
\end{pmatrix}
$$

We note that the inverse $F^{-1} = (\omega^{-ij})$.

Then if $f(x) = a_0 + a_1 x + a_2 x^2 + \ldots + a_7 x^7$ the *discrete Fourier transform* of f is

$$
\begin{pmatrix}
f(\omega^0) \\
f(\omega^1) \\
f(\omega^2) \\
f(\omega^3) \\
f(\omega^4) \\
f(\omega^5) \\
f(\omega^6) \\
f(\omega^7)
\end{pmatrix}
= F \cdot
\begin{pmatrix}
a_0 \\
a_1 \\
a_2 \\
a_3 \\
a_4 \\
a_5 \\
a_6 \\
a_7
\end{pmatrix}
$$

The Fourier transform takes coefficients to points. The inverse transform takes points to coefficients. But the matrix multiplication is an n^2 computation, because it's n rows each dotted with the column vector of height n.

8.2.6   The Cooley–Tukey Fast Fourier Transform

Now for the *fast* part of the FFT; we don't really have to do the n^2 multiplications of the matrix multiplication. We can use the structure of the roots of unity to do the Fourier transform in $\mathcal{O}(n \lg n)$ time.

To evaluate a polynomial $f(x)$ of degree n at the n-th roots of unity, let

$$f^{[0]}(x) = a_0 + a_2 x + a_4 x^2 + \ldots a_{n-2} x^{n/2-1}$$

$$f^{[1]}(x) = a_1 + a_3 x + a_5 x^2 + \ldots a_{n-1} x^{n/2-1}$$

The first polynomial has even subscript coefficients and the second one has odd subscript coefficients so we have

$$f(x) = f^{[0]}(x) + x f^{[1]}(x),$$

and to evaluate $f(x)$ at the n-th roots of unity we need to evaluate $f^{[0]}(x)$ and $f^{[1]}(x)$ at

$$(\omega^0)^2, (\omega^1)^2, (\omega^2)^2, \ldots, (\omega^{n-1})^2$$

and then in n multiplications we will get $f(x)$ at all n-th roots.

Theorem 8.4 *If n is positive and even, the squares of the n-th roots of unity are identical to the $n/2$-th roots of unity.*

We apply this reduction recursively: To compute the n-th order FT, we need to evaluate two polynomials at the $n/2$-th roots of unity and then do n multiplications.

That is, to compute the n-th order Fourier Transform, we need to do two $n/2$-th order Fourier Transforms and then do n multiplications.

Recursively,

$$T(n) = 2T\left(\frac{n}{2}\right) + n$$
$$= 4T\left(\frac{n}{4}\right) + n + n/2$$
$$= \ldots$$
$$= n\lg n + n(1 + 1/2 + 1/4 + \ldots)$$
$$= n\lg n + 2n$$
$$= \mathcal{O}(n\lg n)$$

We will do an example first, and then we will present the algorithmic process that implements the FFT.

8.2.7 An Example

We're going to multiply

$$f(x) = 1 + 2x + 3x^2$$

and

$$g(x) = 9 + 8x + 7x^2 + 6x^3$$

using a Fourier Transform.

First of all, we'll do the multiplication the long way

```
        1  2  3  0  0  0
     ×  9  8  7  6  0  0
     ─────────────────────
        9 18 27  0  0  0
     +  0  8 16 24  0  0
     +  0  0  7 14 21  0
     +  0  0  0  6 12 18
     ─────────────────────
        9 26 50 44 33 18
```

or

$$h(x) = 9 + 26x + 50x^2 + 44x^3 + 33x^4 + 18x^5$$

Remark 8.1 In many applications it is natural to write integers and polynomials left to right instead of right to left. This comes in large part from an underlying issue of how to work with arrays in software. If we write things left to right, and implement the computation in an array, then the extension of the array (in this case to accommodate the coefficients of x^4 and x^5, or in the case of ordinary arithmetic perhaps to accommodate an extra carry at the high end), can be done simply by adding storage elements at the end of the array. If we were to work in the opposite direction, we would have to play painful games with subscripts, or perhaps shift the array up one space to insert a carry-out into the zero-subscript location in the array.

Now, to do this multiplication as a power-of-two transform, we'll have to do an eight point transform, since 8 is the least power of 2 larger than the degree of the product (which is 5).

We do the multiplication

$$\begin{pmatrix} \omega^0 & \omega^0 & \omega^0 & \omega^0 & \omega^0 & \omega^0 & \omega^0 & \omega^0 \\ \omega^0 & \omega^1 & \omega^2 & \omega^3 & \omega^4 & \omega^5 & \omega^6 & \omega^7 \\ \omega^0 & \omega^2 & \omega^4 & \omega^6 & \omega^0 & \omega^2 & \omega^4 & \omega^6 \\ \omega^0 & \omega^3 & \omega^6 & \omega^1 & \omega^4 & \omega^7 & \omega^2 & \omega^5 \\ \omega^0 & \omega^4 & \omega^0 & \omega^4 & \omega^0 & \omega^4 & \omega^0 & \omega^4 \\ \omega^0 & \omega^5 & \omega^2 & \omega^7 & \omega^4 & \omega^1 & \omega^6 & \omega^3 \\ \omega^0 & \omega^6 & \omega^4 & \omega^2 & \omega^0 & \omega^6 & \omega^4 & \omega^2 \\ \omega^0 & \omega^7 & \omega^6 & \omega^5 & \omega^4 & \omega^3 & \omega^2 & \omega^1 \end{pmatrix} \cdot \begin{pmatrix} 1 \\ 2 \\ 3 \\ 0 \\ 0 \\ 0 \\ 0 \\ 0 \end{pmatrix}$$

and the multiplication

$$\begin{pmatrix} \omega^0 & \omega^0 & \omega^0 & \omega^0 & \omega^0 & \omega^0 & \omega^0 & \omega^0 \\ \omega^0 & \omega^1 & \omega^2 & \omega^3 & \omega^4 & \omega^5 & \omega^6 & \omega^7 \\ \omega^0 & \omega^2 & \omega^4 & \omega^6 & \omega^0 & \omega^2 & \omega^4 & \omega^6 \\ \omega^0 & \omega^3 & \omega^6 & \omega^1 & \omega^4 & \omega^7 & \omega^2 & \omega^5 \\ \omega^0 & \omega^4 & \omega^0 & \omega^4 & \omega^0 & \omega^4 & \omega^0 & \omega^4 \\ \omega^0 & \omega^5 & \omega^2 & \omega^7 & \omega^4 & \omega^1 & \omega^6 & \omega^3 \\ \omega^0 & \omega^6 & \omega^4 & \omega^2 & \omega^0 & \omega^6 & \omega^4 & \omega^2 \\ \omega^0 & \omega^7 & \omega^6 & \omega^5 & \omega^4 & \omega^3 & \omega^2 & \omega^1 \end{pmatrix} \cdot \begin{pmatrix} 9 \\ 8 \\ 7 \\ 6 \\ 0 \\ 0 \\ 0 \\ 0 \end{pmatrix}$$

to get two column vectors

$$
\begin{pmatrix}
1 \cdot \omega^0 + 2 \cdot \omega^0 + 3 \cdot \omega^0 + 0 \cdot \omega^0 + 0 \cdot \omega^0 + 0 \cdot \omega^0 + 0 \cdot \omega^0 + 0 \cdot \omega^0 \\
1 \cdot \omega^0 + 2 \cdot \omega^1 + 3 \cdot \omega^2 + 0 \cdot \omega^3 + 0 \cdot \omega^4 + 0 \cdot \omega^5 + 0 \cdot \omega^6 + 0 \cdot \omega^7 \\
1 \cdot \omega^0 + 2 \cdot \omega^2 + 3 \cdot \omega^4 + 0 \cdot \omega^6 + 0 \cdot \omega^0 + 0 \cdot \omega^2 + 0 \cdot \omega^4 + 0 \cdot \omega^6 \\
1 \cdot \omega^0 + 2 \cdot \omega^3 + 3 \cdot \omega^6 + 0 \cdot \omega^1 + 0 \cdot \omega^4 + 0 \cdot \omega^7 + 0 \cdot \omega^2 + 0 \cdot \omega^5 \\
1 \cdot \omega^0 + 2 \cdot \omega^4 + 3 \cdot \omega^0 + 0 \cdot \omega^4 + 0 \cdot \omega^0 + 0 \cdot \omega^4 + 0 \cdot \omega^0 + 0 \cdot \omega^4 \\
1 \cdot \omega^0 + 2 \cdot \omega^5 + 3 \cdot \omega^2 + 0 \cdot \omega^7 + 0 \cdot \omega^4 + 0 \cdot \omega^1 + 0 \cdot \omega^6 + 0 \cdot \omega^3 \\
1 \cdot \omega^0 + 2 \cdot \omega^6 + 3 \cdot \omega^4 + 0 \cdot \omega^2 + 0 \cdot \omega^0 + 0 \cdot \omega^6 + 0 \cdot \omega^4 + 0 \cdot \omega^2 \\
1 \cdot \omega^0 + 2 \cdot \omega^7 + 3 \cdot \omega^6 + 0 \cdot \omega^5 + 0 \cdot \omega^4 + 0 \cdot \omega^3 + 0 \cdot \omega^2 + 0 \cdot \omega^1
\end{pmatrix}
$$

and

$$
\begin{pmatrix}
9 \cdot \omega^0 + 8 \cdot \omega^0 + 7 \cdot \omega^0 + 6 \cdot \omega^0 + 0 \cdot \omega^0 + 0 \cdot \omega^0 + 0 \cdot \omega^0 + 0 \cdot \omega^0 \\
9 \cdot \omega^0 + 8 \cdot \omega^1 + 7 \cdot \omega^2 + 6 \cdot \omega^3 + 0 \cdot \omega^4 + 0 \cdot \omega^5 + 0 \cdot \omega^6 + 0 \cdot \omega^7 \\
9 \cdot \omega^0 + 8 \cdot \omega^2 + 7 \cdot \omega^4 + 6 \cdot \omega^6 + 0 \cdot \omega^0 + 0 \cdot \omega^2 + 0 \cdot \omega^4 + 0 \cdot \omega^6 \\
9 \cdot \omega^0 + 8 \cdot \omega^3 + 7 \cdot \omega^6 + 6 \cdot \omega^1 + 0 \cdot \omega^4 + 0 \cdot \omega^7 + 0 \cdot \omega^2 + 0 \cdot \omega^5 \\
9 \cdot \omega^0 + 8 \cdot \omega^4 + 7 \cdot \omega^0 + 6 \cdot \omega^4 + 0 \cdot \omega^0 + 0 \cdot \omega^4 + 0 \cdot \omega^0 + 0 \cdot \omega^4 \\
9 \cdot \omega^0 + 8 \cdot \omega^5 + 7 \cdot \omega^2 + 6 \cdot \omega^7 + 0 \cdot \omega^4 + 0 \cdot \omega^1 + 0 \cdot \omega^6 + 0 \cdot \omega^3 \\
9 \cdot \omega^0 + 8 \cdot \omega^6 + 7 \cdot \omega^4 + 6 \cdot \omega^2 + 0 \cdot \omega^0 + 0 \cdot \omega^6 + 0 \cdot \omega^4 + 0 \cdot \omega^2 \\
9 \cdot \omega^0 + 8 \cdot \omega^7 + 7 \cdot \omega^6 + 6 \cdot \omega^5 + 0 \cdot \omega^4 + 0 \cdot \omega^3 + 0 \cdot \omega^2 + 0 \cdot \omega^1
\end{pmatrix}
$$

where we have left in all the coefficients because we're going to make them all collapse later.

We do the componentwise multiplication and we know what we're going to get because this problem is small enough that we can do the multiplication by hand.

$$hvec = \begin{pmatrix} 9 \cdot \omega^0 + 26 \cdot \omega^0 + 50 \cdot \omega^0 + 44 \cdot \omega^0 + 33 \cdot \omega^0 + 18 \cdot \omega^0 + 0 \cdot \omega^0 + 0 \cdot \omega^0 \\ 9 \cdot \omega^0 + 26 \cdot \omega^1 + 50 \cdot \omega^2 + 44 \cdot \omega^3 + 33 \cdot \omega^4 + 18 \cdot \omega^5 + 0 \cdot \omega^6 + 0 \cdot \omega^7 \\ 9 \cdot \omega^0 + 26 \cdot \omega^2 + 50 \cdot \omega^4 + 44 \cdot \omega^6 + 33 \cdot \omega^0 + 18 \cdot \omega^2 + 0 \cdot \omega^4 + 0 \cdot \omega^6 \\ 9 \cdot \omega^0 + 26 \cdot \omega^3 + 50 \cdot \omega^6 + 44 \cdot \omega^1 + 33 \cdot \omega^4 + 18 \cdot \omega^7 + 0 \cdot \omega^2 + 0 \cdot \omega^5 \\ 9 \cdot \omega^0 + 26 \cdot \omega^4 + 50 \cdot \omega^0 + 44 \cdot \omega^4 + 33 \cdot \omega^0 + 18 \cdot \omega^4 + 0 \cdot \omega^0 + 0 \cdot \omega^4 \\ 9 \cdot \omega^0 + 26 \cdot \omega^5 + 50 \cdot \omega^2 + 44 \cdot \omega^7 + 33 \cdot \omega^4 + 18 \cdot \omega^1 + 0 \cdot \omega^6 + 0 \cdot \omega^3 \\ 9 \cdot \omega^0 + 26 \cdot \omega^6 + 50 \cdot \omega^4 + 44 \cdot \omega^2 + 33 \cdot \omega^0 + 18 \cdot \omega^6 + 0 \cdot \omega^4 + 0 \cdot \omega^2 \\ 9 \cdot \omega^0 + 26 \cdot \omega^7 + 50 \cdot \omega^6 + 44 \cdot \omega^5 + 33 \cdot \omega^4 + 18 \cdot \omega^3 + 0 \cdot \omega^2 + 0 \cdot \omega^1 \end{pmatrix}$$

Now we multiply this column vector by the inverse matrix for the Fourier Transform. This matrix is

$$F^{-1} = \left(\omega^{-ij} \right) = \begin{pmatrix} \omega^0 & \omega^0 & \omega^0 & \omega^0 & \omega^0 & \omega^0 & \omega^0 & \omega^0 \\ \omega^0 & \omega^7 & \omega^6 & \omega^5 & \omega^4 & \omega^3 & \omega^2 & \omega^1 \\ \omega^0 & \omega^6 & \omega^4 & \omega^2 & \omega^0 & \omega^6 & \omega^4 & \omega^2 \\ \omega^0 & \omega^5 & \omega^2 & \omega^7 & \omega^4 & \omega^1 & \omega^6 & \omega^3 \\ \omega^0 & \omega^4 & \omega^0 & \omega^4 & \omega^0 & \omega^4 & \omega^0 & \omega^4 \\ \omega^0 & \omega^3 & \omega^6 & \omega^1 & \omega^4 & \omega^7 & \omega^2 & \omega^5 \\ \omega^0 & \omega^2 & \omega^4 & \omega^6 & \omega^0 & \omega^2 & \omega^4 & \omega^6 \\ \omega^0 & \omega^1 & \omega^2 & \omega^3 & \omega^4 & \omega^5 & \omega^6 & \omega^7 \end{pmatrix}$$

So let's do the multiplication line by line. The first line of the result will be the dot product of the first line of F^{-1} with $hvec$, that is, of

$$\left(\omega^0 \quad \omega^0 \quad \omega^0 \quad \omega^0 \quad \omega^0 \quad \omega^0 \quad \omega^0 \quad \omega^0 \right)$$

with *hvec*. What we get is just the sum of the lines of *hvec*, since $\omega^0 = 1$: This is

$$9 \cdot \omega^0 + 26 \cdot \omega^0 + 50 \cdot \omega^0 + 44 \cdot \omega^0 + 33 \cdot \omega^0 + 18 \cdot \omega^0 + 0 \cdot \omega^0 + 0 \cdot \omega^0$$
$$+$$
$$9 \cdot \omega^0 + 26 \cdot \omega^1 + 50 \cdot \omega^2 + 44 \cdot \omega^3 + 33 \cdot \omega^4 + 18 \cdot \omega^5 + 0 \cdot \omega^6 + 0 \cdot \omega^7$$
$$+$$
$$9 \cdot \omega^0 + 26 \cdot \omega^2 + 50 \cdot \omega^4 + 44 \cdot \omega^6 + 33 \cdot \omega^0 + 18 \cdot \omega^2 + 0 \cdot \omega^4 + 0 \cdot \omega^6$$
$$+$$
$$9 \cdot \omega^0 + 26 \cdot \omega^3 + 50 \cdot \omega^6 + 44 \cdot \omega^1 + 33 \cdot \omega^4 + 18 \cdot \omega^7 + 0 \cdot \omega^2 + 0 \cdot \omega^5$$
$$+$$
$$9 \cdot \omega^0 + 26 \cdot \omega^4 + 50 \cdot \omega^0 + 44 \cdot \omega^4 + 33 \cdot \omega^0 + 18 \cdot \omega^4 + 0 \cdot \omega^0 + 0 \cdot \omega^4$$
$$+$$
$$9 \cdot \omega^0 + 26 \cdot \omega^5 + 50 \cdot \omega^2 + 44 \cdot \omega^7 + 33 \cdot \omega^4 + 18 \cdot \omega^1 + 0 \cdot \omega^6 + 0 \cdot \omega^3$$
$$+$$
$$9 \cdot \omega^0 + 26 \cdot \omega^6 + 50 \cdot \omega^4 + 44 \cdot \omega^2 + 33 \cdot \omega^0 + 18 \cdot \omega^6 + 0 \cdot \omega^4 + 0 \cdot \omega^2$$
$$+$$
$$9 \cdot \omega^0 + 26 \cdot \omega^7 + 50 \cdot \omega^6 + 44 \cdot \omega^5 + 33 \cdot \omega^4 + 18 \cdot \omega^3 + 0 \cdot \omega^2 + 0 \cdot \omega^1$$

and now we can see the advantage of not collapsing things earlier. Adding up the first column of the above tableau we get

$$9 \cdot \omega^0 = 9 \cdot 1 = 9$$

added up 8 times, which is 72. In every other column we get the coefficient times

$$\omega^0 + \omega^1 + \omega^2 + \omega^3 + \omega^4 + \omega^5 + \omega^6 + \omega^7$$

But this sum is zero, because these are roots of unity, so we have

$$0 = \omega^8 - 1 = (\omega^1 - 1) \cdot (\omega^0 + \omega^1 + \omega^2 + \omega^3 + \omega^4 + \omega^5 + \omega^6 + \omega^7)$$

The product is zero, but since the first factor $(\omega^1 - 1)$ isn't zero, the second factor must be zero.

So, going down every column except the column for the coefficient 9, we get a coefficient (26, 50, 44, 33, 18) times zero. The first line of the product of F^{-1} and *hvec* is thus just the 72.

Now we'll do the second line, and this will be all we'll need to see the pattern. Take the second line of F^{-1},

$$\left(\omega^0 \ \omega^7 \ \omega^6 \ \omega^5 \ \omega^4 \ \omega^3 \ \omega^2 \ \omega^1 \right),$$

and multiply this times $hvec$. We get

$$9 \cdot \omega^0 + 26 \cdot \omega^0 + 50 \cdot \omega^0 + 44 \cdot \omega^0 + 33 \cdot \omega^0 + 18 \cdot \omega^0 + 0 \cdot \omega^0 + 0 \cdot \omega^0$$
$$+$$
$$9 \cdot \omega^7 + 26 \cdot \omega^0 + 50 \cdot \omega^1 + 44 \cdot \omega^2 + 33 \cdot \omega^3 + 18 \cdot \omega^4 + 0 \cdot \omega^5 + 0 \cdot \omega^6$$
$$+$$
$$9 \cdot \omega^6 + 26 \cdot \omega^0 + 50 \cdot \omega^2 + 44 \cdot \omega^4 + 33 \cdot \omega^6 + 18 \cdot \omega^0 + 0 \cdot \omega^2 + 0 \cdot \omega^4$$
$$+$$
$$9 \cdot \omega^5 + 26 \cdot \omega^0 + 50 \cdot \omega^3 + 44 \cdot \omega^6 + 33 \cdot \omega^1 + 18 \cdot \omega^4 + 0 \cdot \omega^7 + 0 \cdot \omega^2$$
$$+$$
$$9 \cdot \omega^4 + 26 \cdot \omega^0 + 50 \cdot \omega^4 + 44 \cdot \omega^0 + 33 \cdot \omega^4 + 18 \cdot \omega^0 + 0 \cdot \omega^4 + 0 \cdot \omega^0$$
$$+$$
$$9 \cdot \omega^3 + 26 \cdot \omega^0 + 50 \cdot \omega^5 + 44 \cdot \omega^2 + 33 \cdot \omega^7 + 18 \cdot \omega^4 + 0 \cdot \omega^1 + 0 \cdot \omega^6$$
$$+$$
$$9 \cdot \omega^2 + 26 \cdot \omega^0 + 50 \cdot \omega^6 + 44 \cdot \omega^4 + 33 \cdot \omega^2 + 18 \cdot \omega^0 + 0 \cdot \omega^6 + 0 \cdot \omega^4$$
$$+$$
$$9 \cdot \omega^1 + 26 \cdot \omega^0 + 50 \cdot \omega^7 + 44 \cdot \omega^6 + 33 \cdot \omega^5 + 18 \cdot \omega^4 + 0 \cdot \omega^3 + 0 \cdot \omega^2$$

Now, let's look carefully at this. In the 26 column, we get ω^0 all the way down, so that column sum is $8 \cdot 26 = 228$. In the 9, 50, and 33 columns and the first 0 column, we get the previous sum

$$\omega^0 + \omega^1 + \omega^2 + \omega^3 + \omega^4 + \omega^5 + \omega^6 + \omega^7,$$

so these columns sum to zero. In the 44 and the second 0 column we have

$$\omega^0 + \omega^2 + \omega^4 + \omega^6 + \omega^0 + \omega^2 + \omega^4 + \omega^6$$
$$= 1 + \omega^2 - 1 - \omega^2 + 1 + \omega^2 - 1 - \omega^2$$
$$= 0$$

and in the 18 column we have

$$\omega^0 + \omega^4 + \omega^0 + \omega^4 + \omega^0 + \omega^4 + \omega^0 + \omega^4$$
$$= 1 - 1 + 1 - 1 + 1 - 1 + 1 - 1$$
$$= 0.$$

So what we get as the final sum for the second line entry in the column vector for $h(x)$ is just the 228.

If we now look at the third line, we'll get something entirely similar to what just happened for the second line. Everything will sum to zero except the 50 column, and we'll get $8 \cdot 50 = 400$ there.

Because we're doing the Fourier Transform with power-of-2 roots of unity, we'll get

$$F^{-1} \cdot hvec = \begin{pmatrix} 8 \cdot 9 \\ 8 \cdot 26 \\ 8 \cdot 50 \\ 8 \cdot 44 \\ 8 \cdot 33 \\ 8 \cdot 18 \\ 8 \cdot 0 \\ 8 \cdot 0 \end{pmatrix}$$

and when we divide out the 8, we get the coefficients for $h(x)$.

8.2.8 The FFT Butterfly

Now, how do we implement this so as to be efficient? Details can be found in several references [3,4]. The key is the communication pattern known as the FFT butterfly, shown in Fig. 8.2. The key to the butterfly is first that the communication from the first column of nodes to the second is to locations one away, from the second to the third is to locations two away, from the third to the fourth to locations four away, and so forth, depending on how many stages are needed, and second, that the flow from one column of nodes to the next is a single multiplication and a single addition of the intermediate data at each respective node. For the butterfly shown, the eight locations are for an 8-point FFT, for which there are $\log_2 8 = 3$ stages.

The computation itself is as follows, where ω is an eighth root of unity. (The powers of ω that multiply in are called "twiddle factors" by those who do FFTs.) In the first stage we combine at stride one.

a_0	$a_0 + a_4$
a_4	$a_0 + a_4\omega^4$
a_2	$a_2 + a_6$
a_6	$a_2 + a_6\omega^4$
a_1	$a_1 + a_5$
a_5	$a_1 + a_5\omega^4$
a_3	$a_3 + a_7$
a_7	$a_3 + a_7\omega^4$

Then we combine at stride two.

$a_0 + a_4$	$a_0 + a_4 + a_2 + a_6$
$a_0 + a_4\omega^4$	$a_0 + a_4\omega^4 + (a_2 + a_6\omega^4)\omega^2$
$a_2 + a_6$	$a_0 + a_4 + (a_2 + a_6)\omega^4$
$a_2 + a_6\omega^4$	$a_0 + a_4\omega^4 + (a_2 + a_6\omega^4)\omega^6$
$a_1 + a_5$	$a_1 + a_5 + a_3 + a_7$
$a_1 + a_5\omega^4$	$a_1 + a_5\omega^4 + (a_3 + a_7\omega^4)\omega^2$
$a_3 + a_7$	$a_1 + a_5 + (a_3 + a_7)\omega^4$
$a_3 + a_7\omega^4$	$a_1 + a_5\omega^4 + (a_3 + a_7\omega^4)\omega^6$

And in the final stage we have

$a_0 + a_4 + a_2 + a_6$	$a_0 + a_4 + a_2 + a_6 + a_1 + a_5 + a_3 + a_7$
$a_0 + a_4\omega^4 + a_2\omega^2 + a_6\omega^6$	$a_0 + a_4\omega^4 + a_2\omega^2 + a_6\omega^6 + (a_1 + a_5\omega^4 + a_3\omega^2 + a_7\omega^6)\omega$
$a_0 + a_4 + (a_2 + a_6)\omega^4$	$a_0 + a_4 + a_2\omega^4 + a_6\omega^4 + (a_1 + a_5 + a_3\omega^4 + a_7\omega^4)\omega^2$
$a_0 + a_4\omega^4 + (a_2 + a_6\omega^4)\omega^6$	$a_0 + a_4\omega^4 + a_2\omega^6 + a_6\omega^2 + (a_1 + a_5\omega^4 + a_3\omega^6 + a_7\omega^2)\omega^3$
$a_1 + a_5 + a_3 + a_7$	$a_0 + a_4 + a_2 + a_6 + (a_1 + a_5 + a_3 + a_7)\omega^4$
$a_1 + a_5\omega^4 + (a_3 + a_7\omega^4)\omega^2$	$a_0 + a_4\omega^4 + a_2\omega^2 + a_6\omega^6 + (a_1 + a_5\omega^4 + a_3\omega^2 + a_7\omega^6)\omega^5$
$a_1 + a_5 + (a_3 + a_7)\omega^4$	$a_0 + a_4 + a_2\omega^4 + a_6\omega^4 + (a_1 + a_5 + a_3\omega^4 + a_7\omega^4)\omega^6$
$a_1 + a_5\omega^4 + (a_3 + a_7\omega^4)\omega^6$	$a_0 + a_4\omega^4 + a_2\omega^6 + a_6\omega^2 + (a_1 + a_5\omega^4 + a_3\omega^6 + a_7\omega^2)\omega^7$

Rearranging the terms of the second column of this tableau by subscript coefficient, we get the same pattern as in the example.

Each of the node dots in Fig. 8.2 represents one multiplication (and some additions that we don't worry about because addition is much cheaper than multiplication. By computing with the butterfly pattern, we have n multiplications down each column of the butterfly, and $\lg n$ columns to effect the entire computation. This gives us the $\mathcal{O}(n \lg n)$ running time of an FFT.

8.3 Montgomery Multiplication

The FFT allows us to multiply quickly. However, much of public-key cryptography is not just multiplication, but *modular* multiplication: at each step of the cryptographic algorithm, we multiply two residues modulo N, that are $\lg N$ bits long, to get a product that is $2 \lg N$ bits in length, and then we have to reduce that product modulo N to get a residue in the range 0 to $N - 1$, of $\lg N$ bits. That modular reduction naively requires a division with remainder. Division with remainder naively is done with a repetition of subtractions and bit shifts. For N of, say, 2048 or 4096 bits, that could be very slow indeed.

Reduction modulo N, as is needed for most public-key cryptography, can be made much faster using *Montgomery multiplication*, invented by Peter Montgomery and published in 1985 [5]. The idea is so important that hardware has been designed for doing Montgomery multiplication [6,7].

The basic idea is an extraordinary extrapolation from the trick used for arithmetic modulo Mersenne numbers. Thrown in for good measure is the trick used to make division itself computationally faster: if we wish to divide n by m, we would normally have the trial-and-error of finding a trial quotient, and then correcting the trial quotient, but that trial and correction can be made simpler if we premultiply the operands by an appropriate integer. (See Knuth [8] for the details.) Montgomery multiplication works in much the same way.

Assume we're going to do a lot of arithmetic modulo some fixed N. Choose $R = 2^k > N$ for a suitable k. Assuming that R and N are relatively prime (and if not, bump k by one and we should be able to get an R that is relatively prime), then we can solve for R' and N' such that $RR' - NN' = 1$.

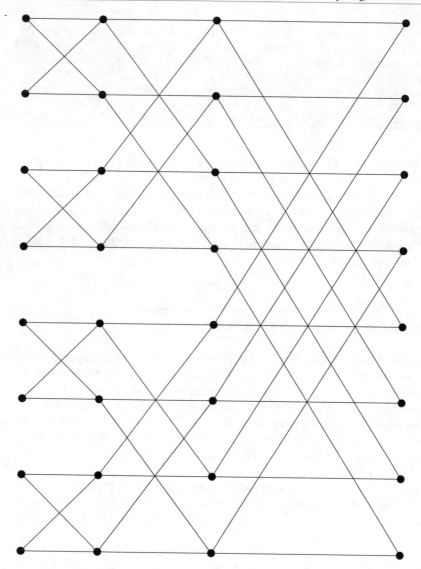

Fig. 8.2 An Eight-Point FFT Butterfly

What we will then do is multiply everything by R. All the constants, all the numbers, etc., will be multiplied by R. So instead of doing arithmetic with integers a and b, say, we will be doing arithmetic with integers aR and bR. And then, at the very end of the computation, we multiply any result by R'. Since $RR' \equiv 1 \pmod{N}$, we recover the result we would have had.

Addition and subtraction are fine, since

$$a + b = c \Leftrightarrow aR + bR = cR.$$

The problem is with multiplication:

$$aR \cdot bR = abR^2$$

which means that we have an extra factor of R. What we want to do is have a function to which we can pass the product abR^2 and that will return abR. We could do this by multiplying modulo N by R', but that would be a multiplication modulo N, and it's exactly that we are trying to avoid.

Here's how we do it. Start with $T = abR^2$.

$$m \leftarrow (T \pmod{R}) \cdot N' \pmod{R}$$
$$t \leftarrow (T + mN)/R$$

and we return either t or $t - N$, whichever lies in the range 0 to $N - 1$.

One might think that if we are trying to avoid modular reduction, then we would not get a win by doing reduction by R twice. But ... remember that R was deliberately chosen to be a power of 2, and reduction by a power of 2 is just picking off the (roughly) rightmost half of the bits of the double-sized product and then throwing away the top half.

Example Let $N = 79$, and instead of using a power of 2 for R, we'll use $R = 100$ for readability with decimal numbers. We find that $64 \cdot 100 - 81 \cdot 79 = 1$, so we have $R = 100$, $R' = 64$, $N = 79$, $N' = 81$.

Now let's say that we multiply $a = 17$ times $b = 26$ to get 442. The number 17 is really $a' \cdot 100$ modulo 79 for some a'. Multiplying $17 \cdot 64 \equiv 61 \pmod{79}$, we find that $a' = 61$. Similarly, $26 \cdot 64 \equiv 5 \pmod{79}$. So when we multiply 17 and 26 in this representation, we're really trying to multiply $61 \cdot 5 = 305 \equiv 68 \pmod{79}$.

Knowing that we can in fact work modulo 79, we know that what we have is

$$17 \cdot 26 = 442 \equiv (61 \cdot 100) \cdot (5 \cdot 100)$$
$$\equiv 305 \cdot 100 \cdot 100$$
$$\equiv 68 \cdot 100 \cdot 100 \pmod{79}$$

and if we multiply by 64 and reduce modulo 79 we should get the right answer:

$$442 \cdot 64 \equiv 28288 \equiv 6 \equiv 68 \cdot 100 \pmod{79}.$$

The function we want is the function that will take as input the 442 and return 6. And the function described above does exactly that:

$$m = (442 \pmod{100}) \cdot 81 \pmod{100}$$
$$= 42 \cdot 81 \pmod{100}$$
$$= 3402 \pmod{100}$$
$$\equiv 2 \pmod{100}$$
$$t = (442 + 2 \cdot 79)/100$$
$$= (442 + 158)/100$$
$$= 600/100$$
$$= 6$$

and we return $t = 6$ as the result.

The proof that the algorithm works runs as follows. We assume that T is a product, and hence is double length. Since we choose $R > N$ but not too much bigger, the products can be taken to be double length in R.

The first modular reduction simply converts T to a single length number modulo R. Again, modulo R, we have that $m = TN'$. Thus

$$mN \equiv TN'N \equiv -T \quad (\bmod R).$$

So when we take $T + mN$ we get an integer that is zero modulo R and we can legitimately divide out the R and get an integer quotient for t.

Now the fact that we get the right quotient comes from the fact that

$$tR = T + mN \equiv T \quad (\bmod N)$$

so that modulo N we have $t \equiv TR'$.

8.3.1 The Computational Advantage

Montgomery multiplication replaces a multiprecise division of two integers by a reduction modulo R, a multiplication modulo R to produce m, an addition, and then a division by R. This doesn't sound at first like a win, but ... if R is a power of two (and not the power of 10 of the example), then reduction of the right hand side used to produce m modulo R is simply taking the rightmost bits of that product, and then division by R is simply taking the leftmost bits. There is, of course, just as with the Mersenne prime trick, the possibility that our integers wind up one bit too long, but the possible one more subtraction to correct that is a very small price.

8.4 Arithmetic in General

We remark finally that arithmetic on large integers is crucial to public-key cryptography, and it, as with computations in number theory in general, has thus been studied extensively [9]. Hardware has been designed and built [7,10–15]. Software and algorithms have been devised [16–20]. This continues to be topic of study, especially as key sizes increase; the theoretically faster algorithms that might not have been practically faster for smaller key sizes might become practical for larger keys.

8.5 Exercises

1. (Programming exercise.) Verify the primality of $M_{13} = 8191$ by implementing the Lucas–Lehmer test. Note that this is the largest Mersenne prime for which the arithmetic can be done using 32-bit arithmetic without multiprecision routines.

If you have access to computer than can handle 64-bit arithmetic, you can test your code on M_{17}, M_{19}, and M_{31}.

You may want to do M_{13} first without the arithmetic trick, and then improve your code after you know you have the algorithm implemented properly. If you can do the larger Mersenne primes, you might want to check the difference in running times and notice the growth pattern.

2. Do the example of Sect. 8.2.7, but do it using the FFT butterfly of Fig. 8.2.
3. Do the Montgomery multiplication example of 17 times 26, but this time do it modulo $N = 83$.
4. (Programming exercise.) Do a program for Montgomery multiplication. Test it using the example, and then make sure it works for 123 times 456 modulo 1009.

References

1. M. Agrawal, N. Kayal, N. Saxena, PRIMES is in P. Ann. Math. **160**, 781–793 (2004)
2. G.H. Hardy, E.M. Wright, *An Introduction to the Theory of Numbers*, 4th edn. (Oxford, 1960), pp. 223–225
3. F.T. Leighton, *Introduction to Parallel Algorithms and Architectures* (Morgan Kaufmann, Burlington, 1992)
4. M.J. Quinn, *Parallel Computing: Theory and practice*, 2nd edn. (McGraw-Hill, New York, 1994)
5. P.L. Montgomery, Modular multiplication without trial division. Math. Comput. **44**, 519–521 (1985)
6. J.-C. Bajard, L.-S. Dider, An RNS Montgomery modular multiplication algorithm, in *Proceedings. IEEE Symposium on Computer Arithmetic* (1997), pp. 234–239
7. S.E. Eldridge, C.D. Walter, Hardware implementation of Montgomery's modular multiplication algorithm. IEEE Trans. Comput. 693–699 (1993)
8. D.E. Knuth, *The Art of Computer Programming*. Seminumerical Algorithms, vol. 2, 2nd edn. (Addison-Wesley, Boston, 1981)
9. D.H. Lehmer, Computer technology applied to the theory of numbers, in *Studies in Number Theory*. MAA Studies in Mathematics (1969), pp. 117–151
10. E.F. Brickell, A survey of hardware implementations of RS, in *Advances in Cryptology - CRYPTO'89. Proceedings, CRYPTO 1989*, ed. by G. Brassard. Lecture Notes in Computer Science, vol. 435 (1990), pp. 368–370
11. D.M. Chiarulli, W.G. Rudd, D.A. Buell, DRAFT-a dynamically reconfigurable processor for integer arithmetic, in *IEEE 7th Symposium on Computer Arithmetic (ARITH)* (1985), pp. 309–317
12. D.M. Chiarulli, A fast multiplier for very large operands, Technical Report (University of Pittsburgh Technical Report CSTR 86-11, 1986)
13. D.M. Chiarulli, A horizontally reconfigurable architecture for extended precision arithmetic. PhD thesis, Baton Rouge, Louisiana, 1986
14. W.G. Rudd, D.M. Chiarulli, D.A. Buell, A high performance factoring machine, in *Proceedings of 11th Annual International Symposium on Computer Architecture* (1984), pp. 297–300
15. A.F. Tenca, C.K. Koc, A scalable architecture for Montgomery multiplication, ed. by C. K. Koc, C. Paar. Lecture Notes in Computer Science, vol. 1717 (1999), pp. 94–108
16. S.E. Eldridge, A faster modular multiplication algorithm. Int. J. Comput. Math. 63–68 (1991)

17. T. Granlund, GNU MP: the GNU multiple precision arithmetic library (Free Software Foundation, Inc., 2001)
18. V. MüCller, Fast multiplication on elliptic curves over small fields of characteristic two. J. Cryptol. **11**, 219–234 (1998)
19. A. Schönhage, V. Strassen, Schnelle multiplikation grosser zahlen. Computing 281–292 (1971)
20. C.D. Walter, S.E. Eldridge, A verification of Brickell's fast modular multiplication algorithm. Int. J. Comput. Math. 153–169 (1990)

Modern Symmetric Ciphers—DES and AES

9

Abstract

In a symmetric cryptosystem, the key used for encrypting a message is the same as the key used for decrypting a message. Although this does place a burden of proper key management and security on the users of such a cryptosystem, there have been two major cryptosystems, the Digital Encryption Standard (DES) and the Advanced Encryption Standard (AES), promulgated by the National Institute of Standards and Technology. DES was controversial due to the manner in which it was promulgated, and it has largely been superseded by the AES, about which almost no controversy exists. AES is currently in wide use in part because it is the NIST standard and in part because its design makes it fast and usable on a variety of platforms with different computational capabilities. This chapter covers the technical aspects of AES. Code for AES and test results appear in Appendix B so that code testing can be done and the encryption process observed.

9.1 History

Early in the 1970s, it was realized by the United States National Bureau of Standards (NBS)[1] that a cryptographically secure algorithm for electronic communication was needed. The search began in 1972. A proposal was published in 1975, and was criticized for several reasons at the time. Nonetheless, the Data Encryption Standard (DES) was published on 15 January 1977 as FIPS (Federal Information Processing Standard) Publication 46 [1]. The standard was reaffirmed several times and not revoked until well after its expected time for secure use. A primary reason for establishing a cryptographic standard was to enable financial institutions to conduct their business over secured communication channels; even into the late 1970s and

---

[1]The name was changed in 1988 to the National Institute for Standards and Technology (NIST).

© The Author(s), under exclusive license to Springer Nature Switzerland AG 2021
D. Buell, *Fundamentals of Cryptography*, Undergraduate Topics in Computer Science,
https://doi.org/10.1007/978-3-030-73492-3_9

early 1980s many banks[2] were reconciling accounts data with the regional Federal Reserve banks over unencrypted telephone lines.

9.1.1   Criticism and Controversy

The precursor to DES was an IBM cryptographic algorithm called LUCIFER. Unlike LUCIFER, which had a 112-bit key, the key for DES is only 56 bits. Given the fact that the United States National Security Agency (NSA) was known to have been involved in the design of DES,[3] there were many conspiracy theories floated about how DES had been deliberately done as a version of LUCIFER that was sufficiently weakened that NSA could crack it.

Almost immediately, a plan for how to crack DES was laid out [2]. The Diffie–Hellman plan called for parallel computing, perhaps enhanced with special purpose hardware. One version was for a $20-million computer that would crack a DES key in 12 h. In essence, the attack was a parallel brute-force attack; breaking up the 2^{56} possible keys into chunks and then testing all the keys in a given chunk is a perfect example of an embarrassingly parallel computation.

Additional criticism was that part of the encryption system (famously known as the "S-boxes") had deliberately been created to be a group operating on the input bits. As will be discussed later in the context of discrete logarithms, if part of the encryption is a group operation

$$g : bits \rightarrow other\_bits$$

then there is an inverse g^{-1} in the group to the operation g, and this inverse could be a back door that would allow those who knew about the group structure (presumably, the NSA) to undo without any real effort the ostensibly cryptographically important action of the S-boxes.

Although there is something in human nature that would have us be enamored with conspiracy theories, it is not clear that any of these have substance. Don Coppersmith, for example [3], showed that the S-boxes did not have a group structure to them. His proof was, in essence, a computational demonstration that if there were a group structure, then the order of the group would have to be much larger than the largest possible group that could operate on the input bits.

So much for the group structure.

More to the point, it was in fact true that the Electronic Frontier Foundation (EFF) cracked DES, using distributed parallel computing, in 22 h and 15 min, in 1999. This feat was entirely consistent with the original proposal for how to crack a 56-bit key

---

[2]Including the author's own, apparently.

[3]NIST is a branch of the Department of Commerce, charged with making standards that benefit U.S. commercial activity. NIST has expertise in cryptography in-house, but is generally required under federal law to work with NSA on matters of technical expertise (like cryptography) for which NSA is the official government agency.

of this nature using parallel computation, as that computation improved in capability over time.

What seems to be overlooked by those who love conspiracy theories, however, is that although DES was reaffirmed several times, the original plan was that it would be an algorithm to provide cryptographic security for 15 years.

A 1977 publication, plus 15 years, takes us to 1992, seven years before the EFF cracks DES in the obvious way. Yes, DES can be cracked, and yes, DES can be cracked in exactly the way it was shown, when promulgated, to be crackable. But there were many people and institutions with a somewhat vested interest in demonstrating that DES was flawed from the start, and it is not at all clear that they have made their point [4,5].

9.2 The Advanced Encryption Standard

In part due to concerns about security, many of those using DES by the 1990s were using "Triple DES," encrypting three times instead of just once. It was clear to NIST by the middle 1990s that a new encryption standard was necessary. In spite of the fact that the conspiracy theories about DES did not seem to be justified, NIST took a totally different approach to cipher design when it began work in 1997 on the Advanced Encryption Standard (AES) that would be the successor to DES. This would be an algorithm to be used for sensitive, but not for classified, information.

This time, very little was done in secret. In fact, the design determination was opened up as a competition in January of 1997.

All contenders were asked to submit proposed designs, and all contenders were permitted to implement and to attack the proposals.

A number of NIST criteria were outlined in advance. The goal was a cryptosystem that was at least as secure as Triple DES that was in moderately wide use, but a cryptosystem that was much more efficient than Triple DES.

The constraints on speed and implementation on low-capability devices required serious contenders to be implementable on such devices. The Rijndael/AES algorithm, for example, is strongly byte-oriented, making it clean and efficient in a high-level language on a standard processor but also relatively straightforward to implement on the kind of minimal-capability processor as might be found on a smart card. The NIST specification was for a block length of 128 bits and for key lengths of 128, 192, and 256 bits.

Finally, there were stringent standards set regarding intellectual property issues. No proposal would be adopted, for example, if its implementation and use were limited by intellectual property constraints; NIST intended AES to be an open standard without encumbrances from patents or other claimed proprietary content.

Submissions were made and evaluated in a series of public conferences [6–8] before the final announcement was made in 2001 [9].

There were 15 original submissions accepted for the first AES round of evaluation. These were presented at a conference held in Ventura, California, in August 1988,

Cryptosystem	Submitter(s)
CAST-256	Entrust (Canada)
Crypton	Future Systems (KR)
DEAL	Outerbridge and Knudsen (USA and Denmark)
DFC	ENS-CNRS (France)
E2	NTT (Japan)
Frog	TecApro (CR)
HPC	Schroeppel (USA)
LOKI97	Brown, et al. (Australia)
Magenta	Deutsche Telekom (Germany)
MARS	IBM (USA)
RC6	RSA (USA)
Rijndael	Daemen and Rijmen (Belgium)
SAFER+	Cylink (USA)
Serpent	Anderson, Biham, Knudsen (UK, Israel, Denmark)
Twofish	Counterpane (USA)

Fig. 9.1 The original AES candidates

and are shown in Fig. 9.1. A second conference was held in March 1999, coinciding with the annual Fast Software Encryption Workshop at which researchers presented implementations, analyses, and criticisms of the 15 submissions. In August of 1999 the list of fifteen candidates was reduced to five—MARS, RC6, Rijndael, Serpent, and Twofish, and researchers presented work on these five at the Fast Software Encryption Workshop in April 2000.

The initial three criteria of security, cost, and implementation characteristics were modified somewhat during the evaluation process. Although security remained the primary concern, the analysis of the proposed algorithms resulted in a refinement of the other two criteria. The cost criteria included both software efficiency and the cost, both in general silicon area and in memory required, of a hardware implementation. Implementation characteristics included the specifics of implementation in silicon, in Field Programmable Gate Arrays, and on general purpose processors with a high degree of instruction level parallelism. Also considered were the flexibility of the algorithm to accommodate parameters outside the original requirements of AES (in case attacks on the original algorithm were discovered).

At the end of that third conference, a survey of the cryptographers overwhelmingly backed Rijndael, the submission of Vincent Rijmen and Joan Daemen. The selection of Rijndael as the AES was announced in a press release on 2 October 2000 and followed by the publication of FIPS-197 on 26 November 2001 [9]. The security of all the finalists had been judged to be adequate. In general, the choice of Rijndael can be traced to the simplicity of the operations it requires and the byte orientation of those operations. These led to relatively high execution efficiency both in software and hardware, although the extensive use of memory tables results in a relatively large silicon area among the finalist algorithms. Finally, Rijndael as proposed incorporated the variations in key and block size beyond the original specifications for AES that would be needed in a flexible algorithm.

Although a few weaknesses have been found in AES, none have been fundamental or lead to attacks that would cause the use of AES to be abandoned.

9.3   The AES Algorithm

AES is a *key-alternating block cipher*, with plaintext encrypted in blocks of 128 bits. The key sizes in AES can be 128, 192, or 256 bits. It is an *iterated block cipher* because a fixed encryption process, usually called a *round*, is applied a number of times to the block of bits. Finally, we mean by *key-alternating* that the cipher key is XORed to the *state* (the running version of the block of input bits) alternately with the application of the round transformation.

The original Rijndael design allows for any choice of block length and key size between 128 and 256 in multiples of 32 bits. In this sense, Rijndael is a superset of AES; the two are not identical, but the difference is only in these configurations initially put into Rijndael but not used in AES.

The only other distinction to be noted is in the labelling of the transformations of AES. We will follow the labelling of the FIPS and of the inventors' book [10] and not that of the original submission of Rijndael to the AES competition. For example, the original submission referred to a `ByteSub` transformation, and the FIPS now refers to `SubBytes`.

9.3.1   Polynomial Preliminaries: The Galois Field $GF(2^8)$

AES makes extensive use of the polynomial

$$m(x) = x^8 + x^4 + x^3 + x + 1,$$

of degree eight, and the finite field of $2^8 = 256$ elements generated by this polynomial.

We now note that we can dispense with the polynomial notation and view the polynomials simply as bit strings, with the 8-bit byte that is the bit string $b_7b_6b_5b_4b_3b_2b_1b_0$ being used as a shorthand notation for the degree-seven polynomial

$$b_7x^7 + b_6x^6 + b_5x^5 + b_4x^4 + b_3x^3 + b_2x^2 + b_1x^1 + b_0x^0$$

that is an element of the finite field of 256 elements defined by $m(x)$.

AES makes extensive use of the fact that bit strings can be taken a byte at a time and interpreted in this way as coefficients of polynomials. What is crucial to the performance of AES is the fact that the nonzero polynomials can be generated as powers of a single polynomial $x + 1$. This permits us to use the powers of the generator to create a table of logarithms and do multiplication in the Galois field by table lookup. Indeed, much of what it takes to understand software that implements AES is to understand that the byte-oriented table lookup does in fact implement the more sophisticated mathematics.

9.3.1.1 More Polynomial Arithmetic

As part of the encryption and decryption processes, AES uses groups of four bytes to define polynomials $f(X)$ of degree three in an indeterminate X; each byte is taken to define an element of $GF(2^8)$ that is one of the coefficients of $f(X)$. The AES process then does arithmetic on these polynomials modulo the polynomial $X^4 + 1$. We will write these polynomials as

$$a_3 \odot X^3 + a_2 \odot X^2 + a_1 \odot X + a_0$$

and write the coefficients a_i in hexadecimal notation, so a specific coefficient $a_3 = x^5 + x^3 + 1 \leftrightarrow 00101001$ would be written as 29.

Although there is a mathematical basis for these operations, from a computational point of view we can regard this almost as a positional notation for the arithmetic. Since $X^4 \equiv 1 \pmod{x^4 + 1}$, multiplication of a polynomial $f(X)$ by $b \odot X$ modulo $X^4 + 1$ is really a coefficient-wise multiplication by b in $GF(2^8)$ and a left circular shift of the coefficients:

$$(b \odot X) \cdot (a_3 \odot X^3 + a_2 \odot X^2 + a_1 \odot X + a_0) \equiv$$
$$(b * a_2) \odot X^3 + (b * a_1) \odot X^2 + (b * a_0) \odot X(b * a_3) \pmod{X^4 + 1}$$

where the multiplication $*$ of the coefficients takes place in $GF(2^8)$. It is in part to recognize this purely formal nature of these polynomials that we use the $\odot$ symbol for multiplication by the coefficients.

9.3.2 Byte Organization

The input to AES is the *plaintext*, a sequence of blocks of 128 bits each of the message to be encrypted, and the *key*, a block of $K = 128$, 192, or 256 bits, with the size an option of the user. The blocks of plaintext are encrypted using the key to produce a *ciphertext* of blocks of bits of 128 bits each. AES is a *symmetric* cipher, in that the ciphertext produced by plaintext and key is converted back to plaintext using the same key.

Viewed simplistically, AES is almost (but not quite) an outer loop of N_r iterations, each called a *round*, of bit-transformations, and an inner set of four stages of transformations per round. The current pattern of bits as input to or output from one of these transformations is referred to as the *state*.

The AES plaintext block is 128 bits long. AES is strongly byte-oriented; if we view the stream of bytes of both plaintext and key as being numbered in increasing order

$$p_0 p_1 \cdots p_{15}$$

and

$$k_0 k_1 \ldots k_{K/8},$$

p_0	p_4	p_8	p_{12}
p_1	p_5	p_9	p_{13}
p_2	p_6	p_{10}	p_{14}
p_3	p_7	p_{11}	p_{15}

Fig. 9.2 Byte-by-byte view of the 128 bits of a plaintext block

then the bytes of both plaintext and key are usually viewed as a two-dimensional array in column-major order, shown for the plaintext in Fig. 9.2; the key can be represented similarly.

A key would be arranged in a similar pattern of four rows and $K/32 = 4$, 6, or 8 columns, respectively, for the key lengths of $K = 128$, 192, or 256 bits.

9.4 The Structure of AES

9.4.1 The Outer Structure of the Rounds

The Rijndael reference book [10] has code for AES and test data in its Appendices D and E. The code in those appendices is slightly different from what is shown in the text of the book. We present here and in an appendix in this book (our Appendix B) a modified version of the C implementation from Appendix E of [10]. For the most part, the differences are simply a renaming of functions; original names in the Rijndael proposal were changed in the AES standard. One change is less minor—the Appendix E (and our) implementation stores the expanded key as a three-dimensional array, with the outer subscript being the subscript for the round number, while the text of the reference book uses a two-dimensional array with the key for each round coming from a slice of columns of the two-dimensional array.

A more substantive, but easily remedied, problem with the code of Appendix E is that the decryption function as presented does the bit transformation in the same order as encryption, instead of in reverse order. As a symmetric cipher, the AES decryption is the same process as encryption, but run in the opposite direction, and with some of the functions replaced with their inverses. Fortunately, it is easy to know that one has the decryption function done properly, because it will reverse the encryption and change ciphertext back into plaintext.

The outer structure of encryption using AES is shown in Fig. 9.3. For key lengths of $K = 128$, 192, and 256 bits, we use $N_r = 10$, 12, and 14 round transformations respectively.

9.4.2 General Code Details

We remark that the code fragments shown here, and shown more completely in our Appendix B, use several global definitions, which we list in Fig. 9.4 The MAXBC

```
Rijndael(State, CipherKey) {
  KeyExpansion(CipherKey, ExpandedKey);
  AddRoundKey(State, ExpandedKey[0]);
  for( i = 1; i < Nr; i++) {
    SubBytes(State);
    ShiftRows(State);
    MixColumns(State);
    AddRoundKey(State, ExpandedKey[i]);
  }

  SubBytes(State);
  ShiftRows(State);
  AddRoundKey(State, ExpandedKey[Nr]);
}
```

Fig. 9.3 Outer encryption structure of AES

```
typedef unsigned char word8;
typedef unsigned int word32;

#define MAXBC 8
#define MAXKC 8
#define MAXROUNDS 14

bool testd2, testd3, testtext;
int BC, KC, ROUNDS;

static int numrounds[5][5] = {{10, 11, 12, 13, 14},
                              {11, 11, 12, 13, 14},
                              {12, 12, 12, 13, 14},
                              {13, 13, 13, 13, 14},
                              {14, 14, 14, 14, 14} };
```

Fig. 9.4 (Some of the) global definitions

constant is the maximum number of 32-bit sub-blocks in a plaintext block, which is set to 8 for the more general Rijndael but would be taken as 4 for AES. In the implementation of the Daemen and Rijmen reference [10], the variable BC set to 4, 6, or 8 allows for testing all of the Rijndael options.

The MAXKC constant is the maximum number of 32-bit sub-blocks in a key, also set to 8; The KC variable can be 4, 6, or 8 for keys of lengths 128, 192, or 256.

The MAXROUNDS constant is set at 14, and the ROUNDS value for different key lengths is set using the global numrounds array.

9.4.3   KeyExpansion

The input key is first expanded with the KeyExpansion function to produce a key that is $N_r + 1$ times its original size. The expanded key is then taken in blocks of K bits at a time. One block is added to the state prior to the round iterations, $N_r - 1$

blocks are added in, one at the end of each of the rounds in the loop, and the final block is added in as the last of the transformations.

The key addition steps require significant numbers of bits of key. These bits are obtained from the initial key by an expansion process. Care must be taken, of course, when expanding an input key, since the resulting key bits will not contain any more inherent randomness than is present in the initial key prior to the deterministic expansion.

With ten, twelve, or fourteen rounds in AES, the algorithm will need $128 \cdot 11 = 1408$, $128 \cdot 13 = 1664$, or $128 \cdot 15 = 1920$ bits of key in order to perform the `AddRoundKey` step. One 128-bit block of key is used prior to the iteration of the rounds, and then additional 128-bit blocks are used for each iteration within the rounds. The key bits are obtained via the `KeyExpansion` function that is applied to the initial key value.

For a version of AES with N_r rounds, the expanded key can be viewed as a three-dimensional array, with the outer subscript being the round number and the inner part of the array being four rows and 4, 6, or 8 columns of key for keys of length 128, 192, or 256 bits. This is the representation of the key in the code in Appendix E of the reference book [10]. The text of the reference, however, views the key as a two-dimensional array (using the last two dimensions of the 3-d array), and we discuss the simpler form that is Fig. 9.7 rather than the 3-d version of Fig. 9.5.

For a version of AES with N_r rounds, we view the expanded key as a two-dimensional array of four rows and $4 \cdot (N_r + 1)$ columns, which we subscript as $W[0..3][0..4 \cdot (N_r + 1)]$. If we set N_k to 4, 6, or 8 according as the key length is 128, 192, or 256 bits, then the first $4 \times N_k$ block receives the original key in column-major order as in Fig. 9.16, and the key is then expanded by the application of the recursive function detailed below. Columns of bytes of key are produced recursively:

1. If the column subscript $j \geq N_k$ is neither 0 modulo N_k nor 4 modulo N_k for $N_k = 8$, then we have

$$
\begin{bmatrix} W[0][j] \\ W[1][j] \\ W[2][j] \\ W[3][j] \end{bmatrix} = \begin{bmatrix} W[0][j - N_k] \\ W[1][j - N_k] \\ W[2][j - N_k] \\ W[3][j - N_k] \end{bmatrix} \oplus \begin{bmatrix} W[0][j - 1] \\ W[1][j - 1] \\ W[2][j - 1] \\ W[3][j - 1] \end{bmatrix}
$$

2. If $N_k = 8$ (256-bit keys) and the column subscript j is 4 modulo 8, then we XOR the $(j - N_k)$-th column not with the $(j - 1)$-st column but with the bits obtained by first applying S to that column. That is, we have the bit operations below. In this, S is the combined $GF(2^8)$ and affine transformation used in `SubBytes`.

$$
\begin{bmatrix} W[0][j] \\ W[1][j] \\ W[2][j] \\ W[3][j] \end{bmatrix} = \begin{bmatrix} W[0][j - N_k] \\ W[1][j - N_k] \\ W[2][j - N_k] \\ W[3][j - N_k] \end{bmatrix} \oplus \begin{bmatrix} S_{RD}(W[0][j - 1]) \\ S_{RD}(W[1][j - 1]) \\ S_{RD}(W[2][j - 1]) \\ S_{RD}(W[3][j - 1]) \end{bmatrix}
$$

```
int KeyExpansion(word8 k[4][MAXKC], word8 W[MAXROUNDS+1][4][MAXBC]) {
  // Calculate the required round keys.
  int i, j, t, RCpointer = 1;
  word8 tk[4][MAXKC];
  for (j = 0; j < KC; j++) {
    for (i = 0; i < 4; i++) {
      tk[i][j] = k[i][j];
    }
  }
  t = 0;
  // Copy values into round key array.
  for (j = 0; (j < KC) && (t < (ROUNDS+1)*BC); j++, t++) {
    for (i = 0; i < 4; i++) {
      W[t / BC][i][t % BC] = tk[i][j];
    }
  }
  while (t < (ROUNDS+1)*BC) {
    // While not enough round key material calculated, calc new values.
    for (i = 0; i < 4; i++) {
      tk[i][0] ^= S[tk[(i+1)%4][KC-1]];
    }
    tk[0][0] ^= RC[RCpointer++];
    if (KC <= 6) {
      for (j = 1; j < KC; j++) {
        for (i = 0; i < 4; i++) {
          tk[i][j] ^= tk[i][j-1];
        }
      }
    }
    else {
      for (j = 1; j < 4; j++) {
        for (i = 0; i < 4; i++) {
          tk[i][j] ^= tk[i][j-1];
        }
      }
      for (i = 0; i < 4; i++) {
        tk[i][4] ^= S[tk[i][3]];
      }
      for (j = 5; j < KC; j++) {
        for (i = 0; i < 4; i++) {
          tk[i][j] ^= tk[i][j-1];
        }
      }
    }
    // Copy values into round key array.
    for (j = 0; (j < KC) && (t < (ROUNDS+1)*BC); j++, t++) {
      for (i = 0; i < 4; i++) {
        W[t / BC][i][t % BC] = tk[i][j];
      }
    }
  }
  return 0;
}
```

Fig. 9.5 Key expansion

```
word32 RC[30] = {0x00, 0x01, 0x02, 0x04, 0x08, 0x10,
                 0x20, 0x40, 0x80, 0x1b, 0x36, 0x6c,
                 0xd8, 0xab, 0x4d, 0x9a, 0x2f, 0x5e,
                 0xbc, 0x63, 0xc6, 0x97, 0x35, 0x6a,
                 0xd4, 0xb3, 0x7d, 0xfa, 0xef, 0xc5};
```

Fig. 9.6 The RC lookup table for $GF(2^8)$ arithmetic in key expansion

3. If the column subscript i is 0 modulo N_k, then we have the bit operations below. In addition to the S_{RD} operation, we have a circular shift down of the bytes of column $j - 1$ before the application of S_{RD} and the XOR in byte 0 of a **round constant** RC, where

$$
\begin{bmatrix} W[0][j] \\ W[1][j] \\ W[2][j] \\ W[3][j] \end{bmatrix} = \begin{bmatrix} W[0][j - N_k] \\ W[1][j - N_k] \\ W[2][j - N_k] \\ W[3][j - N_k] \end{bmatrix} \oplus \begin{bmatrix} S_{RD}(W[1][j-1]) \oplus RC[j/N_k] \\ S_{RD}(W[2][j-1]) \\ S_{RD}(W[3][j-1]) \\ S_{RD}(W[0][j-1]) \end{bmatrix}
$$

$$
RC[1] = x^0 \quad \text{that is, } 01
$$

$$
RC[2] = x^1 \quad \text{that is, } 02
$$

$$
\cdots
$$

$$
RC[j] = x^{j-1} \quad \text{in} \quad GF(2^8)
$$

and as always we can do the $GF(2^8)$ arithmetic with lookup tables, using in this case the table of Fig. 9.6:

The ExpandedKey[i] value as used in the pseudo-code description of the algorithm refers to columns $N_b \cdot i$ through $N_b \cdot (i + 1) - 1$ when viewed as columns, or bytes $4 \cdot N_b \cdot i$ through $4 \cdot N_b \cdot (i + 1) - 1$ taken in column-major order. Thus, key bits are extracted from the ExpandedKey in blocks of 128 bits at a time, but the key bits are generated column by column as needed, not necessarily in blocks of 128 bits.

Specifically, for key lengths of 128 or 192 bits, the ExpandedKey is created with the function of Fig. 9.7. For key lengths of 256 bits, the ExpandedKey is created with the function of Fig. 9.8.

9.4.4 SubBytes

9.4.4.1 Encryption

The SubBytes step is nonlinear, and is in fact the only nonlinear step in AES. Each individual byte

$$
a = a_7 a_6 a_5 a_4 a_3 a_2 a_1 a_0
$$

```
def KeyExpansion(byte K[4][Nk], byte W[4][Nb*(Nr+1)]):
    for j in range(0, Nk):
        for i in range(0, 4):
            W[i][j] = K[i][j]

    for j in range(Nk, Nb*(Nr+1)):
        if j % Nk == 0:
            W[0][j] = W[0][j-Nk] XOR S[W[1][j-1]] XOR RC[j/Nk]
            for i in range(1, 4):
                W[i][j] = W[i][j-Nk] XOR S[W[i+1 % 4][j-1]]
        else:
            for i in range(0, 4):
                W[i][j] = W[i][j-Nk] XOR W[i][j-1]
```

Fig. 9.7 Key expansion for 128- or 192-bit keys (2-dimensional version)

(written as a string of bits) of the state is subjected (at least conceptually) to a two-stage transformation

$$a \rightarrow a^{-1} \text{ in } GF(2^8) \rightarrow f(a^{-1})$$

where $y = f(x)$ is the transformation of Fig. 9.9 and the $GF(2^8)$ arithmetic is defined by the polynomial $m(x)$ above.

9.4.4.2   Decryption

For decryption, the inverse to SubBytes would be accomplished with the function f^{-1} of Fig. 9.10 followed by a byte inversion in $GF(2^8)$. In point of fact, it can be done with the same C code but with a lookup table that is inverse to the table used in encryption.

9.4.4.3   Implementation—The S Function

A crucial feature of AES is that its predilection for computation on bytes makes for efficient implementation. Although the SubBytes operation is conceptually a Galois field inversion followed by an affine transformation, these two can be combined and implemented with a 256-long table lookup, which is the function S in the code in our Appendix B and shown in Fig. 9.11. The inverse operation, used in decryption, is the same function but with the inverse lookup table Si.

For high level language code or for implementation on any standard processor, this is almost certainly the most efficient approach, since the intra-word bit manipulations of Galois inversion and the affine transformation will not be supported by CPU instructions. For hardware implementations, implementation of the actual arithmetic is not out of the question, as we will discuss later.

```
def KeyExpansion(byte K[4][Nk], byte W[4][Nb*(Nr+1)]):
    for j in range(0, Nk):
        for i in range(0, 4):
            W[i][j] = K[i][j]
    for j in range(Nk, Nb*(Nr+1)):
        if j % Nk == 0:
            W[0][j] = W[0][j-Nk] XOR S[W[1][j-1]] XOR RC[j/Nk]
            for i in range(1, 4):
                W[i][j] = W[i][j-Nk] XOR S[W[i+1 % 4][j-1]]
        else:
            for i in range(0, 4):
                W[i][j] = W[i][j-Nk] XOR W[i][j-1]


KeyExpansion(byte K[4][Nk], byte W[4][Nb*(Nr+1)])
{

  for(j = Nk; j < Nb*(Nr+1); j++) } /* expansion loop on columns */
  {
    if(0 == j mod Nk) /* if-then for bytes down columns */
    {
      W[0][j] = W[0][j-Nk] XOR S[W[1][j-1]] XOR RC[j/Nk];
      for(i = 1; i < 4 i++)
      {
        W[i][j] = W[i][j-Nk] XOR S[W[i+1 mod 4][j-1]];
      }
    }
    else if(4 == j mod Nk)
    {
      for(i = 0; i < 4 i++)
      {
        W[i][j] = W[i][j-Nk] XOR S[W[i][j-1]];
      }
    }
    else
    {
      for(i = 0; i < 4 i++)
      {
        W[i][j] = W[i][j-Nk] XOR W[i][j-1];
      }
    } /* end if-then down columns */
  } /* end expansion loop on columns */
} /* end KeyExpansion */
```

Fig. 9.8 Key expansion for 256-bit keys (2-dimensional version)

$$
\begin{pmatrix}
1 & 1 & 1 & 1 & 1 & 0 & 0 & 0 \\
0 & 1 & 1 & 1 & 1 & 1 & 0 & 0 \\
0 & 0 & 1 & 1 & 1 & 1 & 1 & 0 \\
0 & 0 & 0 & 1 & 1 & 1 & 1 & 1 \\
1 & 0 & 0 & 0 & 1 & 1 & 1 & 1 \\
1 & 1 & 0 & 0 & 0 & 1 & 1 & 1 \\
1 & 1 & 1 & 0 & 0 & 0 & 1 & 1 \\
1 & 1 & 1 & 1 & 0 & 0 & 0 & 1
\end{pmatrix}
\times
\begin{pmatrix}
x_7 \\ x_6 \\ x_5 \\ x_4 \\ x_3 \\ x_2 \\ x_1 \\ x_0
\end{pmatrix}
\oplus
\begin{pmatrix}
0 \\ 1 \\ 1 \\ 0 \\ 0 \\ 0 \\ 1 \\ 1
\end{pmatrix}
=
\begin{pmatrix}
y_7 \\ y_6 \\ y_5 \\ y_4 \\ y_3 \\ y_2 \\ y_1 \\ y_0
\end{pmatrix}
$$

Fig. 9.9 The function $f(x)$ in SubBytes

$$
\begin{pmatrix}
0\ 1\ 0\ 1\ 0\ 0\ 1\ 0 \\
0\ 0\ 1\ 0\ 1\ 0\ 0\ 1 \\
1\ 0\ 0\ 1\ 0\ 1\ 0\ 0 \\
0\ 1\ 0\ 0\ 1\ 0\ 1\ 0 \\
0\ 0\ 1\ 0\ 0\ 1\ 0\ 1 \\
1\ 0\ 0\ 1\ 0\ 0\ 1\ 0 \\
0\ 1\ 0\ 0\ 1\ 0\ 0\ 1 \\
1\ 0\ 1\ 0\ 0\ 1\ 0\ 0
\end{pmatrix}
\times
\begin{pmatrix}
y_7 \\ y_6 \\ y_5 \\ y_4 \\ y_3 \\ y_2 \\ y_1 \\ y_0
\end{pmatrix}
\oplus
\begin{pmatrix}
0 \\ 0 \\ 0 \\ 0 \\ 0 \\ 1 \\ 0 \\ 1
\end{pmatrix}
=
\begin{pmatrix}
x_7 \\ x_6 \\ x_5 \\ x_4 \\ x_3 \\ x_2 \\ x_1 \\ x_0
\end{pmatrix}
$$

Fig. 9.10 The function $f^{-1}(x)$ for inverting SubBytes

```
void SubBytes(word8 a[4][MAXBC], word8 box[255]) {
  // Replace every byte of the input by the byte
  // at that place in the non-linear S-box.
  int i, j;
  for (i = 0; i < 4; i++) {
    for (j = 0; j < BC; j++) {
      a[i][j] = box[a[i][j]];
    }
  }
}
```

Fig. 9.11 SubBytes

Fig. 9.12 Byte transformations of the ShiftRows step

B_0	B_4	B_8	B_{12}
B_1	B_5	B_9	B_{13}
B_2	B_6	B_{10}	B_{14}
B_3	B_7	B_{11}	B_{15}

$\rightarrow$

B_0	B_4	B_8	B_{12}
B_5	B_9	B_{13}	B_1
B_{10}	B_{14}	B_2	B_6
B_{15}	B_3	B_7	B_{11}

9.4.5 ShiftRows

9.4.5.1 Encryption

The second stage of the inner loop of AES is the ShiftRows operation. In this stage, the bytes of the four rows of the state are circularly shifted left. Row 0 of the state is not shifted; row 1 is shifted left one byte, row 2 shifted two bytes, and row 3 shifted left circularly by three bytes. A graphical tableau for ShiftRows is as in Fig. 9.12. Code for the function is shown in Fig. 9.13.

9.4.5.2 Decryption

In decryption, the inverse of the ShiftRows step is simply the appropriate right circular shift of the bytes of the state.

```
                // (Global value included here for completeness.)
                static word8 shifts[5][4] = {{0, 1, 2, 3},
                                             {0, 1, 2, 3},
                                             {0, 1, 2, 3},
                                             {0, 1, 2, 4},
                                             {0, 1, 3, 4} };

        void ShiftRows(word8 a[4][MAXBC], word8 d) {
          // Row 0 remains unchanged.
          // The other three rows are shifted a variable amount.
          word8 tmp[MAXBC];
          int i, j;

          if (d == 0) {
            for (i = 1; i < 4; i++) {
              for (j = 0; j < BC; j++) {
                tmp[j] = a[i][(j + shifts[BC-4][i]) % BC];
              }
              for (j = 0; j < BC; j++) {
                a[i][j] = tmp[j];
              }
            }
          }
          else {
            for (i = 1; i < 4; i++) {
              for (j = 0; j < BC; j++) {
                tmp[j] = a[i][(BC + j - shifts[BC-4][i]) % BC];
              }
              for (j = 0; j < BC; j++) {
                a[i][j] = tmp[j];
              }
            }
          }
        }
```

Fig. 9.13 ShiftRows

9.4.6 MixColumns

9.4.6.1 Encryption

In the SubBytes stage, the bits

$$b_7 b_6 b_5 b_4 b_3 b_2 b_1 b_0$$

of a byte were viewed as coefficients of a polynomial

$$b_7 x^7 + b_6 x^6 + b_5 x^5 + b_4 x^4 + b_3 x^3 + b_2 x^2 + b_1 x^1 + b_0$$

that represented an element of the finite field $GF(2^8)$, and this element was inverted in $GF(2^8)$. In the MixColumns stage, we carry that representation one step further. The four bytes of a column in the state are each viewed as elements of $GF(2^8)$ that are now coefficients of a cubic polynomial. For example, a column of state (with bytes written as two hexadecimal digits)

1F
3D
5B
79

would be taken to represent the polynomial

$$1F \odot X^3 + 3D \odot X^2 + 5B \odot X + 79$$

with, for example, the last coefficient $79 = 01111001$ being taken to mean the polynomial

$$0 \cdot x^7 + 1 \cdot x^6 + 1 \cdot x^5 + 1 \cdot x^4 + 1 \cdot x^3 + 0 \cdot x^2 + 0 \cdot x^1 + 1 \cdot x^0$$

as an element of $GF(2^8)$.

The columns of the state, viewed as polynomials in X with coefficients in $GF(2^8)$, are multiplied by

$$c(X) = 03 \odot X^3 + 01 \odot X^2 + 01 \odot X + 02$$

modulo $X^4 + 1$. The polynomial $c(X)$ is invertible modulo $X^4 + 1$, with inverse

$$d(X) = c^{-1}(X) = 0B \odot X^3 + 0D \odot X^2 + 09 \odot X + 0E.$$

Since this is more complicated than most of the stages of AES, we will go into somewhat more detail. Assume we have a column of state

a_3
a_2
a_1
a_0

Then the multiplication of MixColumns is

$$\left(a_3 \odot X^3 + a_2 \odot X^2 + a_1 \odot X + a_0\right) \cdot \left(03 \odot X^3 + 01 \odot X^2 + 01 \odot X + 02\right)$$

which is rewritten as

$$
\begin{aligned}
X^6 \cdot (&& 03 \odot a_3 \;) \\
X^5 \cdot (&& 03 \odot a_2 + 01 \odot a_3 \;) \\
X^4 \cdot (& +03 \odot a_1 + 01 \odot a_2 + 01 \odot a_3 \;) \\
X^3 \cdot (\; 03 \odot a_0 &+ 01 \odot a_1 + 01 \odot a_2 + 02 \odot a_3 \;) \\
X^2 \cdot (\; 01 \odot a_0 &+ 01 \odot a_1 + 02 \odot a_2 &) \\
X^1 \cdot (\; 01 \odot a_0 &+ 02 \odot a_1 &) \\
X^0 \cdot (\; 02 \odot a_0 &&)
\end{aligned}
$$

and which reduces to

$$
\equiv
\begin{aligned}
X^5 \cdot (&& 03 \odot a_2 + 01 \odot a_3 \;) \\
X^4 \cdot (& +03 \odot a_1 + 01 \odot a_2 + 01 \odot a_3 \;) \\
X^3 \cdot (\; 03 \odot a_0 &+ 01 \odot a_1 + 01 \odot a_2 + 02 \odot a_3 \;) \\
X^2 \cdot (\; 01 \odot a_0 &+ 01 \odot a_1 + 02 \odot a_2 + 03 \odot a_3 \;) \\
X^1 \cdot (\; 01 \odot a_0 &+ 02 \odot a_1 &) \\
X^0 \cdot (\; 02 \odot a_0 &&)
\end{aligned}
$$

then to

$$
\equiv
\begin{aligned}
X^4 \cdot (& +03 \odot a_1 + 01 \odot a_2 + 01 \odot a_3 \;) \\
X^3 \cdot (\; 03 \odot a_0 &+ 01 \odot a_1 + 01 \odot a_2 + 02 \odot a_3 \;) \\
X^2 \cdot (\; 01 \odot a_0 &+ 01 \odot a_1 + 02 \odot a_2 + 03 \odot a_3 \;) \\
X^1 \cdot (\; 01 \odot a_0 &+ 02 \odot a_1 + 03 \odot a_2 + 01 \odot a_3 \;) \\
X^0 \cdot (\; 02 \odot a_0 &&)
\end{aligned}
$$

and finally to

$$
\equiv
\begin{aligned}
X^3 \cdot (\; 03 \odot a_0 &+ 01 \odot a_1 + 01 \odot a_2 + 02 \odot a_3 \;) \\
X^2 \cdot (\; 01 \odot a_0 &+ 01 \odot a_1 + 02 \odot a_2 + 03 \odot a_3 \;) \\
X^1 \cdot (\; 01 \odot a_0 &+ 02 \odot a_1 + 03 \odot a_2 + 01 \odot a_3 \;) \\
X^0 \cdot (\; 02 \odot a_0 &+ 03 \odot a_1 + 01 \odot a_2 + 01 \odot a_3 \;)
\end{aligned}
$$

where the reduction is done modulo $X^4 + 1$.

The entire operation on columns of the state can thus be done as a matrix multiplication in $GF(2^8)$:

$$
\begin{pmatrix} b_3 \\ b_2 \\ b_1 \\ b_0 \end{pmatrix} =
\begin{pmatrix}
03 & 01 & 01 & 02 \\
01 & 01 & 02 & 03 \\
01 & 02 & 03 & 01 \\
02 & 03 & 01 & 01
\end{pmatrix}
\begin{pmatrix} a_3 \\ a_2 \\ a_1 \\ a_0 \end{pmatrix}
$$

9.4.6.2 Decryption

The inverse to MixColumns, called InvMixColumns, is a multiplication of the columns by the inverse $d(X)$, all taken modulo $X^4 + 1$. As above, the operation can

```
word8 mul(word8 a, word8 b) {
  // multiply two elements of GF(256)
  // required for MixColumns and InvMixColumns
  if (a && b) return Alogtable[(Logtable[a] + Logtable[b])%255];
  else return 0;
}

void MixColumns(word8 a[4][MAXBC]) {
  // Mix the four bytes of every column in a linear way.
  word8 b[4][MAXBC];
  int i, j;

  for (j = 0; j < BC; j++) {
    for (i = 0; i < 4; i++) {
      b[i][j] = mul(2, a[i][j])
              ^ mul(3, a[(i+1)%4][j])
              ^ a[(i+2)%4][j]
              ^ a[(i+3)%4][j];
    }
  }
  for (i = 0; i < 4; i++) {
    for (j = 0; j < BC; j++) {
      a[i][j] = b[i][j];
    }
  }
}
```

Fig. 9.14 Code for the MixColumns function

be condensed into a matrix operation on the columns of state as follows.

$$
\begin{pmatrix} a_3 \\ a_2 \\ a_1 \\ a_0 \end{pmatrix} = \begin{pmatrix} 0E & 0B & 0D & 09 \\ 09 & 0E & 0B & 0D \\ 0D & 09 & 0E & 0B \\ 0B & 0D & 09 & 0E \end{pmatrix} \begin{pmatrix} b_3 \\ b_2 \\ b_1 \\ b_0 \end{pmatrix}
$$

9.4.6.3 Implementation

The code for MixColumns and for InvMixColumns are presented in Figs. 9.14 and 9.15.

9.4.7 AddRoundKey

The key addition step is labelled AddRoundKey. Since this is an XOR of bits of the expanded key with the state, the AddRoundKey step is its own inverse. The key addition is displayed in Fig. 9.16; the code itself is displayed in Fig. 9.17.

```
void InvMixColumns(word8 a[4][MAXBC]) {
  // Mix the four bytes of every column in a linear way.
  // This is the opposite operation of MixColumns.
  word8 b[4][MAXBC];
  int i, j;

  for (j = 0; j < BC; j++) {
    for (i = 0; i < 4; i++) {
      b[i][j] = mul(0xe, a[i][j])
              ^ mul(0xb, a[(i+1)%4][j])
              ^ mul(0xd, a[(i+2)%4][j])
              ^ mul(0x9, a[(i+3)%4][j]);
    }
  }
  for (i = 0; i < 4; i++) {
    for (j = 0; j < BC; j++) {
      a[i][j] = b[i][j];
    }
  }
}
```

Fig. 9.15 Code for the `InvMixColumns` function

$$
\begin{array}{|c|c|c|c|}
\hline
p_0 & p_4 & p_8 & p_{12} \\\hline
p_1 & p_5 & p_9 & p_{13} \\\hline
p_2 & p_6 & p_{10} & p_{14} \\\hline
p_3 & p_7 & p_{11} & p_{15} \\\hline
\end{array}
\ \oplus\
\begin{array}{|c|c|c|c|}
\hline
k_0 & k_4 & k_8 & k_{12} \\\hline
k_1 & k_5 & k_9 & k_{13} \\\hline
k_2 & k_6 & k_{10} & k_{14} \\\hline
k_3 & k_7 & k_{11} & k_{15} \\\hline
\end{array}
\ =\
\begin{array}{|c|c|c|c|}
\hline
p'_0 & p'_4 & p'_8 & p'_{12} \\\hline
p'_1 & p'_5 & p'_9 & p'_{13} \\\hline
p'_2 & p'_6 & p'_{10} & p'_{14} \\\hline
p'_3 & p'_7 & p'_{11} & p'_{15} \\\hline
\end{array}
$$

Fig. 9.16 `AddRoundKey` operating on the 128 bits of a plaintext block

```
void AddRoundKey(word8 a[4][MAXBC], word8 rk[4][MAXBC]) {
  // XOR corresponding text input and round key input bytes.
  int i, j;
  for (i = 0; i < 4; i++) {
    for (j = 0; j < BC; j++) {
      a[i][j] ^= rk[i][j];
    }
  }
}
```

Fig. 9.17 Code for the `AddRoundKey` function

9.5 Implementation Issues

AES was designed so that it would perform well on a range of processors, including smart cards with small 8-bit processors, fast standard processors, and even on special purpose hardware. Because the functions of AES are bit manipulations, and because many of these functions are not provided in the Instruction Set Architecture (ISA) of a standard processor, some accommodation for the bit-processing must be made in an implementation on a standard processor. On the other hand, AES has been designed so that these tweaks are relatively straightforward and so that high performance can be achieved even on relatively low-performance processors.

Just to review the operations necessary, we summarize the operations to be performed:

1. KeyExpansion: Most of the key expansion operations are XORs. The other operation is the application of the S function from SubBytes.
2. SubBytes: Mathematically, the computation in SubBytes includes the $GF(2^8)$ arithmetic followed by the affine transformation $f(x)$. Computationally, this can all be done by table lookup in a 256-long table and is referred to as the S function.
3. ShiftRows: This consists entirely of byte-oriented memory moves of the array of state.
4. MixColumns: Mathematically, the MixColumns operation involves modular polynomial operations using polynomials in X whose coefficients are elements of $GF(2^8)$. Computationally, the polynomial arithmetic is just byte moves in memory following arithmetic on the coefficients in $GF(2^8)$. In the case of encryption, the coefficient arithmetic is very easy because one needs only to multiply coefficients by 1, x, and $x + 1$. In the case of decryption, the multipliers are more complicated and the arithmetic is thus harder to implement in hardware. In the case of a software implementation, neither is a complicated operation since the multiplication is usually done with a table lookup.
5. AddRoundKey: This operation is simply an XOR of the key for the round and the state.

9.5.1   Software Implementations

The primary points of concern for any software implementation clearly come down to three computations.

1. The $GF(2^8)$ arithmetic appearing in several places.
2. The byte-oriented finite field operations in MixColumns.
3. The issue of memory storage and/or access for the expanded key bits.

Since AES operates entirely on bytes, we can ignore the XOR operations and the byte movements of the ShiftRows step; there are no operations here that are not well-supported by the ISA of a standard processor.

We have already pointed out that the combined SubBytes operation can be done by table lookup with the S function. If not for this, then at other points in the computation one will need to be able to do arithmetic in $GF(2^8)$. Fortunately, this can be done with fixed arithmetic steps and does not need complex loops with decisions. The polynomial modulus is

$$m(x) = x^8 + x^4 + x^3 + x + 1,$$

so we have

$$x \cdot \sum_{i=0}^{7} a_i x^i = \sum_{i=0}^{7} a_i x^{i+1}$$

$$\equiv a_6 x^7 + a_5 x^6 + a_4 x^5 + (a_3 \oplus a_7) x^4 + (a_2 \oplus a_7) x^3 + a_1 x^2 +$$

$$(a_0 \oplus a_7) x^1 + a_7 \pmod{m(x)}$$

The modulus $m(x)$ is a 9-bit pattern $1 \mid 00011011$. Multiplication of the 8-bit pattern $a_7 a_6 a_5 a_4 a_3 a_2 a_1 a_0$ produces the 9-bit pattern

$$a_7 \mid a_6 a_5 a_4 a_3 a_2 a_1 a_0 0,$$

so in the case that $a_7 = 1$ we XOR the right-hand 8 bits with a mask 00011011 to perform the reduction modulo $m(x)$. In software, this can be implemented as a shift left that is possibly followed by an XOR with a mask 00011011. Multiplication by any element of $GF(2^8)$ can be accomplished by breaking that element down into its powers of x (in effect, by using the usual recursive doubling approach), so that the fundamental operation of multiplication by x (a.k.a. 02) is sufficient as a kernel.

One of the reasons for the choice of the polynomial $c(x)$ was that the coefficients 01, 02, and 03 allow for multiplication as a simple operation. Multiplication by 01 is in fact not multiplication; multiplication by 02 is the operation defined above, and multiplication by 03 is multiplication by 02 followed by an XOR. Unfortunately, the coefficients 09, $0B$, and $0D$, and $0E$ of the `InvMixColumns` step are not inherently so simple, if only because the nontrivial entries are more dense and the number of 1-bits greater, making for more bit operations required for the $GF(2^8)$ operation.

Fortunately, as pointed out by Daemen and Rijmen [10], P. Barreto has observed that the `InvMixColumns` multiplication is separable into two matrix products as follows.

$$\begin{pmatrix} 0E & 0B & 0D & 09 \\ 09 & 0E & 0B & 0D \\ 0D & 09 & 0E & 0B \\ 0B & 0D & 09 & 0E \end{pmatrix} = \begin{pmatrix} 02 & 03 & 01 & 01 \\ 01 & 02 & 03 & 01 \\ 01 & 01 & 02 & 03 \\ 03 & 01 & 01 & 02 \end{pmatrix} \times \begin{pmatrix} 05 & 00 & 04 & 00 \\ 00 & 05 & 00 & 04 \\ 04 & 00 & 05 & 00 \\ 04 & 04 & 00 & 05 \end{pmatrix}$$

This permits the `InvMixColumns` to be implemented with the following preprocessing step followed by the same multiplication as used in `MixColumns`.

On 32-bit or larger processor platforms, the same intraword operations can be implemented as on 8-bit platforms, but the longer wordlength can be an advantage in that one can handle four-byte columns in a single step.

Software for AES is relatively straightforward to implement, and use of the software features mentioned above mitigates substantially any complexities due to ISA shortcomings. As part of the original AES competition and selection process, it was necessary for reference code for each algorithm to be submitted. Reference code by P. Barreto and V. Rijmen appears in Daemen and Rijmen [10] and totals fewer than 350 lines of C, including four major tables for lookup of the $GF(2^8)$ arithmetic.

Several authors have reported during and then soon after the selection of AES the processing rate of software implementations of AES. Timings are notoriously quick to become obsolete, and timings are often difficult to compare. Lipmaa reported [11]

260 cycles per encryption, or 1.437 gigabits per second, for encryption and 257 cycles per decryption, or 1.453 gigabits per second, for decryption, with assembly language programs on a 3.05 MHz Pentium 4 processor, and 319 cycles (0.861 Gbit per second) and 344 cycles (0.798 Gbit per second) for encryption and decryption, respectively, with C programs (gcc 3.0.2) on a 2.25 MHz Athlon processor. Other implementations are reported at between 226 and 376 cycles on lesser processors, with the faster implementations being in assembly language and the slower implementations in C or C++. Gladman reported similar timings [12].

It is worth pointing out that the speed of AES in software is somewhat slower than either DES or Triple DES, but not significantly slower [13].

9.5.2 Hardware Implementations

AES was designed so that it might be suitable for smart-card and similar applications. Thus, although software implementations are of interest, the various hardware or programmable-logic implementations of AES are of interest, and in addition to speed, issues of silicon resources and attendant power consumption become relevant. Many of the hardware implementations were done prior to the adoption of Rijndael as the AES, and the papers were published in the AES conference proceedings. A number of these papers provide a comparative analysis of the five finalist algorithms. Some comparisons have also been published in other journals or conferences [14].

Hardware implementations of AES have been quite varied, in part due to the varied many different uses to which AES could be put. Many of these implementations have either been specific ASICs or ASIC designs; some have been architectural specifications for a processor that would support AES computations in a "native" mode. A large number of implementations have been made on Field Programmable Gate Arrays (FPGAs). Work continues on algorithmic means by which processing could be sped up under the assumption that one has, in hardware, substantial flexibility in how the bits are manipulated; among these studies are some on the best way by which the Galois Field arithmetic can be supported in hardware.

Hardware implementations, although varied, can generally be said to address one or more of the following questions.

1. If one were designing an ASIC for AES, what design would yield the absolutely the fastest throughput?
2. If one were designing an ASIC for AES, what design would yield the fastest throughput and use no more hardware than might be available on a smart card?
3. If one were designing an ASIC for AES, what design would yield the fastest throughput and use no more hardware than might be available on a network interface card?
4. If one were implementing AES on reconfigurable hardware (FPGAs), what design would yield the absolutely the fastest throughput?

5. If one were implementing AES on reconfigurable hardware, what design would yield the fastest throughput and use no more hardware than might be available on a smart card?
6. If one were implementing AES on reconfigurable hardware, what design would yield the fastest throughput and use no more hardware than might be available on a network interface card?

The FPGA-based implementations add another dimension to the definition of "best" in that they permit designing an implementation with the look and feel of an ASIC, but they must be placed on specific commercial chips. Where software implementations are constrained by the ISA of the processor, the FPGA implementations are constrained by the size and nature of the FPGA resources. In most instances, the eventual constraint on throughput is not on the AES core but on the bandwidth through the device of which the FPGA is a part.

Further, on either ASICs or FPGAs, there are methods either for improving performance or for decreasing size by rearranging the steps of the algorithm. If hardware size is not an issue, then the iterative loop of the rounds can be unrolled to pipeline the rounds themselves. This should permit increased throughput, at the cost of a latency that will not be noticed in steady state, but which will require hardware for each individual round instead of a single hardware module used repeatedly.

One effect of the loop unrolling is that the number of lookup tables might increase dramatically, since one would prefer to keep the tables physically close to the logic that uses the stored values. To avoid the hardware cost of the $GF(2^8)$ lookup tables, one can perform the arithmetic in hardware; one comparison showed a very dramatic decrease in hardware utilization and an increase in speed when this change was made to a design. An additional benefit is that memory access is inherently going to be sequential, working against the parallelism of hardware, and the on-chip memory resources of FPGAs are not sufficient to provide for all the tables needed in a fully unrolled AES design.

Even if the outer loop of rounds cannot be fully unrolled, there is also the possibility in hardware for combining the flow of processing inside the rounds. In general, the larger the hardware circuit to be synthesized by design tools, the more efficient and higher-performing the circuit will be (until the circuit is so large that the tools can no longer function properly). Larger designs provide more opportunity for synthesis tools to extract parallelism. Also, breaking a large design into modules often requires signals that must propagate from one module to another to be registered both on output and on input; if multiple modules are synthesized together, then such signals can be dealt without the artificial modularization.

9.6 Security

The primary reason for existence of a cryptographic algorithm is to maintain **confidentiality** of data, that is, to prevent disclosure of data to unauthorized parties. In its simplest application, a user would encrypt a data file so that it could be transmitted "in the clear" without fear that the contents could be read by someone not possessing the key. Conscious user action to encrypt the data can provide the security required, although in a corporate setting the data transmission software could be configured to make this transparent. Either way, the data need only be encrypted and decrypted once per transmission in this end-to-end method, and the management of keys is simplest of all the scenarios because keys need only be distributed to users.

A more complicated setting would exist if the goal were to encrypt the data payloads of individual packets after the transmission process has begun, and if the process of decryption and re-encryption were to take place at every link along the path from sender to receiver. Since the number of packets and the number of links would normally each be much larger than the number of files transmitted, and since the process would now have to be completely transparent to the users involved, this situation requires a much higher speed of encryption and decryption. This also requires a much different standard for the integrity of the key distribution process, since all the link-to-link connections must be provided with keys.

Regardless of the application, the fundamental question to be addressed with regard to any cryptographic algorithm is, "Is it secure?" The initial attempts at cryptanalysis, done as part of the AES evaluation process, are detailed in the NIST report. There has been subsequent work attacking AES, and one summary of some of perhaps most prominently by Courtois, who maintains (or maintained) a website [15]. Courtois is clearly skeptical about AES. In response to the NESSIE (New European Schemes for Signatures, Integrity and Encryption) press release (2003) that states that no weakness has been found in AES (or in 16 other algorithms submitted to the European competition), Courtois argues "This is simply not true and such a recommendation could have serious consequences." Much more positive, or at least less skeptical, about the status of AES is Landau [16], who writes "The cryptography community is a rather contentious lot, but it has been virtually unanimous in its praise of NIST's AES effort and the choice of Rijndael as the Advanced Encryption Standard. This is high praise indeed."

In spite of the complaints of Courtois, then, the future of AES seems assured. The NIST website, in the response to a frequently-asked-question, says that AES "has the potential to remain secure well beyond twenty years." It seems likely, then, that AES will continue to be an approved algorithm for U. S. government use for many years to come.

9.7 Exercises

1. (Programming exercise.) Verify that $x + 1$ is in fact of order 256 modulo the polynomial
$$m(x) = x^8 + x^4 + x^3 + x^1 + 1.$$

2. (Possible programming exercise.) Verify that $c(x)$ and $d(x)$ are inverses modulo $X^4 + 1$.

3. (Programming exercise.) Download the code from Appendix B, compile it, and verify that you are producing the same results as are in Appendix B.
4. (Programming exercise.) Download the code from Appendix B, compile it, and verify that you are producing the same results as are in Appendix B.
5. (Programming exercise.) Download the code from Appendix B, compile it, and verify that you have it correct by encrypting and then decrypting the message "this is the secret message". Notice that this will require two blocks (with padding on the second) of text, since this is more than 16 bytes in length.

References

1. NIST, Fips 46-3: data encryption standard (reaffirmed) (1999), http://csrc.nist.gov/publications/fips/fips46-3/fips46-3.pdf
2. W. Diffie, M.E. Hellman, Exhaustive cryptanalysis of the NBS DES. IEEE Comput. 74–84 (1977)
3. D. Coppersmith, A.M. Odlyzko, R. Schroeppel, Discrete logarithms in GF(p). Algorithmica 1–15 (1986)
4. S. Landau, Standing the test of time: The Data Encryption Standard. Not. Am. Math. Soc. **47**, 341–349 (2000)
5. NIST, Data Encryption Standard (1999), https://nvlpubs.nist.gov/nistpubs/sp958-lide/250-253.pdf
6. NIST, in *1st AES Candidate Conference* (1998), http://csrc.nist.gov/CryptoToolkit/aes/round1/conf1/aes1conf.htm
7. NIST, in *2nd AES Candidate Conference* (1998), http://csrc.nist.gov/CryptoToolkit/aes/round1/conf2/aes2conf.htm
8. NIST, in *3rd AES Candidate Conference* (2000), http://csrc.nist.gov/CryptoToolkit/aes/round2/conf3/aes3conf.htm
9. NIST, FIPS 197: announcing the advanced encryption standard (AES) (2000), http://csrc.nist.gov/encryption/aes/index.html
10. J. Daemen, V. Rijmen, *The Design of Rijndael*, 2nd edn. (Springer, Berlin, 2020)
11. H. Lipmaa, AES candidates: a survey of implementations (2004), http://www.tcs.hut.fi/~helger/aes
12. B. Gladman, Implementation experience with AES candidate algorithms, in *Proceedings, 2nd AES Candidate Conference* (1998)
13. C. Sanchez-Avila, R. Sanchez-Reillo, The Rijndael block cipher (AES proposal): a comparison with DES, in *Proceedings, 35th IEEE Carnahan Conference on Security Technology* (2001), pp. 229–234
14. A.A. Dandalis, V.K. Prasanna, J.D. Rolim, "A comparative study of performance of AES final candidate, in *Proceedings, 2nd International Workshop, Cryptographic Hardware and Embedded Systems*, ed. by Ç.K. Koç, C. Paar. Lecture Notes in Computer Science, vol. 1965 (2000), pp. 125–140
15. N.T. Courtois, Is AES a secure cipher? (2004) http://www.cryptosystem.net/aes. Accessed 17 Jun 2020
16. S. Landau, Communications security for the twenty-first century: the advanced encryption standard. Not. Am. Math. Soc. **47**, 450–459 (2000)

Asymmetric Ciphers—RSA and Others

10

Abstract

The notion of an asymmetric encryption system dates to the 1970s, with the first and still primary version of asymmetric encryption being the RSA algorithm of Rivest, Shamir, and Adleman. In asymmetric encryption, an encryption key that is made public is used to encrypt a message that is sent to the owner of the public key. That owner then uses a privately held key to decrypt. The RSA algorithm relies on a choice of two large primes p and q, multiplied together to produce a modulus $N = pq$. The public encryption key e and private decryption key d are chosen so that $ed \equiv 1 \pmod{\phi(N)}$. Current knowledge of the mathematics is that if N and e are public, but p, q, and d are kept private, then decrypting a message requires factoring N into p times q, and that is computationally hard. In this chapter we lay out the foundation of the RSA process, with an example, and we comment on the current records in factoring as a estimate of the security of RSA.

10.1 History

AES is at present the state of the art in symmetric encryption. The algorithm was vetted in a rigorous competition, promulgated by NIST as a U. S. national standard, and has proven to be resistant to all attempts at finding practical attacks. But AES is nonetheless a symmetric encryption system that requires both sender and receiver to know the key, and this therefore requires that sender and receiver have had some other, secure, mechanism by which to transmit that key.

The problem of secure key distribution has plagued throughout the centuries all those who would use cryptography. Anyone who uses cryptography must always remember that the best symmetric cryptography available is totally compromised if the keys have not been kept secret.

© The Author(s), under exclusive license to Springer Nature Switzerland AG 2021   149
D. Buell, *Fundamentals of Cryptography*, Undergraduate Topics in Computer Science,
https://doi.org/10.1007/978-3-030-73492-3_10

It was thus a major new idea when Whit Diffie and Martin Hellman published a paper that argued that asymmetric encryption might be possible, in which the key used to encrypt was not the same as the key used to decrypt [1]. Diffie and Hellman proposed a scheme by which a publicly-available key would allow anyone to encrypt a message to be sent to a receiver, but encryption would not be the same as decryption, and it would require a separate, private, key, held only by the receiver, to decrypt the message.

Diffie and Hellman did not propose an algorithm that might permit this "non-secret" encryption. That came almost immediately from Rivest, Shamir, and Adleman, in their seminal paper describing what is now known as the RSA algorithm [2] and that almost (due to the efforts of the U. S. government) never saw the light of day. The two papers have been the classic public beginnings of public-key cryptography.

As of today, because their papers were the first to be, published, these authors remain the ones credited with the discoveries (or inventions?). There is a contrary view, however, from the United Kingdom. In the late 1990s, the British government released documents that suggest that its researchers should get credit for first having these ideas. The work of Diffie, Hellman, Rivest, Shamir, and Adleman, was in fact perhaps already done by Clifford Cocks, James Ellis, and Malcolm Williamson, with some prodding by Nick Patterson, at GCHQ (Government Communications Headquarters) in the United Kingdom nearly a decade earlier [3]. The actual origins of public-key cryptography are thus up for discussion, but the utility is accepted.

10.2 RSA Public-Key Encryption

The fundamental question for public-key cryptography is this: Is there an algorithm that will allow publication of an encryption key, that anyone can see and use, that will produce via encryption a "random" bits version of a message, and that can only be decrypted by the intended recipient by use of a private key held private by the recipient?

The answer to this, by Rivest, Shamir, and Adleman, is "yes", provided we accept the assumptions that encryption should be fast, that decryption by those who know the private key should be fast, but that decryption (by something possibly better than brute-force encryption) should be at least "computationally impossible" even for adversaries with state-of-the-art computational facilities.

And the answer comes from one of the deep and as-yet-still-difficult problems in computational number theory.

10.2.1 The Basic RSA Algorithm

Let us choose two primes, p and q, each of 1024 bits, say, and consider the 2048-bit product $N = pq$. We can view a 2048-bit block of a message to be an integer M modulo 2^{2048}. If the message is in 8-bit ASCII, for example, then the 2048 bit blocks can be taken to be an integer base $2^8 = 256$ of $2048/8 = 256$ digits. We choose an exponent e, an integer modulo 2^{2048}, as the publicly-known encryption exponent. We publish e to the known universe, and we thus allow anyone to send us the value $E = M^e \pmod{N}$; this is the encryption of the message M.

We know the values of p and q, but we have kept them secret. We know that the order of the group modulo N is $\phi(N) = (p-1)(q-1)$, but no one else knows this, because no one else has the factoring of N into p and q, and because computing $\phi(N)$ without factoring N is, as far as is known now, a computationally hard problem.

Since the integer residues modulo N form a group modulo N of order $\phi(N)$, and since we know the value of $\phi(N)$, we know that we can determine a value d such that $ed \equiv 1 \pmod{\phi(N)}$. Since $\phi(N)$ is the order of the group modulo the composite integer N, we know that $x^{ed} \equiv x^1 \pmod{N}$ for any x.

Therefore, ...

$$E^d \equiv (M^e)^d \equiv M^{ed} \equiv M^1 \equiv M \pmod{N}$$

We publish the product N and the encryption exponent e. We keep secret the factoring of N into the product $N = pq$, the value of $\phi(N)$, and the decryption exponent d. Anyone who wants to send us a secure message M can send $M^e \equiv E \pmod{N}$. Only we have the value of d and can decrypt.

This is the basic RSA encryption scheme, which relies for security on the difficulty of determining d given only e and N.

Current theory is that there is no good computational mechanism for getting d from e and N without knowing $\phi(N)$, and that there is no good computational mechanism for knowing $\phi(N)$ without factoring N into p times q.

Current theory thus says that breaking the RSA algorithm requires the ability to factor large integers (of, say, 2048 bits), and current theory and practice say that this is in general a computationally infeasible problem.

10.3 Implementation

To implement an RSA encryption scheme, we must first find large primes p and q, each of (say) 1024 bits. That is not in fact all that difficult. The prime number theorem says that the number of primes less than or equal to x is approximately

$$\frac{x}{\log x}.$$

This means that there are approximately

$$2^{1024}/1024$$

primes of 1024 bits or less, and approximately

$$2^{1023}/1023$$

primes of 1023 bits or less, so by a rough count there are almost as many 1024-bit primes as there are primes of less than or equal to 1023 bits. Finding primes is not that hard. The prime number theorem is an asymptotic result, and there are issues of which logarithms one might use, but 2^{1023} is a number of more than 300 decimals, and we don't need to worry about gaining or losing a factor of 10 or even 100 in estimating computational cost.

(We will see in Chaps. 11 and 12 that there are certain kinds of primes to avoid, but this is an easy thing to determine, and the primes that are poor choices can easily be avoided.)

We need to determine e, and then d. As with the choice of primes, there are certain values of e to avoid, but there are lots of suitable e to use. Given e, determining d is no more difficult than two applications of a generalized Euclidean algorithm, followed by one application of the Chinese Remainder Theorem. The hard part of setting up an RSA cryptosystem, then, is determining suitable p, q, and then e.

Given that, we can publish N and e and wait for messages to be sent to us with the cryptosystem.

10.3.1   An Example

We will illustrate the RSA cryptosystem with an example. As can be inferred from Chaps. 3 and 4, the order of the group modulo $N = pq$ is $\phi(N) = (p - 1)(q - 1)$. If we were to choose p and q such that both $(p - 1)/2$ and $(q - 1)/2$ were prime, we would have the longest possible multiplicative cycle and fewest number of zero divisors for any group of size about N for which N had exactly two prime factors.

We will choose

$$p = 4294900427 = 2 \times 2147450213 + 1$$

and

$$q = 4294901243 = 2 \times 2147450621 + 1.$$

2147450213 and 2147450621 are both prime. These happen to be two such primes of 32 bits each, so the product

$$N = 18446173182483530761$$

is 64 bits in length, and

$$\phi(N) = (4294900427 - 1) * (4294901243 - 1) = 18446173173893729092.$$

We need an encryption exponent e and a decryption exponent d chosen such that

$$ed \equiv 1 \pmod{\phi(N)}.$$

If we choose $e = 1111111111$, a simple Euclidean algorithm shows that the decryption exponent $d = 13522443910346794455$ and that

$$1111111111 * 13522443910346794455 \equiv 1 \pmod{18446173173893729092}.$$

If our message to be encrypted is the eight-byte message "the text", this becomes

$$\begin{array}{cccccccc} t & h & e & & t & e & x & t \\ 74 & 68 & 65 & 32 & 74 & 65 & 78 & 74 \end{array}$$

with the second row being the ASCII code in hexadecimal, and thus the message, in ASCII, whose bits are interpreted as a 64-bit integer, is the integer

$$8392569455039047796.$$

We now encrypt, compute

$$8392569455039047796^{1111111111} \pmod{N} \equiv 2134423211333931089$$

and then (miracle of miracles) decrypt as a check:

$$2134423211333931089^{13522443910346794455} \pmod{N} \equiv 8392569455039047796.$$

Clearly, for longer messages, we can break the message into eight-byte blocks and encrypt each block separately. For a serious implementation of RSA, we might choose p and q each to be 1024 bits long, for N of 2048 bits, and then encrypt in 256-byte blocks.

10.4 How Hard Is It to Break RSA?

Clearly, RSA is only secure if it is computationally infeasible to determine the decryption exponent d given the modulus N and the encryption exponent e. The current state of the theory is that there is no way to compute d from e without knowing $\phi(N)$, and that there is no way to know the value of $\phi(N)$ without factoring N. The security of RSA, then, relies on the difficulty of factoring large integers N, then, where N might be 2048 bits long and is the product of two primes p and q of about equal size.

There are certainly bad choices of p and q that can be made, as we will see in the next chapters. There are also bad choices of e. But as mentioned above, there are lots of primes, and choosing good ones is not really a difficult task. Further, factoring was a difficult computational problem even before it became something of cryptographic interest, and it has remained difficult even with the enormous interest that comes with its cryptographic significance. The recent history of factoring records includes the following in Table 10.1 from a list of challenge numbers published by Rivest, Shamir, and Adleman. In many instances, the computations needed to factor these challenge values took months or years of computing.

10.5 Other Groups

It should be clear that there is no real magic in the choice of integer factoring for this kind of asymmetric cryptography for which knowing how to encrypt a message does not imply knowing how to decrypt someone else's messages. What is key to using RSA as a cryptographic algorithm is that one has a group modulo N, and that, given a public value e used to encrypt, it is difficult to determine the inverse value d in the group because it is difficult to determine the order $\phi(N)$ of the group. We need to

Table 10.1 Record factorings from the RSA challenge numbers

Name	Decimals	Bits	Factoring announced
RSA-129	129	426	April 1994
RSA-130	130	430	April 1996
RSA-140	140	463	February 1999
RSA-150	150	496	2004
RSA-160	160	530	April 2003
RSA-170	170	563	December 2009
RSA-576	174	576	December 2003
RSA-180	180	596	May 2010
RSA-190	190	629	November 2010
RSA-640	193	640	November 2005
RSA-200	200	633	May 2005
RSA-210	210	696	September 2013
RSA-704	212	704	July 2012
RSA-220	220	729	May 2016
RSA-230	230	762	August 2018
RSA-232	232	768	February 2020
RSA-768	232	768	December 2009
RSA-240	240	795	November 2019
RSA-250	250	829	February 2020

have a large cycle in the group order (hence our choice, in the example, of primes p and q for which $p - 1$ and $q - 1$ were twice a prime) in order to make brute force attacks infeasible.

We recall that Fermat's Little Theorem on which determining e and d is based is really Lagrange's Theorem that applies to any group. Other groups could be used and have been suggested in the literature. The most important of these is the group of points on an elliptic curve, and cryptography using elliptic curves is the topic of Chap. 14. The two major advantages of elliptic curves lie in the ability to get the same degree of computational infeasibility with far fewer bits (and thus less computation) and in the absence of even the kind of attack that is the General Number Field Sieve for factoring.

Other than elliptic curves, however, the suggestions for using other groups, while cryptographically as secure, have failed to be promising alternatives. At the heart of an RSA-like method is the exponentiation of an element in a group. For RSA, that exponentiation is modular multiplication so as to compute a^b in a group. For the other groups that have been suggested, the basic group operation is much more complicated and thus much slower, hence the lack of adoption of such ideas. Virtually all the other group-based suggestions require modular arithmetic modulo large integers, and it is essentially impossible to do the same mathematics with fewer arithmetic operations than RSA needs. One squaring for each bit of N, and one multiplication for the (roughly) half that many bits that happen to be 1, is about as simple as could be imagined.

On the other hand, RSA as a cryptographic algorithm is slower than, say, AES, and RSA *per se* is not extensively used for cryptography. One of the major features of AES is that it is byte-oriented and can be made table-driven, while exponentiation modulo N requires multiplication with multiprecise integers and is inherently slow. For this reason, as we will see in Chap. 13, although RSA is not widely used for cryptography, a variant idea, based on largely the same underlying number theory, is used for key exchange.

10.6 Exercises

1. (Probable programming exercise.) Use $N = 193 \times 223 = 43039$ as the modulus for an RSA cryptosystem and $e = 23$. Compute d. Then encrypt and decrypt (for verification purposes) the message "message" one byte at a time (padding the last with a blank). Note that since 43039 is smaller than 46340, all the arithmetic can be done using 32-bit signed arithmetic, almost regardless of the programming language used.

2. (Programming exercise.) Using a programming language that allows for multiprecise arithmetic, either natively (Python) or with packages (C++ or Java), extend your solution to the previous exercise to do the computation of the example of Sect. 10.3.1.

3. (Probable programming exercise.) It is tempting to think of choosing two primes p and q of 1024 bits each, say, and then breaking the message in $2048/8 = 256$ blocks. There can be a problem with this, though, because the modulus N will be less than 2^{2048} and could be smaller than the integer that encodes the message. Test this using $p = 241$ and $q = 251$, so $N = 60491$, and verify that a two-byte message that encodes to an integer 60492 through 65536 will result in a decryption to the wrong message.

References

1. W. Diffie, M.E. Hellman, New directions in cryptography. IEEE Trans. Inf. Theory IT-**22**, 644–654 (1976)
2. R.L. Rivest, A. Shamir, L. Adleman, A method for obtaining digital signatures and public-key cryptosystems. Commun. ACM 120–126 (1978)
3. J.H. Ellis, The history of non-secret encryption. Cryptologia **23**, 267–273 (1999)

How to Factor a Number

11

Abstract

The security of the RSA cryptosystem is based on the difficulty of factoring integers N that are the products of two large primes p and q. If p and q are chosen well, then factoring N is indeed hard, but there are also factoring methods that work very quickly on certain kinds of integers. In order to ensure security of an RSA system, one must be careful to choose an N that does not succumb to one of the faster methods. We will discuss the Pollard rho and Pollard $p - 1$ methods first. These are not only used in general for factoring, but have been generalized to be applicable in other attacks against cryptographic systems. We then move on to CFRAC, a precursor to the state-of-the-art factoring method that is the primary topic of Chap. 12.

Dedication

We dedicate this chapter to the memory of Richard Guy, whose paper with the same title [1] as this chapter is a legendary contribution to the literature on factoring (and thus on cryptography). Richard Guy died, at 103 years old, on 9 March 2020, contributing to mathematics until only a few weeks before his death. It is our hope that this chapter does justice to a great scholar and friend.

Introduction

In general, we are going to look at RSA encryption using a modulus $N = pq$, where p and q are large primes (of, say, 2048 bits each). It is generally agreed that even the heavy-duty factoring algorithms won't succeed on moduli N of 4096 bits with well-chosen p and q factors. But there are a number of factoring algorithms that are relatively cheap to run and that will provide a factoring of N if p and q are chosen badly, and there are middle-grade algorithms that will also succeed some of the time. It is incumbent on anyone who might choose to implement RSA encryption that one bangs at N with these lesser algorithms just to make sure that good primes have been used, or at least to avoid primes known likely to lead to a lower-cost factoring of N.

Some of the factoring methods described below are heuristics and won't always produce a factor quickly. Some will essentially always produce a factoring, but with a running time that is provably too long to be of use in attacking a well-chosen RSA implementation.

We remark at the outset that at least one factor of any integer N must be smaller than the square root of N, but that trial division of N by all the primes less than $\sqrt{N}$ is so infeasible as to be dismissed outright as a possibility. The Prime Number Theorem [2] says that the number of primes less than or equal to x, which we write as $\pi(x)$, satisfies

$$\lim_{x \to \infty} \frac{\pi(x)}{\frac{x}{\ln x}} = 1$$

and for values of x as large as come up in RSA encryption, the limit of 1 is nearly reached. That is, there are, within at worst a factor not much different from 1, more than 10^{600} primes of 2048 bits. If we thus assume $N = pq$ with p and q each of 2048 bits, we would need to do trial division by more than 10^{600} primes, which is simply impossible; planet Earth has only been in existence for about $4.5 \cdot 10^{18}$ nanoseconds.

Factoring was a curious academic enterprise prior to the publication of the RSA algorithm. For many years the standard reference of "hard" factorings to be attempted was the "Cunningham tables" first done by Allan J. C. Cunningham beginning in 1925 and then updated by a number of authors [3]. An extensive literature exists from before the invention of the Number Field Sieve (the NFS, which we almost introduce in Chap. 12) [4–19]. Since the introduction of the NFS, most work on factoring has been to improve the running time, but not the basic algorithm.

11.1 Pollard rho

The Pollard rho factoring method [1,20] is a heuristic that only works for certain integers one might want to factor. However, it is a simple and fast method and can always be tried just to see if it's going to work.

Let's assume we are trying to factor $N = 1037 = 17 \cdot 61$.

We iterate a simple function, like $x_n^2 = x_{n-1}^2 - 1$ repeatedly. We start with x_1 and x_2, and then iterate x_1 to x_2 and iterate x_2 twice to get x_3 and then x_4. We then iterate x_2 once and x_4 twice. In steady state, we do three iterations of the function to obtain the values of x_m and x_{2m}, all taken modulo $N = 1037$. As we go, we take $\gcd(x_m - x_{2m}, N)$ and hope to get a factor of N popping out.

m	x_m	x_{2m}	$x_m - x_{2m}$	gcd
1	2	8	−6	1
2	3	63	−60	1
3	8	252	−244	61
4	63	369	−306	17
5	857			
6	252			
7	246			
8	369			

What happens is this: As one runs the x_i at single speed and double speed, the values x_i and x_{2i} must eventually collide, because there are only finitely many values modulo p for any prime factor p of N. The "rho" comes from the appearance of the cycle, and we use the term *epact* for the prime p for the least m such that we have $x_{2m} \equiv x_m$ (mod p) and m is not less than the tail length that leads in to the cycle. If N is the product of two primes, we hope that the epacts for the two factors will not be the same, or else we would get N for the gcd and not just one of the two factors. In practice, with large primes, this won't be a problem.

And in general, rather than take the gcd with every step, we would accumulate a running product modulo N and only take gcd's every 100 steps, or perhaps every 1000 steps, depending on one's taste.

Finally, we present a scatter plot of all epacts for primes to ten million. The scatter plot is actually of

$$\frac{epact(p)}{\sqrt{p} \ln p}$$

which can be seen to be a slowly decreasing constant generally smaller than 0.2 for primes p of this size.

We note, however, that this method almost certainly won't factor integers that would be used for RSA encryption. If $N = pq$ and the primes p and q are each 2048 bits long, then we would expect to have to step the iteration more than $2^{1024} \approx 10^{308}$ times before we hit the epact and found a factor.

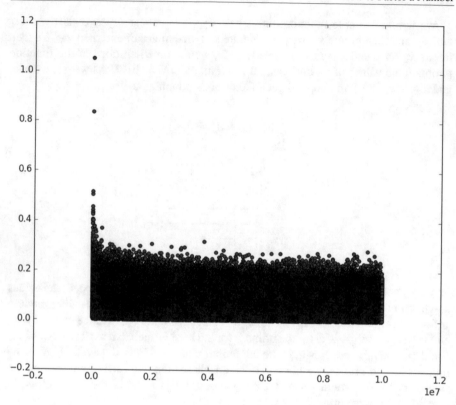

11.2 Pollard $p - 1$

The Pollard $p - 1$ factoring method [21] is the forerunner of a number of methods.

We remember Lagrange's Theorem, that the order of the multiplicative group mod a prime p is $p - 1$ and that any element raised to the order of the group is the identity.

To factor an integer N, then, we first compute an enormous exponent $M = \prod q_i^{e_i}$ that is the product of all small primes q_i to high powers e_i, for some vague definitions of "all", "small", and "high". For example, one could take the 78498 primes up to one million raised to the highest exponent such that $q_i^{e_i}$ is still a 32-bit number. This value of M is an integer of about 3 million bits.

We now choose a residue a (like 3) and compute

$$a^M \equiv b \pmod{N}.$$

Now, if it happens that N is divisible by a prime p for which $p - 1$ divides M, then we have

$$a^M \equiv b \equiv 1 \pmod{p}$$

and by taking

$$\gcd(b - 1, N)$$

we extract the factor p.

In general, we would not expect to be able to factor RSA-type N using this approach. In order for the $p-1$ method to work, the order of the group modulo some factor of N would have to be "crumbly", that is, would have to comprise only small prime factors, and that's not likely. However, the existence of this factoring attack implies that one should specifically guard against being susceptible to it when one chooses the two primes with which to create N. Part of choosing primes p and q with which to create $N = pq$ must be to verify that each of $p-1$ and $q-1$ have a very large prime factor; that would prevent a Pollard $p-1$ attack from succeeding.

11.2.1 The General Metaphysics of $p-1$

The $p-1$ method is the forerunner of a number of such algorithms.

We assume that we have a group, such as the group of residues under multiplication modulo a prime. We assume that we have a way to "hack for" the order of the group to a factor of N; in the case of traditional $p-1$, that's the $\gcd(b-1, N)$ part. The entire method is a bit of a hack in the original sense of the term. But it works.

So we simply exponentiate a group element to a large power M in hopes of getting the factor to pop out from the group structure.

This basic approach shows up later in other factoring methods that use different groups instead of just the integers themselves modulo N.

11.2.2 Step Two of $p-1$

What has been described above is Step One of the $p-1$ method. Step Two is as follows:

Beyond a certain point, one would not expect $p-1$, the order of the group, to be divisible by the square of a prime, so we need only include in M primes to the first power. And beyond a certain point we might assume that we were missing only a single prime in the order of the group, that is, that M contained all of $p-1$ except for one last prime somewhat larger than the primes we included in our calculation of M. So we exponentiate one more prime at a time.

If we have originally chosen to take the primes to 100 thousand, then the next primes would be 100003, 100019, 100043, 100049, and 100057. We exponentiate to the 100003-rd power to add 100003 to M, and either take the gcd or multiply in the $b-1$ value to a running product just as we did with Pollard rho. Then we exponentiate only 16 more steps to replace 100003 by 100019, then 24 more steps to replace 100019 with 100043, and so forth. This is cheap and can be effective.

11.3 CFRAC

CFRAC, the continued fraction algorithm, was first proposed by Lehmer and Powers back about 1930, but was not implemented seriously until 1970, because it doesn't always work. That makes it tediously annoying if done by hand, but less so if it's the computer that simply fails several times before succeeding. Indeed, Morrison and Brillhart's [22,23] use of it in 1970 to factor $F_7 = 2^{2^7} + 1$, an integer of 39 decimals, began an entirely new era in research on factoring.

Mersenne, as far back as 1643, used the difference-of-squares method for factoring integers. If an integer N to be factored can be written as a difference of squares, say

$$N = x^2 - y^2, \tag{11.1}$$

then we have an algebraic factoring

$$N = (x + y)(x - y).$$

the problem, of course, is that for large N this is impractical, since there isn't much that can be tested that looks much better than trial division.

CFRAC, and the sieve methods that have followed it and that are now the workhorse methods for factoring large N, are based on a simplification of the above equation: rather than solving Eq. (11.1) as an *equation*, we solve the *congruence*

$$x^2 - y^2 \equiv 0 \quad (\text{mod } N)$$

and then we compute

$$m = \gcd(N, x + y)$$

and

$$n = \gcd(N, x - y).$$

We have an algebraic factoring of N into $x + y$ times $x - y$, and we hope that if $N = pq$ for a cryptographic N that is the product of two large primes p and q, we don't get the trivial factorings $(m, n) = (1, N)$ or $(m, n) = (N, 1)$ when we compute the two gcd's. If we do get one of these two results, we continue to find another pair of x and y values to be used. (This is the failure part that would make it tedious to calculate by hand.)

11.3.1 Continued Fractions

We illustrate the concept of a continued fraction by example. Consider the value $267/111$. We write this as

$$267/111 = 2 + 45/111$$

The algorithm should be obvious (although it might not necessarily be clear why anyone would care to implement such an algorithm):

- Write the quantity as $a_0 + z_0$, where $0 \le z_0 < 1$.
- Write z_0 as $\frac{1}{1/z_0}$, noting that $1/z_0 > 1$.

- Write $\frac{1}{1/z_0}$ as $\frac{1}{a_1+z_1}$, where $0 \leq z_1 < 1$.
- Rinse and repeat.

Let's motivate the recurrences to follow with something that isn't quite a proof but is close and should make the recurrences more understandable.

Let's say we have a continued fraction

$$a_0 + \cfrac{1}{a_1 + \cfrac{1}{a_2 + \cfrac{1}{a_3 + \cfrac{1}{\cdots}}}}$$

which we will write as

$$R = [a_0, a_1, a_2, a_3, \ldots]$$

for integers a_i, and for the moment we won't care whether it's a finite or infinite continued fraction.

We're going to evaluate

$$R_0 = p_0/q_0 = [a_0]$$
$$R_1 = p_1/q_1 = [a_0, a_1]$$
$$R_2 = p_2/q_2 = [a_0, a_1, a_2]$$
$$R_3 = p_3/q_3 = [a_0, a_1, a_2, a_3]$$

These are all rational numbers, since the a_i are integers, and thus we can assume p_i and q_i are integers. We will call p_i and q_i the *convergents*.

So let's unwind the algebra.

$$R_0 = p_0/q_0 = [a_0]$$

so we have

$$p_0 = a_0$$
$$q_0 = 1$$

Now

$$R_1 = p_1/q_1 = a_0 + \frac{1}{a_1} = \frac{a_0 a_1 + 1}{a_1}$$

so we have

$$p_1 = a_0 a_1 + 1 = a_1(p_0) + 1$$
$$q_1 = a_1 = a_1(q_0) + 0$$

Continuing, we have

$$R_2 = p_2/q_2 = a_0 + \cfrac{1}{a_1 + \frac{1}{a_2}}$$

$$= a_0 + \cfrac{1}{\frac{a_1 a_2 + 1}{a_2}}$$

$$= a_0 + \cfrac{a_2}{a_1 a_2 + 1}$$

$$= \frac{a_0 a_1 a_2 + a_0 + a_2}{a_1 a_2 + 1}$$

$$= \frac{a_2(a_0 a_1 + 1) + a_0}{a_2(a_1) + 1}$$

$$= \frac{a_2(p_1) + p_0}{a_2(q_1) + q_0}$$

so we have

$$p_2 = a_2(a_0 a_1 + 1) + a_0 = a_2(p_1) + p_0$$
$$q_2 = a_2(a_1) = a_2(q_1) + q_0$$

Finally,

$$R_3 = p_3/q_3 = a_0 + \cfrac{1}{a_1 + \cfrac{1}{a_2 + \frac{1}{a_3}}}$$

$$= a_0 + \cfrac{1}{a_1 + \cfrac{1}{\frac{a_2 a_3 + 1}{a_3}}}$$

$$= a_0 + \cfrac{1}{a_1 + \cfrac{a_3}{a_2 a_3 + 1}}$$

$$= a_0 + \cfrac{1}{\frac{a_1 a_2 a_3 + a_1 + a_3}{a_2 a_3 + 1}}$$

$$= a_0 + \cfrac{a_2 a_3 + 1}{a_1 a_2 a_3 + a_1 + a_3}$$

$$= \frac{a_0 a_1 a_2 a_3 + a_0 a_1 + a_0 a_3 + a_2 a_3 + 1}{a_1 a_2 a_3 + a_1 + a_3}$$

$$= \frac{a_3(a_0 a_1 a_2 + a_0 + a_2) + a_0 a_1 + 1}{a_3(a_1 a_2 + 1) + a_1}$$

so we have

$$p_3 = a_3(a_0 a_1 a_2 + a_0 + a_2) + a_0 a_1 + 1 = a_3(p_2) + p_1$$
$$q_3 = a_3(a_1 a_2 + 1) + a_1 = a_3(q_2) + q_1$$

We have used the term *convergent* for the successive initial parts of the continued fraction. Although we will not prove it, we can observe why that term is used by looking at the convergents from our example of $267/111 = 89/37 \approx 2.405$.

$$R_0 = [2] = 2 = 2.0$$

$$R_1 = [2, 2] = 2 + \frac{1}{2} = 2.5$$

$$R_2 = [2, 2, 2] = 2 + \frac{1}{2 + \frac{1}{2}} = \frac{12}{5} = 2.4$$

$$R_3 = [2, 2, 2, 7] = 2 + \frac{1}{2 + \frac{1}{2+1/7}} = \frac{89}{37}$$

We notice that the even-subscripted R_i are smaller and the odd-subscripted are larger than the value whose continued fraction we are computing. The R_i can be shown to be converging.

Theorem 11.1 *If r is a rational number, then it has a finite continued fraction expansion.*

Theorem 11.2 *If $z \in \mathbb{R}$, then it has a continued fraction expansion that is eventually periodic if and only if it is $a + b\sqrt{n}$, where $n \in \mathbb{Z}$.*

The second of these theorems says that quadratic irrationals have continued fraction expansions that are eventually periodic.

11.3.2 The CFRAC Algorithm

Our goal is to factor N. We expand what is essentially the continued fraction for $\sqrt{N}$. What motivates us is the thought that if we can create a congruence

$$X^2 \equiv Y^2 \pmod{N},$$

then we would have

$$(X - Y)(X + Y) \equiv 0 \pmod{N},$$

and it just might happen that one of the two factors of N would divide $X - Y$ and the other would divide $X + Y$. If this were the case, then computing $\gcd(N, X - Y)$ would cause a factor of N to pop out.

Let

$$i = 0$$
$$P_0 = 0$$
$$Q_0 = 1$$
$$a_0 = [\sqrt{N}]$$
$$p_{-2} = 0$$
$$p_{-1} = 1$$
$$q_{-2} = 1$$
$$q_{-1} = 0$$

We now repeat:

$$p_i = a_i \cdot p_{i-1} + p_{i-2} \pmod{N}$$
$$q_i = a_i \cdot q_{i-1} + q_{i-2} \pmod{N}$$
$$P_{i+1} = a_i \cdot Q_i - P_i$$
$$Q_{i+1} = \frac{N - P_{i+1}^2}{Q_i}$$
$$a_i = \left[\frac{P_{i+1} + \sqrt{N}}{Q_{i+1}} \right]$$

We note that we always have

$$p_i^2 - Nq_i^2 = (-1)^{i+1} Q_{i+1}. \tag{11.2}$$

We are trying to create

$$X^2 \equiv Y^2 \pmod{N},$$

and the square value on one side, p_i^2, is always present. The essence of all modern heavy-duty factoring methods is to find a subset of the $(-1)^i Q_i$ which, when multiplied together, forms a square.[1]

To find this subset of $(-1)^i Q_i$, we factor the $(-1)^i Q_i$ over a *factor base* of "small" primes, where we only save the parity of the exponents. If we get to a point where we have a subset of subscripts S such that

$$\prod_{i \in S} (-1)^i Q_i \pmod{N}$$

is a square, then we have a congruence as desired with

$$X = \prod_{i \in S} p_{i-1} \pmod{N}$$

and

$$Y = \sqrt{\prod_{i \in S} (-1)^i Q_i} \pmod{N}$$

with Y an integer, and

$$X^2 \equiv Y^2 \pmod{N}.$$

Unless we are extremely unlucky, we will find that $\gcd(X - Y, N)$ and $\gcd(X + Y, N)$ will yield factors of N.

We will call an integer *smooth* if it factors completely over the factor base. The CRAC algorithm succeeds if one can get enough smooth numbers, with their factorings, to allow for the linear combinations that produce two squares congruent to each other modulo N. The size of the factor base is important. If it is chosen too small,

---

[1]This isn't quite true; the number field sieve uses roots of polynomials not of degree 2 but of degrees usually 5 or 6, and some more algebraic number theory, but the essence of the computational part is the same.

not enough of the Q_i will factor completely. If it is chosen too large, then testing individual integers for smoothness will be too slow. And what is important to know, but that we shall not prove, is that the magnitudes of the Q_i are bounded by $\sqrt{N}$; we have a control on the size of the integers we are testing for smoothness.

And we remark that the only primes we need to worry about in the factor base are the primes for which N is a quadratic residue; for any prime q dividing the Q_i of Eq. (11.2) we must have

$$p_i^2 - Nq_i^2 \equiv 0 \pmod{q}.$$

There is always the possibility that we will be unlucky and will get a gcd that is either 1 or all of N. This is the place where the algorithm can fail and was the reason it was not pursued when first invented. When humans do the calculations, success needs to be the outcome; when computers are used, one can simply have the program keep working until success is finally achieved.

11.3.3 Example

Let $N = 1000009$, and use as our factor base the primes 19 and smaller. (We can skip 7 and 11 since N is not a quadratic residue modulo those primes.) We include -1 as a "prime" since the signs on the Q_i alternate. The primes in boldface are larger than the largest prime in our factor base, and the corresponding Q_i are not smooth.

i	p_{i-1}	q_{i-1}	P_i	Q_i	a_i	Q_i factored
1	1000	1	1000	9	222	$[-1, 3, 3]$
2	222001	222	998	445	4	$[2, 3, \mathbf{37}]$
3	889004	889	782	873	2	$[3, 3, \mathbf{97}]$
4	1000000	2000	964	81	24	$[3, 3, 3, 3]$
5	888788	48889	980	489	4	$[3, \mathbf{163}]$
6	555116	197556	976	97	20	$[\mathbf{97}]$
7	991009	999982	964	729	2	$[-1, 3, 3, 3, 3, 3, 3]$
8	537116	197502	494	1037	1	$[17, \mathbf{61}]$
9	528116	197475	543	680	2	$[-1, 2, 2, 2, 5, 17]$
10	593339	592452	817	489	3	$[3, \mathbf{163}]$
11	308115	974822	650	1181	1	$[\mathbf{1181}]$
12	901454	567265	531	608	2	$[2, 2, 2, 2, 2, 19]$
13	111005	109334	685	873	1	$[3, 3, \mathbf{97}]$
14	12450	676599	188	1105	1	$[5, 13, 17]$
15	123455	785933	917	144	13	$[-1, 2, 2, 2, 2, 3, 3]$
16	617356	893638	955	611	3	$[13, \mathbf{47}]$
17	975514	466820	878	375	5	$[-1, 3, 5, 5, 5]$
18	494881	227711	997	124	16	$[2, 2, 2, 2]$
19	340200	702732	987	1615	1	$[-1, 5, 17, 19]$
20	835081	930443	628	375	4	$[3, 5, 5, 5]$
21	680497	424468	872	639	2	$[3, 3, \mathbf{71}]$
22	196057	779370	406	1307	1	$[\mathbf{1307}]$
23	876554	203829	901	144	13	$[-1, 2, 2, 2, 2, 3, 3]$
24	591160	429120	971	397	4	$[\mathbf{397}]$
25	241167	920300	617	1560	1	$[-1, 2, 2, 2, 3, 5, 13]$

We now look for subsets of this list where the factorings have exponents that all sum to zero mod 2 (meaning that the product of the corresponding Q_i would be a perfect square). We note that we treat -1 as if it were a prime; we need an even number of -1 values in our factorings in order to get a square (and not the negative of a square). We find that

$$\{4\}$$
$$\{18\}$$
$$\{1, 7\}$$
$$\{1, 15\}$$
$$\{1, 23\}$$
$$\{1, 17, 20\}$$
$$\{9, 12, 19\}$$
$$\{9, 14, 20, 25\}$$

are the subsets that work.

If we look at line 18, we have a Q_i that is itself a perfect square, and thus

$$X = 494881$$
$$Y = 4$$

and we find that

$$\gcd(494877, N) = 293$$

for a factoring.

In general, we would not expect to get a Q_i that was a perfect square all by itself, but we could look at lines 1 and 23:

$$X = 1000 \cdot 876554 \equiv 546116 \pmod{N}$$
$$Y = 36$$

and we find that

$$\gcd(546152, N) = 293$$

for a factoring.

11.3.4 Computation

In all factoring methods that actually work, there is an interplay between the mathematics and the computation. In the case of CFRAC, we observe two things that make the computation feasible. First, the Q_i that we try to factor completely over the factor base are always smaller than $\sqrt{N}$. That could still be a large number, but it is at least under control.

Equally important, if not more so, the determination of which Q_i can be multiplied together to form a square can be done with matrix reduction, and with matrix reduction on bits and not actually on integers. We produce a matrix in which only the exponent modulo 2 of the factorings is present, and we reduce that matrix modulo 2. Any row that reduces to all zeros corresponds to a subset of Q_i that provides an $X^2 \equiv Y^2 \pmod{N}$ congruence. In our example above, we would start with a matrix

	−1	2	3	5	13	17	19
1	1 0 0 0				0	0	0
4	0 0 0 0				0	0	0
7	1 0 0 0				0	0	0
9	1 1 0 1				0	1	0
12	0 1 0 0				0	0	1
14	0 0 0 1				1	1	0
15	1 0 0 0				0	0	0
17	1 0 1 1				0	0	0
18	0 0 0 0				0	0	0
19	1 0 0 1				0	1	1
20	0 0 1 1				0	0	0
23	1 0 0 0				0	0	0
25	1 1 1 1				1	0	0

Indeed, for an RSA-sized N to factor, this will be a large matrix, and we will also need the identity matrix as we reduce in order to determine which rows of the matrix combine to generate products of Q_i that are perfect squares, but the fact that we need only reduce modulo 2 is an enormous computational advantage. We will see later, in the context of the discrete logarithm problem, a matrix similar to this but for which we will need to keep all the integer values of the matrix reduction.

11.4 Factoring with Elliptic Curves

The sieve methods to be described next, in Chap. 12, are "middle grade" methods.

Another middle grade method uses elliptic curves [24], and is essentially an application of a Pollard $p - 1$ approach to the group of points on an elliptic curve.

We recall that in projective notation, the identity of the group modulo a prime p is the point with projective coordinates and $z \equiv 0 \pmod{p}$. If we run a $p - 1$-like multiplication of points (recall that the curve group is written additively, so we use the term "multiplication" instead of the term "exponentiation"), but take the coordinates modulo N (the integer to be factored) instead of the unknown factor p of N, then a gcd of the z coordinate with N will extract the p when we hit the identity of the group.

In the $p - 1$ method the order of the group is $p - 1$, and thus in order to achieve a factoring we need an exponent that has in it all the factors of $p - 1$. By Hasse's Theorem, the order of the curve group modulo a prime p is in the range $p + 1 - 2\sqrt{p}$ to $p + 1 + 2\sqrt{p}$, so we are not much worse off here than with the naive $p - 1$. We lose computational speed with elliptic curves in that the arithmetic for adding two points takes about a dozen multiplications of integers (the number varies depending on exactly which curve representation is used and how the arithmetic steps are arranged) instead of just the one that is used in $p - 1$.

However, we get a huge win with elliptic curves, as we do with the MPQS of Chap. 12, in that we can run the computation using a large number of different curves, all in parallel. With $p - 1$, we have only the one group order of $p - 1$, which could have a large prime factor that would prevent the $p - 1$ method from succeeding. With elliptic curves, we know from the mathematics that essentially all values in the range $p + 1 - 2\sqrt{p}$ to $p + 1 + 2\sqrt{p}$ are in fact orders of curve groups, and we only need one of those group orders to be crumbly in order to succeed. This has led to the use of the ECM as a standard method for removing relatively small factors from any large integer that needs to be factored.

11.5 Exercises

1. Factor $29 \times 53 = 1537$ using Pollard rho.
2. (Programming exercise.) Implement a simple version of Pollard $p - 1$ (simple meaning that you can run a loop over the prime powers that would make up M rather than building a single value of M). Use this to factor 43039.
3. (Programming exercise.) The set of 2×2 matrices with integer coefficients, taken modulo an integer N, with determinant 1, form a finite group. One could therefore run an analog of Pollard $p - 1$ factoring by taking powers of such a matrix. Implement this algorithm, and use it to factor 1037, 1537, and 43039. This is an example of the metaphysics of $p - 1$ applied to a different group. What is the cost of each step of this algorithm, and how does that compare to the original $p - 1$?
4. (Programming exercise.) Program the continued fraction algorithm, using trial division to test for smoothness, and use this to set up the factoring of 1537 with a factor base of primes up through 11. You won't need to code the linear algebra, because you should be able to compute X and Y by hand.

References

1. R.K. Guy, How to factor a number. Congressus Numerantium, 49–89 (1976)
2. G.H. Hardy, E.M. Wright, *An Introduction to the Theory of Numbers*, 4th edn. (Oxford, 1960), pp. 223–225
3. J. Brillhart, D.H. Lehmer, J.L. Selfridge, B. Tuckerman, S.S. Wagstaff, *Factorizations of $b^n +/- 1, b = 2, 3, 5, 6, 7, 10, 11, 12, up to high powers* (American Mathematical Society, 1983)
4. R.P. Brent, An improved Monte Carlo factorization algorithm. BIT, 176–184 (1980)
5. R.P. Brent, J.M. Pollard, Factorisation of the eighth Fermat number. Math. Comput. 627–630 (1981)
6. D.A. Buell, Factoring: algorithms, computers, and computations. J. Supercomput. 191–216 (1987)

7. J.P. Buhler, H.W. Lenstra, C. Pomerance, Factoring integers with the number field sieve, in *The Development of the Number Field Sieve*, vol. 1554, Lecture Notes in Mathematics, ed. by A.K. Lenstra, H.W. Lenstra Jr. (1993), pp. 50–94

8. D. Coppersmith, Specialized integer factorization, in *Advances in Cryptology- EUROCRYPT '98*, vol. 1403, Lecture Notes in Computer Science, ed. by K. Nyberg (1998), pp. 542–545

9. J.D. Dixon, Asymptotically fast factorization of integers. Math. Comput. 255–260 (1981)

10. J.D. Dixon, Factorization and primality tests. Am. Math. Mon. 333–352 (1984)

11. J.L. Gerver, Factoring large numbers with a quadratic sieve. Math. Comput. 287–294 (1983)

12. J. Cowie, B. Dodson, R.M. Elkenbracht-Huizing, A.K. Lenstra, P.L. Montgomery, J. Zayer, A world wide number field sieve factoring record: on to 512 bits, in *Advances in Cryptology - ASIACRYPT '96*, vol. 1163, Lecture Notes in Computer Science, ed. by K. Kim, T. Matsumoto (1996), pp. 382–394

13. H.W. Lenstra Jr., A.K. Lenstra, M.S. Manasse, J.M. Pollard, The factorization of the ninth Fermat number. Math. Comput. 319–349 (1993)

14. H.W. Lenstra Jr., C. Pomerance, A rigorous time bound for factoring integers. J. AMS 483–516 (1992)

15. C. Pomerance, Analysis and comparison of some integer factoring algorithms, in *Computational Methods in Number Theory*, Math Centre Tracts-Part 1, ed. by H.W. Lenstra Jr., R. Tijdeman (1982), pp. 89–139

16. C. Pomerance, The quadratic sieve factoring algorithm, in *Advances in Cryptology - EUROCRYPT 1984*, vol. 209, Lecture Notes in Computer Science, ed. by T. Beth, N. Cot, I. Ingemarsson (1985), pp. 169–182

17. S.S. Wagstaff, J. Smith, Methods of factoring large integers, in *Number Theory*, vol. 1240, Lecture Notes in Computer Science, ed. by D.V. Chudnovsky, G.V. Chudnovsky, H. Cohn, M.B. Nathanson (1987), pp. 281–303

18. H.C. Williams, A $p + 1$ method of factorization. Math. Comput. 225–234 (1982)

19. H.C. Williams, An overview of factoring, in *Advances in Cryptology*, ed. by D. Chaum (Springer, Boston, MA, 1984), pp. 71–80

20. J.M. Pollard, A Monte Carlo method for factorization. BIT 331–334 (1975)

21. J.M. Pollard, Theorems on factorization and primality testing. Math. Proc. Camb. Philos. Soc. **76**, 521–528 (1974)

22. M.A. Morrison, J. Brillhart, The factorization of F 7. Bull. AMS 264 (1971)

23. M.A. Morrison, J. Brillhart, A method of factoring and the factorization of F7. Math. Comput. 183–205 (1975)

24. H.W. Lenstra Jr., Factoring integers with elliptic curves. Ann. Math. **126**, 649–673 (1987)

How to Factor More Effectively

12

Abstract

In Chap. 11 we described several factoring methods. Each will succeed in factoring some integers, but none of these is a state-of-the-art method that we would expect to succeed on a well-chosen RSA $N = pq$. Even the best of these, CFRAC, suffers from the need to do trial division that will fail most of the time to provide any forward motion toward factoring N. In this chapter we discuss sieve methods for factoring. The primary computational benefit of a sieve method is that all the computational steps taken actually work toward finding factors, and that a sieve, stepping at constant stride through an array in memory, is highly efficient at the very lowest levels of a computing process. We discuss the Quadratic Sieve and the Multiple Polynomial Quadratic Sieve, and then finish with a nod to the current best method for factoring large "hard" integers, the Number Field Sieve.

12.1 Shortcomings of CFRAC

One major advantage of CFRAC was the fact that in order to factor an integer N, one needed only to test integers of size $\sqrt{N}$ for smoothness.

The major shortcoming of CFRAC was that there was no structure or order to the numbers that one was testing for smoothness, and thus smoothness testing for CFRAC is a process that is essentially trial division that fails most of the time.

12.2 The Quadratic Sieve

Carl Pomerance usually gets most of the credit for the quadratic sieve (QS) algorithm, but its roots go back to ideas of Kraitchik. However, just as CFRAC was conceived

© The Author(s), under exclusive license to Springer Nature Switzerland AG 2021 173
D. Buell, *Fundamentals of Cryptography*, Undergraduate Topics in Computer Science,
https://doi.org/10.1007/978-3-030-73492-3_12

of but not reasonable to implement in the days before computers, the QS was not something that Kraitchik would have implemented in his era.

The basic idea of QS is quite similar to CFRAC: we will look at a long list of values Q for which we have a solution A to the congruence $A^2 \equiv Q$. We will factor the Q using a factor base. And we will then do the linear algebra on the factorings of the Q to be able to complete a difference-of-squares congruence

$$\left(\prod A_i\right)^2 \equiv \prod Q_{i_j} \equiv Y^2 \quad (\text{mod } N)$$

in hopes that the gcd of the algebraic factoring of the congruence yields something nontrivial.

12.2.1 The Algorithm

To factor N, we first compute $R = [\sqrt{N}]$.

We then set up a long vector L for subscripts n running $-k$ to k whose values are the *logarithms* of

$$Q_n = (R + n)^2 - N$$

and we note that, just as with CFRAC, we have the values that square modulo N to the Q_n that we are going to test for smoothness. As with CFRAC, if we can collect a set S of the Q_n whose product is a perfect square, then we will have the desired congruence

$$Y^2 = \prod_{n \in S} Q_n \equiv \prod_{n \in S} (R + n)^2 = X^2$$

We choose, as before, a factor base FB of small primes p.

Now, for each $p \in FB$, we determine an entry point n_0 for which

$$(R + n_0)^2 - N = Q_{n_0} \equiv 0 \quad (\text{mod } p)$$

and for all subscripts $n_0 \pm kp$ we subtract $\log p$ from the array L.

If, when we finish with the factor base, we have entries in L that are zero or near zero (we must allow for roundoff of floating point values), then these likely correspond to Q_n that factor completely over the factor base. We refactor those values using trial division.

We then do the linear algebra step just as we did for CFRAC.

12.2.2 The Crucial Reasons for Success and Improvement over CFRAC

The values Q_n are small (just as they were in CFRAC) because we have $R + n$ nearly equal to $\sqrt{N}$, so the Q_n are not really much bigger than N^2.

What is crucial to notice, however, and what makes the QS successful, is that we have provided structure to the values we test for smoothness. They lie in an array, and we can *sieve at constant stride* through that array. Not all values will prove to be smooth, but we have replaced expensive integer trial division, that will usually fail, with subtraction at constant stride, for only those locations where subtraction is necessary, as we walk through a very long array. Since we know which array locations need to have a log p subtracted, no compute step is totally wasted. The only "wasted" computation is subtraction in locations that eventually turn out not to correspond to smooth integers.

We can speed things up (perhaps) by scaling all the floating point values and then using fixed point integer arithmetic.

We note that what we are actually testing for smoothness are the *norms* of algebraic integers

$$\frac{-(R+n)+\sqrt{N}}{2}$$

in the quadratic number field $\mathbb{Q}(\sqrt{N})$ (or maybe $4N$; we will not be pedantic about discriminant N or $4N$). This theme will continue; the multiple polynomial quadratic sieve uses a number of quadratic number fields with N as a factor of the discriminant, and the more general number field sieve, now the best of the factoring methods, does the same thing with norms in fields of higher degree than 2.

12.3   Once More Unto the Breach

So let's factor 1037 yet again ...

$$R = [\sqrt{1037}] = 32$$

n	$R+n$	Q_n	Factoring
−8	24	−461	$-1 \cdot 461$
−7	25	−412	$-1 \cdot 2^2 \cdot 10311$
−6	26	−361	$-1 \cdot 2^2 \cdot 19 \cdot 19$
−5	27	−308	$-1 \cdot 2^2 \cdot 7 \cdot 11$
−4	28	−253	$-1 \cdot 11 \cdot 23$
−3	29	−196	$-1 \cdot 2^2 \cdot 7^2$
−2	30	−137	$-1 \cdot 137$
−1	31	−76	$-1 \cdot 2^2 \cdot 17$
0	32	−13	$-1 \cdot 13$
1	33	52	$2^2 \cdot 13$
2	34	119	$7 \cdot 17$
3	35	188	$4 \cdot 47$
4	36	259	$7 \cdot 37$
5	37	332	$4 \cdot 83$
6	38	407	$11 \cdot 37$
7	39	484	$4 \cdot 121$
8	40	563	563
9	41	644	$4 \cdot 7 \cdot 23$

We see that $n = -3, 0, 1$ produce

$$29^2 \cdot 32^2 \cdot 33^2 \equiv 364^2 \pmod{1037}$$

and that $30624 - 364 = 30260$ has the factor 17 and $30624 + 364 = 30988$ has the factor 61.

12.4   The Multiple Polynomial Quadratic Sieve

The crucial improvement with CFRAC was the notion of factor base and the linear algebra to get a $X^2 \equiv Y^2 \pmod{N}$ congruence.

The crucial improvement with QS was to turn the smoothness testing into a vector sieving operation.

The problem with QS is that we have only one quadratic polynomial $X^2 - N$ whose values we are trying to keep small in order to make them more likely to be smooth over the factor base. Since this is a parabola rising to the right and left from $X_0 = \sqrt{N}$, the values will increase steadily the further away we go from the square root of N, and the yield of smooth values will decrease.

Let's fix that problem.

The N to factor is big, maybe 1024 bits (300 decimals) or more. The array we are working with is limited by physical memory in a computer, so for a machine with 4 gigabytes, we have space for maybe 10^9 things, which is tiny by comparison.

We won't go into all the details of the math, but the gist of the approach is this. Instead of being satisfied with the one polynomial $X^2 - N$, we can do a little calculus to optimize the choice of polynomials $aX^2 + bXY + cY^2$ of discriminants $b^2 - 4ac = kN$ for small values of k, so that when we complete the square we have

$$(2an + b)^2 - kN$$

small for a large range of values n.

The details are very clear in Silverman's original paper [1]. In essence, one is using the fact that there are lots of polynomials, and thus there are lots of polynomials with long arrays of small norm values to test for smoothness. When one polynomial has its values getting too big, the program shifts to a different polynomial and continues as before. The goal, after all, is to harvest as many smooth numbers as possible for later use in the linear algebra step.

Everything else proceeds as before. We do run the risk, for cryptographic numbers $N = pq$, then we might get a trivial factoring $k \cdot N$ instead of $(kp) \cdot (q)$ (or perhaps even $(k_1) \cdot (k_2 N)$ for a factoring of $k = k_1 k_2$), but that is a chance we take, and if we have sufficiently many smooth Q_n, we will eventually get a factoring that splits the p from the q.

It was the MPQS that was used by Lenstra and Manasse [2] in the first factoring ever of a "hard" number of 100 decimal digits.

12.4.1 Yet One More Advantage

A final advantage gained by MPQS, which was exploited extensively by Silverman and was the prototype of all the embarrassingly parallel crowdsourcing of computational capability (GIMPS, SETI At Home, etc.), is that this is an embarrassingly parallel computation that can be done on computers that are only loosely coupled in a network. Because N is large, we can assume all the polynomials lead to a different range of numbers to test for smoothness, so there is no overlap or redundancy in doing all the smoothness testing in parallel. Even if there were a redundancy, it wouldn't change the ability of the computation eventually to get a factoring, but rather would only slow down its progress. Silverman's experience was that changing polynomials very frequently was a very good thing, so he farmed out the different computations to a number of different machines. Since there are relatively few residues that come up smooth, the data of smooth numbers coming back to a central repository is small compared to the sieving work being done on the different computers, so we there is no need for a high bandwidth connection to all the various computers. This use of embarrassing parallelism has become routine for such computations.

12.5 The Number Field Sieve

The MPQS was superseded in the early 1990s by the Number Field Sieve [3], which we won't go into in detail because the algebra is much more complicated.

Suffice it to say, however, that the basic approach to factoring is much the same in the NFS as in MPQS and QS. We sieve to test numbers for smoothness over a factor base, using formulas that give us for free one side of a congruence

$$X^2 \equiv Y^2 \pmod{N}$$

and then we do linear algebra modulo 2 to find a subset of our smooth numbers that multiply together to give a perfect square. Finally, we test

$$\gcd(X - Y, N)$$

and

$$\gcd(X + Y, N)$$

in hopes of finding a factor.

The improvement provided by the NFS over the MPQS is the same as that of the MPQS over the QS. We use more of the algebraic structure of number fields to get a better set of small numbers to test for smoothness, so we get more such smooth numbers faster.

Asymptotically, the General Number Field Sieve runs in time

$$L[1/3, (64/9)^{1/3}] = \exp\left(\left((64/9)^{1/3} + o(1)\right)(\ln N)^{1/3}(\ln \ln N)^{2/3}\right)$$

time when used to factor an integer N.

12.6 Exercises

1. (Programming exercise.) Code the sieve part of the quadratic sieve, and use it to factor first 1037 as in the example, and then 1537 and 43039. Doing 1037 and 1537 won't require much thinking about the factor base, but 43039 and 1000009 will require tinkering with the size of the factor base and the length of the sieve array.

2. (Programming exercise.) Having coded the quadratic sieve and used it to factor $N = 1000009$, try sieving kN for small k and see if you can collect the same number of smooth numbers but using a shorter sieve array.

References

1. R.D. Silverman, The multiple polynomial quadratic sieve. Math. Comput. **48**, 329–339 (1987)
2. A.K. Lenstra, M.S. Manasse, Factoring by electronic mail, in *Advances in Cryptology - Eurocrypt '89*, ed. by J.-J. Quisquater, J. Vandewalle (1990), pp. 355–371
3. A.K. Lenstra, H.W. Lenstra Jr., *The Development of the Number Field Sieve*, vol. 1554, Lecture Notes in Mathematics (Springer, Berlin, Heidelberg, 1993)

Cycles, Randomness, Discrete Logarithms, and Key Exchange

13

Abstract

With symmetric cryptography, it is necessary for the two parties who wish to communicate to have access to a common key so that one party can encrypt a message and the other party can decrypt the message. This would limit the ability of two parties who have not communicated in the past to engage in the kind of secure communication necessary for electronic commerce, for example. In this chapter we describe how number-theoretic constructs that create seemingly-random sequences of integers can be used to allow two parties to exchange information that would allow them to agree upon a common cryptographic key, even if no other communication has taken place between them. This exchange of key information can be done by exponentiation modulo a large prime number, in a manner similar to that of RSA encryption, or using elliptic curve groups in the same fashion. We will also cover the basics of the index calculus method that can be used, although with difficulty, to attack this kind of key exchange.

13.1 Introduction

The classic problem in cryptography has always been the desire of two parties to communicate with each other but prevent others from reading and understanding those communications. With the expansion of computing and the development of computer networks, a new version of this problem has become critically important: How can two parties (Armadillo and Bobcat, say), who have never met, and whose only connection is a first-time communication via computers on the internet, authenticate their identities to each other? How can a secure and asymmetric communication link be established so that they can exchange information that cannot be read by other entities?

We remark that this is a problem that is specific to asymmetric encryption algorithms. In a symmetric world, both Armadillo and Bobcat would have shared a

© The Author(s), under exclusive license to Springer Nature Switzerland AG 2021   179
D. Buell, *Fundamentals of Cryptography*, Undergraduate Topics in Computer Science,
https://doi.org/10.1007/978-3-030-73492-3_13

cryptographic key and the ability of either to provide any meaningful communication to the other would have demonstrated that the party at the end of the communication link had access to the key. (We will admit that interception, coercion, and such could co-opt such legitimate use of the key, but in fact that vulnerability exists in any such attempt at secure communication between parties.)

And we note up front that this is a fundamental problem in electronic commerce. We buy things online, but we make these purchases at times with vendors with whom we have not done business before.

The current solution to this communication problem invariably all seems to point back to the use of a discrete logarithm. In this chapter we present the basic math behind discrete logarithms in several relevant groups.

We remark that, just as with factoring, there is an extensive literature on the computation of discrete logs [1–7].

13.2 The Discrete Logarithm Problem

Definition 13.1 Let G be a cyclic group with a known generator g. If the group is cyclic, then any element $a \in G$ can be written as some power g^e in G. Given such an element $a \in G$, the *discrete logarithm problem* in G is the determination of the integer exponent e such that $g^e = a$.

The use of the word "discrete" is in reference to the more ordinary logarithm, where we would write

$$g^e = a$$
$$e = \log_g a$$

Some discrete logarithm (DL) problems are easy. For example, let group G be the group of integers modulo n under addition. The generator is $g = 1_G$. Given any element m_G in the group, it is trivial to see that

$$m_G = m \cdot 1_G$$

where we have subscripted 1_G and m_G for the purpose of identifying these as elements in the group, which happen to be different from the m on the right hand side that represents repeated application m times of the group operation.

We can also relax our constraints somewhat. We will be looking at groups for which the entire group is cyclic, so that powers of the generator generate the entire group. What we really need is only that the cycle generated by the powers of g be sufficiently large that the discrete log problem is hard.

13.3 Difficult Discrete Log Problems

It is a *hugely important fact* that for a number of useful groups, the discrete logarithm problem is hard to solve because taking powers of a generator g will cycle through the group in a reasonably random order. For the integers under addition, the DL problem is trivial. For the integers modulo a prime number under multiplication, the problem is very hard indeed.

What we will see is that the discrete log problem is a hard problem (for some definition of "hard") in many groups for which exponentiation/computation is simple. That is, doing the exponentiation to get $a = g^e$ given g and e is easy, but undoing the exponentiation to get e from a and g is hard.

For example, modulo 11, with primitive root 2, we have

$$2^1 \equiv 2$$
$$2^2 \equiv 4$$
$$2^3 \equiv 8$$
$$2^4 \equiv 5$$
$$2^5 \equiv 10$$
$$2^6 \equiv 9$$
$$2^7 \equiv 7$$
$$2^8 \equiv 3$$
$$2^9 \equiv 6$$
$$2^{10} \equiv 1$$

In this case, because 2 is small, we can predict some of the sequences (2 to 4 to 8, for example). But if we choose a primitive root for which the "wrap" modulo 11 is almost guaranteed, say 7, then there is (apparently) no simple way to follow the sequence:

$$7^1 \equiv 7$$
$$7^2 \equiv 5$$
$$7^3 \equiv 2$$
$$7^4 \equiv 3$$
$$7^5 \equiv 10$$
$$7^6 \equiv 4$$
$$7^7 \equiv 6$$
$$7^8 \equiv 9$$
$$7^9 \equiv 8$$
$$7^{10} \equiv 1$$

This is the key fact used in many cryptographic schemes.

13.4 Cycles

We mentioned in Sect. 4.4.1 the concept of a primitive root. Let's continue with that.

Definition 13.2 A *primitive root* in a cyclic group G of order n is an element g that is of order n.

Theorem 13.1 *For n an integer, the order of the multiplicative group of integers modulo n is $\phi(n)$.*

Theorem 13.2 *For p a prime and k a positive integer, we have $\phi(p^k) = (p-1)p^{k-1}$.*

Theorem 13.3 *The only integers n for which primitive roots exist are 2, 4, prime powers p^k for k a positive integer, and $2p^k$ for k a positive integer.*

Remark 13.1 We go back to the multiplicative structure of the integers mod 15 for an example of these results. Since $15 = 3 \cdot 5$, we have Since $\phi(15) = \phi(3)\phi(5) = 2 \cdot 4 = 8$. Since 15 is not of the form mentioned in Theorem 13.3, it is not multiplicatively a cyclic group, but is instead the product of a 2-cycle (from the 3) and a 4-cycle (from the 5). The multiplicative group is the direct product

$$\{1, 11\} \times \{1, 2, 4, 8\}$$

Theorem 13.4 *There are exactly $\phi(p-1)$ primitive roots of the multiplicative group of integers modulo a prime p.*

Proof To see this, we look at the powers of the primitive root in exponent order

$$g^1, g^2, g^3, \ldots g^{p-1} = 1$$

and we remember that multiplying these elements is the same as adding the exponents.

Clearly, an exponent e that is prime to $p-1$ will generate additively a complete cycle of the exponents 1 through $p-1$, and an exponent e that has factors in common with $p-1$ will short-cycle.   □

13.5 Cocks-Ellis-Williamson/Diffie-Hellman Key Exchange

Let us assume that Armadillo and Bobcat wish to share secret information over an insecure communication channel. This would be simple for them to do if they had a cryptographic key to be used for encryption. But what if they have never met? What if this is their first interaction? What if Armadillo is an ordinary user, and Bobcat a large commercial enterprise from which Armadillo wants to purchase goods?

The basis for creating a joint key that both Armadillo and Bobcat both have, but which is computationally infeasible for others to determine, is the key exchange protocol invented by Cocks, Ellis, and Williamson (if one is British) or by Diffie and Hellman (if one is from the United States).

13.5.1   The Key Exchange Algorithm

Armadillo determines a prime number P, a primitive root g for the group of integers mod P and a secret exponent e_A. Armadillo publishes the prime number P and the primitive root g as public information, computes $m_A \equiv g^{e_A} \pmod{P}$, and sends m_A to Bobcat.

Bobcat reads the values of P, g, and m_A, and determines her own secret exponent e_B. She computes $m_B \equiv g^{e_B} \pmod{P}$ and sends that to Armadillo.

Armadillo uses Bobcat's submitted m_B to compute, using her secret e_A,

$$S = (m_B)^{e_A} \equiv (g^{e_B})^{e_A} \equiv g^{e_A e_B} \pmod{P}.$$

Bobcat for her part uses Armadillo's submitted m_A to compute, using her secret e_B,

$$S = (m_A)^{e_B} \equiv (g^{e_A})^{e_B} \equiv g^{e_A e_B} \pmod{P};$$

and Armadillo and Bobcat now have a shared secret S.

An outsider who has seen only P, g, m_A, and m_B cannot reproduce the computation of either Armadillo or Bobcat without solving the discrete log problem modulo P to determine one or the other of the secret exponents e_A or e_B. (Or at least it is not known publicly of a way to find e_A or e_B without solving the discrete log problem.)

The CEW/DH protocol is often used to exchange a key to be used in a cryptographic setting, hence the term "key exchange". In fact, a great deal of electronic commerce is done exactly this way; the discrete log is used for two parties to agree on a secret key, and then the key is used in AES because AES is regarded as secure and it is fast.

We remark on good choices for primes P. A *safe prime* is a prime P for which $(P-1)/2$ is also prime. Safe primes have the longest possible cycle compared against the number of bits in the prime.

13.6   The Index Calculus

Solving a discrete logarithm problem modulo a prime P uses the *index calculus* and is related to the sieve methods for factoring. The idea again goes back to Kraitchik but was reinvented in the late 1970s when cryptographic applications made computational number theory suddenly more fashionable.

The classic description of the algorithm is that of Coppersmith, Odlyzko, and Schroeppel [8], usually referred to as C-O-S; some additional references are by

LaMacchia [9] and Odlyzko [10]. A somewhat intuitive notion of the algorithm is this:

- the integers have a multiplicative basis of the prime numbers, in that any integer is a product of primes;
- if we can determine the appropriate logarithms mod P of sufficiently many small primes, then we can add the logs in the factoring of an integer M to get the discrete log modulo P.

We illustrate the algorithm with an example, using the C-O-S description. Although there are computationally better methods, they require more mathematical background but don't actually improve on an understanding of how the algorithm works.

13.6.1   Our Example

We will choose 1019 as our prime, noting that $(1019 - 1)/2 = 509$ is also a prime, so the cycle of powers would be as long as possible. We note that 2 is a primitive root.

13.6.2   Smooth Relations

We compute $H = [\sqrt{1019} + 1] = 32$. As with sieve methods for factoring, we choose a factor base $Q = \{q_i\}$ of small primes $-1, 2, 3, 5, 7, 11, 13$ (including -1 as a "prime" just as with the factoring algorithms).

We now run a double loop on c_1 and c_2 for small values of $c_1\, c_2$, computing

$$(H + c_1)(H + c_2) \quad (\text{mod } P)$$

and attempting to factor these (which are the analogs of the Q_i in the sieve for factoring) over the factor base. Since H is about $\sqrt{P}$, this product will be about P in size, so these products should be "small" compared to P itself.

For those products that do factor, we have

$$\prod q_i^{e_i} \equiv (H + c_1)(H + c_2) \quad (\text{mod } P)$$

and thus

$$\sum_i e_i \log q_i - \log(H + c_1) - \log(H + c_2) \equiv 0 \quad (\text{mod } P - 1)$$

We expand our factor base to include the $H + c_1$ and $H + c_2$, and we add the one inhomogeneous log of which we are sure:

$$\log 2 = 1,$$

because we are using 2 as our primitive root.

13.6.3 Matrix Reduction

If we run the double loop on c_1 from -5 to 4 and on c_2 from $c_1 + 1$ to 5, inclusive, and do the factorings, we the following tableau, where we have split for readability the columns from the factor base and the columns from the $H + c_i$.

-1	2	3	5	7	11	13	27	28	29	30	31	32	33	34	35	36	37	
0	1	0	0	0	0	0	0	0	0	0	0	0	0	0	0	0	0	1
1	1	0	0	1	0	1	-1	0	0	0	-1	0	0	0	0	0	0	0
1	0	0	1	0	0	0	-1	0	0	0	1	-1	0	0	0	0	0	0
1	7	0	0	0	0	0	-1	0	0	0	0	0	-1	0	0	0	0	0
1	1	0	0	0	0	0	-1	0	0	0	0	0	0	0	-1	0	1	0
1	2	0	1	0	0	0	-1	0	0	0	0	0	0	0	0	0	-1	0
1	0	1	0	0	0	1	0	-1	0	0	0	0	0	0	-1	0	0	0
1	0	0	0	0	1	0	0	-1	0	0	0	0	0	0	0	-1	0	0
1	3	1	1	0	0	0	0	0	-1	0	-1	0	0	0	0	0	0	0
1	0	0	0	1	0	1	0	0	-1	0	0	-1	0	0	0	0	0	0
1	1	0	0	0	0	0	0	0	-1	0	1	0	-1	0	0	0	0	0
1	0	1	0	0	1	0	0	0	-1	0	0	0	0	-1	0	0	0	0
1	2	0	0	0	0	0	0	0	-1	0	0	0	0	0	-1	0	0	0
0	0	0	2	0	0	0	0	0	-1	0	0	0	0	0	0	-1	0	0
0	1	3	0	0	0	0	0	0	-1	0	0	0	0	0	0	0	-1	0
1	0	0	0	0	0	0	0	0	1	-1	0	0	-1	0	0	0	0	0
0	0	0	0	0	0	0	0	0	0	-1	0	0	0	-1	0	0	0	0
0	0	0	0	0	0	0	0	0	0	-1	1	0	0	0	-1	0	0	0
0	0	0	0	1	0	1	0	0	0	-1	0	0	0	0	0	0	-1	0
1	0	3	0	0	0	0	0	0	0	0	-1	-1	0	0	0	0	0	0
0	2	0	0	0	0	0	0	0	0	0	-1	0	-1	0	0	0	0	0
0	0	0	1	1	0	0	0	0	0	0	-1	0	0	-1	0	0	0	0
0	1	1	0	0	1	0	0	0	0	0	-1	0	0	0	-1	0	0	0
0	7	0	0	0	0	0	0	0	0	0	-1	0	0	0	0	0	-1	0
0	0	0	0	0	0	0	0	0	0	0	0	-1	-1	0	0	0	1	0
0	0	1	1	0	1	0	0	0	0	0	0	-1	0	0	0	0	-1	0
0	0	0	0	0	0	2	0	0	0	0	0	0	-1	0	0	-1	0	0

The first line below the header is the inhomogeneous $\log 2 = 1$. The second line represents the factoring

$$-1 \cdot 2 \cdot 7 \cdot 13 = -182 \equiv 27 \cdot 31 = (32 - 5)(32 - 1) \pmod{1019}$$

If we want, when doing an example, we can cheat and compute the logs from the primitive root:

$$\log(-1) = 509$$
$$\log 2 = 1$$
$$\log 7 = 363$$
$$\log 13 = 289$$
$$\log 27 = 838$$
$$\log 31 = 324$$

and we can compute

$$509 + 1 + 363 + 289 - 838 - 324 = 0.$$

We now reduce this matrix over the integers modulo 1018. This is computationally an enormous difference between factoring and discrete logarithms. In the factoring algorithm, we were only required to consider the parity of the matrix entries and could do mod-2 arithmetic, relatively cheap in both time and memory, even with a matrix of tens if not hundreds of thousands of rows and columns. With discrete logarithms, we need to do arithmetic on multiprecise integers as large as $P - 1$.

We can do our simple example without such difficulty, though, and we get

-1	2	3	5	7	11	13	27	28	29	30	31	32	33	34	35	36	37	
0	1	0	0	0	0	0	0	0	0	0	0	0	0	0	0	0	0	1
1	0	0	0	0	0	0	0	0	0	0	0	0	0	0	0	0	0	509
0	0	1	0	0	0	0	0	0	0	0	0	0	0	0	0	0	0	958
0	0	0	1	0	0	0	0	0	0	0	0	0	0	0	0	0	0	10
0	0	0	0	1	0	0	0	0	0	0	0	0	0	0	0	0	0	363
0	0	0	0	0	1	0	0	0	0	0	0	0	0	0	0	0	0	756
0	0	0	0	0	0	1	0	0	0	0	0	0	0	0	0	0	0	289
0	0	0	0	0	0	0	1	0	0	0	0	0	0	0	0	0	0	838
0	0	0	0	0	0	0	0	1	0	0	0	0	0	0	0	0	0	365
0	0	0	0	0	0	0	0	0	1	0	0	0	0	0	0	0	0	138
0	0	0	0	0	0	0	0	0	0	1	0	0	0	0	0	0	0	969
0	0	0	0	0	0	0	0	0	0	0	1	0	0	0	0	0	0	324
0	0	0	0	0	0	0	0	0	0	0	0	1	0	0	0	0	0	5
0	0	0	0	0	0	0	0	0	0	0	0	0	1	0	0	0	0	696
0	0	0	0	0	0	0	0	0	0	0	0	0	0	1	0	0	0	49
0	0	0	0	0	0	0	0	0	0	0	0	0	0	0	1	0	0	373
0	0	0	0	0	0	0	0	0	0	0	0	0	0	0	0	1	0	900
0	0	0	0	0	0	0	0	0	0	0	0	0	0	0	0	0	1	701
0	0	0	0	0	0	0	0	0	0	0	0	0	0	0	0	0	0	0
0	0	0	0	0	0	0	0	0	0	0	0	0	0	0	0	0	0	0
0	0	0	0	0	0	0	0	0	0	0	0	0	0	0	0	0	0	0
0	0	0	0	0	0	0	0	0	0	0	0	0	0	0	0	0	0	0
0	0	0	0	0	0	0	0	0	0	0	0	0	0	0	0	0	0	0
0	0	0	0	0	0	0	0	0	0	0	0	0	0	0	0	0	0	0
0	0	0	0	0	0	0	0	0	0	0	0	0	0	0	0	0	0	0
0	0	0	0	0	0	0	0	0	0	0	0	0	0	0	0	0	0	0
0	0	0	0	0	0	0	0	0	0	0	0	0	0	0	0	0	0	0

These are the values we obtained from our small-example cheat, so we know we got this matrix reduction correct. Our reduction was almost just Gaussian elimination. We write "almost" because we are doing a reduction modulo a composite integer and can't guarantee that we can divide, so instead we apply what is essentially a gcd process in the row-reduction. In a real problem, more sophisticated matrix reduction techniques, usually a variant of the Lanczos method, would be used.

13.6.4 Individual Logarithms

Having produced the logs for the elements of our (expanded) factor base, the eventual problem would be to compute an individual logarithm. We assume that we have a value b, and that we wish to compute the logarithm x such that $g^x \equiv b \pmod{P}$ in our example, where we chose $g = 2$ as our primitive root. To this end we compute

$$g^w b \pmod{P}$$

for some randomly chosen value of w, and we factor this into

$$g^w b \equiv \prod q_i^{e_i} u_i^{f_i} \pmod{P}$$

for some "medium-sized" primes u_i. This gives us more values for which to find the logs, just as we expanded the small primes factor base to include the $H + c_j$. We can repeat the above sieving and matrix reduction to find the logs of the u_i, and then the log of b is determined. We have not done this with our example because the integers are so small that "medium-sized" would provide little enlightenment.

13.6.5 Asymptotics

The simple version of an index calculus algorithm runs in time

$$L[1/2, c] = \exp\left((c + o(1))\, (\ln N)^{1/2} (\ln \ln N)^{1/2}\right)$$

time, for some constant c, but this can be improved using an analog of the Number Field Sieve to the same $L[1/3, c]$ running time (with a different constant c) as the NFS itself.

13.7 Key Exchange with Elliptic Curves

Note that key exchange as described above is not really a result depending only on the integers modulo P. It is really a result about computations in cyclic groups for which the discrete log problem is hard. As with RSA, compared to other groups that could be used for encryption, it just happens that using the integers mod P is computationally very simple as a baseline for how such an algorithm should work. In balancing the complexity of computations mod P against the difficulty of a mod-P discrete log problem, it's very hard to find another group whose discrete log problem is just as hard but is not more costly to use for key exchange. On the other hand, there does exist the index calculus attack, and this does not work with some of the other groups that could be used (like the group of an elliptic curve).

Key exchange using elliptic curves is entirely analogous to the basic algorithm using a large prime. Armadillo and Bobcat agree upon an elliptic curve $\mathcal{E}$ modulo a large prime P, so that the order of the curve is too difficult to compute, and a base point Q on that curve. Armadillo and Bobcat choose their own secret exponents

e_A, e_B as before. Armadillo computes $e_A \cdot Q$ in the curve group and sends that to Bobcat. Bobcat computes $e_B \cdot Q$ in the curve group and sends that to Armadillo. They can now both compute $e_A \cdot e_B \cdot Q$ and obtain the same point on the curve, from whose x coordinate a shared secret key can be derived.

The salient feature of elliptic curve groups for key exchange is that there is no obvious index calculus. The ordinary integers (not the integers modulo P) are generated using the primes as a multiplicative basis and the Fundamental Theorem of Arithmetic. The index calculus works modulo P because the multiplicative generation of residues provides sufficient information mod P that computing the logs of sufficiently many small primes permits computing the logs for the rest of the residues. The second step is a bootstrap from a smallish factor base to an expanded factor base that contains only the primes that we happen to need, not all the primes (which would be too many).

We do not have this situation with elliptic curves. There is no clear analog to the index calculus, because there is no known multiplicative basis for the points on an elliptic curve taken modulo a prime, although Joseph Silverman proposed an algorithm he referred to as "the Xedni calculus" [11]. ("Xedni" is "index" backwards.) The Xedni calculus has not been used effectively, although it remains of some interest.

What is normally used for discrete log computations in elliptic curves is a parallelizable variant of the Pollard rho algorithm. We will take this up in Chap. 14.

13.8 Key Exchange in Other Groups

Just as with analogies to RSA for cryptography, there are other groups (besides elliptic curves) that have properties similar to those of the integers modulo a prime, and these groups have been proposed for key exchange algorithms. The class groups of complex quadratic fields are generally nearly-cyclic, and the class group of discriminant N is approximately $\sqrt{N}$ in size. Just as with the integers modulo P, exponentiation in class groups is a straightforward process, and the reduction of forms (or ideals) to reduced forms/ideals is similar to the "wrap" of powers of a primitive root modulo a large prime. However, an approach entirely similar to the index calculus can be used for these groups, because multiplication of classes is almost the same as multiplication of the lead coefficients of forms (it is when the products that are the lead coefficients are reduced to produce the canonical reduced form of the class that the obscuring of the product takes place).

However, although the cryptographic security of such a mathematical structure might be just as good as that of the integers modulo P, the same problem exists for these groups as for cryptography itself—the computational simplicity of multiplication modulo a prime cannot be compared to the cost of compounding forms and classes, which requires at least a gcd operation with every multiplication. The level of random behavior needed for cryptography is present, but the cost of the computations is much greater than for arithmetic modulo large primes, with no real benefit to security.

Table 13.1 Record discrete log computations modulo primes

Decimals	Bits	Announced	Notes
130	431	18 June 2005	
160	530	5 February 2007	Safe prime
180	596	11 June 2014	Safe prime
232	765	16 June 2016	Safe prime
240	795	2 December 2019	Safe prime

Table 13.2 Record discrete log computations in elliptic curves

Bits	Announced
112	July 2009
113	April 2014
114	21 August 2017
114	June 2020

13.9   How Hard Is the Discrete Logarithm Problem?

Just as with RSA, it is worth taking a look at record achievements in computing discrete logarithms. The recent records for computing discrete logs modulo primes are shown in Table 13.1.

For discrete logs in elliptic curve groups, a standard challenge has been that issued by Certicom Corporation. Their Level I challenges involve curves modulo 109-bit and 131-bit primes, and the Level II challenges have primes of 163, 191, 239, and 359 bits. Certicom asserts that all the Level II challenges are currently infeasible. Records for computing discrete logs in elliptic curves are shown in Table 13.2.

One can see, in the comparison of record computations, the inherent advantage of elliptic curves. Although the group operations are more complicated than merely multiplying large integers, one can obtain comparable security using elliptic curves with moduli much smaller than with prime moduli.

13.10   Exercises

1. (Possible programming exercise.) Set up a key exchange process as in Sect. 13.5.1. Test first with the prime 31 to make sure you understand the process. Then try with the prime 257.
2. (Programming exercise.) If you have not already done so for the previous exercise, write the code for key exchange as in Sect. 13.5.1. Test first with the prime 31 to make sure you understand the process. Then try with the prime 257. Finally, use

the prime 46301, which will be large enough to ensure that you have the code correct, but will not require multiprecise arithmetic even if done in C++ or Java.

3. (Programming exercise.) Write simple code (that is, go ahead and use trial division) for the index calculus, and verify the example of Sect. 13.6.1.

4. (Programming exercise.) Do the next step of the index calculus by computing the logs of 41, 43, and 47, using the process sketched out in Sect. 13.6.4.

References

1. T. Elgamal, A subexponential-time algorithm for computing discrete logarithms over $GF(p^2)$. IEEE Trans. Inf. Theory 473–481 (1985)
2. D.M. Gordon, Discrete logarithms in $GF(p)$ using the number field sieve. SIAM J. Discrete Math. **6**, 124–138 (1993)
3. D.M. Gordon, K.S. McCurley, Computation of discrete logarithms in fields of characteristic two. Crypto 91 rump session paper (1991)
4. J.M. Pollard, Monte Carlo methods for index computation mod p. Math. Comput. 918–924 (1978)
5. D. Weber, An implementation of the general number field sieve to compute discrete logarithms mod p. Proc. Eurocrypt **95**, 95–105 (1995)
6. D. Weber, Computing discrete logarithms with the general number field sieve. Proceedings, ANTS II (1996)
7. D. Weber, Computing discrete logarithms with quadratic number rings, in *Advances in Cryptology - EUROCRYPT '98*, vol. 1403, Lecture Notes in Computer Science, ed. by K. Nyberg (1998), pp. 171–183
8. D. Coppersmith, A.M. Odlyzko, R. Schroeppel, Discrete logarithms in $GF(p)$. Algorithmica 1–15 (1986)
9. B.A. LaMacchia, A.M. Odlyzko, Computation of discrete logarithms in prime fields. Des. Codes Cryptogr. **1**, 47–62 (1991)
10. A.M. Odlyzko, Discrete logarithms in finite fields and their cryptographic significance, in *Advances in Cryptology - EUROCRYPT '84*, vol. 209, Lecture Notes in Computer Science, ed. by T. Beth, N. Cot, I. Ingemarsson (1985), pp. 224–314
11. J.H. Silverman, The Xedni calculus and the elliptic curve discrete logarithm problem. Des. Codes Cryptogr. **20**, 5–40 (2000)

Elliptic Curve Cryptography

14

Abstract

The first proposed asymmetric encryption scheme was that of Rivest, Shamir, and Adleman, using exponentiation in the group of integers modulo the product of two large primes. Koblitz and Miller independently proposed the use of the groups of points on elliptic curves. In this chapter we cover the algorithm for using curves for cryptography both for encryption and for key exchange. Since the arithmetic to do point addition is expensive, we include the formulas for adding points efficiently. Finally, we include the Pohlig-Hellman attack, which should not be successful if the curves are chosen properly, and the Pollard rho attack, which is the current best attack on the elliptic curve discrete log problem.

14.1 Introduction

The use of elliptic curves in cryptography was suggested independently at almost the same time in the mid-1980s by Neal Koblitz [1] and Victor Miller [2], and since the introduction of this idea, there has been an explosion in the study of curves.

We review the basic (high-school) algebra defining an elliptic curve $\mathcal{E}$.

We start with a polynomial equation that is quadratic in Y and cubic in X

$$\mathcal{E} : Y^2 + a_1 XY + a_3 Y = X^3 + a_2 X^2 + a_4 X + a_6$$

and, although we will shortly make a change of base field, consider this to be an equation with rational constants a_1, a_3, a_2, a_4, a_6 and rational values of X and Y. The curve $\mathcal{E}$ is the set of pairs of rational numbers (X, Y) together with the *point at infinity* $\mathcal{O}$.

Key to understanding curves is that fact that, since we are considering rational (X, Y), we are permitted to make rational changes of variable without changing the set of points that lie on the curve. If we make the change of variable

$$Y' = Y + a_1/2X + a_3/2$$

© The Author(s), under exclusive license to Springer Nature Switzerland AG 2021
D. Buell, *Fundamentals of Cryptography*, Undergraduate Topics in Computer Science,
https://doi.org/10.1007/978-3-030-73492-3_14

we obtain

$$\mathcal{E} : (Y')^2 = X^3 + a_2'X^2 + a_4'X + a_6'$$

and then with

$$X' = X + a_2/3$$

we obtain

$$\mathcal{E} : (Y')^2 = (X')^3 + a_4''X' + a_6''.$$

Since these transformations do not affect whether or not solutions are rational numbers, we can take this last,

$$\mathcal{E} : Y^2 = X^3 + a_4X + a_6$$

as the canonical definition for an elliptic curve over the rationals.

CAVEAT: We shall have occasion to consider curves over fields other than the rational numbers, namely fields modulo prime integers and finite fields of characteristic 2. Since we will be using large primes P, division by 2 and by 3 in these two transformations do not cause problems, but over fields of characteristic 2, the first of these transformations cannot be done, and we will have a canonical representation

$$\mathcal{E} : Y^2 + a_3Y = X^3 + a_4X + a_6$$

14.1.1   Jacobian Coordinates

We remark that although the high-school algebra seems a little bit more clean when we write the curves using rational numbers, the switch to Jacobian coordinates is almost required when looking at actual computation. The curve over the rational numbers, with solutions x and y rational,

$$\mathcal{E} : y^2 = x^3 + a_4x + a_6,$$

is really the curve

$$\mathcal{E} : (Y/Z^3)^2 = (X/Z^2)^3 + a_4(X/Z^2) + a_6,$$

with solutions X, Y, and Z that are integers. We can clear away the need for denominators by multiplying by Z^6 to get

$$\mathcal{E} : Y^2 = X^3 + a_4XZ^4 + a_6Z^6,$$

in *Jacobian coordinates*. And now all of X, Y, and Z are integers, and we know how to compute with integers.

14.2 Elliptic Curve Discrete Logarithms

The potential use of elliptic curves for discrete logarithms, and thus for key exchange, is something of a no-brainer once one thinks to use such things. The order of the group modulo a large prime P is known to be "about" P. The sequence of points Q generated by taking multiples of a particular base point have coordinate values that appear "as random" as would be needed for cryptographic purposes. And, unlike the groups modulo primes P under multiplication, for which the index calculus method solves the discrete log problem in subexponential time, none of the attacks on elliptic curve discrete logs are better than $\sqrt{P}$, which means that much smaller P can be used.

The key question would be whether the additional expense of the elliptic curve addition and doubling were worth it. We will look at the cost of the arithmetic in curves in Sect. 14.4, but the answer in general is an unequivocal "yes".

14.3 Elliptic Curve Cryptography

The group of points on an elliptic curve would seem to be a perfectly-reasonable set of "random" points, so these would seem to be fruitful mathematical constructs for key exchange. Doing cryptography using elliptic curves requires a little bit more of an explanation.

Armadillo, who wants to communicate securely, chooses an elliptic curve $\mathcal{E}$, a base point P of large prime order n, and makes those public. Armadillo also chooses a private key d and computes the public key

$$Q = dP.$$

When Bobcat wishes to send a secure message to Armadillo, she knows $\mathcal{E}$, P, and Q, but not d. The plaintext message m is converted to represent a point M on the curve. Bobcat computes a random k and then computes $R_1 = kP$ and $R_2 = M + kQ$ on the curve and sends those to Armadillo.

Armadillo now computes

$$dR_1 = dkP = kdP = kQ$$

and then uses this to compute

$$R_2 - kQ = M + kQ - kQ = M$$

and thus gets the curve version M of the plaintext m.

In order for Coati, who has intercepted the message, to get to M, she would have to get d from $Q = dP$, or k from kQ, since both P and Q, but neither d nor k, are public. Either of these is the elliptic curve discrete logarithm problem.

14.4   The Cost of Elliptic Curve Operations

The benefit of using elliptic curves instead of arithmetic modulo large primes is that the same level of security can be obtained with smaller numbers on which to perform arithmetic. The down side is that a single group operation on an elliptic curve is much more complicated than just the multiplication modulo P required for RSA. It's worth looking at the group operations to consider what it takes to use elliptic curves for cryptography.

We will illustrate the arithmetic using the Weierstrass form of a curve, which we will take modulo N, and to avoid the problem of inversions modulo N (which would require a gcd operation every time), we will consider the Jacobian version of the curve

$$\mathcal{E} : Y^2 = X^3 + aXZ^4 + bZ^6.$$

and will keep track of triples (X, Y, Z) instead of pairs (X, Y).

We also remember that squaring an integer is less costly than multiplying two integers together, so we will consider squaring to be different from multiplication.

14.4.1   Doubling a Point

If our goal is to double a point $P = (X, Y, Z)$, using Jacobian coordinates, as described in [3] and elsewhere, we can compute the triple (x_3, y_3, z_3) with six squarings, four multiplications, and some additions and shifts that are inexpensive by comparison with the squaring and multiplication as shown here.

$P_3 = (x_3, y_3, z_3)$ with

$$m_{num} = 3x_1^2 + az_1^4$$
$$x_3 = m_{num}^2 - 8x_1y_1^2$$
$$y_3 = m_{num}(4x_1y_1^2 - x_3) - 8y_1^4$$
$$z_3 = 2y_1z_1$$

done in sequence as

$A = y_1^2$	square
$B = 4x_1A$	multiply, shift
$C = 8A^2$	square, shift
$D = 3x_1^2 + az_1^4$	square, square, square, multiply, add
$x_3 = D^2 - 2B$	square, shift, add
$y_3 = D(B - x_3) - C$	add, multiply
$z_3 = 2y_1z_1$	multiply, shift

We note that some of these computations can be done in parallel; this might not be relevant if done in software (although threading could be possible), but it is something that could be considered if one were actually building hardware specifically for doing elliptic curve arithmetic.

14.4.2   Left-to-Right "Exponentiation"

A further simplification of the arithmetic in elliptic curve cryptography comes when one looks at the algorithms used for computing $m \cdot Q$ for a multiplier m and a point Q on the curve. We commented in Sect. 6.4 about exponentiation done by looking at the bits of the exponent. We don't exponentiate with elliptic curves, but rather compute the point mQ for some multiplier m and a base point Q. The usual right-to-left multiplication is as in the Python code here.

```
# Compute P = m times point Q
# expanding the bits of m right to left.
P = identity
point_to_add_in = Q
while m != 0:
    if m % 2 == 1:
        P = P + point_to_add_in
    m = m // 2
    point_to_add_in = point_to_add_in + point_to_add_in
return P
```

We can, however, get the same result by expanding the bits left to right, as in the code below.

The left to right method is slightly more tedious to get started, since we need a power of two to be able to find the leftmost 1-bit of the exponent. In the right-to-left algorithm, we have to double the point to be added in for each bit of the exponent, and in the left-to-right algorithm, we double the running return point P. There is no savings there. The savings is that when the bit is a 1, we add in the base point, so if that curve arithmetic is cheaper than a general-purpose point addition because we have chosen a distinguished point as our base, we save time.

```
# Compute P = m times point Q
# expanding the bits of m left to right.
P = identity
poweroftwo = A LARGE POWER OF TWO
while m != 0:
    P = P + P
    if power_of_two <= m:
        P = P + Q
        m = m - power_of_two
    power_of_two = power_of_two // 2
return P
```

Curve arithmetic is inherently expensive, so if we can maintain the same level of security, but choose the base point Q to be a point for which addition is cheap, we get a win in terms of the running time.

14.4.2.1 Adding a Distinguished Point to Any Point

Adding $P_1 = (x_1, y_1, z_1)$ to a distinguished "easy" point $P_2 = (x_2, y_2, 1)$ can be done as follows to produce $P_3 = (x_3, y_3, z_3)$.

$$x_3 = (y_2 z_1^3 - y_1)^2 - (x_2 z_1^2 - x_1)^2 (x_1 + x_2 z_1^2)$$
$$y_3 = (y_2 z_1^3 - y_1)(x_1(x_2 z_1^2 - x_1)^2 - x_3) - y_1(x_2 z_1^2 - x_1)^3$$
$$z_3 = (x_2 z_1^2 - x_1)z_1$$

As with doubling, these can be sequenced in an efficient way, as described in [3] and elsewhere, requiring three squarings, eight multiplications, and some shifts and adds.

$A = z_1^2$	square
$B = z_1 A$	multiply
$C = x_2 A$	multiply
$D = y_2 B$	multiply
$E = C - x_1$	add
$F = D - y_1$	add
$G = E^2$	square
$H = GE$	multiply
$I = x_1 G$	multiply
$x_3 = F^2 - H - 2I$	square, shift, add, add
$y_3 = F(I - x_3) - y_1 H$	add, multiply, multiply, add
$z_3 = z_1 E$	multiply

In the latter case of distinct points P_1 and P_2, we can compute the triple (x_3, y_3, z_3) with two squarings, twelve multiplications, seven additions, and two shifts, where once again we note that the operations inside each step can be done in parallel.

There has been extensive work on how best to perform this arithmetic, because it would be expensive if done naively.

14.5 The NIST Recommendations

Given the extent to which one can play games with the arithmetic needed for public key encryption, it is not surprising that the elliptic curves recommended for use by NIST are curves for which the arithmetic games work well. The NIST FIPS 186-4 (Federal Information Processing Standard), dated July 2013, recommends [4]

Bit Length	Prime Field	Binary Field
$161 - 223$	$P_{192} = 2^{192} - 2^{64} - 1$	$t^{163} + t^7 + t^6 + t^3 + 1$
$224 - 255$	$P_{224} = 2^{224} - 2^{96} + 1$	$t^{233} + t^{74} + 1$
$246 - 383$	$P_{256} = 2^{256} - 2^{224} + 2^{192} + 2^{96} - 1$	$t^{283} + t^{12} + t^7 + t^5 + 1$
$384 - 511$	$P_{384} = 2^{384} - 2^{128} - 2^{96} + 2^{32} - 1$	$t^{409} + t^{87} + 1$
> 511	$P_{521} = 2^{521} - 1$	$t^{571} + t^{10} + t^5 + t^2 + 1$

In the case of the prime fields, the recommended curves are of the form

$$\mathcal{E} : y^2 = x^3 - 3x + b \quad (\text{mod } P)$$

and random base points are recommended.

In the case of the binary fields, the recommended curves are either of the form

$$\mathcal{E} : y^2 + xy = x^3 + x^2 + b$$

for suggested values of b or are *Koblitz curves*

$$\mathcal{E} : y^2 + xy = x^3 + ax^2 + 1$$

with $a = 0$ or 1.

In all instances, the recommended base points are of a large prime order n and the number of points on the curve is hn, for a cofactor h that is 1, 2, or 4.

The FIPS 186-4 standard comes complete with the games to be played to enable efficient arithmetic, which are simple generalizations of the arithmetic game used, and in Chap. 8, when proving a Mersenne number to be prime. For example, for the 192-bit prime field, every integer less than P_{192}^2 (and thus the result of every multiplication step) can be written as

$$A = A_5 \cdot 2^{320} + A_4 \cdot 2^{256} + A_3 \cdot 2^{192} + A_2 \cdot 2^{128} + A_1 \cdot 2^{64} + A_0$$

where each of the A_i is a 64-bit integer. The value

$$B \equiv A \quad (\text{mod } P_{192})$$

can be computed as

$$B \equiv T + S_1 + S_2 + S_3 \quad (\text{mod } P_{192})$$

where the 192-bit summands are produced by concatenating the A_i appropriately:

$$T = A_2 || A_1 || A_0$$
$$S_1 = A_3 || A_3$$
$$S_2 = A_4 || A_4 || A_0$$
$$S_3 = A_5 || A_5 || A_5$$

The modular reduction has been replaced by bit extraction, concatenation, addition, and perhaps a few subtractions of the modulus.

The arithmetic needed to reduce modulo the other primes is also present in the FIPS, and analogous arithmetic games are presented for working in the binary fields.

14.6 Attacks on Elliptic Curves

We have already stated that the index calculus approach does not work in attacking the discrete log problem for elliptic curves, or at least the potential attack using Xedni has not been made effective [5,6].

What, then, are the attacks that are used?

14.6.1 Pohlig-Hellman Attacks

The most obvious attack on an elliptic curve discrete log problem would be that of Pohlig-Hellman [7]. This attack, however, is only efficient if the order of the group N is a smooth number, since it runs in time that is $\sqrt{N}$, where N is the order of the group. If the group order is smooth, Pohlig-Hellman runs by determining the discrete logs for each factor of N and then creates the desired discrete log using the Chinese Remainder Theorem. This is unlikely to be relevant to cryptanalytic problems, because a professional designer would not choose to use curves susceptible to this attack. It is specifically to prevent such an attack that the NIST curves, and any curves chosen by real professionals, would have a large prime factor dividing the order of the group, and a cofactor (referred to as h in the NIST FIPS, and chosen so that $h = 1, 2, 4$) that is as small as possible.

14.6.2 Pollard Rho Attacks

The Pollard rho attack on discrete log problems is derived from the Pollard rho factoring algorithm. It is a $\mathcal{O}(\sqrt{P})$ algorithm, which is why the index calculus is generally preferred for discrete logs modulo large primes. However, in the absence of an effective index calculus for elliptic curves, the best algorithm for curves is a variant of Pollard rho.

14.6.2.1 Pollard Rho Modulo Primes

If we were to follow Pollard's original approach for logs modulo primes [8], we start with a primitive root r and a value q for which we need the discrete log, and we compute sequences of exponents a_i and b_i and use them to compute

$$x_i \equiv q^{a_i} r^{b_i} \pmod{p}.$$

We want the a_i and b_i to provide a more-or-less-random walk through the integers modulo p, and choose

$$a_{i+1} \equiv a_i + 1 \pmod{p-1} \quad \text{if} \ \ 0 < x_i < p/3$$
$$\equiv 2a_i \pmod{p-1} \quad \text{if} \ \ p/3 < x_i < 2p/3$$
$$\equiv a_i \pmod{p-1} \quad \text{if} \ \ 2p/3 < x_i < p$$

and

$$b_{i+1} \equiv b_i \quad (\text{mod } p-1) \quad \text{if } \ 0 < x_i < p/3$$
$$\equiv 2b_i \quad (\text{mod } p-1) \quad \text{if } \ p/3 < x_i < 2p/3$$
$$\equiv b_i + 1 \quad (\text{mod } p-1) \quad \text{if } \ 2p/3 < x_i < p$$

We can now, using essentially no memory, compute x_i and x_{2i} by stepping one sequence once and the other twice, keeping track of the values of a_i and b_i, and look for a collision

$$x_i = x_{2i}.$$

When we get a collision, we have

$$q^{a_i} r^{b_i} \equiv q^{a_{2i}} r^{b_{2i}} \quad (\text{mod } p)$$

and thus

$$q^m \equiv q^{a_i - a_{2i}} \equiv r^{b_{2i} - b_i} \equiv r^n \quad (\text{mod } p)$$

We have q to the m-th power as a power of the primitive root r; we want q to the first power in terms of r. So we solve using the extended Euclidean algorithm

$$g = \lambda m + \mu(p-1)$$

for λ and μ, and exponentiate both sides:

$$q^g \equiv (q^m)^\lambda \equiv (r^n)^\lambda \equiv r^{gk} \quad (\text{mod } p)$$

We can divide n by g and try r^k, r^{2k}, r^{3k}, ...until we hit upon q. Since g should be small, this last step is not difficult.

Let's do an example, with $p = 31$, $r = 3$, and $q = 22$. Just for reference, we'll table the powers of 3.

Power	Value	Power	Value	Power	Value
1	3	11	13	21	15
2	9	12	8	22	14
3	27	13	24	23	11
4	19	14	10	24	2
5	26	15	30	25	6
6	16	16	28	26	18
7	17	17	22	27	23
8	20	18	4	28	7
9	29	19	12	29	21
10	25	20	5	30	1

Now, we'll run the Pollard algorithm:

Subscript	a_i	q^{a_i}	b_i	r^{b_i}	$q^{a_i}r^{b_i}$
1	0	1	0	1	1
2	1	22	0	1	22
2	1	22	0	1	22
4	2	19	1	3	26
3	1	22	1	3	4
6	4	20	4	19	8
4	2	19	1	3	26
8	5	6	5	26	1
5	2	19	2	9	16
10	6	8	6	16	4
6	4	20	4	19	8
12	7	21	7	17	16
7	5	6	4	19	21
14	15	30	14	10	21

We get the collision with $i = 7$, $a_7 = 5$, $a_{14} = 15$, $b_7 = 4$, $b_{14} = 14$. This gives us $m = 5 - 15 \equiv 20 \pmod{30}$ and $n = 14 - 4 \equiv 10 \pmod{30}$, and $22^{20} \equiv 3^{10} \equiv 25 \pmod{31}$. We get $\lambda = 2$ and $g = 10$, and we exponentiate

$$22^{10} \equiv 22^{40} \equiv 3^{20} \pmod{31}$$

We start with $3^2 \equiv 9 \pmod{31}$, because $20/10 = 2$, and then multiply in the 10-th roots of unity modulo 31; these would be $3^3, 3^6, 3^9, \ldots 3^{27}, 3^{30}$.

We get $3^2 \equiv 9 \pmod{31}$, $3^5 \equiv 26 \pmod{31}$, $3^8 \equiv 20 \pmod{31}$, $3^{11} \equiv 13 \pmod{31}$, $3^{14} \equiv 10 \pmod{31}$, $3^{17} \equiv 22 \pmod{31}$, and we are done.

14.6.3 Pollard Rho for Curves

Given points P and Q on a curve, the basic goal is to find distinct pairs of pairs, (a, b) and (a', b'), such that

$$aP + bQ = a'P + b'Q$$

on the curve. If this can be done, then we know that

$$(a - a')P = (b - b')Q = (b - b')dP$$

where P and Q are public information, but d is the private key. this would mean that

$$(a - a') \equiv (b - b')d \pmod{n}$$

where n is the order of the point P on the curve. Since n is known, we can invert $b - b'$ to get

$$d \equiv (a - a')(b - b')^{-1} \pmod{n}$$

The Pollard rho version of the attack is to choose a randomization function for stepping through the curve. Instead of just stepping once and twice, as in the factoring algorithm, we step forward at different rates (and this can be parallelized quite effectively) until we get the collision that would be expected. When we get the collision, with

$$aP + bQ = a'P + b'Q$$

for $a \neq a'$ and $b \neq b'$, then we will get our solution. This runs, as does Pollard rho for factoring, in time proportional to the square root of the order of the group.

14.6.4 Pollard Rho in Parallel

The algorithm as presented is a single path through the rho diagram. But we observe that once a collision is found, nothing in the rest of the algorithm that relies on the collision having been found for particular subscripts i and $2i$. We need the triples a_i, b_i, and $q^{a_i} r^{b_i}$, for two subscripts that result in a collision, but there is no use made of the value i.

If we had all the memory in the world, and a fast search tree, we could start a number of parallel steppings from different initial subscripts, store the a_i, b_i, pairs with an index of $q^{a_i} r^{b_i}$, and then search for collisions in the tree.

Better yet, although we would benefit from a search tree, we don't need it if all we want to do is detect the existence of a collision. We do need to store the triples a_i, b_i, and $q^{a_i} r^{b_i}$, but for detecting collisions what we need is a good hash function using $q^{a_i} r^{b_i}$ as input. We are going to be computing in parallel for a very long time and we are only going to get collisions at very rare intervals (there are some collisions that could be useless, for example if we somehow hit upon the same a_i, b_i, values). Storing the triples is a back-end process. Checking for $q^{a_i} r^{b_i}$ collisions happens all the time and needs to be as efficient as possible, and since collisions are rare, checking for the essence of a collision (that it's from identical $q^{a_i} r^{b_i}$ values and not from hash function collisions), we can afford to do a little more searching when we do think we have found something.

If the cycle is large, as it would be in cryptography for prime moduli or for elliptic curves, the stumbling block here is the need for enormous memory resources. That can be mitigated somewhat by choosing to save not all the steppings, but only those a subset, perhaps only those for which $q^{a_i} r^{b_i}$ is "small". This then becomes a standard computational balancing act:

- How many processors do we have?
- How much memory do we have for storing pairs?
- How fast can we look up values using a hash function?
- How do we balance the rate of stepping with the cost of collision lookup with the cost of doing more computing because we don't have enough memory?

As with everything in the computations done for factoring, for doing the index calculus, or for the Pollard rho attack on an elliptic curve discrete log, the most efficient approach is a moving target based in part on the computing resources available and the nature of the underlying hardware and system software. The art (and not science)

Table 14.1 Security–AES versus RSA versus elliptic curves

Security bits	AES	Minimum bits RSA	Minimum bits ECC
128	AES-128	3072	256
192	AES-192	7680	384
256	AES-256	15360	512

of doing the computations on commodity computers would be much different from what might be the best approach if one were using FPGAs or GPUs or designing special purpose hardware.

14.7   A Comparison of Complexities

A white paper published by Atmel Corporation compares the cryptographic security of different cryptosystems based on the bit lengths of the operands. Their results [9] cite an earlier NSA document and are in Table 14.1. Although these may be moving targets based on the computational capability of different kinds of hardware platforms (supercomputers, desktops, computers augmented with FPGAs or GPUS, etc.), this table provides one starting point for comparison.

14.8   Exercises

1. (Programming exercise.) Implement a general class for elliptic curve arithmetic modulo a prime, using Jacobian coordinates but with a reduction to the point with $z = 1$ so you can see with less effort that you have the arithmetic done properly.
2. (Programming exercise.) Implement an elliptic curve key exchange using the base point $Q = (1, 6)$ on the curve $x^3 + x + 3$ taken modulo 31. This curve has a cycle of prime length 41.
3. (Programming exercise.) Implement an elliptic curve cryptographic system using the curve $x^3 + x + 3$ taken modulo 31. This curve has a cycle of prime length 41, with a base point $P = (1, 6)$.

References

1. N. Koblitz, Elliptic curve cryptosystems. Math. Comput. **48**, 203–209 (1987)
2. V.S. Miller, Use of elliptic curves in cryptography, in *Advances in Cryptology -CRYPTO '85*, vol. 218, Lecture Notes in Computer Science (1986), pp. 417–426

3. D. Hankerson, A. Menezes, S. Vanstone, *Guide to Elliptic Curve Cryptography* (Springer, 2004)
4. NIST, *Fips 186-4: digital signature standard* (2013). https://csrc.nist.gov/publications/detail/fips/186/4/final
5. M.J. Jacobson, N. Koblitz, J.H. Silverman, A. Stein, E. Teske, Analysis of the Xedni calculus attack. Des. Codes Cryptogr. **20**, 41–64 (2000)
6. J.H. Silverman, The Xedni calculus and the elliptic curve discrete logarithm problem. Des. Codes Cryptogr. **20**, 5–40 (2000)
7. S. Pohlig, M. Hellman, An improved algorithm for computing logarithms over $GF(p)$ and its cryptographic significance. IEEE Trans. Inf. Theory **24**, 106–110 (1978)
8. J.M. Pollard, Monte Carlo methods for index computation mod p. Math. Comput. 918–924 (1978)
9. K. Maletski, *RSA vs ECC Comparison for Embedded Systems* (Atmel Corporation white paper, 2015)

Lattice-Based Cryptography and NTRU

15

Abstract

With the publication of Peter Shor's seminal paper that factoring and discrete log computations would be entirely feasible on a quantum computer, and with advances in the building of quantum computers, there has been a focus on what is referred to as "post-quantum cryptography". Among the most viable candidates for post-quantum cryptography are cryptosystems based on the problem of finding short vectors in lattices. In this chapter we outline briefly why quantum computers can make RSA-type cryptosystems obsolete and how lattices can be used in cryptography. We concentrate on perhaps the best-known lattice system, NTRU, and explain how it is used and why attacks on it still seem computationally infeasible.

15.1 Quantum Computing

To become a physicist, you must sign in blood that you won't be upset by things that make no sense and can't be explained. (Ed Fredkin [1])

Very informally, one can say that the power of a quantum computer is its ability to compute everthing all at once. That's not quite right, but it is an insight into how a quantum computer can attack RSA-type factoring and Diffie-Hellman-type discrete log problems. A quantum computer is at any point in the computation in a superposition of states

$$\sum_i a_i |S_i\rangle$$

where each $|S_i\rangle$ is a state of the computer and the a_i are complex numbers that are the amplitudes. Quantum physics says that examining the system changes it, but if the computer is examined at any point, the probability of observing state $|S_i\rangle$ is $|a_i|^2$, and these are in fact probabilities: we have $\Sigma_i |a_i|^2 = 1$.

© The Author(s), under exclusive license to Springer Nature Switzerland AG 2021
D. Buell, *Fundamentals of Cryptography*, Undergraduate Topics in Computer Science,
https://doi.org/10.1007/978-3-030-73492-3_15

Although fully-functional, general-purpose, quantum computers have not yet been built, progress is being made, and there will likely be a point in the not-too-distant future when quantum computers can be used on real computational problems. One of the most significant consequences of the ability to build a real quantum computer is that all the public key cryptography based on number theory as presented in Chaps. 10–14 will be attackable and will no longer provide security. This was the primary result of a seminal paper published in 1994 by Peter Shor [2–4]. Since the publication of that paper, and more especially in recent years as progress toward building real quantum computers has increased, there has been a focus on cryptographic systems that are not susceptible to attacks on quantum computers.

We will only give an overview of factoring with a quantum computer, rather than the details, which require perhaps more mathematics and more physics than is necessary to understand the need for the development of alternative cryptosystems.

We recall that the RSA cryptosystem is hard to attack because it is based on arithmetic modulo $N = pq$ for two large primes p and q, because attacking the system requires (or at least at present seems to) knowing the Euler phi function $\phi(N) = (p - 1)(q - 1)$, and because computing $\phi(N)$ seems to be as hard as factoring. The sieve methods for factoring rely on finding X and Y such that

$$X^2 - Y^2 = (X + Y)(X - Y) \equiv 0 \pmod{N}$$

and finding sufficiently many such X and Y that eventually we have $\gcd(X + Y, N)$ and $\gcd(X - Y, N)$ each containing one of p and q, but not both multiplied together in one of the gcds.

If we can produce X such that $X^2 - 1 \equiv 0 \pmod{N}$ by finding a nontrivial square root of 1, then we can probably factor N.

As an example, let's factor $1457 = 31 \times 47$. We have $\phi(1457) = 1380 = 2^2 \times 3 \times 5 \times 23$; the part modulo 31 is crumbly, but 47 is twice a prime plus 1.

The nontrivial square roots of 1 modulo 31 and 47, respectively, are, of course, 30 and 46. We can compute directly (because this is a small example) that the nontrivial square roots of 1 modulo 1457 are $187 = 6 \times 31 + 1 = 4 \times 47 - 1$ and $1270 = 41 \times 31 - 1 = 27 \times 47 + 1$; the four square roots of 1 modulo the product of two primes will have the pattern of $(1, 1)$, $(-1, 1)$, $(1, -1)$, and $(-1, -1)$, modulo the two primes.

More to the point of the algorithm, we can compute the orders of the residues modulo 1457. We know that the maximal order is 690, and we find that 3 has order 690. Backing off one factor of 2 in the exponent, which is taking the square root, we find that

$$\gcd(3^{345} + 1 \pmod{1457}, \quad 1457) = 31$$

and

$$\gcd(3^{345} - 1 \pmod{1457}, \quad 1457) = 47.$$

Now, on a standard computer, choosing random residues and computing the order would be inefficient, because we would have no good way to power up a residue and check all the powers to find the one value that happened to be 1. With a quantum computer, however, the superposition of states permits us essentially to check all the powers simultaneously. By performing a quantum Fourier transformation (which we won't explain), we obtain approximations to the order, and can determine in polynomial time whether the approximation is close enough to let us determine the order exactly. Since we can determine the order of a randomly chosen residue in quantum polynomial time, we can find in polynomial time a factor of N.

15.2 Lattices: An Introduction

Definition 15.1 We consider row vectors $\mathbf{b_i}$, for $i = 1, \ldots, n$, that are of length n, have coefficients in the real numbers $\mathbb{R}$, and are linearly independent over $\mathbb{R}^n$. A *lattice* over the basis $\{\mathbf{b_i}\}$ is the set

$$L(\mathbf{b_1}, \ldots, \mathbf{b_n}) = \left\{ \sum_{i=1}^{n} x_i \mathbf{b_i} : x_i \in \mathbb{Z} \right\}$$

Clearly, we can phrase this as in the language of matrices. If we write

$$\mathbf{B} = \begin{pmatrix} \mathbf{b_1} \\ \ldots \\ \mathbf{b_n} \end{pmatrix}$$

then the lattice can be written as the set of matrix products

$$L(\mathbf{B}) = \left\{ \mathbf{xB} : \mathbf{x} \in \mathbb{Z}^n \right\}$$

We observe that if $\mathbf{U}$ is a matrix with integer coefficients and determinant ± 1, then there exists an inverse matrix $\mathbf{U}^{-1}$ whose coefficients are also integers, and we have that

$$L(\mathbf{B}) = L(\mathbf{UB}).$$

The matrix $\mathbf{U}$ is a change-of-basis matrix, and some matrices $\mathbf{U}$ can be obtained by doing by doing matrix reduction on $\mathbf{B}$. Indeed, if we apply any of the standard matrix reduction steps

- Interchange two rows of $\mathbf{B}$
- Multiply all entries in a row by -1
- Add an integer multiple of one row to another row.

and do the operations on the matrix of k rows and $2k$ columns $\mathbf{BI}$ of $\mathbf{B}$ with an identity appended on the right, then the identity matrix is transformed into the matrix that does the change of basis. The only thing that makes this different from ordinary Gaussian elimination is that we must take care not to multiply or divide by values other than ± 1, because we need to maintain the matrix coefficients as integers.

We can illustrate the reduction of $\mathbf{B}$ to a basis with more constraints this with a simple example.

Example 15.1 Let's assume that we have a lattice in three dimensions given by

$$\mathbf{B} = \begin{pmatrix} 1 & 4 & 9 \\ 2 & 7 & 2 \\ 3 & 9 & 5 \end{pmatrix}$$

We can augment the matrix with the identity to get

$$\begin{pmatrix} 1 & 4 & 9 & X & 1 & 0 & 0 \\ 2 & 7 & 2 & X & 0 & 1 & 0 \\ 3 & 9 & 5 & X & 0 & 0 & 1 \end{pmatrix}$$

where the X is merely a marker to separate the two matrices.

We reduce on the first column:

$$\begin{pmatrix} 1 & 4 & 9 & X & 1 & 0 & 0 \\ 0 & -1 & -16 & X & -2 & 1 & 0 \\ 0 & -3 & -22 & X & -3 & 0 & 1 \end{pmatrix}$$

We can then reduce on the second column:

$$\begin{pmatrix} 1 & 4 & 9 & X & 1 & 0 & 0 \\ 0 & 1 & 16 & X & 2 & -1 & 0 \\ 0 & 0 & 26 & X & 3 & -3 & 1 \end{pmatrix}$$

At this point we can observe that

$$\mathbf{U} \cdot \mathbf{B} = \mathbf{B}' = \begin{pmatrix} 1 & 0 & 0 \\ 2 & -1 & 0 \\ 3 & -3 & 1 \end{pmatrix} \cdot \begin{pmatrix} 1 & 4 & 9 \\ 2 & 7 & 2 \\ 3 & 9 & 5 \end{pmatrix} = \begin{pmatrix} 1 & 4 & 9 \\ 0 & 1 & 16 \\ 0 & 0 & 26 \end{pmatrix}$$

and we have a change of basis matrix $\mathbf{U}$ taking $\mathbf{B}$ to $\mathbf{B}'$.
We note that this matrix is its own inverse.

15.3 Hard Lattice Problems

Cryptography based on lattices relies primarily (though not exclusively) on the fact
that there are two lattice problems that are computationally very hard to solve.

Problem 1. (Shortest Vector Problem) Given a lattice L, what is the shortest
vector in the lattice? That is, among all vectors $\mathbf{v} = \mathbf{xB}$, for $\mathbf{x} \in \mathbb{Z}^n$, what is the
vector $\mathbf{v} = (v_1, \ldots, v_n)$ whose length

$$\|\mathbf{v}\| = \sqrt{\sum_{i=1}^{n} v_i^2}$$

is minimal?

Problem 2. (Closest Vector Problem) Given a lattice L, and a point $\mathbf{r} \in \mathbb{R}^n$, what
is the lattice vector that is closest to $\mathbf{r}$?

These are very similar problems. Both have been studied extensively, and there
are algorithms which provide approximations, but there are also proofs that under
appropriate conditions, these problems are computationally infeasible to solve in
practice.

Example 15.2 In our example above, we can determine (because the dimension is small) that the shortest vector in the lattice is

$$(1\ 3\ -3)\begin{pmatrix} 1 & 4 & 9 \\ 2 & 7 & 2 \\ 3 & 9 & 5 \end{pmatrix} = (-2\ -2\ 0)$$

of length $\sqrt{8}$.

We can also verify that

$$(-2\ 6\ -3)\begin{pmatrix} 1 & 4 & 9 \\ 0 & 1 & 16 \\ 0 & 0 & 26 \end{pmatrix} = (-2\ -2\ 0)$$

and that

$$(-2\ 6\ -3)\begin{pmatrix} 1 & 0 & 0 \\ 2 & -1 & 0 \\ 3 & -3 & 1 \end{pmatrix} = (1\ 3\ -3)$$

as it must be: if $\mathbf{B'} = \mathbf{UB}$, and $\mathbf{x'B'} = \mathbf{xB}$, then we must have $\mathbf{x'U} = \mathbf{x}$.

15.4 NTRU

Although it might not be obvious at first, the NTRU cryptosystem, proposed by Hoffstein, Pipher, and Silverman[1] [5], is a lattice-based cryptosystem. We consider the ring R of polynomials $f(X)$, with integer coefficients, reduced modulo $X^N - 1$. The value of N, the degree of the modulus, will be one of the factors influencing the security of the cryptosystem. The addition of elements in this ring is the usual polynomial addition (remembering that in this case we are *not* reducing the coefficients modulo 2). The multiplication is the usual multiplication and subsequent reduction. The fact that we have $X^N \equiv 1$ means that we can write the multiplication as a convolution product

$$h(X) = f(X) \circledast g(X)$$

where the coefficients h_k are

$$h_k = \sum_{\substack{i+j \equiv k \pmod{N}}} f_i \cdot g_j$$

We note that the convolution product is commutative.

Example 15.3 If we have $X^3 - 1$ as our modulus and

$$f(X) = 1 + 2X + 3X^2$$
$$g(X) = 2 + 5X + 7X^2$$

---

[1] We will refer to these authors as "HPS" in the text here.

then
$$f(X) \circledast g(X) = 2 + 5X + 7X^2 + 4X + 10X^2 + 14X^3 + 6X^2 + 15X^3 + 21X^4$$
$$= (2 + 14 + 15) + (5 + 4 + 21)X + (7 + 10 + 6)X^2$$
$$= 31 + 30X + 23X^2.$$

Finally, we will use the notation
$$f(X) \equiv g(X) \quad (\text{mod } X^N - 1, q)$$
to indicate that we would obtain polynomial $g(X)$ by reducing $f(X)$ modulo $X^N - 1$ as a polynomial and then reduce the coefficients of the polynomial modulo an integer q.

15.5 The NTRU Cryptosystem

Extensive descriptions of NTRU can be found in the original paper by Hoffstein, Pipher, and Silverman [5] and in the later book by the same authors [6].

15.5.1 Parameters

A given instance of NTRU has three integer parameters, the degree N of the polynomial used as a modulus and two integers p and q; and four sets of polynomials L_f, L_g, L_r, and L_m of degrees $N - 1$ with integer coefficients. We do not actually need p and q to be prime, only that they are coprime with $\gcd(p, q) = 1$, but we will often take them to be prime, and we will take q to be much larger than p for reasons that will appear later.

Working in the ring R defined above, we write polynomials or vectors
$$F = \sum_{i=0}^{N-1} F_i x^i = [F_0, \ldots, F_{N-1}]$$
with the sequence of coefficients corresponding to increasing powers of x.

We define a lattice by
$$L(d_1, d_2) = \left\{ F \in R : F \text{ has } \begin{cases} d_1 \text{ coefficients that are } 1, \\ d_2 \text{ coefficients that are } -1, \\ \text{and all other coefficients are } 0 \end{cases} \right\}$$
We use d_f, d_g, and d as integer bounds on the numbers of nonzero coefficients of polynomials f, g, r in R, and we define lattices
$$L_f = L(d_f, d_f - 1)$$
$$L_g = L(d_g, d_g)$$
$$L_r = L(d, d)$$
We deliberately choose $L_f = L(d_f, d_f - 1)$ so that f is invertible.

15.5.2 Creating Keys

NTRU is an asymmetric, public-key, cryptosystem. To create a key, Armadillo will choose random polynomials f and g from L_f and L_g, respectively. The polynomial f must be invertible modulo both p and q, and we denote its inverses by F_p and F_q. By "inverses" we mean that

$$F_p \circledast f \equiv 1 \quad (\bmod \ x^N - 1, p)$$
$$F_q \circledast f \equiv 1 \quad (\bmod \ x^N - 1, q)$$

We note that computing the inverses is one-time work prior to establishing a cryptographic system, and for efficiency the inverses could be stored for later use.

Armadillo then creates her public key

$$h = F_q \circledast g \quad (\bmod \ q)$$

but keeps f (and F_p, if it is being saved) private.

15.5.3 Encrypting a Message

Given a message to send, Bobcat writes the message as a polynomial m of degree $N - 1$ with coefficients taken in the range $\frac{-p}{2}$ to $\frac{p}{2}$. Bobcat then randomly chooses a polynomial $r \in L_r$ as a one-time key, computes the ciphertext[2]

$$e = p \cdot r \circledast h + m \quad (\bmod \ q).$$

and sends e to Armadillo.

15.5.4 Decrypting a Message

After receiving the ciphertext e, Armadillo, knowing her private key f, computes

$$a \equiv f \circledast e \quad (\bmod \ q)$$

and reduces the coefficients a_i to satisfy the bounds

$$\frac{-q}{2} \leq a_i < \frac{q}{2}.$$

With this, Armadillo recovers m as

$$m \equiv F_p \circledast a \quad (\bmod \ p). \tag{15.1}$$

---

[2]We note that some presentations include the multiplication by p as part of the public key h, while the HPS presentation multiplies by p when the ciphertext is produced.

Example 15.4 Let's look at an example. We choose parameters $N = 5$, so we reduce all polynomials modulo $X^5 - 1$, the small modulus $p = 3$, and the large modulus $q = 17$. We choose $d_f = 2, d_g = 2, d_r = 1$; These are the bounds on the numbers of nonzero coefficients of the polynomials.

With this, we can choose

$$f = -1 + X^2 + X^4 = [-1, 0, 1, 0, 1]$$

and

$$g = -1 + X + X^2 - X^3 = [-1, 1, 0, 1, -1]$$

and compute

$$F_p = -1 - X + X^3 - X^4 = [-1, -1, 0, 1, -1]$$

and

$$F_q = 6 + 5X + +8X^2 + 2X^3 + 14X^4 = [6, 5, 8, 2, 14]$$

noting that the computation of F_p and of F_q is one-time work that is essentially a gcd operation in the appropriate rings.

We can now compute the public key

$$h = 11 + 12X + 9X^2 + 15X^3 + 4X^4 = [11, 12, 9, 15, 4]$$

Now, let's assume the message is the polynomial/vector

$$m = [-1, 0, 1, 1, 0]$$

where we take the vector to be increasing powers of X.

We randomly choose $r = X - X^4$ and compute the ciphertext

$$e = p \cdot h \circledast r + m \quad (\text{mod } q),$$

which yields

$$e = 8 + 2X + 6X^2 + 8X^3 + 11X^4 = [8, 2, 6, 8, 11] \quad (\text{mod } q),$$

Decryption requires computing

$$a' \equiv f \circledast e \equiv [2, -2, -7, 5, 3] \quad (\text{mod } q).$$

We then compute

$$F_p \circledast a \equiv [-1, 0, 1, 1, 0] \quad (\text{mod } p).$$

and we recover, modulo p, the original message.

15.5.5 Why This Works

The first step in decryption is to multiply e on the left by f, which is

$$
\begin{aligned}
a' &= f \circledast e \\
&\equiv f \circledast pr \circledast h + f \circledast m \quad (\text{mod } q) \\
&\equiv f \circledast pr \circledast F_q \circledast g + f \circledast m \quad (\text{mod } q) \\
&\equiv pr \circledast g + f \circledast m \quad (\text{mod } q)
\end{aligned}
\tag{15.2}
$$

We now reduce a' to a, with all the coefficients in the interval $[-q/2, q/2)$. If we have chosen p and q correctly, the reduction modulo q produces the exact coefficients of this last polynomial, not just the coefficients modulo q, so when this last is reduced modulo p we get back the exact polynomial

$$
f \circledast m
$$

and can multiply by F_p modulo p to get back the plaintext m.

15.5.6 Preventing Errors in Decryption

We would not normally expect reduction modulo p and modulo q to produce an unambiguous result. The argument that this process is unambiguous runs as follows.

We remember that the coefficients of f, g, and r were chosen to be only $0, 1, -1$. We have chosen p to be much smaller than q, and we can choose the coefficients of m to be small, since they represent an encoding of the plaintext.

This means that the *actual integer* coefficients of

$$
pr \circledast g + f \circledast m
$$

are likely to be small and the reduction modulo q into the range $-q/2$ to $q/2$ may not actually be needed. Reducing this polynomial modulo p produces $f \circledast m$ and then multiplication by F_p modulo p produces m.

One can prove a bound; the following is Proposition 6.48 from [6].

Theorem 15.1 *If the parameters N, p, q, d are chosen such that*

$$
q > (6d + 1)p
$$

then the polynomial computed by Armadillo as Eq. (15.1) is equal to Bobcat's plaintext message m, where we assume that $d_f - 1 = d_g = d_r = d$.

Proof We know from Eq. (15.2) that

$$
a' \equiv pr \circledast g + f \circledast m \quad (\text{mod } q).
\tag{15.3}
$$

The polynomials r and g have d coefficients each of values either $+1$ or -1. If all the coefficients match up, then the largest coefficient in the convolution product $r \circledast g$ will be $2d$. Similarly, the largest possible coefficient in the second term $f \circledast m$ will be $p(2d + 1)/2$, so the largest possible coefficient of (15.3) is

$$p(2d) + p(2d + 1)/2 = p\left(3d + \frac{1}{2}\right) < q/2.$$

If we have chosen q as in the assumption of the theorem, this last value is less than $q/2$ and the coefficients computed modulo q as residues symmetric about 0 will be the same as the coefficients we would obtain from computing the coefficients as ordinary integers. The reduction modulo p of a' to a must then result in the recovery of the original message polynomial m.   □

Theorem 15.1 is a worst-case result. Since the polynomials are sparse, and their coefficients small, it is unlikely that one would normally encounter this worst case. We note that in our example, with $p = 3$ and $d = 2$, this bound would require q to be larger than 17, and yet we recover at least this one message with $q = 17$. This bound, however, is not so excessive that one cannot use it in practice, and indeed this has been done.

15.6 Lattice Attacks on NTRU

It might not be apparent that NTRU can be viewed as a lattice-based cryptosystem; this becomes easier to see when one looks at various attacks on NTRU. This attack is from the work of Coppersmith and Shamir [7]. We will do an example first and then look at the theory.

We let $(N, p, q) = (7, 3, 19)$, with

$$f = 1 - x + x^4 = [1, -1, 0, 0, 1, 0, 0]$$
$$g = -1 - x + x^3 - x^5 = [-1, 1, 0, 1, 0, -1, 0]$$

and we get the public key

$$h = [2, 18, 14, 6, 4, 4, 9]$$

as coefficients of increasing powers of x.

We produce a matrix of $2N$ rows and columns:

```
1 0 0 0 0 0 0 | 2  18 14 6  4  4  9
0 1 0 0 0 0 0 | 9  2  18 14 6  4  4
0 0 1 0 0 0 0 | 4  9  2  18 14 6  4
0 0 0 1 0 0 0 | 4  4  9  2  18 14 6
0 0 0 0 1 0 0 | 6  4  4  9  2  18 14
0 0 0 0 0 1 0 | 14 6  4  4  9  2  18
0 0 0 0 0 0 1 | 18 14 6  4  4  9  2
0 0 0 0 0 0 0 | 19 0  0  0  0  0  0
0 0 0 0 0 0 0 | 0  19 0  0  0  0  0
0 0 0 0 0 0 0 | 0  0  19 0  0  0  0
0 0 0 0 0 0 0 | 0  0  0  19 0  0  0
0 0 0 0 0 0 0 | 0  0  0  0  19 0  0
0 0 0 0 0 0 0 | 0  0  0  0  0  19 0
0 0 0 0 0 0 0 | 0  0  0  0  0  0  19
```

We have blocked off the four quadrants, with the identity upper left, the identity times q down the diagonal lower right, a zero matrix lower left, and the circulant of the h coefficients in the upper right. This matrix defines a lattice, which we will refer to as the NTRU lattice. The difficulty of attacking a lattice-based cryptosystem depends on the difficulty of finding short vectors in the lattice.

The state-of-the-art algorithms for finding short vectors in lattices are variants of the Lenstra-Lenstra-Lovász (LLL) algorithm [8]. Using the LLL algorithms of Sage Math [9], we find short vectors in the lattice. Using the default LLL algorithm, for example, produces the following, where we have prepended each row with the length of the vector that follows.

```
7   | 0  0  -1 1  0  0  -1 | 1  0  1  -1 0  -1 0
7   | -1 0  0  -1 1  0  0  | 0  1  0  1  -1 0  -1
7   | 1  0  0  -1 0  0  -1 | -1 0  -1 0  1  0  1
7   | -1 1  0  0  -1 0  0  | 1  -1 0  -1 0  1  0
7   | 1  1  1  1  1  1  1  | 0  0  0  0  0  0  0
7   | 0  1  0  0  1  -1 0  | 1  0  -1 0  -1 1  0
7   | 0  0  -1 0  0  -1 1  | 0  -1 0  1  0  1  -1
95  | 1  4  -2 -3 -3 -1 3  | 2  1  0  1  0  -6 2
95  | -3 -3 -1 3  1  4  -2 | 1  0  -6 2  2  1  0
104 | 0  -1 1  1  3  0  -3 | 1  0  6  2  1  5  4
95  | -3 -1 -4 2  3  3  1  | -2 -2 -1 0  -1 0  6
104 | 0  3  0  1  -1 -1 -3 | -5 -4 -1 0  -6 -2 -1
96  | -3 -1 4  1  4  -1 -4 | 0  -5 2  1  1  -1 2
104 | -1 1  1  3  0  -3 0  | 0  6  2  1  5  4  1
```

If we split the left and right halves of the fourth row we get

$$-f = [-1, 1, 0, 0, -1, 0, 0]$$
$$-g = [1, -1, 0, -1, 0, 1, 0]$$

These are exactly the negatives of the coefficient sequences for f and g. Looking more closely at all the rows of length 7 except the fifth, we see that they are plus or minus circular shifts of each other, and a circular shift of the coefficients of the polynomials is the same as the star multiplication by a power of x.

$$f = 1 - x + x^4 = [1, -1, 0, 0, 1, 0, 0]$$
$$g = -1 - x + x^3 - x^5 = [-1, 1, 0, 1, 0, -1, 0]$$

15.7 The Mathematics of the Lattice Reduction Attack

There is, we admit, a bit of a chicken-and-egg problem regarding lattice reduction, lattice cryptography, and NTRU in particular. So let's go back to the theory of lattices.
   Let

$$h(x) = h_0 + h_1 x + \ldots + h_{N-1} x^{N-1}$$

be a public key for an instance of NTRU.
   The lattice L associated with that public key is the $2N$-dimensional lattice spanned by the rows of the matrix M given by

$$M = \begin{pmatrix} 1 & 0 & \ldots & 0 & h_0 & h_1 & \ldots & h_{N-1} \\ 0 & 1 & \ldots & 0 & h_{N-1} & h_0 & \ldots & h_{N-2} \\ \ldots & \ldots & \ldots & & \ldots & \ldots & \ldots \\ 0 & 0 & \ldots & 1 & h_1 & h_2 & \ldots & h_0 \\ 0 & 0 & \ldots & 0 & q & 0 & \ldots & 0 \\ 0 & 0 & \ldots & 0 & 0 & q & \ldots & 0 \\ \ldots & \ldots & \ldots & & \ldots & \ldots & \ldots \\ 0 & 0 & \ldots & 0 & 0 & 0 & \ldots & q \end{pmatrix}$$

We can view the rows of this matrix as providing the coefficients for two polynomials

$$(a, b) = ((a_0, a_1, \ldots, a_{N-1})(b_0, b_1, \ldots, b_{N-1}))$$

If we assume that the private key $h(x)$ was created using two polynomials $f(x)$ and $g(x)$, then we can turn an attack on the NTRU instance into a lattice problem with the following proposition.

Proposition 15.1 *Assuming that $f(x) \circledast h(x) \equiv g(x) \pmod{q}$, then let $u(x)$ be the polynomial satisfying*

$$f(x) \circledast h(x) = g(x) + q u(x)$$

With this definition, we have that

$$(f, -u)M = (f, g)$$

and thus the vector (f, g) is in the lattice L.

The key takeaway here is that the private keys (f, g) are in the lattice L, but they are also (by definition) polynomials with only a few nonzero coefficients, and those coefficients are only 1 in absolute value. The vector (f, g) is thus very likely a very short vector, if not the shortest vector in the lattice. One can prove the probability that this is the shortest vector, and it is dependent on the choices of the parameters for the instance of NTRU.

15.7.1   Other Attacks on NTRU

The attack described just above uses the matrix M to create a lattice in which the private keys f and g are likely to appear when the lattice is reduced. A very similar attack can be launched against ciphertext. If we use instead of

$$M = \begin{pmatrix} I & H \\ 0 & qI \end{pmatrix}$$

where H is the circulant matrix, the matrix

$$\begin{pmatrix} I & H \\ 0 & qI \\ 0 & e \end{pmatrix}$$

then a similar lattice reduction might well produce as one of the short vectors the vector (m, r).

15.7.2   Lattice Reduction

So ..., what does lattice reduction look like?

In the case of two dimensions, the reduction of lattices looks very much like a two-dimensional gcd algorithm, and the algorithm goes back to Gauss.

Given two vectors

$$\mathbf{v_1} = [v_{11}, v_{12}]$$
$$\mathbf{v_2} = [v_{21}, v_{22}]$$

that define a lattice, we can reduce the vector basis to produce the shortest vector in the lattice with the algorithm of Algorithm 1.

Algorithm 1 Gaussian reduction in two dimensions

1: **while** True **do**

2: **if** length(v_2) $\leq$ length(v_1) **then**

3:    Swap v_1 and v_2

4: **end if**
5: Compute $m = round(v_1 \cdot v_2 / length(v_1)^2)$
6: **if** $m = 0$ **then**

7:    Return v_1 and v_2

8: **end if**
9: $v_2 \leftarrow v_2 - mv_1$

10: **end while**

Lattice reduction in higher dimensions is not as simple as the Gauss reduction in two dimensions. The problem of proving the length of the shortest vector in a lattice, the problem of proving the length of some short vector in a lattice, and algorithms for finding such vectors have been studied for more than two centuries. One result that can be useful for studying NTRU is the *Gaussian heuristic*: A randomly chosen lattice defined by an $n \times n$ matrix L will have a nonzero vector v such that

$$||v|| \approx \frac{n}{2\pi e} |det L|^{1/n}$$

The state of the art for lattice reduction is the Lenstra-Lenstra-Lovász algorithm [8], usually referred to simply as "LLL", with pseudocode as in Algorithm 2. In this algorithm the values $\mu_{k,j}$ and the intermediate basis vectors v_i^* are the values from Gram-Schmidt orthogonalization process of Algorithm 3. The pseudocode for Algorithms 2 and 3 are derived from the algorithms shown in [6].

15.8   NTRU Parameter Choices

Research on NTRU is very much still active. Suggestions for parameter choices for NTRU can be found on the Security Innovation website [10] and are presented in the table below. A more in-depth analysis can be found in [11].

	N	q	p
Moderate Security	167	128	3
Standard Security	251	128	3
High Security	347	128	3
Highest Security	503	256	3

Algorithm 2 LLL lattice reduction

1: Input a basis $(\mathbf{v}_1, \ldots, \mathbf{v}_n)$ for a lattice L
2: $k \leftarrow 2$
3: $\mathbf{v}_1^* \leftarrow= \mathbf{v}_1$
4: **while** $k \leq n$ **do**

5:   **for** $j = 1, 2, \ldots, k - 1$ **do**

6:       $\mathbf{v}_k \leftarrow \mathbf{v}_k - round(\mu_{k,j})\mathbf{v}_j^*$ {Size reduction}

7:   **end for**
8:   (Now apply Lovász condition)
9:   **if** $||\mathbf{v}_k^*||^2 \geq \left(\frac{3}{4} - \mu_{k,k-1}^2\right) ||\mathbf{v}_{k-1}^*||^2$ **then**

10:       $k \leftarrow k + 1$

11:   **else**

12:       Swap $\mathbf{v}_{k-1}$ and $\mathbf{v}_k$
13:       $k \leftarrow \max(k - 1, 2)$

14:   **end if**

15: **end while**
16: **return** Reduced basis $(\mathbf{v}_1, \ldots, \mathbf{v}_n)$

Algorithm 3 Gram-Schmidt orthogonalization

1: Input a basis $(\mathbf{v}_1, \ldots, \mathbf{v}_n)$ for a lattice L
2: $\mathbf{v}_1^* \leftarrow \mathbf{v}_1$
3: **for** $i = 2, \ldots, n$ **do**

4:   **for** $j = 1, \ldots, i - 1$ **do**

5:       $\mu_{ij} \leftarrow (\mathbf{v}_i \cdot \mathbf{v}_j^*)/||\mathbf{v}_j^*||^2$

6:   **end for**
7:   $\mathbf{v}_i^* \leftarrow \mathbf{v}_i - \sum_{j=1}^{i-1} \mu_{ij}\mathbf{v}_j^*$

8: **end for**
9: **return** Orthogonal basis $(\mathbf{v}_1^*, \ldots, \mathbf{v}_n^*)$

15.9 Exercises

1. SageMath reports that the (probably) second shortest vector in the lattice of Example 15.1 is $(-1, 0, 3)$ of length $\sqrt{10}$. Verify that this short vector is in the lattice by determining the coefficients $a, b, c \in \mathbb{Z}^3$ such that

$$a(1, 4, 9) + b(2, 7, 2) + c(3, 9, 5) = (-2, -2, 0).$$

2. (Probably requires programming.) Do the same for the 14×14 matrix of the example in Sect. 15.6: verify that the short vector of row 1 of the matrix returned by SageMath is a linear combination of the vectors defining the lattice.

3. (Probably requires programming.) Consider the message xy, of two characters, and 16 bits, in length. Convert this using the ASCII codes for x and y into an integer in the obvious way, and then encrypt and decrypt this message using the NTRU system of Example 15.4. Hint: use the two characters in the message to encode an integer for the ASCII values, and then write that integer base 3 (since the small modulus is 3). That should provide three blocks of coefficients (you'll have to pad the last one with a 0) that you can encrypt and then decrypt.

4. (Probably requires programming.) Verify that parameter choices matter. Do the encryption/decryption of Problem 3 but then shrink the size of q until the decryption is no longer unambiguous.

References

1. D.A. Buell, D.A. Carlson, Y.-C. Chow, K. Culik, N. Deo, R. Finkel, E.N. Houstis, E.M. Jacobson, Z.M. Kedem, J.S. Kowalik, P.J. Kuekes, J.L. Martin, G.A. Michael, N.S. Ostlund, J. Potter, D.K. Pradhan, M.J. Quinn, G.W. Stewart, Q.F. Stout, L. Watson, J. Webb, *Report of the summer workshop on parallel algorithms and architectures*, Report UMIACS TR-86-1, CS-TR-1625 (Supercomputing Research Center and University of Maryland Institute for Advanced Computer Studies, Lanham MD, 1986)
2. C.H. Bennett, G. Brassard, Quantum cryptography: public key distribution and coin tossing, in *International Conference on Computers, Systems, and Signal, Processing* (1984), pp. 175–179
3. T. Monz, D. Nigg, E. Martinez, M.B.l, P. Schindler, R. Rines, S. Wang, I. Chuang, R. Blatt, Realization of a scalable Shor algorithm, in *Science* (2016), pp. 1068–1070
4. P.W. Shor, Algorithms for quantum computation: discrete log and factoring, in *Proceedings 35th Annual Symposium on Foundations of Computer Science* (1994), pp. 124–134
5. J. Hoffstein, J. Pipher, J.H. Silverman, NTRU: a ring-based public key cryptosystem, in *Proceedings of the Third International Symposium on Algorithmic Number Theory, ANTS-III* (1998), pp. 267–288
6. J. Hoffstein, J. Pipher, J.H. Silverman, *An Introduction to Mathematical Cryptography* (Springer, 2010)
7. D. Coppersmith, A. Shamir, Lattice attacks on NTRU, in *EUROCRYPT*, vol. 1233, Lecture Notes in Computer Science, ed. by W. Fumy (1997), pp. 52–61
8. A.K. Lenstra, H.W. Lenstra Jr., L. Lov, Factoring polynomials with rational coefficients. Mathematische Annalen **261**, 515–534 (1982)

9. The Sage Developers, *Sagemath, the Sage Mathematics Software System (Version 9.2)* (2020). https://www.sagemath.org
10. Security Innovation, *NTRU PKCS Tutorial* (2021). http://www.securityinnovation.com/security-lab/crypto/155.html
11. J. Hoffstein, J. Pipher, J.M. Schanck, J.H. Silverman, M. Whyte, Z. Zhang, Choosing parameters for NTRUEncrypt, in *Topics in Cryptology - CT-RSA 2017*, vol. 10159, Lecture Notes in Computer Science, ed. by H. Handschuh (2017)

Homomorphic Encryption

16

16.1 Introduction

Shortly after the original RSA paper [1], a question was posed by Rivest, Adleman, and Dertouzos [2]: would it be possible to have a database of encrypted information (such as financial or health data), stored in an external location, that would nonetheless allow computations on the encrypted data without decrypting it? This would permit, for example, external storage, and computation on the encrypted data stored at the external site, without having to trust the owner or operator of the external site.

As originally proposed, one has plaintext S, ciphertext S', and a decrypting function $\phi : S' \to S$ and encrypting function $\phi^{-1} : S \to S'$.

Given a function f one would like to apply to plaintext (an original suggestion was the average value of outstanding loans from a financial institution), we would need a corresponding function f' that would operate on the ciphertext. And given two documents $d_1, d_2 \in S$, for which we have encrypted versions $\phi^{-1}(d_1) = d_1'$ and $\phi^{-1}(d_2) = d_2'$, we might ask for the value of $f(d_1, d_2) = f'(d_1', d_2')$.

Now, if the encrypting/decrypting function ϕ were a homomorphism, we would have

$$\phi(f'(d_1', d_2')) = \phi(f'(\phi^{-1}(d_1), \phi^{-1}(d_2))) = f(d_1, d_2),$$

that is to say, the decryption of the output of the function f' would be the result of applying f to the plaintext.

Now, what would it mean for the decryption function ϕ to be a homomorphism? Since functions used in computation rely on arithmetic operations, we might imagine that the homomorphism be a ring-to-ring mapping that preserves the addition and multiplication operations, and is thus a homomorphism of rings. This is consistent with the notion that the function f' to be performed on the encrypted data is a circuit; circuits compute things using Boolean operations for which addition and multiplication are the obvious examples.

The details of homomorphic encryption require rather more background than the rest of the material in this book. That, together with the fact that research on homomorphic encryption is still very active, makes it unrealistic that we could provide details that would be both understandable and would survive for very long as the state of the art. For this reason, we will provide only an overview of this important topic that is sure to be at the forefront of cryptography for many years to come.

16.2   Somewhat Homomorphic Encryption

There are a number of cryptosystems that have been characterized as *somewhat homomorphic*. For example, RSA-like systems operate homomorphically with respect to multiplications modulo N: if we have messages m_1 and m_2, and a private key e, then we have $m_1^e m_2^e \equiv (m_1 m_2)^e$ (mod N); modulo N, the encryption of the product is clearly the product of the encryptions.

16.3   Fully Homomorphic Encryption

There are many cryptosystems that are somewhat homomorphic, in the sense that RSA, for example, operates homomorphically with respect to multiplication. The notion of homomorphic encryption was proposed in 1978, but it was not until Craig Gentry's doctoral dissertation and subsequent publications [3–5] that it was shown to be possible to have a cryptosystem that was *fully homomorphic* in the sense that the cryptosystem would permit any Boolean operations to be performed on the ciphertext and maintain the homomorphic requirements. Since Gentry's dissertation, a number of systems have been proposed, most of which have substantial overhead. The need for encrypted data to be stored and computed upon external to the owner of the plaintext makes for an active area of study.

We will focus on one such system, proposed by Brakerski, Gentry, and Vaikuntanathan [6,7], which we will refer to as BGV.

16.4   Ideal Lattices

Many recent cryptographic proposals have used as the basis for the cryptographic masking of plaintext the context of an *ideal* in a ring.

Definition 16.1 Given a ring R with addition $+$ and multiplication $\times$, an *ideal I* in R is a set $I \subseteq R$ such that I is a subgroup under addition of the additive group in R, and I is closed under multiplication by elements of R, that is, for any $r \in R$ and any $i \in I$, we have $r \times i \in I$.

Given an ideal I in a commutative ring R, we can define the *quotient ring* R/I. We observe first that an ideal generates an equivalence relation: for elements r and s in R, we have $r \equiv s$ if and only if $r - s \in I$. This allows us to define the elements of the quotient ring to be, for any element $r \in R$, $r + I = \{r + i \mid i \in I\}$. The operations in the quotient ring derive from the operations in R:

$$(r + I) + (s + I) \equiv (r + s) + I$$
$$(r + I) \times (s + I) \equiv (r \times s) + I$$

where we conflate notation somewhat by using the same $+$ and $\times$ symbols for both R and R/I.

Example 16.1 We have been using the canonical example of ideals and quotient rings throughout this text: given any integer n, then the set of all integer multiples of n is an ideal we can write as $n\mathbb{Z}$, and the quotient ring can be written as

$$\mathbb{Z}/n\mathbb{Z} = \{k + n\mathbb{Z}\}$$

and consists of a complete set of reduced residues modulo n. For $n = 4$, the ideal consists of all integers $4k$ that are multiples of r, and the arithmetic in the quotient ring is congruence arithmetic modulo 4:

$$(r + 4t) + (s + 4u) = (r + s) + 4t + 4u = (r + s) + 4(t + u)$$
$$(r + 4t) \times (s + 4u) = (r \times s) + 4ru + 4st + 16tu = (r \times s) + 4(ru + st + 4tu)$$

Cryptographic schemes that rely on ideals generally work as follows: given a plaintext message m, a random element $i \in I$ is chosen and the ciphertext is $m + i$ in the ring. This provides homomorphic addition and multiplication. With a careful eye toward the choice of rings and ideals, one can build in a trapdoor as a decryption secret key, permitting the conversion of an arbitrary ring element into its residue class modulo I. Without the secret key, converting an arbitrary ideal element into the element that is the plaintext is computationally difficult.

One somewhat homomorphic encryption scheme is as follows, as described in Dijk et al. [8] and elsewhere. We choose a large odd integer (perhaps a prime) p in the range $[2^{n-1}, 2^n]$. The encryption of a single bit m is an integer congruent modulo p to the parity of the bit m. To encrypt, we choose q and r at random, and set the ciphertext integer c to be $c = pq + 2r + m$. Knowing p, we can reduce c modulo p, and the result $2r + m$ is 0 or 1 exactly when m is.

With this scheme, it can be shown that one can evaluate low-degree polynomials of the ciphertext while permitting arithmetic on the ciphertext itself. For sufficiently small q, r, perhaps $r \approx 2^{\sqrt{n}}$ and $q \approx 2^{n^3}$, the system is secure [8].

What we see in this rather simple approach is similar to what we observe with NTRU: the ciphertext can be viewed as a small "error" added to a much larger value. With integers, we take "large" in the usual sense. With polynomials over rings we are more concerned with high dimension and sparse polynomials with small coefficients.

A more sophisticated version of the cryptosystem just above, which becomes a public-key cryptosystem, is as follows. With suitable bounds conditions, we choose p and sample for a set of q_i and r_i, and keep these as our private key. We compute

$x_i = q_i p + 2r_i$ for the public key. For each bit m of the plaintext, we choose a set of 0, 1-bits b_i randomly, compute the integer $B = \sum_i b_i x_i$, and transmit the ciphertext bit $c = m + B$. Decryption is thus reduction of c modulo p to produce an integer whose parity is the same as that of the plaintext bit m.

The conventional attack on this system is what is referred to as the *approximate gcd problem*. Namely, we are given a set of integers x_i which (assuming we have chosen our bounds properly) are random large multiples of a common value p perturbed slightly by the addition of a "errors" r_i. The naive attack would be, for any two x_j, x_k, to try all possible gcds

$$\gcd(x_j - s, x_k - t)$$

for all possible pairs s, t within the bounds for the r_i.

A better approach is to reduce this to a lattice problem. Given any two $x_j = q_j p + r_j, x_k = q_k p + r_k$, we observe that the difference $q_k x_j - q_j x_k = q_k r_j - q_j r_k$ is small compared to the x_i, because we are multiplying the random q_i by small values r_i instead of the much larger p.

We can convert this into a lattice problem, choosing K to be twice as large as the largest possible value for r_i.

$$(q_0, \ldots, q_t) \begin{pmatrix} K & x_1 & \cdots & x_t \\ -x_0 & \cdots & & \\ & -x_0 & \cdots & \\ & & \cdots & -x_0 \end{pmatrix} = (q_0 K, q_0 x_1 - q_1 x_0, \ldots, q_0 x_t - q_t x_0)$$

and this would be a vector with small coefficients, and thus a short vector in the lattice.

Example 16.2 We illustrate with a simple example. We let $p = 2047$ and the (q_i, r_i) chosen from $(25, 1)$ through $(34, 10)$ with the multipliers q_i and addins r_i increasing by 1 each time. This gives us

$$[x_0, \ldots, x_9] = [51176, 53224, 55272, 57320, 59368, 61416, 63464, 65512, 67560, 69608].$$

If we then build the matrix

$$\begin{pmatrix} 16 & 53224 & 55272 & 57320 & 59368 & 61416 & 63464 & 65512 & 67560 & 69608 \\ 0 & 53224 & 0 & 0 & 0 & 0 & 0 & 0 & 0 & 0 \\ 0 & 0 & -51176 & 0 & 0 & 0 & 0 & 0 & 0 & 0 \\ 0 & 0 & 0 & -51176 & 0 & 0 & 0 & 0 & 0 & 0 \\ 0 & 0 & 0 & 0 & -51176 & 0 & 0 & 0 & 0 & 0 \\ 0 & 0 & 0 & 0 & 0 & -51176 & 0 & 0 & 0 & 0 \\ 0 & 0 & 0 & 0 & 0 & 0 & -51176 & 0 & 0 & 0 \\ 0 & 0 & 0 & 0 & 0 & 0 & 0 & -51176 & 0 & 0 \\ 0 & 0 & 0 & 0 & 0 & 0 & 0 & 0 & -51176 & 0 \\ 0 & 0 & 0 & 0 & 0 & 0 & 0 & 0 & 0 & -51176 \end{pmatrix}$$

and reduce it using the LLL algorithm of SageMath, we get as the first row of the reduced matrix the vector

$$[400, 24. 48, 72, 96, 120, 144, 168, 192, 216]$$

and a solution to the problem of determining the q_i and r_i.

16.5 Learning with Errors

The cryptosystem proposed in [8] is easy to understand, and it has been elaborated upon both with regard to implementation and the analysis of its security. Other homomorphic systems have been proposed that use polynomials and lattice problems.

BGV, as well as other proposed systems, relies on the problem of *learning with errors (LWE)*. The *ring learning with errors (RLWE)*. problem resembles the lattice problem posed by the NTRU cryptosystem. A version of this problem can be described as follows [6].

We start with a degree-N polynomial $f(x)$ in a variable x with integer coefficients. Using this we can form a ring R of polynomials with integer coefficients taken modulo $f(x)$, and we can form the ring R_q of the polynomials in R with their coefficients reduced modulo an odd integer q (which need not be prime). The ring operations of addition and multiplication are the obvious operations of polynomial addition and multiplication followed by reduction modulo $f(x)$ and modulo q, just as we have done in Chaps. 6 and 15. As we have done earlier, we can represent a polynomial element in R with a vector of coefficients

$$g(x) = g_0 + \cdots + g_{N-1}x^{N-1} = [g_0, \ldots, g_{N-1}]$$

where the coefficients are integers modulo q and we order the coefficients in increasing powers of x. We let $||g|| = \max(|g_i|)$ be the maximum absolute value of the coefficients of $g(x)$.

The various LWE problems over a ring such as R can be described intuitively more or less as follows. Given polynomially-many polynomials g_i chosen uniformly randomly from R, given a random ring element s, and given a randomly chosen set of elements e_i with small coefficients, is it computationally feasible to distinguish the set of pairs $(a_i, a_i \cdot s + e_i)$ from a random set of pairs chosen from $R \times R$? From an intuitive standpoint, this is a cryptographic problem: how many pairs will be needed before we can determine s by removing the noise contributed by adding in the e_i? Without the e_i, we would have a problem in linear algebra. With the e_i, we have a problem that reduces to the problem of finding short vectors in lattices, and is thus resistant (as far is is known today) to quantum computer attacks.

We build a secret-key symmetric cryptosystem as follows. We begin with a secret key polynomial s chosen from R_q. We then sample R_q to obtain a polynomial a and a noise polynomial e. The ciphertext bit that is the encryption of a message bit m is the pair

$$(a, a \cdot s + 2e + m)$$

computed in R_q. Decryption is accomplished by using a and the secret key s to compute the product $a \cdot s$ in the ring R, using that to extract $2e + m$ from the second element of the pair, and then reducing modulo 2 to recover the bit m. The value q is odd, so 2 is invertible, and provided q is chosen large enough, and the sampled e has sufficiently small coefficients, the extraction modulo q of $a \cdot s + 2e + m$ to obtain $2e + m$ is, as in NTRU, not a congruence but an actual equality.

16.6 Security, and Homomorphic Evaluation of Functions

We have not commented before now either on the parameters and their impact on
security, or on the functions that can be evaluated on ciphertext. Details of both of
these are unfortunately beyond the scope of this text, but we can reason somewhat
by analogy. With NTRU, we had a large integer parameter q and a small integer
parameter p and the degree N of the polynomial $f(x) = x^N - 1$ that defined the
ring in which encryption and decryption took place. Reduction modulo $f(x)$ and
modulo q was expected to produce not just polynomials in congruence classes, but
the actual polynomials with coefficients modulo p, because p was much smaller than
q. And the dimension N of the lattice was assumed to be large enough that lattice
reduction attacks would be computationally infeasible.

Most of the same heuristics apply here for homomorphic encryption, with one
difference being that proof of security can be done for the methods suggested in this
chapter. The degree N is usually taken to be a power of 2, and needs to be large
enough to make lattice reductions difficult to compute.

More importantly, it is necessary to consider what functions f might be able
to compute on the ciphertexts in a meaningful way. By "compute" we mean the
application of addition and multiplication on ciphertext. Clearly, these operations
propagate the "error", and thus arbitrary computation of polynomials on ciphertext
will not result in an output that can be unambiguously decrypted. One of Gentry's
main contributions was the introduction of a recursive procedure by which high-
degree polynomials could be applied to ciphertext, and one of the primary areas of
current research is the simplification of this process [3–5, 7].

16.7 An Apologetic Summary

At one level, we apologize for the lack of detail in this chapter. On the other hand,
homomorphic encryption seems not yet to be a settled matter, and thus it seems unrealistic to present too much material that might soon become outdated. The interested
reader should plan to stay abreast of the research literature, because the state of the
art seems ever-changing.

References

1. R.L. Rivest, A. Shamir, L. Adleman, A method for obtaining digital signatures and public-key
   cryptosystems. Commun. ACM 120–126 (1978)
2. R.L. Rivest, L. Adleman, M. Dertouzos, On data banks and privacy homo-morphisms. Foundations of Secure Computation 169–180 (1978)
3. C. Gentry, A fully homomorphic encryption scheme, Ph.D. thesis (Stanford University, 2009)

4. C. Gentry, Fully homomorphic encryption using ideal lattices, in *Symposium on the Theory of Computing (STOC '09)*, ed. by M. Mitzenmacher (2009), pp. 169–178
5. C. Gentry, Toward basing fully homomorphic encryption on worst-case hardness, in *Advances in Cryptology - CRYPTO 2010*, vol. 6223, Lecture Notes in Computer Science, ed. by T. Rabin (2010), pp. 116–137
6. Z. Brakerski, V. Vaikuntanathan, Efficient fully homomorphic encryption from (sta dard) LWE, in *52nd Annual Symposium on Foundations of Computer Science* (2011), pp. 97–106
7. Z. Brakerski, V. Vaikuntanathan, C. Gentry, Fully homomorphic encryption without botstrapping, in *Innovations in Theoretical Computer Science* (2012)
8. M. van Dijk, C. Gentry, S. Halevi, V. Vaikuntanathan, Fully homomorphic encryption over the integers, in *Advances in Cryptology - EUROCRYPT 2010*, ed. by H. Gilbert (2010), pp. 24–43

An Actual World War I Cipher

A

A.1 Introduction

In Chap. VII of Herbert Yardley's *The American Black Chamber* [1], the method for deciphering one German diplomatic message is presented, and a second message, alleged to be produced by the same system, dated 10 January 1919, is given without the decryption process, although the resulting message is given in English translation. In this paper we will trace the decipherment of this message.

A.2 The Message

The message itself is given on pages 150–151 of Yardley's book and displayed here as Fig. A.1.

A.3 Language Determination

On the one hand, we are fairly certain that this is a German message from Yardley's context and that it is a transposition and not a substitution cipher. On the other hand, it never hurts to have confirmation of one's assumptions, so we do a frequency count of letters, which appears as Fig. A.2. We note that there are 1367 characters overall in the message.

These frequencies fit a model of German rather well [2] so we continue with our assumption that this is transposition and not substitution.

© The Editor(s) (if applicable) and The Author(s), under exclusive license to Springer Nature Switzerland AG 2021
D. Buell, *Fundamentals of Cryptography*, Undergraduate Topics in Computer Science, https://doi.org/10.1007/978-3-030-73492-3_A_A

```
nogaaaimue saeesntraa seienewwei heuamaoeid zcdkeftedt edgeigunri
eceutnninb mhbebanais iteaarukss tdscmoorob aeuoermotd hzzzdigbtt
fceumlreri eeoemffcea iqeirenuef drisrrbnle enznuhbtpf kgtineenel
anvescalrr adngdceoeu tiailuiorl bkrnnoeeqe hhananvsdf niemineiee
eetreegdmp eilsbihlnu hodciageef sttheetdbe ugmuaudnuu dnsfnenenn
umtralgtnu rehnemenbe mntngefsae kltzedrkii rhficnvaks onbtguhewn
thitzmsrmd lghireicsc enpneiette nhvdnvhbvn nrsnecnemn ngepniceuh
eortsgesie eneonfiend wnpkcevemd isrhwlften amucnosazr ahelnehiln
crseamilnb eutceszrth rsaeoszclx mneouhslcu nmenenefae eckerglnra
bgfireubli roznnsseuz csthpusica ufohunnbdn betfmmcirt unfrnsrbna
dsukouiust bmgdreninu lusneadash scecfaonen ehsmnrgoot erzruierne
incneinfee etkstnbika zeugdednkr ibhideeree aeuneinzet dendaoerea
ighueuoanu uzasruoddi eeemcutiee teanchchdd igrrrrrnso esiereerde
emiehdeade nhdthmnosm elolmeennd rhktendend uockehaete eresfjhouk
fhbmkttemn ledsetuehl enimliaern ehzeuesesg snmeuhaimd rrensshikh
rahdhennjh osesedfhin meerneaseh udzsgifmri uoisoehsna deitfeebsa
ekamhceant eaoabeunou flrnneizua nfpbhmnfon gusdiporth fhrsmdndrl
tmaurrwini ulnezsknts hdrsdbbnip osedlsuctb ctidafsaue ttunwirhbr
ngnedumiis veurakklne enrcmtdtea nsinleimgr iehnlemnlg gkhegdatee
eaaeegtero arusrelari graenuinbi eeikdnspni ribhhpkuze tkrseshdne
haravntsee ipreicseuu emozusmudh ipitnndark nalccssgle ursttrlecp
irbdnsaend recoeteian mdtnnheamt ntzeomtier nukwmttcke ucebdihtnf
eswgowgeen notzreasnu caahnbgeil ceernsnrta lgghcue
```

Fig. A.1 The original message

Fig. A.2 Letter frequencies
in the message

a	79	g	38	m	51	s	81	y	0
b	35	h	65	n	148	t	73	z	24
c	44	i	92	o	46	u	75		
d	65	j	2	p	14	v	9		
e	224	k	29	q	2	w	10		
f	31	l	39	r	90	x	1		

A.4 An Initial Blocking

The original message does not appear to be reasonable text in any language. Following Yardley's sample decryption, we assume that all letters in the message have been shifted a fixed number of positions from their original location. To bring the letters back into their correct relative positions, we consider that in German the letter 'c' is always followed by 'h' or 'k'. We therefore compute the distances (modulo 1367, of course) between the 44 instances of the letter 'c' and the 65 instances of 'h'. We write a program that produces those differences and feed the output to a convenient Unix hack

```
Abchdiffs <message | sort -n | uniq -c | sort -n | tail >diffs
```

whose output is unambiguous. The most frequent letter position differences between 'c' and 'h' are

5	−744
5	778
6	−111
6	124
6	−181
6	−273
6	331
6	446
6	71
26	378

It is obvious that we should block the message with letters at a difference of 378 from one another. We do this with a program that produces the message sequence number and character tetragrams of Fig. A.3.

A.5 Cribbing the Sequence

Unlike the original cipher text, this collection of tetragrams (we will refer to all as tetragrams, even those that happen to be trigrams) clearly bears resemblance to German.

If this cipher were created using the same system as the cipher used by Yardley as an example, then our next task is to look for a sequence of sequence number differences, taken modulo 378, and to try to connect the tetragrams using that sequence. We start, following Yardley, with a crib on the punctuation. The Unix hack

```
grep 'k '    tetragrams  >cribkomma
grep 'ko '   tetragrams  >>cribkomma
grep 'kom '  tetragrams  >>cribkomma
grep 'omm '  tetragrams  >>cribkomma
grep 'mma '  tetragrams  >>cribkomma
grep ' kom'  tetragrams  >>cribkomma
grep ' omm'  tetragrams  >>cribkomma
grep ' mma'  tetragrams  >>cribkomma
grep ' ma'   tetragrams  >>cribkomma
grep ' a'    tetragrams  >>cribkomma
```

will collect from the list of tetragrams (in the file tetragrams) all those that could be connected together to produce the word komma ("comma"). We do the same for punkt ("period") and klammer ("parenthesis") and then by hand compute the differences between the tetragram sequence numbers.

At this point we have to start hoping for good luck, because the letter sequences are not long enough to provide unambiguous information. For punkt, for example, we get the data of Fig. A.4, and none of the differences are repeated. For komma,

0 nscg	1 ochd	2 geda	3 andt	4 apie	5 ange	6 iere	7 mira
8 uera	9 etre	10 stre	11 aeng	12 enst	13 ehoe	14 sver	15 ndso
16 tnia	17 rver	18 ahru	19 abes	20 sver	21 enre	22 indl	23 erea
24 nser	25 enmi	26 weig	27 wcer	28 enha	29 iede	30 hmen	31 enau
32 undi	33 agen	34 menb	35 aphi	36 onde	37 eite	38 ichi	39 demk
40 zund	41 chon	42 dess	43 komp	44 eren	45 ftli	46 tsor	47 egli
48 demb	49 tseh	50 eieh	51 denp	52 genk	53 endu	54 ierz	55 gohe
56 unkt	57 nftk	58 rier	59 iens	60 ende	61 cdes	62 ewnh	63 undd
64 tpun	65 nkoe	66 ncch	67 ieka	68 nver	69 beha	70 mmav	71 hden
72 bitt	73 eses	74 bree	75 ahre	76 nwei	77 alsp	78 iffr	79 stje
80 iehi	81 tnoc	82 eaus	83 amke	84 aufu	85 rchu	86 unbe	87 komm
88 ssko	89 satz	90 tztu	91 dres	92 samm	93 chnu	94 meld	95 oleh
96 ondi	97 resp	98 ohei	99 bitt	100 alun	101 enen	102 uchd	103 orla
104 eser	105 renk	106 main	107 omma	108 till	109 dlic	110 hnac	111 zbes
112 zers	113 zung	114 dtel	115 iche	116 gezu	117 bser	118 tzus	119 tret
120 ftst	121 cher	122 ersl	123 usge	124 masc	125 lenp	126 romi	127 eser
128 rzub	129 ichd	130 elan	131 exis	132 omma	133 ende	134 mern	135 ford
136 fuer	137 chne	138 essc	139 also	140 iche	141 quit	142 enke	143 imhi
144 rera	145 enan	146 nehm	147 undd	148 eeht	149 ffen	150 dann	151 renh
152 ieje	153 scha	154 rkom	155 rest	156 bren	157 ngst	158 llez	159 ende
160 erfo	161 nahm	162 zbit	163 ngni	164 ufme	165 hier	166 bren	167 teru
168 punk	169 fbew	170 klam	171 gist	172 tret	173 iohc	174 nzuk	175 ende
176 enzu	177 nssc	178 esge	179 leib	180 aufd	181 nzmi	182 vcrh	183 esit
184 stun	185 chof	186 apie	187 luss	188 rsow	189 rieg	190 acho	191 dasw
192 nung	193 gfae	194 dode	195 chen	196 euin	197 onto	198 enft	199 ubez
200 tder	201 inbe	202 absa	203 ieas	204 lten	205 ufku	206 imac	207 omma
208 rcha	209 lich	210 bren	211 ktab	212 rung	213 nnte	214 nfei	215 oral
216 enoc	217 esae	218 qrbe	219 eber	220 hnun	221 hans	222 adon	223 nsur
224 auft	225 nkla	226 vorl	227 sung	228 ding	229 fueh	230 nsic	231 itzu
232 ebue	233 mma	234 ign	235 ndf	236 erp	237 ieb	238 enh	239 eim
240 enn	241 euf	242 tlo	243 run	244 esg	245 enu	246 ges	247 dad
248 mdi	249 pap	250 eso	251 ihr	252 lst	253 sch	254 bef	255 ich
256 hfr	257 las	258 nom	259 und	260 hen	261 ond	262 der	263 chl
264 ist	265 amm	266 gna	267 eru	268 egr	269 for	270 sow	271 tti
272 ten	273 hri	274 ezu	275 erl	276 tun	277 die	278 bez	279 ers
280 unk	281 gen	282 mit	283 uns	284 ach	285 und	286 der	287 nis
288 und	289 ufb	290 deb	291 nen	292 sei	293 ftp	294 nko	295 ess
296 nte	297 end	298 nbl	299 nis	300 uku	301 mac	302 tzt	303 reb
304 auc	305 lgt	306 gdi	307 ted	308 nda	309 unf	310 rks	311 era
312 hiu	313 nbe	314 eht	315 mit	316 edu	317 nen	318 bew	319 eri
320 mer	321 neh	322 tab	323 ner	324 gun	325 eng	326 fen	327 sie
328 and	329 ezu	330 kem	331 lti	332 tdi	333 zes	334 env	335 dde
336 rau	337 kor	338 iea	339 irk	340 rek	341 hal	342 fin	343 ige
344 che	345 nun	346 ver	347 auc	348 kom	349 sat	350 ond	351 nut
352 bue	353 tza	354 gan	355 uss	356 hri	357 eun	358 wol	359 nde
360 tdi	361 him	362 ieg	363 ter	364 zei	365 mme	366 sch	367 run
368 mtl	369 die	370 lem	371 gen	372 htl	373 ieg	374 rag	375 enk
376 ich	377 che						

Fig. A.3 Message tetragrams from blocking at 378

43 komp	16 tnia	307 ted
51 denp	46 tsor	322 tab
77 alsp	49 tseh	332 tdi
97 resp	64 tpun	353 tza
125 lenp	81 tnoc	360 tdi
236 erp	90 tztu	363 ter
249 pap	108 till	
293 ftp	118 tzus	
	119 tret	
64 tpun	167 teru	
	172 tret	
168 punk	200 tder	
	242 tlo	
280 unk	271 tti	
56 unkt	272 ten	
	276 tun	
211 ktab	302 tzt	

64 tpun	→	211 ktab	$\delta = 147$
43 komp	→	56 unkt	$\delta = 13$
51 denp	→	56 unkt	$\delta = 5$
77 alsp	→	56 unkt	$\delta = 357$
97 resp	→	56 unkt	$\delta = 337$
125 lenp	→	56 unkt	$\delta = 309$
236 erp	→	56 unkt	$\delta = 198$
249 pap	→	56 unkt	$\delta = 185$
293 ftp	→	56 unkt	$\delta = 141$
43 komp	→	280 unk	$\delta = 240$
51 denp	→	280 unk	$\delta = 229$
77 alsp	→	280 unk	$\delta = 203$
97 resp	→	280 unk	$\delta = 183$
125 lenp	→	280 unk	$\delta = 155$
236 erp	→	280 unk	$\delta = 44$
249 pap	→	280 unk	$\delta = 31$
293 ftp		280 unk	$\delta = 365$

Fig. A.4 Cribs for 'punkt'

however, there are fewer unambiguous possibilities, and yet the difference 154 is repeated. Finally, for klammer, although we have no repetitions, we also have only three possible differences from the longer cribs. The cribs for komma and klammer are shown in Fig. A.5. We also note some unusual (for German) tetragrams: exis and quit. The first almost requires that the next tetragram begin with t, and the second almost requires that the next tetragram begin with ten or tun. Finally, we notice several tetragrams that could be used to form the common suffix lich. Considering all these together, we guess that distances of 135, 140, 141, 145, 150, and 154 might be in the cryptogram because they occur more than once among our cribs.

We therefore generate all pairs at these distances and filter to get those that look as if they might be legitimate German. These pairs are shown in Figs. A.5, A.6, A.7, A.8, A.9 and A.10.

225 nkla	→	365 mme	$\delta = 140$
170 klam	→	320 mern	$\delta = 150$
170 klam	→	134 mern	$\delta = 342$
88 ssko	→	233 mma	$\delta = 145$
88 ssko	→	70 mmav	$\delta = 360$
294 nko	→	233 mma	$\delta = 317$
294 nko	→	70 mmav	$\delta = 154$
154 rkom	→	106 main	$\delta = 330$
154 rkom	→	124 masc	$\delta = 348$
154 rkom	→	301 mac	$\delta = 157$
348 kom	→	106 main	$\delta = 136$
348 kom	→	124 masc	$\delta = 154$
348 kom	→	301 mac	$\delta = 331$

Fig. A.5 Cribs for 'komma' and 'klammer'

2	geda	137	chne	91	dres	226	vorl	246	ges	3	andt
12	enst	147	undd	102	uchd	237	ieb	249	pap	6	iere
15	ndso	150	dann	123	usge	258	nom	253	sch	10	stre
24	nser	159	ende	137	chne	272	ten	257	las	14	sver
26	weig	161	nahm	140	iche	275	erl	282	mit	39	demk
28	enha	163	ngni	141	quit	276	tun	285	und	42	dess
30	hmen	165	hier	145	enan	280	unk	286	der	43	komp
33	agen	168	punk	150	dann	285	und	291	nen	48	demb
37	eite	172	tret	156	bren	291	nen	296	nte	53	endu
40	zund	175	ende	187	luss	322	tab	300	uku	57	nftk
41	chon	176	enzu	192	nung	327	sie	315	mit	72	bitt
44	eren	179	leib	207	omma	342	fin	318	bew	75	ahre
48	demb	183	esit	209	lich	344	che	320	mer	77	alsp
51	denp	186	apie	210	bren	345	nun	327	sie	84	aufu
69	beha	204	lten	211	ktab	346	ver	336	rau	93	chnu
75	ahre	210	bren	212	rung	347	auc	354	gan	111	zbes
77	alsp	212	rung	213	nnte	348	kom	364	zei	121	cher
84	aufu	219	eber	219	eber	354	gan	372	htl	129	ichd
86	unbe	221	hans	228	ding	363	ter	373	ieg	130	elan
87	komm	222	adon	242	tlo	377	che	374	rag	131	exis
89	satz	224	auft	245	enu	2	geda	376	ich	133	ende

Fig. A.6 Pairs at a distance of 135

A.6 Putting It All Together

At this point we definitely begin moving to the art of cryptanalysis as practiced
before the computer age. We assume that the tetragrams are to be strung together
from pairs into triples, then quadruples, and so forth. To this end we start looking at
"good German" pairs for one initial distance for which the second tetragram of one
pair is also the first tetragram of another pair.

2	geda	142	enke	113	zung	253	sch	201 inbe 341 hal
4	apie	144	rera	115	iche	255	ich	207 omma 347 auc
6	iere	146	nehm	127	eser	267	eru	209 lich 349 sat
15	ndso	155	rest	131	exis	271	tti	211 ktab 351 nut
30	hmen	170	klam	135	ford	275	erl	216 enoc 356 hri
37	eite	177	nssc	136	fuer	276	tun	225 nkla 365 mme
43	komp	183	esit	137	chne	277	die	259 und 21 enre
44	eren	184	stun	140	iche	280	unk	275 erl 37 eite
45	ftli	185	chof	150	dann	290	deb	277 die 39 demk
60	ende	200	tder	153	scha	293	ftp	286 der 48 demb
63	undd	203	ieas	155	rest	295	ess	315 mit 77 alsp
90	tztu	230	nsic	156	bren	296	nte	327 sie 89 satz
94	meld	234	ign	159	ende	299	nis	349 sat 111 zbes
99	bitt	239	eim	175	ende	315	mit	351 nut 113 zung
103	orla	243	run	184	stun	324	gun	369 die 131 exis
105	renk	245	enu	188	rsow	328	and	374 rag 136 fuer
107	omma	247	dad	189	rieg	329	ezu	

Fig. A.7 Pairs at a distance of 140

5	ange	146	nehm	195	chen	336	rau	293 ftp 56 unkt
24	nser	165	hier	200	tder	341	hal	320 mer 83 amke
84	aufu	225	nkla	203	ieas	344	che	347 auc 110 hnac
99	bitt	240	enn	228	ding	369	die	358 wol 121 cher
131	exis	272	ten	265	amm	28	enha	365 mme 128 rzub
136	fuer	277	die	269	for	32	undi	373 ieg 136 fuer
139	also	280	unk	275	erl	38	ichi	376 ich 139 also
140	iche	281	gen	285	und	48	demb	

Fig. A.8 Pairs at a distance of 141

29	iede	174	nzuk	134	mern	279	ers	238 enh 5 ange
31	enau	176	enzu	136	fuer	281	gen	270 sow 37 eite
44	eren	189	rieg	137	chne	282	mit	272 ten 39 demk
56	unkt	201	inbe	153	scha	298	nbl	286 der 53 endu
72	bitt	217	esae	160	erfo	305	lgt	304 auc 71 hden
80	iehi	225	nkla	180	aufd	325	eng	320 mer 87 komm
85	rchu	230	nsic	189	rieg	334	env	322 tab 89 satz
88	ssko	233	mma	192	nung	337	kor	342 fin 109 dlic
99	bitt	244	esg	204	lten	349	sat	358 wol 125 lenp
113	zung	258	nom	209	lich	354	gan	360 tdi 127 eser
131	exis	276	tun	213	nnte	358	wol	373 ieg 140 iche
132	omma	277	die	216	enoc	361	him	

Fig. A.9 Pairs at a distance of 145

3 andt	153 scha	136 fuer	286 der	265 amm	37 eite
6 iere	156 bren	144 rera	294 nko	273 hri	45 ftli
30 hmen	180 aufd	147 undd	297 end	276 tun	48 demb
39 demk	189 rieg	160 erfo	310 rks	288 und	60 ende
45 ftli	195 chen	165 hier	315 mit	309 unf	81 tnoc
56 unkt	206 imac	170 klam	320 mer	314 eht	86 unbe
57 nftk	207 omma	183 esit	333 zes	315 mit	87 komm
89 satz	239 eim	192 nung	342 fin	317 nen	89 satz
92 samm	242 tlo	201 inbe	351 nut	320 mer	92 samm
101 enen	251 ihr	204 lten	354 gan	327 sie	99 bitt
107 omma	257 las	219 eber	369 die	332 tdi	104 eser
110 hnac	260 hen	224 auft	374 rag	359 nde	131 exis
111 zbes	261 ond	226 vorl	376 ich	363 ter	135 ford
129 ichd	279 ers	233 mma	5 ange	368 mtl	140 iche
132 omma	282 mit	237 ieb	9 etre	369 die	141 quit
134 mern	284 ach	242 tlo	14 sver		
135 ford	285 und	251 ihr	23 erea		

Fig. A.10 Pairs at a distance of 150

12 enst	166 bren	150 dann	304 auc	277 die	53 endu
23 erea	177 nssc	157 ngst	311 era	284 ach	60 ende
24 nser	178 esge	159 ende	313 nbe	292 sei	68 nver
30 hmen	184 stun	161 nahm	315 mit	294 nko	70 mmav
37 eite	191 dasw	168 punk	322 tab	296 nte	72 bitt
56 unkt	210 bren	180 aufd	334 env	297 end	73 eses
104 eser	258 nom	186 apie	340 rek	313 nbe	89 satz
111 zbes	265 amm	189 rieg	343 ige	325 eng	101 enen
115 iche	269 for	192 nung	346 ver	328 and	104 eser
125 lenp	279 ers	195 chen	349 sat	341 hal	117 bser
134 mern	288 und	204 lten	358 wol	348 kom	124 masc
136 fuer	290 deb	219 eber	373 ieg	362 ieg	138 essc
137 chne	291 nen	227 sung	3 andt	366 sch	142 enke
140 iche	294 nko	262 der	38 ichi	374 rag	150 dann
144 rera	298 nbl	264 ist	40 zund		

Fig. A.11 Pairs at a distance of 154

If we start with 135, then a number of triples of "good German" could be formed with any of the other sets of pairs in Figs. A.7, A.8, A.9, A.10 and A.11. However, one triple,

```
282 mit (135) 39 demk (150) 189 rieg
```

stands out. In the context of the First World War, a crib that looked like `mit dem krieg[e]` is tantalizing, especially when we look at the tetragrams beginning with `e` and see that both distances of 140 and 145 are possible. We also notice the possible triple

Fig. A.12 Quadruples at
distances of 135, 150, and
140

```
  2 geda 137 chne 287 nis  49 tseh
 12 enst 147 undd 297 end  59 iens
 30 hmen 165 hier 315 mit  77 alsp
 48 demb 183 esit 333 zes  95 oleh
 66 ncch 201 inbe 351 nut 113 zung
 69 beha 204 lten 354 gan 116 gezu
 84 aufu 219 eber 369 die 131 exis
 89 satz 224 auft 374 rag 136 fuer
102 uchd 237 ieb    9 etre 149 ffen
138 essc 273 hri   45 ftli 185 chof
156 bren 291 nen   63 undd 203 ieas
174 nzuk 309 unf   81 tnoc 221 hans
192 nung 327 sie   99 bitt 239 eim
246 ges    3 andt 153 scha 293 ftp
249 pap    6 iere 156 bren 296 nte
254 bef   11 aeng 161 nahm 301 mac
264 ist   21 enre 171 gist 311 era
282 mit   39 demk 189 rieg 329 ezu
300 uku   57 nftk 207 omma 347 auc
318 bew   75 ahre 225 nkla 365 mme
336 rau   93 chnu 243 run    5 ange
354 gan  111 zbes 261 ond   23 erea
375 enk  132 omma 282 mit   44 eren
```

```
246 ges (135) 3 andt (150) 153 scha[ft]
```

and recognize the German word Gesandtschaft, or "legation." Better yet, we
notice only three tetragrams (45 ftli, 120 ftst, and 293 ftp) that begin
with the necessary ft, and the third of these is located at a distance of 140 from
(153 scha. This corroborates our finding many instances of triples at distances of
150 followed by 140 that appear to be good German. We take a wild guess and put
together quadruples of tetragrams from distances 135, 150, and 140, and we find at
least the instances of possible good German shown in Fig. A.12. We note that there
may be a garble or two in this list, notably with those quadruples beginning with
tetragrams 48 and 66, but this list seems quite promising.

A.7   Further Guessing

Now we hunker down further in hopes of guessing the right connections. The quadruple beginning with tetragram 84 cries out for an initial letter t to follow, the quadruples beginning with tetragrams 254 and 347 need to be followed by quadruples with
the initial letter c, and the quadruple beginning with 318 would seem to need a
tetragram beginning with r. If we search for distances for these tetragrams, we get
repeated possibilities of distances 9, 71, and 141. However, the 141 also allows us
to complete

Fig. A.13 Quintuples at
distances of 135, 150, 140,
141

```
12 enst 147 undd 297 end 59 iens 200 tder
30 hmen 165 hier 315 mit 77 alsp 218 qrbe
48 demb 183 esit 333 zes 95 oleh 236 erp
66 ncch 201 inbe 351 nut 113 zung 254 bef
69 beha 204 lten 354 gan 116 gezu 257 las
84 aufu 219 eber 369 die 131 exis 272 ten
89 satz 224 auft 374 rag 136 fuer 277 die
102 uchd 237 ieb 9 etre 149 ffen 290 deb
138 essc 273 hri 45 ftli 185 chof 326 fen
156 bren 291 nen 63 undd 203 ieas 344 che
174 nzuk 309 unf 81 tnoc 221 hans 362 ieg
228 ding 363 ter 135 ford 275 erl 38 ichi
233 mma 368 mtl 140 iche 280 unk 43 komp
246 ges 3 andt 153 scha 293 ftp 56 unkt
282 mit 39 demk 189 rieg 329 ezu 92 samm
300 uku 57 nftk 207 omma 347 auc 110 hnac
318 bew 75 ahre 225 nkla 365 mme 128 rzub
336 rau 93 chnu 243 run 5 ange 146 nehm
354 gan 111 zbes 261 ond 23 erea 164 ufme
```

```
246 ges (135) 3 andt (150) 153 scha (140) 293 ftp
```

to be

```
246 ges (135) 3 andt (150) 153 scha (140) 293 ftp (141) unkt
```

and we decide to try this. The resulting possible German strings are shown in
Fig. A.13.

We aren't done yet. We probably need a z to follow tetragram 272. We need an
h to follow tetragram 110. And we might guess that en would follow tetragram 92.
If we look for duplicate distances among these, we come up with 146, 298, and 339
as possibilities. The choice of 146 seems good, however, when we notice that this
would continue

```
354 gan  (135) 111 zbes (150) 261 ond (140) 23 erea (141) 164 ufme
```

to become

```
354 gan  111 zbes 261 ond  23 erea 164 ufme 310 rks
```

A.8   Continuing the Sequence

We collect sextuples of pairs in Fig. A.14. Some things are becoming very clear. The
odd pqr in the string beginning with 30 must be a name, since the text says that
"herewith as". Tetragram 95 in line 3 is a garble, as is tetragram 66 in line 4. We

```
 12 enst 147 undd 297 end  59 iens 200 tder 346 ver
 30 hmen 165 hier 315 mit  77 alsp 218 qrbe 364 zei
 48 demb 183 esit 333 zes  95 oleh 236 erp    4 apie
 66 ncch 201 inbe 351 nut 113 zung 254 bef  22 indl
 69 beha 204 lten 354 gan 116 gezu 257 las  25 enmi
 84 aufu 219 eber 369 die 131 exis 272 ten  40 zund
 89 satz 224 auft 374 rag 136 fuer 277 die  45 ftli
102 uchd 237 ieb    9 etre 149 ffen 290 deb  58 rier
138 essc 273 hri  45 ftli 185 chof 326 fen  94 meld
156 bren 291 nen  63 undd 203 ieas 344 che 112 zers
174 nzuk 309 unf  81 tnoc 221 hans 362 ieg 130 elan
228 ding 363 ter 135 ford 275 erl  38 ichi 184 stun
233 mma  368 mtl 140 iche 280 unk  43 komp 189 rieg
246 ges    3 andt 153 scha 293 ftp  56 unkt 202 absa
282 mit   39 demk 189 rieg 329 ezu  92 samm 238 enh
300 uku   57 nftk 207 omma 347 auc 110 hnac 256 hfr
318 bew   75 ahre 225 nkla 365 mme 128 rzub 274 ezu
336 rau   93 chnu 243 run    5 ange 146 nehm 292 sei
354 gan  111 zbes 261 ond  23 erea 164 ufme 310 rks
```

Fig. A.14 Sextuples at distances 135, 150, 140, 141, 146

```
 12 enst 147 undd 297 end  59 iens 200 tder 346 ver 119 tret
 30 hmen 165 hier 315 mit  77 alsp 218 qrbe 364 zei 137 chne
 48 demb 183 esit 333 zes  95 oleh 236 erp    4 apie 155 rest
 66 ncch 201 inbe 351 nut 113 zung 254 bef  22 indl 173 iohc
 84 aufu 219 eber 369 die 131 exis 272 ten  40 zund 191 dasw
102 uchd 237 ieb    9 etre 149 ffen 290 deb  58 rier 209 lich
138 essc 273 hri  45 ftli 185 chof 326 fen  94 meld 245 enu
156 bren 291 nen  63 undd 203 ieas 344 che 112 zers 263 chl
174 nzuk 309 unf  81 tnoc 221 hans 362 ieg 130 elan 281 gen
228 ding 363 ter 135 ford 275 erl  38 ichi 184 stun 335 dde
246 ges    3 andt 153 scha 293 ftp  56 unkt 202 absa 353 tza
282 mit   39 demk 189 rieg 329 ezu  92 samm 238 enh  11 aeng
300 uku   57 nftk 207 omma 347 auc 110 hnac 256 hfr  29 iede
318 bew   75 ahre 225 nkla 365 mme 128 rzub 274 ezu  47 egli
336 rau   93 chnu 243 run    5 ange 146 nehm 292 sei  65 nkoe
354 gan  111 zbes 261 ond  23 erea 164 ufme 310 rks  83 amke
```

Fig. A.15 Septuples at distances 135, 150, 140, 141, 146, 151

have moved some of the odd lines to the bottom. Line 8 beginning with tetragram 156 speaks of "burning" and of doing something with the ashes.

Cribs from here forward are somewhat harder. The only lines that look promising are the second line and the last line above the middle dividing line. The first might start as [ne]hmen and end as qrbe zei [ch]. We might take from the last line a need for aufmerksam. Both of these can be accommodated with a distance of 151, and since there are only two choices for aufmerksam, we feel reasonably certain that this is correct. We present septuples in Fig. A.15.

Further cribs and observations: Line 3, tetragram 95, is probably olch. Line 4, tetragram 66, is probably noch. Line 4, tetragram 173, is probably ichc.

Line 2 should probably be followed with an n or a t.

Line 8: "Burn, and the ashes ..." One consults the dictionary and finds that *zer-schlagen* is the word, so we would want to look for agen to follow this line. There is only one tetragram, 33 agen, that would fit, at a distance of 148.

Line 12: We might look for *zusammenhaengen*.... Tetragram 159, ende, would fit a distance of 148.

Line 14: We almost certainly need to follow this with ch. Tetragram 195, chen, would fit a distance of 148.

We present octuples in Fig. A.16. Clearly many of these have garbles, which we would expect. However, at this point (or somewhat sooner, if we were more clever), we would notice that the lines differ in tetragram sequence numbers most often by 18. Since $378 = 18 \cdot 21$, we guess that the message is blocked in 21 lines, 18 tetragrams to the line, and we include in our strings of putative German all the lines, even if they don't necessarily look like good German at this point.

We now look in front of our sequences, after first removing all 168 tetragrams that appear in Fig. A.16.

We guess that tetragram 12 might be preceded by a d. For this we get distances of 30, 58, 84, 142, 294, and 358.

We guess that tetragram 102 might be preceded by a a. For this we get distances of 35, 74, 86, 94, 95, 142, 214, 247, 272, 336, 348, 373, and 377.

We guess that tetragram 300 might be preceded by a z. For this we get distances of 22, 101, 142, 211, and 246.

The common value here is 142, and in Fig. A.17 we present sequences of length nine.

From the remaining tetragrams, the only good choice to follow tetragram 141, quit, would be tetragram 276, tun   at a distance of 135. This give us Fig. A.18.

Now for some more cribbing.

At the end of line 1 we might expect a t.

At the end of line 2 we might expect an r.

At the end of line 7 we might expect a g.

At the end of line 8 we might expect an mma.

At the end of line 11 we might expect an ma.

These latter two provide some clue, since there are only two tetragrams for line 8, namely 70, mmav and 233, mma, at distances 154 and 84.

Further, there are only two tetragrams for line 11, namely 106, main, 124, masc, and 301, mac, at distances 136, 154, and 331.

We go with the common 154, noting that we get the expected letters for lines 1, 2, and 7.

Now, in the last line, we need to find a tetragram that begins with h, and there are only three left: 71, hden, 260, hen, and 341, hal, at distances 145, 334, and 37. All three are legal, in none would require use to use a tetragram that we have already used, but 145 produces clearly superior German.

With the verb at the end of line 3, we suspect we need to follow with unk, which would now be only tetragram 280 at a distance of 155.

This works.

Fig. A.16 Octuples at distances 135, 150, 140, 141, 146, 151, 148

12	147	297	59	200	346	119	267
enst	undd	end	iens	tder	ver	tret	eru
30	165	315	77	218	364	137	285
hmen	hier	mit	alsp	qrbe	zei	chne	und
48	183	333	95	236	4	155	303
demb	esit	zes	oleh	erp	apie	rest	reb
66	201	351	113	254	22	173	321
ncch	inbe	nut	zung	bef	indl	iohc	neh
84	219	369	131	272	40	191	339
aufu	eber	die	exis	ten	zund	dasw	irk
102	237	9	149	290	58	209	357
uchd	ieb	etre	ffen	deb	rier	lich	eun
120	255	27	167	308	76	227	375
ftst	ich	wcer	teru	nda	nwei	sung	enk
138	273	45	185	326	94	245	15
essc	hri	ftli	chof	fen	meld	enu	ndso
156	291	63	203	344	112	263	33
bren	nen	undd	ieas	che	zers	chl	agen
174	309	81	221	362	130	281	51
nzuk	unf	tnoc	hans	ieg	elan	gen	denp
192	327	99	239	2	148	299	69
nung	sie	bitt	eim	geda	eeht	nis	beha
210	345	117	257	20	166	317	87
bren	nun	bser	las	sver	bren	nen	komm
228	363	135	275	38	184	335	105
ding	ter	ford	erl	ichi	stun	dde	renk
246	3	153	293	56	202	353	123
ges	andt	scha	ftp	unkt	absa	tza	usge
264	21	171	311	74	220	371	141
ist	enre	gist	era	bree	hnun	gen	quit
282	39	189	329	92	238	11	159
mit	demk	rieg	ezu	samm	enh	aeng	ende
300	57	207	347	110	256	29	177
uku	nftk	omma	auc	hnac	hfr	iede	nssc
318	75	225	365	128	274	47	195
bew	ahre	nkla	mme	rzub	ezu	egli	chen
336	93	243	5	146	292	65	213
rau	chnu	run	ange	nehm	sei	nkoe	nnte
354	111	261	23	164	310	83	231
gan	zbes	ond	erea	ufme	rks	amke	itzu
372	129	279	41	182	328	101	249
htl	ichd	ers	chon	vcrh	and	enen	pap

Line 12 now requires the word *punkt* to be completed, for a distance of 147 to tetragram 211.

The trail seems to stall at this point, so we work on the other end of the strings. Line 9 needs a vowel preceding tetragram 158. We try the `uera`, since it's the only a left, and note that this also matches up our long-delayed `klam` and `mer`.

We now have *oheimdienst* in line 5. Surely the leading o is a garble, and this is meant to be *geheimdienst*. Only 0 `nscg`, which must also be garbled, and 325

248	12	147	297	59	200	346	119	267
mdi	enst	undd	end	iens	tder	ver	tret	eru
266	30	165	315	77	218	364	137	285
gna	hmen	hier	mit	alsp	qrbe	zei	chne	und
284	48	183	333	95	236	4	155	303
ach	demb	esit	zes	oleh	erp	apie	rest	reb
302	66	201	351	113	254	22	173	321
tzt	ncch	inbe	nut	zung	bef	indl	iohc	neh
320	84	219	369	131	272	40	191	339
mer	aufu	eber	die	exis	ten	zund	dasw	irk
338	102	237	9	149	290	58	209	357
iea	uchd	ieb	etre	ffen	deb	rier	lich	eun
356	120	255	27	167	308	76	227	375
hri	ftst	ich	wcer	teru	nda	nwei	sung	enk
374	138	273	45	185	326	94	245	15
rag	essc	hri	ftli	chof	fen	meld	enu	ndso
14	156	291	63	203	344	112	263	33
sver	bren	nen	undd	ieas	che	zers	chl	agen
32	174	309	81	221	362	130	281	51
undi	nzuk	unf	tnoc	hans	ieg	elan	gen	denp
50	192	327	99	239	2	148	299	69
eieh	nung	sie	bitt	eim	geda	eeht	nis	beha
68	210	345	117	257	20	166	317	87
nver	bren	nun	bser	las	sver	bren	nen	komm
86	228	363	135	275	38	184	335	105
unbe	ding	ter	ford	erl	ichi	stun	dde	renk
104	246	3	153	293	56	202	353	123
eser	ges	andt	scha	ftp	unkt	absa	tza	usge
122	264	21	171	311	74	220	371	141
ersl	ist	enre	gist	era	bree	hnun	gen	quit
140	282	39	189	329	92	238	11	159
iche	mit	demk	rieg	ezu	samm	enh	aeng	ende
158	300	57	207	347	110	256	29	177
llez	uku	nftk	omma	auc	hnac	hfr	iede	nssc
176	318	75	225	365	128	274	47	195
enzu	bew	ahre	nkla	mme	rzub	ezu	egli	chen
194	336	93	243	5	146	292	65	213
dode	rau	chnu	run	ange	nehm	sei	nkoe	nnte
212	354	111	261	23	164	310	83	231
rung	gan	zbes	ond	erea	ufme	rks	amke	itzu
230	372	129	279	41	182	328	101	249
nsic	htl	ichd	ers	chon	vcrh	and	enen	pap

Fig. A.17 Length nine sequences, distances 142,135,150,140,141,146,151,148

14	156	291	63	203	344	112	263	33	168
sver	bren	nen	undd	ieas	che	zers	chl	agen	punk
32	174	309	81	221	362	130	281	51	186
undi	nzuk	unf	tnoc	hans	ieg	elan	gen	denp	apie
50	192	327	99	239	2	148	299	69	204
eieh	nung	sie	bitt	eim	geda	eeht	nis	beha	lten
68	210	345	117	257	20	166	317	87	222
nver	bren	nun	bser	las	sver	bren	nen	komm	adon
86	228	363	135	275	38	184	335	105	240
unbe	ding	ter	ford	erl	ichi	stun	dde	renk	enn
104	246	3	153	293	56	202	353	123	258
eser	ges	andt	scha	ftp	unkt	absa	tza	usge	nom
122	264	21	171	311	74	220	371	141	276
ersl	ist	enre	gist	era	bree	hnun	gen	quit	tun
140	282	39	189	329	92	238	11	159	294
iche	mit	demk	rieg	ezu	samm	enh	aeng	ende	nko
158	300	57	207	347	110	256	29	177	312
llez	uku	nftk	omma	auc	hnac	hfr	iede	nssc	hiu
176	318	75	225	365	128	274	47	195	330
enzu	bew	ahre	nkla	mme	rzub	ezu	egli	chen	kem
194	336	93	243	5	146	292	65	213	348
dode	rau	chnu	run	ange	nehm	sei	nkoe	nnte	kom
212	354	111	261	23	164	310	83	231	366
rung	gan	zbes	ond	erea	ufme	rks	amke	itzu	sch
230	372	129	279	41	182	328	101	249	6
nsic	htl	ichd	ers	chon	vcrh	and	enen	pap	iere
248	12	147	297	59	200	346	119	267	24
mdi	enst	undd	end	iens	tder	ver	tret	eru	nser
266	30	165	315	77	218	364	137	285	42
gna	hmen	hier	mit	alsp	qrbe	zei	chne	und	dess
284	48	183	333	95	236	4	155	303	60
ach	demb	esit	zes	oleh	erp	apie	rest	reb	ende
302	66	201	351	113	254	22	173	321	78
tzt	ncch	inbe	nut	zung	bef	indl	iohc	neh	iffr
320	84	219	369	131	272	40	191	339	96
mer	aufu	eber	die	exis	ten	zund	dasw	irk	ondi
338	102	237	9	149	290	58	209	357	114
iea	uchd	ieb	etre	ffen	deb	rier	lich	eun	dtel
356	120	255	27	167	308	76	227	375	132
hri	ftst	ich	wcer	teru	nda	nwei	sung	enk	omma
374	138	273	45	185	326	94	245	15	150
rag	essc	hri	ftli	chof	fen	meld	enu	ndso	dann

Fig. A.18 Length ten sequences, distances 142, 135, 150, 140, 141, 146, 151, 148, 145

eng would work for this. The differences are 98 and 151. We try both and the 151 produces more consistent German.

At this point we have only one column left. Brute force on a sliding strip of tetragrams, or else a guess that tetragram 0 to 145 with a distance of 145 fits the pattern of the cryptogram, yields the final message.

A.9   Putting Together the Final Message

We present below the text of the message. Our sequence of differences is

145, 151, 150, 142, 135, 150, 140, 141, 146, 151, 148, 135, 154, 145, 155, 147, 138

which we display in Figs. A.19, A.21, and A.23 (Figs. A.20 and A.22).

We include Fig. A.21 to indicate what the tetragrams would look like in the original message as written by the German code clerk. We note that the method of *encryption* is still unclear from this, since the choice of trigrams with a trailing blank versus tetragrams must obviously be made after rearranging.

First we break this on word boundaries to produce Fig. A.24. Then we look hard at the German to rearrange the lines to produce the final message of Fig. A.25. In this last figure we have indicated in bold the letters that were garbled in the original. The garblings come directly from Yardley [1], and it is not clear whether they were in the original message or whether these garblings came from the printing of the book.

Finally, we offer the translation from Yardley (pp. 151–152) in Fig. A.26, and as a final thought, for those who can read the German, we remark that the opening ten lines of the original text seem to exemplify the famous comment from Mark Twain:

> Whenever the literary German dives into a sentence, that is the last you are going to see of him till he emerges on the other side of his Atlantic with his verb in his mouth.
>
> (*A Connecticut Yankee in King Arthur's Court*)

Fig. A.19 Length eighteen sequences

0	145	296	68	210	345	117	257	20	
nscg	enan	nte	nver	bren	nun	bser	las	sver	
	166	317	87	222	376	143	298	67	205
	bren	nen	komm	adon	ich	imhi	nbl	ieka	ufku
18	163	314	86	228	363	135	275	38	
ahru	ngni	eht	unbe	ding	ter	ford	erl	ichi	
	184	335	105	240	16	161	316	85	223
	stun	dde	renk	enn	tnia	nahm	edu	rchu	nsur
36	181	332	104	246	3	153	293	56	
onde	nzmi	tdi	eser	ges	andt	scha	ftp	unkt	
	202	353	123	258	34	179	334	103	241
	absa	tza	usge	nom	menb	leib	env	orla	euf
54	199	350	122	264	21	171	311	74	
ierz	ubez	ond	ersl	ist	enre	gist	era	bree	
	220	371	141	276	52	197	352	121	259
	hnun	gen	quit	tun	genk	onto	bue	cher	und
72	217	368	140	282	39	189	329	92	
bitt	esae	mtl	iche	mit	demk	rieg	ezu	samm	
	238	11	159	294	70	215	370	139	277
	enh	aeng	ende	nko	mmav	oral	lem	also	die
90	235	8	158	300	57	207	347	110	
tztu	ndf	uera	llez	uku	nftk	omma	auc	hnac	
	256	29	177	312	88	233	10	157	295
	hfr	iede	nssc	hiu	ssko	mma	stre	ngst	ess
108	253	26	176	318	75	225	365	128	
till	sch	weig	enzu	bew	ahre	nkla	mme	rzub	
	274	47	195	330	106	251	28	175	313
	ezu	egli	chen	kem	main	ihr	enha	ende	nbe
126	271	44	194	336	93	243	5	146	
romi	tti	eren	dode	rau	chnu	run	ange	nehm	
	292	65	213	348	124	269	46	193	331
	sei	nkoe	nnte	kom	masc	for	tsor	gfae	lti
144	289	62	212	354	111	261	23	164	
rera	ufb	ewnh	rung	gan	zbes	ond	erea	ufme	
	310	83	231	366	142	287	64	211	349
	rks	amke	itzu	sch	enke	nis	tpun	ktab	sat
162	307	80	230	372	129	279	41	182	
zbit	ted	iehi	nsic	htl	ichd	ers	chon	vcrh	
	328	101	249	6	160	305	82	229	367
	and	enen	pap	iere	erfo	lgt	eaus	fueh	run
180	325	98	248	12	147	297	59	200	
aufd	eng	ohei	mdi	enst	undd	end	iens	tder	
	346	119	267	24	178	323	100	247	7
	ver	tret	eru	nser	esge	ner	alun	dad	mira
198	343	116	266	30	165	315	77	218	
enft	ige	gezu	gna	hmen	hier	mit	alsp	qrbe	
	364	137	285	42	196	341	118	265	25
	zei	chne	und	dess	euin	hal	tzus	amm	enmi
216	361	134	284	48	183	333	95	236	
enoc	him	mern	ach	demb	esit	zes	oleh	erp	
	4	155	303	60	214	359	136	283	43
	apie	rest	reb	ende	nfei	nde	fuer	uns	komp
234	1	152	302	66	201	351	113	254	
ign	ochd	ieje	tzt	ncch	inbe	nut	zung	bef	
	22	173	321	78	232	377	154	301	61
	indl	iohc	neh	iffr	ebue	che	rkom	mac	cdes

Fig. A.20 Length eighteen sequences (continued)

252	19	170	320	84	219	369	131	272	
1st	abes	klam	mer	aufu	eber	die	exis	ten	
	40	191	339	96	250	17	172	319	79
	zund	dasw	irk	ondi	eso	rver	tret	eri	stje
270	37	188	338	102	237	9	149	290	
sow	eite	rsow	iea	uchd	ieb	etre	ffen	deb	
	58	209	357	114	268	35	190	337	97
	rier	lich	eun	dtel	egr	aphi	acho	kor	resp
288	55	206	356	120	255	27	167	308	
und	gohe	imac	hri	ftst	ich	wcer	teru	nda	
	76	227	375	132	286	53	208	355	115
	nwei	sung	enk	omma	der	endu	rcha	uss	iche
306	73	224	374	138	273	45	185	326	
gdi	eses	auft	rag	essc	hri	ftli	chof	fen	
	94	245	15	150	304	71	226	373	133
	meld	enu	ndso	dann	auc	hden	vorl	ieg	ende
324	91	242	14	156	291	63	203	344	
gun	dres	tlo	sver	bren	nen	undd	ieas	che	
	112	263	33	168	322	89	244	13	151
	zers	chl	agen	punk	tab	satz	esg	ehoe	renh
342	109	260	32	174	309	81	221	362	
fin	dlic	hen	undi	nzuk	unf	tnoc	hans	ieg	
	130	281	51	186	340	107	262	31	169
	elan	gen	denp	apie	rek	omma	der	enau	fbew
360	127	278	50	192	327	99	239	2	
tdi	eser	bez	eieh	nung	sie	bitt	eim	geda	
	148	299	69	204	358	125	280	49	187
	eeht	nis	beha	lten	wol	lenp	unk	tseh	luss

Fig. A.21 Length eighteen sequences, rearranged

72	217	368	140	282	39	189	329	92	
bitt	esae	mtl	iche	mit	demk	rieg	ezu	samm	
	238	11	159	294	70	215	370	139	277
	enh	aeng	ende	nko	mmav	oral	lem	also	die
180	325	98	248	12	147	297	59	200	
aufd	eng	ohei	mdi	enst	undd	end	iens	tder	
	346	119	267	24	178	323	100	247	7
	ver	tret	eru	nser	esge	ner	alun	dad	mira
252	19	170	320	84	219	369	131	272	
1st	abes	klam	mer	aufu	eber	die	exis	ten	
	40	191	339	96	250	17	172	319	79
	zund	dasw	irk	ondi	eso	rver	tret	eri	stje
90	235	8	158	300	57	207	347	110	
tztu	ndf	uera	llez	uku	nftk	omma	auc	hnac	
	256	29	177	312	88	233	10	157	295
	hfr	iede	nssc	hiu	ssko	mma	stre	ngst	ess
108	253	26	176	318	75	225	365	128	
till	sch	weig	enzu	bew	ahre	nkla	mme	rzub	
	274	47	195	330	106	251	28	175	313
	ezu	egli	chen	kem	main	ihr	enha	ende	nbe
342	109	260	32	174	309	81	221	362	
fin	dlic	hen	undi	nzuk	unf	tnoc	hans	ieg	
	130	281	51	186	340	107	262	31	169
	elan	gen	denp	apie	rek	omma	der	enau	fbew
18	163	314	86	228	363	135	275	38	
ahru	ngni	eht	unbe	ding	ter	ford	erl	ichi	
	184	335	105	240	16	161	316	85	223
	stun	dde	renk	enn	tnia	nahm	edu	rchu	nsur
216	361	134	284	48	183	333	95	236	
enoc	him	mern	ach	demb	esit	zes	oleh	erp	
	4	155	303	60	214	359	136	283	43
	apie	rest	reb	ende	nfei	nde	fuer	uns	komp
126	271	44	194	336	93	243	5	146	
romi	tti	eren	dode	rau	chnu	run	ange	nehm	
	292	65	213	348	124	269	46	193	331
	sei	nkoe	nnte	kom	masc	for	tsor	gfae	lti
324	91	242	14	156	291	63	203	344	
gun	dres	tlo	sver	bren	nen	undd	ieas	che	
	112	263	33	168	322	89	244	13	151
	zers	chl	agen	punk	tab	satz	esg	ehoe	renh
54	199	350	122	264	21	171	311	74	
ierz	ubez	ond	ersl	ist	enre	gist	era	bree	
	220	371	141	276	52	197	352	121	259
	hnun	gen	quit	tun	genk	onto	bue	cher	und
270	37	188	338	102	237	9	149	290	
sow	eite	rsow	iea	uchd	ieb	etre	ffen	deb	
	58	209	357	114	268	35	190	337	97
	rier	lich	eun	dtel	egr	aphi	acho	kor	resp
36	181	332	104	246	3	153	293	56	
onde	nzmi	tdi	eser	ges	andt	scha	ftp	unkt	
	202	353	123	258	34	179	334	103	241
	absa	tza	usge	nom	menb	leib	env	orla	euf
234	1	152	302	66	201	351	113	254	
ign	ochd	ieje	tzt	ncch	inbe	nut	zung	bef	
	22	173	321	78	232	377	154	301	61
	indl	iohc	neh	iffr	ebue	che	rkom	mac	cdes

288	55	206	356	120	255	27	167	308	
und	gohe	imac	hri	ftst	ich	wcer	teru	nda	
	76	227	375	132	286	53	208	355	115
	nwei	sung	enk	omma	der	endu	rcha	uss	iche
144	289	62	212	354	111	261	23	164	
rera	ufb	ewnh	rung	gan	zbes	ond	erea	ufme	
	310	83	231	366	142	287	64	211	349
	rks	amke	itzu	sch	enke	nis	tpun	ktab	sat
162	307	80	230	372	129	279	41	182	
zbit	ted	iehi	nsic	htl	ichd	ers	chon	vcrh	
	328	101	249	6	160	305	82	229	367
	and	enen	pap	iere	erfo	lgt	eaus	fueh	run
306	73	224	374	138	273	45	185	326	
gdi	eses	auft	rag	essc	hri	ftli	chof	fen	
	94	245	15	150	304	71	226	373	133
	meld	enu	ndso	dann	auc	hden	vorl	ieg	ende
0	145	296	68	210	345	117	257	20	
nscg	enan	nte	nver	bren	nun	bser	las	sver	
	166	317	87	222	376	143	298	67	205
	bren	nen	komm	adon	ich	imhi	nbl	ieka	ufku
198	343	116	266	30	165	315	77	218	
enft	ige	gezu	gna	hmen	hier	mit	alsp	qrbe	
	364	137	285	42	196	341	118	265	25
	zei	chne	und	dess	euin	hal	tzus	amm	enmi
360	127	278	50	192	327	99	239	2	
tdi	eser	bez	eieh	nung	sie	bitt	eim	geda	
	148	299	69	204	358	125	280	49	187
	eeht	nis	beha	lten	wol	lenp	unk	tseh	luss

Fig. A.22 Length eighteen sequences rearranged (continued)

bitt esae mtl iche mit demk rieg ezu samm enh aeng ende nko mmav oral lem also die
aufd eng ohei mdi enst undd end iens tder ver tret eru nser esge ner alun dad mira
lst abes klam mer aufu eber die exis ten zund dasw irk ondi eso rver tret eri stje
tztu ndf uera llez uku nftk omma auc hnac hfr iede nssc hiu ssko mma stre ngst ess
till sch weig enzu bew ahre nkla mme rzub ezu egli chen kem main ihr enha ende nbe
fin dlic hen undi nzuk unf tnoc hans ieg elan gen denp apie rek omma der enau fbew
ahru ngni eht unbe ding ter ford erl ichi stun dde renk enn tnia nahm edu rchu nsur
enoc him mern ach demb esit zes oleh erp apie rest reb ende nfei nde fuer uns komp
romi tti eren dode rau chnu run ange nehm sei nkoe nnte kom masc for tsor gfae lti
gun dres tlo sver bren nen undd ieas che zers chl agen punk tab satz esg ehoe renh
ierz ubez ond ersl ist enre gist era bree hnun gen quit tun genk onto bue cher und
sow eite rsow iea uchd ieb etre ffen deb rier lich eun dtel egr aphi acho kor resp
onde nzmi tdi eser ges andt scha ftp unkt absa tza usge nom menb leib env orla euf
ign ochd ieje tzt ncch inbe nut zung bef indl iohc neh iffr ebue che rkom mac cdes
und gohe imac hri ftst ich wcer teru nda nwei sung enk omma der endu rcha uss iche
rera ufb ewnh rung gan zbes ond erea ufme rks amke itzu sch enke nis tpun ktab sat
zbit ted iehi nsic htl ichd ers chon vcrh and enen pap iere erfo lgt eaus fueh run
gdi eses auft rag essc hri ftli chof fen meld enu ndso dann auc hden vorl ieg ende
nscg enan nte nver bren nun bser las sver bren nen komm adon ich imhi nbl ieka ufku
enft ige gezu gna hmen hier mit alsp qrbe zei chne und dess euin hal tzus amm enmi
tdi eser bez eieh nung sie bitt eim geda eeht nis beha lten wol lenp unk tseh luss

Fig. A.23 Decrypted message

bitte saemtliche mit dem kriege zusammen haengenden komma vorallem also die
auf den goheimdienst und den dienst der vertreter unseres general und admira
l stabes klammer auf ueber die existenz und das wirkondie sor vertreter istje
tzt und fuer alle zukunft komma auch nach friedensschiuss komma strengstes s
tillschweigen zu bewahren klammer zu bezueglichen kem main ihren haenden be
findlichen und in zukunft noch ansiegelangenden papiere komma deren auf bew
ahrung nieht unbedingterforderlichistundderen kenntnia nahme durch unsur
e noch immer nach dem besitze s oleh er papieres trebenden feinde fuer uns komp
romittieren dode rauch nur unangenehm sein koennte komma sc fort sorg faelti
g und rest los verbrennen und die asche zerschlagen punkt absatz es gehoeren h
ierzu bezonders listen register abreehnungen quittungen kontobuecher und
soweiter sowie auch die betreffen debrierlich eund telegraphiacho korresp
ondenz mit dieser gesandtschaft punkt absatz ausgenommen bleiben vorlaeuf
ig noch die jetzt ncch in benutzung befindl ioh cneh iffre buecher komma c cdes
und goheim achriftstich wcer ter und anweisungen komma deren durch aussiche
r er auf bewnhrung ganz besondere aufmerksamkeit zu schenken ist punkt absat
z bitte die hinsichtlich der schon vcrhandenen papiere erfolgte aus fuehr un
g dieses auftrages schriftlich offenmelden und so dann auch den vorliegende
n scgenannten verbrennun bser lass verbrennen komma don ich im hinbliek aufku
enftige gezug nahmen hier mit als pqr bezeichne und desseu inhalt zusammen mi
t dieser bezeiehung sie bitte im gedaeehtnis behalten wollen punkt seh luss

Fig. A.24 Decrypted message broken at word boundaries

bitte saemtliche mit dem kriege zusammenhaengenden komma vorallem also die
auf den geheimdienst und den dienst der vertreter unseres general und admira
lstabes klammer auf ueber die existenz und das wirkon dieser vertreter ist je
tzt und fuer alle zukunft komma auch nach friedensschiuss komma strengstes s
tillschweigen zu bewahren klammer zu bezueglichen komma in ihren haenden be
findlichen und in zukunft noch ansiegelangenden papiere komma deren auf bew
ahrung nicht unbedingt erforderlichistundderen kenntnis nahme durch unsur
e noch immer nach dem besitze solcher papieres trebenden feinde fuer uns komp
romittierende der auch nur unangenehm sein koennte komma so fort sorg faelti
g und rest los verbrennen und die asche zerschlagen punkt absatz es gehoeren h
ierzu bezonders listen register abrechnungen quittungen kontobuecher und
soweiter sowie auch die betreffen debrierliche und telegraphische korresp
ondenz mit dieser gesandtschaft punkt absatz ausgenommen bleiben vorlaeuf
ig noch die jetzt noch in benutzung befindl ich en chiffrebuecher komma codes
und goheim schriftstich woerter und anweisungen komma deren durch aussiche
r er auf beanhrung ganz besondere aufmerksamkeit zu schenken ist punkt absat
z bitte die hinsichtlich der schon verhandenen papiere erfolgte aus fuehrun
g dieses auftrages schriftlich offen melden und so dann auch den vorliegende
n sogenannten verbrennun gs erlass verbrennen komma don ich im hinblick aufku
enftige gezug nahmen hier mit als pqr bezeichne und desseu inhalt zusammen mi
t dieser bezeiehnung sie bitte im gedaechtnis behalten wollen punkt schluss

Fig. A.25 Final message

*Please carefully and immediately burn without remainder, and destroy the ashes of, all
papers connected with the war, the preservation of which is not absolutely necessary,
especially papers now in your hands or reaching you hereafter which have to do with the
Secret Service and the service of the representatives of our General Staff and Admiralty
Staff (strictest silence concerning the existence and activity of these representatives is to be
observed now and for all future time, even after the conclusion of peace) which might be
compromising or even unpleasant for us if they came to the knowledge of our enemies, who
are still endeavoring to obtain possession of such papers.*

*Lists, registers, accounts, receipts, account books, etc., are especially included in these
papers, as well as correspondence with this Embassy by letter and telegraph on the subjects
mentioned.*

*Cipher books, codes and cipher keys and directions that are still in use are excepted for the
present, and most particular attention must be paid to keeping them in absolute safety.*

*Please report in writing en claire the execution of this order so far as it relates to papers
now on hand and then burn this so-called order for burning, which, for further reference,
I herewith designate as PQR, and the contents of which together with this designation you
will please retain in memory.*

Fig. A.26 The translated message

AES Code

B

B.1 Introduction

This is a revision of the test vectors and code that appears in the back of [3] as Appendices B and C.

Appendix B.2 of [3] has a trace of Rijndael with plaintext blocks of 128 bits and key size 128. As indicated there (and changed slightly here), the labels on the output are

- r is the round number
- input is the input to the cipher
- start is the state (the 128-bit block that starts with the plaintext input and is traced through the encryption process to result in the ciphertext) at the start of round r
- s_box is the state after the s_box substitution
- s_row is the state after the shift-row transformation
- m_col is the state after the mix-column transformation
- k_sch is the key schedule value for round r
- output is the state after the encryption, that is, the ciphertext.

B.2 A Revised Appendix B.2

This is essentially the same as Appendix B.2. We have changed the labelling slightly, we have traced both the encryption and the decryption (rather than just the encryption), and we have included a translation of the hex bytes into printable characters. The ENC label is for the encryption of the plaintext, DEC label is for the subsequent decryption.

© The Editor(s) (if applicable) and The Author(s), under exclusive license to Springer Nature Switzerland AG 2021
D. Buell, *Fundamentals of Cryptography*, Undergraduate Topics in Computer Science, https://doi.org/10.1007/978-3-030-73492-3 A B

```
block length 128   key length 128
TEXT   32 43 f6 a8 88 5a 30 8d 31 31 98 a2 e0 37 07 34


KEY    2b 7e 15 16 28 ae d2 a6 ab f7 15 88 09 cf 4f 3c


ROUND  0 input    32 43 f6 a8 88 5a 30 8d 31 31 98 a2 e0 37 07 34
ROUND  0 k_sch    2b 7e 15 16 28 ae d2 a6 ab f7 15 88 09 cf 4f 3c


ROUND  1 start    19 3d e3 be a0 f4 e2 2b 9a c6 8d 2a e9 f8 48 08
ROUND  1 s_box    d4 27 11 ae e0 bf 98 f1 b8 b4 5d e5 1e 41 52 30
ROUND  1 s_row    d4 bf 5d 30 e0 b4 52 ae b8 41 11 f1 1e 27 98 e5
ROUND  1 m_col    04 66 81 e5 e0 cb 19 9a 48 f8 d3 7a 28 06 26 4c
ROUND  1 k_sch    a0 fa fe 17 88 54 2c b1 23 a3 39 39 2a 6c 76 05


ROUND  2 start    a4 9c 7f f2 68 9f 35 2b 6b 5b ea 43 02 6a 50 49
ROUND  2 s_box    49 de d2 89 45 db 96 f1 7f 39 87 1a 77 02 53 3b
ROUND  2 s_row    49 db 87 3b 45 39 53 89 7f 02 d2 f1 77 de 96 1a
ROUND  2 m_col    58 4d ca f1 1b 4b 5a ac db e7 ca a8 1b 6b b0 e5
ROUND  2 k_sch    f2 c2 95 f2 7a 96 b9 43 59 35 80 7a 73 59 f6 7f


ROUND  3 start    aa 8f 5f 03 61 dd e3 ef 82 d2 4a d2 68 32 46 9a
ROUND  3 s_box    ac 73 cf 7b ef c1 11 df 13 b5 d6 b5 45 23 5a b8
ROUND  3 s_row    ac c1 d6 b8 ef b5 5a 7b 13 23 cf df 45 73 11 b5
ROUND  3 m_col    75 ec 09 93 20 0b 63 33 53 c0 cf 7c bb 25 d0 dc
ROUND  3 k_sch    3d 80 47 7d 47 16 fe 3e 1e 23 7e 44 6d 7a 88 3b


ROUND  4 start    48 6c 4e ee 67 1d 9d 0d 4d e3 b1 38 d6 5f 58 e7
ROUND  4 s_box    52 50 2f 28 85 a4 5e d7 e3 11 c8 07 f6 cf 6a 94
ROUND  4 s_row    52 a4 c8 94 85 11 6a 28 e3 cf 2f d7 f6 50 5e 07
ROUND  4 m_col    0f d6 da a9 60 31 38 bf 6f c0 10 6b 5e b3 13 01
ROUND  4 k_sch    ef 44 a5 41 a8 52 5b 7f b6 71 25 3b db 0b ad 00


ROUND  5 start    e0 92 7f e8 c8 63 63 c0 d9 b1 35 50 85 b8 be 01
ROUND  5 s_box    e1 4f d2 9b e8 fb fb ba 35 c8 96 53 97 6c ae 7c
ROUND  5 s_row    e1 fb 96 7c e8 ae 9b 35 6c d2 ba 97 4f fb 53
ROUND  5 m_col    25 d1 a9 ad bd 11 d1 68 b6 3a 33 8e 4c 4c c0 b0
ROUND  5 k_sch    d4 d1 c6 f8 7c 83 9d 87 ca f2 b8 bc 11 f9 15 bc


ROUND  6 start    f1 00 6f 55 c1 92 4c ef 7c c8 8b 32 5d b5 d5 0c
ROUND  6 s_box    a1 63 a8 fc 78 4f 29 df 10 e8 3d 23 4c d5 03 fe
ROUND  6 s_row    a1 4f 3d fe 78 e8 03 fc 10 d5 a8 df 4c 63 29 23
ROUND  6 m_col    4b 86 8d 6d 2c 4a 89 80 33 9d f4 e8 37 d2 18 d8
ROUND  6 k_sch    6d 88 a3 7a 11 0b 3e fd db f9 86 41 ca 00 93 fd


ROUND  7 start    26 0e 2e 17 3d 41 b7 7d e8 64 72 a9 fd d2 8b 25
ROUND  7 s_box    f7 ab 31 f0 27 83 a9 ff 9b 43 40 d3 54 b5 3d 3f
ROUND  7 s_row    f7 83 40 3f 27 43 3d f0 9b b5 31 ff 54 ab a9 d3
ROUND  7 m_col    14 15 b5 bf 46 16 15 ec 27 46 56 d7 34 2a d8 43
ROUND  7 k_sch    4e 54 f7 0e 5f 5f c9 f3 84 a6 4f b2 4e a6 dc 4f


ROUND  8 start    5a 41 42 b1 19 49 dc 1f a3 e0 19 65 7a 8c 04 0c
ROUND  8 s_box    be 83 2c c8 d4 3b 86 c0 0a e1 d4 4d da 64 f2 fe
ROUND  8 s_row    be 3b d4 fe d4 e1 f2 c8 0a 64 2c c0 da 83 86 4d
ROUND  8 m_col    00 51 2f d1 b1 c8 89 ff 54 76 6d cd fa 1b 99 ea
ROUND  8 k_sch    ea d2 73 21 b5 8d ba d2 31 2b f5 60 7f 8d 29 2f


ROUND  9 start    ea 83 5c f0 04 45 33 2d 65 5d 98 ad 85 96 b0 c5
ROUND  9 s_box    87 ec 4a 8c f2 6e c3 d8 4d 4c 46 95 97 90 e7 a6
ROUND  9 s_row    87 6e 46 a6 f2 4c e7 8c 4d 90 4a d8 97 ec c3 95
ROUND  9 m_col    47 37 94 ed 40 d4 e4 a5 a3 70 3a a6 4c 9f 42 bc
```

```
ROUND  9 k_sch    ac 77 66 f3 19 fa dc 21 28 d1 29 41 57 5c 00 6e

ROUND 10 start    eb 40 f2 1e 59 2e 38 84 8b a1 13 e7 1b c3 42 d2
ROUND 10 s_box    e9 09 89 72 cb 31 07 5f 3d 32 7d 94 af 2e 2c b5
ROUND 10 s_row    e9 31 7d b5 cb 32 2c 72 3d 2e 89 5f af 09 07 94
ROUND 10 k_sch    d0 14 f9 a8 c9 ee 25 89 e1 3f 0c c8 b6 63 0c a6
ROUND 10 output   39 25 84 1d 02 dc 09 fb dc 11 85 97 19 6a 0b 32

ENC    39 25 84 1d 02 dc 09 fb dc 11 85 97 19 6a 0b 32

ROUND 10 output   39 25 84 1d 02 dc 09 fb dc 11 85 97 19 6a 0b 32
ROUND 10 k_sch    d0 14 f9 a8 c9 ee 25 89 e1 3f 0c c8 b6 63 0c a6
ROUND 10 s_row    e9 31 7d b5 cb 32 2c 72 3d 2e 89 5f af 09 07 94
ROUND 10 s_box    e9 09 89 72 cb 31 07 5f 3d 32 7d 94 af 2e 2c b5
ROUND 10 start    eb 40 f2 1e 59 2e 38 84 8b a1 13 e7 1b c3 42 d2

ROUND  9 k_sch    ac 77 66 f3 19 fa dc 21 28 d1 29 41 57 5c 00 6e
ROUND  9 m_col    47 37 94 ed 40 d4 e4 a5 a3 70 3a a6 4c 9f 42 bc
ROUND  9 s_row    87 6e 46 a6 f2 4c e7 8c 4d 90 4a d8 97 ec c3 95
ROUND  9 s_box    87 ec 4a 8c f2 6e c3 d8 4d 4c 46 95 97 90 e7 a6
ROUND  9 start    ea 83 5c f0 04 45 33 2d 65 5d 98 ad 85 96 b0 c5

ROUND  8 k_sch    ea d2 73 21 b5 8d ba d2 31 2b f5 60 7f 8d 29 2f
ROUND  8 m_col    00 51 2f d1 b1 c8 89 ff 54 76 6d cd fa 1b 99 ea
ROUND  8 s_row    be 3b d4 fe d4 e1 f2 c8 0a 64 2c c0 da 83 86 4d
ROUND  8 s_box    be 83 2c c8 d4 3b 86 c0 0a e1 d4 4d da 64 f2 fe
ROUND  8 start    5a 41 42 b1 19 49 dc 1f a3 e0 19 65 7a 8c 04 0c

ROUND  7 k_sch    4e 54 f7 0e 5f 5f c9 f3 84 a6 4f b2 4e a6 dc 4f
ROUND  7 m_col    14 15 b5 bf 46 16 15 ec 27 46 56 d7 34 2a d8 43
ROUND  7 s_row    f7 83 40 3f 27 43 3d f0 9b b5 31 ff 54 ab a9 d3
ROUND  7 s_box    f7 ab 31 f0 27 83 a9 ff 9b 43 40 d3 54 b5 3d 3f
ROUND  7 start    26 0e 2e 17 3d 41 b7 7d e8 64 72 a9 fd d2 8b 25

ROUND  6 k_sch    6d 88 a3 7a 11 0b 3e fd db f9 86 41 ca 00 93 fd
ROUND  6 m_col    4b 86 8d 6d 2c 4a 89 80 33 9d f4 e8 37 d2 18 d8
ROUND  6 s_row    a1 4f 3d fe 78 e8 03 fc 10 d5 a8 df 4c 63 29 23
ROUND  6 s_box    a1 63 a8 fc 78 4f 29 df 10 e8 3d 23 4c d5 03 fe
ROUND  6 start    f1 00 6f 55 c1 92 4c ef 7c c8 8b 32 5d b5 d5 0c

ROUND  5 k_sch    d4 d1 c6 f8 7c 83 9d 87 ca f2 b8 bc 11 f9 15 bc
ROUND  5 m_col    25 d1 a9 ad bd 11 d1 68 b6 3a 33 8e 4c 4c c0 b0
ROUND  5 s_row    e1 fb 96 7c e8 c8 ae 9b 35 6c d2 ba 97 4f fb 53
ROUND  5 s_box    e1 4f d2 9b e8 fb fb ba 35 c8 96 53 97 6c ae 7c
ROUND  5 start    e0 92 7f e8 c8 63 63 c0 d9 b1 35 50 85 b8 be 01

ROUND  4 k_sch    ef 44 a5 41 a8 52 5b 7f b6 71 25 3b db 0b ad 00
ROUND  4 m_col    0f d6 da a9 60 31 38 bf 6f c0 10 6b 5e b3 13 01
ROUND  4 s_row    52 a4 c8 94 85 11 6a 28 e3 cf 2f d7 f6 50 5e 07
ROUND  4 s_box    52 50 2f 28 85 a4 5e d7 e3 11 c8 07 f6 cf 6a 94
ROUND  4 start    48 6c 4e ee 67 1d 9d 0d 4d e3 b1 38 d6 5f 58 e7

ROUND  3 k_sch    3d 80 47 7d 47 16 fe 3e 1e 23 7e 44 6d 7a 88 3b
ROUND  3 m_col    75 ec 09 93 20 0b 63 33 53 c0 cf 7c bb 25 d0 dc
ROUND  3 s_row    ac c1 d6 b8 ef b5 5a 7b 13 23 cf df 45 73 11 b5
ROUND  3 s_box    ac 73 cf 7b ef c1 11 df 13 b5 d6 b5 45 23 5a b8
ROUND  3 start    aa 8f 5f 03 61 dd e3 ef 82 d2 4a d2 68 32 46 9a

ROUND  2 k_sch    f2 c2 95 f2 7a 96 b9 43 59 35 80 7a 73 59 f6 7f
ROUND  2 m_col    58 4d ca f1 1b 4b 5a ac db e7 ca a8 1b 6b b0 e5
```

```
ROUND   2 s_row    49 db 87 3b 45 39 53 89 7f 02 d2 f1 77 de 96 1a
ROUND   2 s_box    49 de d2 89 45 db 96 f1 7f 39 87 1a 77 02 53 3b
ROUND   2 start    a4 9c 7f f2 68 9f 35 2b 6b 5b ea 43 02 6a 50 49

ROUND   1 k_sch    a0 fa fe 17 88 54 2c b1 23 a3 39 39 2a 6c 76 05
ROUND   1 m_col    04 66 81 e5 e0 cb 19 9a 48 f8 d3 7a 28 06 26 4c
ROUND   1 s_row    d4 bf 5d 30 e0 b4 52 ae b8 41 11 f1 1e 27 98 e5
ROUND   1 s_box    d4 27 11 ae e0 bf 98 f1 b8 b4 5d e5 1e 41 52 30
ROUND   1 start    19 3d e3 be a0 f4 e2 2b 9a c6 8d 2a e9 f8 48 08

ROUND   0 k_sch    2b 7e 15 16 28 ae d2 a6 ab f7 15 88 09 cf 4f 3c
ROUND   0 input    32 43 f6 a8 88 5a 30 8d 31 31 98 a2 e0 37 07 34

DEC       32 43 f6 a8 88 5a 30 8d 31 31 98 a2 e0 37 07 34
```

B.3   A Revised Appendix B.3

This is essentially the same as Appendix B.3.

We have changed the labelling slightly, we have traced both the encryption and the decryption (rather than just the encryption), and we have included a translation of the hex bytes into printable characters. The ENC label is for the encryption of the plaintext, ENC label is for the subsequent repeated encryption.

```
block length 128 key length 128
TEXT 00000000000000000000000000000000
KEY  00000000000000000000000000000000
ENC  66e94bd4ef8a2c3b884cfa59ca342b2e
ENC  f795bd4a52e29ed713d313fa20e98dbc

block length 160 key length 128
TEXT 0000000000000000000000000000000000000000
KEY  00000000000000000000000000000000
ENC  9e38b8eb1d2025a1665ad4b1f5438bb5cae1ac3f
ENC  939c167e7f916d45670ee21bfc939e1055054a96

block length 192 key length 128
TEXT 000000000000000000000000000000000000000000000000
KEY  00000000000000000000000000000000
ENC  a92732eb488d8bb98ecd8d95dc9c02e052f250ad369b3849
ENC  106f34179c3982ddc6750aa01936b7a180e6b0b9d8d690ec

block length 224 key length 128
TEXT 00000000000000000000000000000000000000000000000000000000
KEY  00000000000000000000000000000000
ENC  0623522d88f7b9c63437537157f625dd5697ab628a3b9be2549895c8
ENC  93f93cbdabe23415620e6990b0443d621f6afbd6edefd6990a1965a8

block length 256 key length 128
TEXT 0000000000000000000000000000000000000000000000000000000000000000
KEY  00000000000000000000000000000000
ENC  a693b288df7dae5b1757640276439230db77c4cd7a871e24d6162e54af434891
ENC  5f05857c80b68ea42ccbc759d42c28d5cd490f1d180c7a9397ee585bea770391

block length 128 key length 160
```

```
TEXT  00000000000000000000000000000000
KEY   0000000000000000000000000000000000000000
ENC   94b434f8f57b9780f0eff1a9ec4c112c
ENC   35a00ec955df43417ceac2ab2b3f3e76

block length 160 key length 160
TEXT  0000000000000000000000000000000000000000
KEY   0000000000000000000000000000000000000000
ENC   33b12ab81db7972e8fdc529dda46fcb529b31826
ENC   97f03eb018c0bb9195bf37c6a0aece8e4cb8de5f

block length 192 key length 160
TEXT  000000000000000000000000000000000000000000000000
KEY   0000000000000000000000000000000000000000
ENC   528e2fff6005427b67bb1ed31ecc09a69ef41531df5ba5b2
ENC   71c7687a4c93ebc35601e3662256e10115beed56a410d7ac

block length 224 key length 160
TEXT  0000000000000000000000000000000000000000000000000000000000
KEY   0000000000000000000000000000000000000000
ENC   58a0c53f3822a32464704d409c2fd0521f3a93e1f6fcfd4c87f1c551
ENC   d8e93ef2eb49857049d6f6e0f40b67516d2696f94013c065283f7f01

block length 256 key length 160
TEXT  0000000000000000000000000000000000000000000000000000000000000000
KEY   0000000000000000000000000000000000000000
ENC   938d36e0cb6b7937841dab7f1668e47b485d3acd6b3f6d598b0a9f923823331d
ENC   7b44491d1b24a93b904d171f074ad69669c2b70b134a4d2d773250a4414d78be

block length 128 key length 192
TEXT  00000000000000000000000000000000
KEY   000000000000000000000000000000000000000000000000
ENC   aae06992acbf52a3e8f4a96ec9300bd7
ENC   52f674b7b9030fdab13d18dc214eb331

block length 160 key length 192
TEXT  0000000000000000000000000000000000000000
KEY   000000000000000000000000000000000000000000000000
ENC   33060f9d4705ddd2c7675f0099140e5a98729257
ENC   012cab64982156a5710e790f85ec442ce13c520f

block length 192 key length 192
TEXT  000000000000000000000000000000000000000000000000
KEY   000000000000000000000000000000000000000000000000
ENC   c6348be20007bac4a8bd62890c8147a2432e760e9a9f9ab8
ENC   eb9def13c253f81c1fc2829426ed166a65a105c6a04ca33d

block length 224 key length 192
TEXT  0000000000000000000000000000000000000000000000000000000000
KEY   000000000000000000000000000000000000000000000000
ENC   3856b17bea77c4611e3397066828aadda004706a2c8009df40a811fe
ENC   160ad76a97ae2c1e05942fde3da2962684a92ccc74b8dc23bde4f469

block length 256 key length 192
TEXT  0000000000000000000000000000000000000000000000000000000000000000
KEY   000000000000000000000000000000000000000000000000
ENC   f927363ef5b3b4984a9eb9109844152ec167f08102644e3f9028070433df9f2a
ENC   4e03389c68b2e3f623ad8f7f6bfc88613b86f334f4148029ae25f50db144b80c

block length 128 key length 224
```

```
TEXT  00000000000000000000000000000000
KEY   000000000000000000000000000000000000000000000000000000000
ENC   73f8dff62a36f3ebf31d6f73a56ff279
ENC   3a72f21e10b6473ea9ff14a232e675b4

block length 160 key length 224
TEXT  0000000000000000000000000000000000000000
KEY   000000000000000000000000000000000000000000000000000000000
ENC   e9f5ea0fa39bb6ad7339f28e58e2e7535f261827
ENC   06ef9bc82905306d45810e12d0807796a3d338f9

block length 192 key length 224
TEXT  000000000000000000000000000000000000000000000000
KEY   0000000000000000000000000000000000000000000000000000000000
ENC   ecbe9942cd6703e16d358a829d542456d71bd3408eb23c56
ENC   fd10458ed034368a34047905165b78a6f0591ffeebf47cc7

block length 224 key length 224
TEXT  00000000000000000000000000000000000000000000000000000000
KEY   00000000000000000000000000000000000000000000000000000000
ENC   fe1cf0c8ddad24e3d751933100e8e89b61cd5d31c96abff7209c495c
ENC   515d8e2f2b9c5708f112c6de31caca47afb86838b716975a24a09cd4

block length 256 key length 224
TEXT  0000000000000000000000000000000000000000000000000000000000000000
KEY   00000000000000000000000000000000000000000000000000000000
ENC   bc18bf6d369c955bbb271cbcdd66c368356dba5b33c0005550d2320b1c617e21
ENC   60aba1d2be45d8abfdcf97bcb39f6c17df29985cf321bab75e26a26100ac00af

block length 128 key length 256
TEXT  00000000000000000000000000000000
KEY   0000000000000000000000000000000000000000000000000000000000000000
ENC   dc95c078a2408989ad48a21492842087
ENC   08c374848c228233c2b34f332bd2e9d3

block length 160 key length 256
TEXT  0000000000000000000000000000000000000000
KEY   0000000000000000000000000000000000000000000000000000000000000000
ENC   30991844f72973b3b2161f1f11e7f8d9863c5118
ENC   eef8b7cc9dbe0f03a1fe9d82e9a759fd281c67e0

block length 192 key length 256
TEXT  000000000000000000000000000000000000000000000000
KEY   0000000000000000000000000000000000000000000000000000000000000000
ENC   17004e806faef168fc9cd56f98f070982075c70c8132b945
ENC   bed33b0af364dbf15f9c2f3fb24fbdf1d36129c586eea6b7

block length 224 key length 256
TEXT  00000000000000000000000000000000000000000000000000000000
KEY   0000000000000000000000000000000000000000000000000000000000000000
ENC   9bf26fad5680d56b572067ec2fe162f449404c86303f8be38fab6e02
ENC   658f144a34af44aae66cfddab955c483dfbcb4ee9a19a6701f158a66

block length 256 key length 256
TEXT  0000000000000000000000000000000000000000000000000000000000000000
KEY   0000000000000000000000000000000000000000000000000000000000000000
ENC   c6227e7740b7e53b5cb77865278eab0726f62366d9aabad908936123a1fc8af3
ENC   9843e807319c32ad1ea3935ef56a2ba96e4bf19c30e47d88a2b97cbbf2e159e7
```

B.4   A Revised Appendix C

This is essentially the same as Appendix C, but we have revised the formatting of the code slightly. The major change is that the `Decrypt` function in Appendix C is wrong, in that it retains the order of the calls to the steps of encryption, instead of reversing the order. In addition to correcting for this error, we have included calls to functions that output the tracing information of Appendix B.2.

B.4.1   AES Functions

The functions used in AES are displayed here.

```c
#include <stdio.h>
#include <stdlib.h>
#include <string.h>
#include <stdbool.h>

typedef unsigned char word8;
typedef unsigned int word32;

#define MAXBC 8
#define MAXKC 8
#define MAXROUNDS 14

bool testd2, testd3, testtext;
int BC, KC, ROUNDS;

word8 Logtable[256] = {
    0,    0,   25,    1,   50,    2,   26,  198,   75,  199,   27,  104,   51,  238,  223,    3,
  100,    4,  224,   14,   52,  141,  129,  239,   76,  113,    8,  200,  248,  105,   28,  193,
  125,  194,   29,  181,  249,  185,   39,  106,   77,  228,  166,  114,  154,  201,    9,  120,
  101,   47,  138,    5,   33,   15,  225,   36,   18,  240,  130,   69,   53,  147,  218,  142,
  150,  143,  219,  189,   54,  208,  206,  148,   19,   92,  210,  241,   64,   70,  131,   56,
  102,  221,  253,   48,  191,    6,  139,   98,  179,   37,  226,  152,   34,  136,  145,   16,
  126,  110,   72,  195,  163,  182,   30,   66,   58,  107,   40,   84,  250,  133,   61,  186,
   43,  121,   10,   21,  155,  159,   94,  202,   78,  212,  172,  229,  243,  115,  167,   87,
  175,   88,  168,   80,  244,  234,  214,  116,   79,  174,  233,  213,  231,  230,  173,  232,
   44,  215,  117,  122,  235,   22,   11,  245,   89,  203,   95,  176,  156,  169,   81,  160,
  127,   12,  246,  111,   23,  196,   73,  236,  216,   67,   31,   45,  164,  118,  123,  183,
  204,  187,   62,   90,  251,   96,  177,  134,   59,   82,  161,  108,  170,   85,   41,  157,
  151,  178,  135,  144,   97,  190,  220,  252,  188,  149,  207,  205,   55,   63,   91,  209,
   83,   57,  132,   60,   65,  162,  109,   71,   20,   42,  158,   93,   86,  242,  211,  171,
   68,   17,  146,  217,   35,   32,   46,  137,  180,  124,  184,   38,  119,  153,  227,  165,
  103,   74,  237,  222,  197,   49,  254,   24,   13,   99,  140,  128,  192,  247,  112,    7,
};

word8 Alogtable[256] = {
    1,    3,    5,   15,   17,   51,   85,  255,   26,   46,  114,  150,  161,  248,   19,   53,
   95,  225,   56,   72,  216,  115,  149,  164,  247,    2,    6,   10,   30,   34,  102,  170,
  229,   52,   92,  228,   55,   89,  235,   38,  106,  190,  217,  112,  144,  171,  230,   49,
   83,  245,    4,   12,   20,   60,   68,  204,   79,  209,  104,  184,  211,  110,  178,  205,
   76,  212,  103,  169,  224,   59,   77,  215,   98,  166,  241,    8,   24,   40,  120,  136,
  131,  158,  185,  208,  107,  189,  220,  127,  129,  152,  179,  206,   73,  219,  118,  154,
  181,  196,   87,  249,   16,   48,   80,  240,   11,   29,   39,  105,  187,  214,   97,  163,
  254,   25,   43,  125,  135,  146,  173,  236,   47,  113,  147,  174,  233,   32,   96,  160,
  251,   22,   58,   78,  210,  109,  183,  194,   93,  231,   50,   86,  250,   21,   63,   65,
```

```
195,  94, 226,  61,  71, 201,  64, 192,  91, 237,  44, 116, 156, 191, 218, 117,
159, 186, 213, 100, 172, 239,  42, 126, 130, 157, 188, 223, 122, 142, 137, 128,
155, 182, 193,  88, 232,  35, 101, 175, 234,  37, 111, 177, 200,  67, 197,  84,
252,  31,  33,  99, 165, 244,   7,   9,  27,  45, 119, 153, 176, 203,  70, 202,
 69, 207,  74, 222, 121, 139, 134, 145, 168, 227,  62,  66, 198,  81, 243,  14,
 18,  54,  90, 238,  41, 123, 141, 140, 143, 138, 133, 148, 167, 242,  13,  23,
 57,  75, 221, 124, 132, 151, 162, 253,  28,  36, 108, 180, 199,  82, 246,   1,
};

word8 S[256] = {
 99, 124, 119, 123, 242, 107, 111, 197,  48,   1, 103,  43, 254, 215, 171, 118,
202, 130, 201, 125, 250,  89,  71, 240, 173, 212, 162, 175, 156, 164, 114, 192,
183, 253, 147,  38,  54,  63, 247, 204,  52, 165, 229, 241, 113, 216,  49,  21,
  4, 199,  35, 195,  24, 150,   5, 154,   7,  18, 128, 226, 235,  39, 178, 117,
  9, 131,  44,  26,  27, 110,  90, 160,  82,  59, 214, 179,  41, 227,  47, 132,
 83, 209,   0, 237,  32, 252, 177,  91, 106, 203, 190,  57,  74,  76,  88, 207,
208, 239, 170, 251,  67,  77,  51, 133,  69, 249,   2, 127,  80,  60, 159, 168,
 81, 163,  64, 143, 146, 157,  56, 245, 188, 182, 218,  33,  16, 255, 243, 210,
205,  12,  19, 236,  95, 151,  68,  23, 196, 167, 126,  61, 100,  93,  25, 115,
 96, 129,  79, 220,  34,  42, 144, 136,  70, 238, 184,  20, 222,  94,  11, 219,
224,  50,  58,  10,  73,   6,  36,  92, 194, 211, 172,  98, 145, 149, 228, 121,
231, 200,  55, 109, 141, 213,  78, 169, 108,  86, 244, 234, 101, 122, 174,   8,
186, 120,  37,  46,  28, 166, 180, 198, 232, 221, 116,  31,  75, 189, 139, 138,
112,  62, 181, 102,  72,   3, 246,  14,  97,  53,  87, 185, 134, 193,  29, 158,
225, 248, 152,  17, 105, 217, 142, 148, 155,  30, 135, 233, 206,  85,  40, 223,
140, 161, 137,  13, 191, 230,  66, 104,  65, 153,  45,  15, 176,  84, 187,  22,
};

word8 Si[256] = {
 82,   9, 106, 213,  48,  54, 165,  56, 191,  64, 163, 158, 129, 243, 215, 251,
124, 227,  57, 130, 155,  47, 255, 135,  52, 142,  67,  68, 196, 222, 233, 203,
 84, 123, 148,  50, 166, 194,  35,  61, 238,  76, 149,  11,  66, 250, 195,  78,
  8,  46, 161, 102,  40, 217,  36, 178, 118,  91, 162,  73, 109, 139, 209,  37,
114, 248, 246, 100, 134, 104, 152,  22, 212, 164,  92, 204,  93, 101, 182, 146,
108, 112,  72,  80, 253, 237, 185, 218,  94,  21,  70,  87, 167, 141, 157, 132,
144, 216, 171,   0, 140, 188, 211,  10, 247, 228,  88,   5, 184, 179,  69,   6,
208,  44,  30, 143, 202,  63,  15,   2, 193, 175, 189,   3,   1,  19, 138, 107,
 58, 145,  17,  65,  79, 103, 220, 234, 151, 242, 207, 206, 240, 180, 230, 115,
150, 172, 116,  34, 231, 173,  53, 133, 226, 249,  55, 232,  28, 117, 223, 110,
 71, 241,  26, 113,  29,  41, 197, 137, 111, 183,  98,  14, 170,  24, 190,  27,
252,  86,  62,  75, 198, 210, 121,  32, 154, 219, 192, 254, 120, 205,  90, 244,
 31, 221, 168,  51, 136,   7, 199,  49, 177,  18,  16,  89,  39, 128, 236,  95,
 96,  81, 127, 169,  25, 181,  74,  13,  45, 229, 122, 159, 147, 201, 156, 239,
160, 224,  59,  77, 174,  42, 245, 176, 200, 235, 187,  60, 131,  83, 153,  97,
 23,  43,   4, 126, 186, 119, 214,  38, 225, 105,  20,  99,  85,  33,  12, 125,
};

word32 RC[30] = {0x00, 0x01, 0x02, 0x04, 0x08, 0x10, 0x20, 0x40, 0x80,
                 0x1b, 0x36, 0x6c, 0xd8, 0xab, 0x4d, 0x9a, 0x2f, 0x5e,
                 0xbc, 0x63, 0xc6, 0x97, 0x35, 0x6a, 0xd4, 0xb3, 0x7d,
                 0xfa, 0xef, 0xc5};

static word8 shifts[5][4] = {{0, 1, 2, 3},
                             {0, 1, 2, 3},
                             {0, 1, 2, 3},
                             {0, 1, 2, 4},
                             {0, 1, 3, 4} };

static int numrounds[5][5] = {{10, 11, 12, 13, 14},
                              {11, 11, 12, 13, 14},
                              {12, 12, 12, 13, 14},
                              {13, 13, 13, 13, 14},
```

```
                              {14, 14, 14, 14, 14} };

/*************************************************************************
 * Multiply two elements of GF(256)
 * Required for MixColumns and InvMixColumns
 **/
word8 mul(word8 a, word8 b) {
  if (a && b) return Alogtable[(Logtable[a] + Logtable[b])%255];
  else return 0;
}

/*************************************************************************
 * XOR corresponding text input and round key input bytes
 **/
void AddRoundKey(word8 a[4][MAXBC], word8 rk[4][MAXBC]) {
  int i, j;
  for (i = 0; i < 4; i++) {
    for (j = 0; j < BC; j++) {
      a[i][j] ^= rk[i][j];
    }
  }
}

/*************************************************************************
 * Replace every byte of the input by the byte at that place
 * in the non-linear S-box
 **/
void SubBytes(word8 a[4][MAXBC], word8 box[255]) {
  int i, j;
  for (i = 0; i < 4; i++) {
    for (j = 0; j < BC; j++) {
      a[i][j] = box[a[i][j]];
    }
  }
}

/*************************************************************************
 * Row 0 remains unchanged.
 * The other three rows are shifted a variable amount.
 **/
void ShiftRows(word8 a[4][MAXBC], word8 d) {
  word8 tmp[MAXBC];
  int i, j;

  if (d == 0) {
    for (i = 1; i < 4; i++) {
      for (j = 0; j < BC; j++) {
        tmp[j] = a[i][(j + shifts[BC-4][i]) % BC];
      }
      for (j = 0; j < BC; j++) {
        a[i][j] = tmp[j];
      }
    }
  }
  else {
    for (i = 1; i < 4; i++) {
      for (j = 0; j < BC; j++) {
        tmp[j] = a[i][(BC + j - shifts[BC-4][i]) % BC];
      }
      for (j = 0; j < BC; j++) {
        a[i][j] = tmp[j];
      }
```

```
      }
    }
  }

/***************************************************************
 * Mix the four bytes of every column in a linear way.
 **/
void MixColumns(word8 a[4][MAXBC]) {
  word8 b[4][MAXBC];
  int i, j;

  for (j = 0; j < BC; j++) {
    for (i = 0; i < 4; i++) {
      b[i][j] = mul(2, a[i][j])
              ^ mul(3, a[(i+1)%4][j])
              ^ a[(i+2)%4][j]
              ^ a[(i+3)%4][j];
    }
  }
  for (i = 0; i < 4; i++) {
    for (j = 0; j < BC; j++) {
      a[i][j] = b[i][j];
    }
  }
}


/***************************************************************
 * Mix the four bytes of every column in a linear way.
 * This is the opposite operation of MixColumns.
 **/
void InvMixColumns(word8 a[4][MAXBC]) {
  word8 b[4][MAXBC];
  int i, j;

  for (j = 0; j < BC; j++) {
    for (i = 0; i < 4; i++) {
      b[i][j] = mul(0xe, a[i][j])
              ^ mul(0xb, a[(i+1)%4][j])
              ^ mul(0xd, a[(i+2)%4][j])
              ^ mul(0x9, a[(i+3)%4][j]);
    }
  }
  for (i = 0; i < 4; i++) {
    for (j = 0; j < BC; j++) {
      a[i][j] = b[i][j];
    }
  }
}


/***************************************************************
 *
 **/
int KeyExpansion(word8 k[4][MAXKC], word8 W[MAXROUNDS+1][4][MAXBC]) {
  // Calculate the required round keys.
  int i, j, t, RCpointer = 1;
  word8 tk[4][MAXKC];

  for (j = 0; j < KC; j++) {
    for (i = 0; i < 4; i++) {
      tk[i][j] = k[i][j];
    }
  }
```

```
  t = 0;
  // copy values into round key array
  for (j = 0; (j < KC) && (t < (ROUNDS+1)*BC); j++, t++) {
    for (i = 0; i < 4; i++) {
      W[t / BC][i][t % BC] = tk[i][j];
    }
  }

  while (t < (ROUNDS+1)*BC) {
    // while not enough round key material calculated, calc new values
    for (i = 0; i < 4; i++) {
      tk[i][0] ^= S[tk[(i+1)%4][KC-1]];
    }
    tk[0][0] ^= RC[RCpointer++];

    if (KC <= 6) {
      for (j = 1; j < KC; j++) {
        for (i = 0; i < 4; i++) {
          tk[i][j] ^= tk[i][j-1];
        }
      }
    } // if (KC <= 6)
    else {
      for (j = 1; j < 4; j++) {
        for (i = 0; i < 4; i++) {
          tk[i][j] ^= tk[i][j-1];
        }
      }
      for (i = 0; i < 4; i++) {
        tk[i][4] ^= S[tk[i][3]];
      }
      for (j = 5; j < KC; j++) {
        for (i = 0; i < 4; i++) {
          tk[i][j] ^= tk[i][j-1];
        }
      }
    } // else

    // copy values into round key array
    for (j = 0; (j < KC) && (t < (ROUNDS+1)*BC); j++, t++) {
      for (i = 0; i < 4; i++) {
        W[t / BC][i][t % BC] = tk[i][j];
      }
    }
  } // while (t < (ROUNDS+1)*BC) {

  return 0;
} // int KeyExpansion(word8 k[][], word8 W[][][]) {

/**************************************************************************
 * Encryption of one block.
 **/
int Encrypt(word8 a[4][MAXBC], word8 rk[MAXROUNDS+1][4][MAXBC]) {
  int r;

  dumpvaluesBC(0, "input ", a, 4, BC, testd2);

  // Begin with a key addition.
  AddRoundKey(a, rk[0]);

  dumpvaluesKC(0, "k_sch ", rk[0], 4, KC, testd2);
```

```
      if (testd2) printf("\n");
      dumpvaluesBC(1, "start ", a, 4, BC, testd2);

      // ROUNDS-1 ordinary rounds.
      for (r = 1; r < ROUNDS; r++) {
        SubBytes(a, S);
        dumpvaluesBC(r, "s_box ", a, 4, BC, testd2);

        ShiftRows(a, 0);
        dumpvaluesBC(r, "s_row ", a, 4, BC, testd2);

        MixColumns(a);
        dumpvaluesBC(r, "m_col ", a, 4, BC, testd2);

        AddRoundKey(a, rk[r]);
        dumpvaluesKC(r, "k_sch ", rk[r], 4, KC, testd2);
        if (testd2) printf("\n");
        dumpvaluesBC(r+1, "start ", a, 4, BC, testd2);
      }

      // Last round is special:  there is no MixColums.
      SubBytes(a, S);
      dumpvaluesBC(r, "s_box ", a, 4, BC, testd2);

      ShiftRows(a, 0);
      dumpvaluesBC(r, "s_row ", a, 4, BC, testd2);
      dumpvaluesKC(r, "k_sch ", rk[r], 4, KC, testd2);

      AddRoundKey(a, rk[ROUNDS]);
      dumpvaluesBC(r, "output", a, 4, BC, testd2);

      return 0;
    }

    /***********************************************************************
    * To decrypt:
    *    Apply the inverse operations of the encrypt routine,
    *    in opposite order.
    *
    *    AddRoundKey is equal to its inverse.
    *    The inverse of SubBytes with table S is
    *         SubBytes with the inverse table Si.
    *    The inverse of Shiftrows is Shiftrows over
    *         a suitable distance.
    **/
    int Decrypt(word8 a[4][MAXBC], word8 rk[MAXROUNDS+1][4][MAXBC]) {
      int r;

      // First the special round:
      //    without InvMixColumns
      //    with extra AddRoundKey

      dumpvaluesBC(ROUNDS, "output", a, 4, BC, testd2);
      AddRoundKey(a, rk[ROUNDS]);

      dumpvaluesKC(ROUNDS, "k_sch ", rk[ROUNDS], 4, KC, testd2);
      dumpvaluesBC(ROUNDS, "s_row ", a, 4, BC, testd2);
    // This was the original order of the functions.
    //   SubBytes(a, Si);
    //   dumpvaluesBC(ROUNDS, "s_box ", a, 4, 4, testd2);
    //   ShiftRows(a, 1);
```

```
// This is the revised order of the functions.
// This order works and the original one does not.
  ShiftRows(a, 1);

  dumpvaluesBC(ROUNDS, "s_box ", a, 4, BC, testd2);
  SubBytes(a, Si);

  // ROUNDS-1 ordinary rounds.
  for (r = ROUNDS-1; r > 0; r--) {
    dumpvaluesBC(r+1, "start ", a, 4, BC, testd2);
    if (testd2) printf("\n");
    AddRoundKey(a, rk[r]);

    dumpvaluesKC(r, "k_sch ", rk[r], 4, KC, testd2);
    dumpvaluesBC(r, "m_col ", a, 4, BC, testd2);
    InvMixColumns(a);

    dumpvaluesBC(r, "s_row ", a, 4, BC, testd2);
// This was the original order of the functions.
//  SubBytes(a, Si);
//  ShiftRows(a, 1);

// This is the revised order of the functions.
// This order works and the original one does not.
    ShiftRows(a, 1);
    dumpvaluesBC(r, "s_box ", a, 4, BC, testd2);

    SubBytes(a, Si);
  }

  dumpvaluesBC(r+1, "start ", a, 4, BC, testd2);
  if (testd2) printf("\n");
  dumpvaluesKC(0, "k_sch ", rk[0], 4, KC, testd2);

  AddRoundKey(a, rk[0]);

  dumpvaluesBC(0, "input ", a, 4, BC, testd2);

  return 0;
}
```

B.4.2 AES Main Program

The main program used for the Appendix B.2 and B.3 data is displayed here.

```
#include <stdio.h>
#include <stdlib.h>
#include <string.h>
#include <stdbool.h>

#include "aesutils.c"
#include "aesfunctions.c"

/*******************************************************************
 *
 **/
int main() {
  word8 a[4][MAXBC], rk[MAXROUNDS+1][4][MAXBC], sk[4][MAXKC];
```

```
    char* key;
    char* text;
    int bcupper = 4; // default value
    int kcupper = 4; // default value

    testd2 = false;
    testd3 = false;
    testtext = false;

#ifdef TESTD2
    testd2 = true;
#elif TESTD3
    testd3 = true;
#elif TESTTEXT
    testtext = true;
#else
#error "Must define TESTD2 or TESTD3 or TESTTEXT"
#endif

    text = readstuff("xtext.txt");
    key = readstuff("xkey.txt");

    if (testd3) {
      bcupper = 8;
      kcupper = 8;
    }
    else if (testd2) {
      bcupper = 4;
      kcupper = 4;
    }
    else if (testtext) {
      bcupper = 4;
      kcupper = 8;
    }

    for (KC = 4; KC <= kcupper; KC++) {
      for (BC = 4; BC <= bcupper; BC++) {
        ROUNDS = numrounds[KC-4][BC-4];

        if (testd3) {
          filltextallzeros(a);
          fillkeyallzeros(sk);
        }
        else if (testd2) {
          filltextd2(a);
          fillkeyd2(sk);
        }
        else if (testtext) {
          filltexttest(a);
          fillkeytest(sk);
        }
        else {
          printf("ERROR testd2 testd3\n");
          exit(0);
        }

        KeyExpansion(sk, rk);

#ifdef KEYSCHED
```

```
      // Print key schedule.
      printf("KEY SCHEDULE\n");
      if ((KC == 4) && (BC == 4)) {
        for (int r = 0; r < ROUNDS+1; r++) {
          printf("%2d", r);
          for (j = 0; j < 4; j++) {
            for (i = 0; i < 4; i++) {
              printf(" %02X", rk[r][i][j]);
            }
          }
          printf("\n");
        }
      }
      printf("\n");
#endif

      printf("block length %d  key length %d\n", 32*BC, 32*KC);
      dump2dcolsBC("TEXT", a, 4, BC);
      dump2dcolsBCchar("TEXT", a, 4, BC);
      printf("\n");

      dump2dcolsKC("KEY ", sk, 4, KC);
      dump2dcolsKCchar("KEY ", sk, 4, KC);
      printf("\n");

      Encrypt(a, rk);
      printf("\n");
      dump2dcolsBC("ENC ", a, 4, BC);
      dump2dcolsBCchar("CHAR", a, 4, BC);
      printf("\n");

      if (testd2 || testtext) {
        Decrypt(a, rk);
        printf("\n");
        dump2dcolsBC("DEC ", a, 4, BC);
        dump2dcolsBCchar("CHAR", a, 4, BC);
        printf("\n");
      } // if (testd2) {
      else if (testd3) {
        Encrypt(a, rk);
        dump2dcolsBC("DEC ", a, 4, BC);
        dump2dcolsBCchar("CHAR", a, 4, BC);
        printf("\n");
      } // else if (testd3) {
    } // for (BC = 4; BC <= 8; BC++) {
  } // for (KC = 4; KC <= 8; KC++) {
}
```

B.4.3 AES Input/Output Utilities

We display here some locally produced utility functions. Yes, these are hacks. We don't really apologize, although perhaps we should.

```
#include <stdio.h>
#include <stdlib.h>
#include <string.h>
```

```c
typedef unsigned char word8;
typedef unsigned int word32;

#define MAXBC 8
#define MAXKC 8
#define MAXROUNDS 14

int BC, KC, ROUNDS;

/****************************************************************************
*
**/
void dump2drowsBC(char* label, word8 thevalues[4][MAXBC],
                  int limitrow, int limitcol) {
  int i, j;
  printf("%s by rows\n", label);
  for (i = 0; i < limitrow; i++) {
    printf("%2d", i);
    for (j = 0; j < limitcol; j++) {
      printf(" %02x", thevalues[i][j]);
    }
    printf("\n");
  }
}

/****************************************************************************
*
**/
void dump2drowsKC(char* label, word8 thevalues[4][MAXKC],
                  int limitrow, int limitcol) {
  int i, j;
  printf("%s by rows\n", label);
  for (i = 0; i < limitrow; i++) {
    printf("%2d", i);
    for (j = 0; j < limitcol; j++) {
      printf(" %02x", thevalues[i][j]);
    }
    printf("\n");
  }
}

/****************************************************************************
*
**/
void dump2dcolsBC(char* label, word8 thevalues[4][MAXBC], int limitrow,
                  int limitcol) {
  int i, j;

  // print as one row
  printf("%s by cols ", label);
  for (j = 0; j < limitcol; j++) {
    for (i = 0; i < limitrow; i++) {
      printf(" %02x", thevalues[i][j]);
    }
  }
  printf("\n");
}

/****************************************************************************
```

```
*
**/
void dump2dcolsBCchar(char* label, word8 thevalues[4][MAXBC], int limitrow,
                      int limitcol) {
  int i, j;

  // print as one row
  printf("%s by cols ", label);
  for (j = 0; j < limitcol; j++) {
    for (i = 0; i < limitrow; i++) {
      if ((thevalues[i][j] >= 0x21) && (thevalues[i][j] <= 0x7d)) {
        printf(" %2c", thevalues[i][j]);
      }
      else {
        printf("  ~");
      }
    }
  }
  printf("\n");
}

/************************************************************************
*
**/
void dump2dcolsKC(char* label, word8 thevalues[4][MAXKC], int limitrow,
                  int limitcol) {
  int i, j;

  // print as one row
  printf("%s by cols ", label);
  for (j = 0; j < limitcol; j++) {
    for (i = 0; i < limitrow; i++) {
      printf(" %02x", thevalues[i][j]);
    }
  }
  printf("\n");
}

/************************************************************************
*
**/
void dump2dcolsKCchar(char* label, word8 thevalues[4][MAXKC], int limitrow,
                      int limitcol) {
  int i, j;

  // print as one row
  printf("%s by cols ", label);
  for (j = 0; j < limitcol; j++) {
    for (i = 0; i < limitrow; i++) {
      if ((thevalues[i][j] >= 0x21) && (thevalues[i][j] <= 0x7d)) {
        printf(" %2c", thevalues[i][j]);
      }
      else {
        printf("  ~");
      }
    }
  }
  printf("\n");
}
```

```c
/**************************************************************************
 *
 **/
void dump3d(word8 thevalues[MAXROUNDS+1][4][MAXBC],
            int limitx, int limity, int limitz) {
  int i, j, k;
  for (i = 0; i < limitx; i++) {
    for (j = 0; j < limity; j++) {
      printf("%2d %2d", i, j);
      for (k = 0; k < limitz; k++) {
        printf(" %02x", thevalues[i][j][k]);
      }
      printf("\n");
    }
    printf("\n");
  }
}

/**************************************************************************
 *
 **/
void dump3dcols(word8 thevalues[MAXROUNDS+1][4][MAXBC],
                int limiti, int limitj, int limitk) {
  int i, j, k;
  for (i = 0; i < limiti; i++) {
    printf("%2d ", i);
    for (k = 0; k < limitk; k++) {
      for (j = 0; j < limitj; j++) {
        printf(" %02x", thevalues[i][j][k]);
      }
    }
    printf("\n");
  }
}

/**************************************************************************
 *
 **/
void dumpvaluesBC(int round, char* label, word8 thevalues[4][MAXBC],
                  int limitrow, int limitcol, bool printflag) {
  if (printflag) {
    printf("ROUND %2d ", round);
    dump2dcolsBC(label, thevalues, limitrow, limitcol);
  }
}

/**************************************************************************
 *
 **/
void dumpvaluesKC(int round, char* label, word8 thevalues[4][MAXBC],
                  int limitrow, int limitcol, bool printflag) {
  if (printflag) {
    printf("ROUND %2d ", round);
    dump2dcolsKC(label, thevalues, limitrow, limitcol);
  }
}

/**************************************************************************
 *
 **/
```

```
void fillkeyallzeros(word8 thekey[4][MAXKC]) {
  int i, j;
  for (j = 0; j < KC; j++) {
    for (i = 0; i < 4; i++) {
      thekey[i][j] = 0;
    }
  }
}
/**********************************************************************
 *
 **/
void fillkeyd2(word8 sk[4][MAXKC]) {
  sk[0][0] = 0x2b;
  sk[1][0] = 0x7e;
  sk[2][0] = 0x15;
  sk[3][0] = 0x16;
  sk[0][1] = 0x28;
  sk[1][1] = 0xae;
  sk[2][1] = 0xd2;
  sk[3][1] = 0xa6;
  sk[0][2] = 0xab;
  sk[1][2] = 0xf7;
  sk[2][2] = 0x15;
  sk[3][2] = 0x88;
  sk[0][3] = 0x09;
  sk[1][3] = 0xcf;
  sk[2][3] = 0x4f;
  sk[3][3] = 0x3c;
}
/**********************************************************************
 *
 **/
void fillkeytest(word8 sk[4][MAXKC]) {
  sk[0][0] = 0x2b;
  sk[1][0] = 0x7e;
  sk[2][0] = 0x15;
  sk[3][0] = 0x16;
  sk[0][1] = 0x28;
  sk[1][1] = 0xae;
  sk[2][1] = 0xd2;
  sk[3][1] = 0xa6;
  sk[0][2] = 0xab;
  sk[1][2] = 0xf7;
  sk[2][2] = 0x15;
  sk[3][2] = 0x88;
  sk[0][3] = 0x09;
  sk[1][3] = 0xcf;
  sk[2][3] = 0x4f;
  sk[3][3] = 0x3c;
}
/**********************************************************************
 *
 **/
void filltestd3key(word8 sk[4][MAXKC]) {
  sk[0][0] = 0x00;
  sk[1][0] = 0x00;
  sk[2][0] = 0x00;
```

```
    sk[3][0] = 0x00;
    sk[0][1] = 0x00;
    sk[1][1] = 0x00;
    sk[2][1] = 0x00;
    sk[3][1] = 0x00;
    sk[0][2] = 0x00;
    sk[1][2] = 0x00;
    sk[2][2] = 0x00;
    sk[3][2] = 0x00;
    sk[0][3] = 0x00;
    sk[1][3] = 0x00;
    sk[2][3] = 0x00;
    sk[3][3] = 0x00;
}

/******************************************************************
 *
 **/
void filltextallzeros(word8 thetext[4][MAXBC]) {
    int i, j;
    for (j = 0; j < BC; j++) {
      for (i = 0; i < 4; i++) {
        thetext[i][j] = 0;
      }
    }
}

/******************************************************************
 *
 **/
void filltextd2(word8 a[4][MAXBC]) {
    a[0][0] = 0x32;
    a[1][0] = 0x43;
    a[2][0] = 0xf6;
    a[3][0] = 0xa8;
    a[0][1] = 0x88;
    a[1][1] = 0x5a;
    a[2][1] = 0x30;
    a[3][1] = 0x8d;
    a[0][2] = 0x31;
    a[1][2] = 0x31;
    a[2][2] = 0x98;
    a[3][2] = 0xa2;
    a[0][3] = 0xe0;
    a[1][3] = 0x37;
    a[2][3] = 0x07;
    a[3][3] = 0x34;
}

/******************************************************************
 *
 **/
void filltexttest(word8 a[4][MAXBC]) {
    a[0][0] = 0x74; // t
    a[1][0] = 0x68; // h
    a[2][0] = 0x69; // i
    a[3][0] = 0x73; // s
    a[0][1] = 0x20; // blank
    a[1][1] = 0x69; // i
    a[2][1] = 0x73; // s
```

```
  a[3][1] = 0x20; // blank
  a[0][2] = 0x74; // t
  a[1][2] = 0x68; // h
  a[2][2] = 0x65; // e
  a[3][2] = 0x20; // blank
  a[0][3] = 0x74; // t
  a[1][3] = 0x65; // e
  a[2][3] = 0x78; // x
  a[3][3] = 0x74; // t
}

/*********************************************************************
*
**/
char* readstuff(char* filename) {
  char* text = NULL;
  size_t linecap = 0;
//  ssize_t linelen;
  FILE *fp;

  fp = fopen(filename, "r");
  getline(&text, &linecap, fp);
  fclose(fp);

  return(text);
}
```

References

1. H.O. Yardley, *The American Black Chamber* (Bobbs-Merrill, 1931), pp. 140–171
2. F. Pratt, *Secret and Urgent* (Blue Ribbon Books, 1939)
3. J. Daemen, V. Rijmen, *The Design of Rijndael*, 2nd edn. (Springer, 2020)

Index

A

Abelian group, 50
ADFGX, 20
Advanced Encryption Standard *see* AES
AES, 8, 125
  AddRoundKey, 140
  byte organization, 128
  differences from Rijndael, 127
  implementation issues, 141
  key expansion, 130
  MixColumns, 137
  original candidates, 126
  rounds, 130
  selection process, 125
  ShiftRows, 136
  SubBytes, 133
AKS algorithm, 100
Approximate gcd problem, 226
Argand plane, 107
ASCII, 5, 6
Attack
  chosen ciphertext, 7
  chosen plaintext, 7
  ciphertext only, 7
  known plaintext, 7
Authentication, 5

B

Battle of Midway, 3
BFI *see* Brute force and ignorance
Bletchley Park, 2
Block cipher, 6, 127
  iterated, 127
  key-alternating, 127

Brute force and ignorance, 22

C

Caesar cipher, 12
Carmichael number, 101
Character
  of a group, 67
Characteristic of a field, 60
Chinese Remainder Theorem, 38
Chosen ciphertext attack, 7
Chosen plaintext attack, 7
Cipher, 11
  block cipher, 6
  Caesar cipher, 12
  cipher block chaining, 6
  electronic codebook, 6
  one-time pad, 22
  polyalphabetic, 13
  state of, 127
  stream cipher, 6
  substitution, 11
  transposition, 11
  transposition cipher, 19
  Vernam one-time pad, 22
Cipher block chaining, 6
Ciphertext, 4
Ciphertext only attack, 7
Cocks, Clifford, 150
Codebook, 4, 11
Coding theory, 4
Colossus, 2
Common divisor, 27
Common multiple, 27
Commutative group, 50

© The Editor(s) (if applicable) and The Author(s), under exclusive license to Springer
Nature Switzerland AG 2021
D. Buell, *Fundamentals of Cryptography*, Undergraduate Topics in Computer Science,
https://doi.org/10.1007/978-3-030-73492-3

Commutative ring, 53
Complete set of residues, 36
Composite number, 35
Confidentiality, 5
Congruence, 36
modulus of, 36
Continued fraction, 162
convergent, 163
Convergent, 163
Cribbing, 4
Crumbly integer, 161
Cryptanalysis, 3
Cryptography, 3
Cryptology, 3
Cyclic group, 51

D

Data Encryption Standard *see* DES
D-Day invasion, 3
Deciphering, 4
Decrypting, 4
DES, 7, 123
Digital watermarking, 11
Direct product, 58
Discrete logarithm, 180
Discrete logarithm problem, 56, 180
Division algorithm, 28
polynomial, 79
quotient from, 28
remainder from, 28
Divisor of an integer, 27

E

Electronic codebook, 6
Elliptic curve, 87, 105
factoring, 169
Hasse's Theorem, 96
Jacobian coordinates, 94, 192
Koblitz curve, 197
Mordell-Weil group, 91
point at infinity, 191
projective coordinates, 94
Weierstrass form, 88
Ellis, James, 150
Enciphering, 4
Encrypting, 4
Enigma, 2
Entropy, 16, 17
entropy of English, 18
Entropy of English, 18
Epact, 159

Euclidean algorithm, 29
binary version, 32
polynomial, 79
subtraction version, 33
Euler phi function, 43
Euler totient function, 43
Exponentiation, 44
Exponent of a group, 53
Extended Euclidean algorithm, 31

F

Factor base, 166
Factoring
continued fraction, 162
elliptic curve, 169
multiple polynomial quadratic sieve, 176
number field sieve, 177
Pollard $p - 1$, 160
Pollard rho, 158
quadratic sieve, 173
Factor of an integer, 27
Fast Fourier Transform, 102, 103
Fermat number, 104
Fermat's Little Theorem, 43, 100
FFT *see* Fast Fourier Transform
Field, 54
characteristic of a field, 60
finite, 73
finite field, 54
galois field, 54
Finite field, 54, 73
normal basis, 82
optimal normal basis, 84
Friedman, Elizabeth, 2
Friedman, William, 2
Fully homomorphic encryption, 224
Fundamental Theorem of Arithmetic, 35

G

Galois field, 54
Gaussian heuristic, 218
Greatest common divisor, 28
Group, 49
abelian, 50
commutative, 50
cyclic, 51
direct product, 58
exponent of a group, 53
generator of, 51
homomorphism, 59
identity, 50

inverse, 50
isomorphism, 59
Lagrange's theorem, 100
order of a group, 52
order of an element, 52
subgroup of, 50
Group character, 67
Group generator, 51

H
Hash function, 6
Hasse's Theorem, 96
Hermite Normal Form, 46
Homomorphism, 59

I
Ideal, 224
Identity element, 50
Index calculus, 56, 183
Information theory, 16
Integer
common divisors, 27
common multiple, 27
congruence, 36
divisor of, 27
factor of, 27
prime to one another, 29
relatively prime, 29
Integrity, 5
Inverse element, 50
Irreducible polynomial, 79
Isomorphism, 59
Iterated block cipher, 127

J
Jacobian coordinates, 192
Jacobi symbol, 68
Jefferson, Thomas, 2

K
Kerckhoff, Auguste, 9
Kerckhoffs Principle, 9
Key, 4
Key-alternating block cipher, 127
Key exchange
safe prime, 183
Klein-4 group, 60
Known plaintext attack, 7
Koblitz curve, 197

L
Lagrange's theorem, 100
Law of quadratic reciprocity, 68, 69
Learning with errors, 227
Least common multiple, 28
Least positive residue, 36
Legendre symbol, 67
Linear feedback shift register, 75
period of, 75
Lucas–Lehmer test, 101, 104

M
M-94, 2
Mary, Queen of Scots, 2
Matrix reduction, 45
Mersenne number, 100
Mersenne prime, 99
Modular arithmetic, 38
Modulus, 36
Montgomery multiplication, 117
Mordell-Weil group, 91
Multiple Polynomial Quadratic Sieve (MPQS),
176
Multiplicative identity, 53

N
Non-repudiation, 5
Normal basis, 82
optimal, 84
Number field sieve, 177

O
One-time pad, 22
Optimal normal basis, 84
Order of a group, 52
Order of an element, 52

P
Patterson, Nick, 150
Phi function, 43
Plaintext, 4
Playfair, Baron, 20
Playfair cipher, 20
Point at infinity, 191
Pollard $p - 1$, 160
Pollard rho, 158
Polyalphabetic cipher, 13
Polynomial
irreducible, 79
prime, 79
primitive, 75

Primality proving, 99
Prime
  Mersenne, 99
Prime number, 35
  primality proving, 99
Prime Number Theorem, 158
Prime polynomial, 79
Prime to one another, 29
Primitive polynomial, 75
Primitive root, 55, 182
Primitive trinomial, 74
Proving primality, 100
Purple, 2

Q

Quadratic reciprocity, 68, 69
Quadratic sieve, 173
Quotient ring, 225

R

Reading ciphertext, 4
Relatively prime, 29
Residue
  complete set of, 36
  least positive, 36
Rijndael *see* AES
Ring, 53
  commutative, 53
  multiplicative identity, 53
  zero divisors, 57
Ring learning with errors, 227
Riverbank Laboratories, 2
Rochefort, Joseph, 3
Round, 127

S

Safe prime, 183
S-box, 124
Shannon, Claude, 9

Shift register, 75
  period of, 75
Smooth number, 166
Somewhat homomorphic encryption, 224
Square roots modulo primes, 63
Square roots of 1, 64
State, 127
Steganography, 11
Stimson, Henry, 2
Stream cipher, 6
Subgroup, 50
Substitution cipher, 11

T

Totient function, 43
Transposition cipher, 11, 19
  ADFGX, 20
  Playfair, 20
Trinomial
  primitive, 74
Turing, Alan, 2

U

Unicode, 6

V

Vernam one-time pad, 22

W

Weierstrass form, 88
Wheatstone, Sir Charles, 20
Williamson, Malcolm, 150

Y

Yardley, Herbert O., 2

Z

Zero divisors, 57

Printed in the United States
by Baker & Taylor Publisher Services